WILLIAM WILKINS
1778–1839

E. H. Baily. Bust of William Wilkins, R.A. 1830.

WILLIAM WILKINS
1778 – 1839

R. W. LISCOMBE

Associate Professor of Fine Arts, University of British Columbia

CAMBRIDGE UNIVERSITY PRESS

Cambridge

London   New York   New Rochelle

Melbourne   Sydney

CAMBRIDGE UNIVERSITY PRESS
Cambridge, New York, Melbourne, Madrid, Cape Town, Singapore,
São Paulo, Delhi, Dubai, Tokyo, Mexico City

Cambridge University Press
The Edinburgh Building, Cambridge CB2 8RU, UK

Published in the United States of America by Cambridge University Press, New York

www.cambridge.org
Information on this title: www.cambridge.org/9780521144674

First published 1980
First paperback printing 2010

A catalogue record for this publication is available from the British Library

Library of Congress Cataloguing in Publication data
Liscombe, R W 1946–
William Wilkins, 1778–1839.

Bibliography: p.
Includes index.
Wilkins, William, 1778–1839. 2. Architects – England – Biography.
3. Architecture, Regency – England.
NA997.W48L57   720′.92′4 [B]   78-73247

ISBN 978-0-521-22528-1 Hardback
ISBN 978-0-521-14467-4 Paperback

CONTENTS

TO
PHILIPPA WINDSOR
LISCOMBE

THE PLATES

PLATES 1 TO 107 ARE AT THE END
OF THE BOOK

ACKNOWLEDGEMENTS

This book could not have been completed without the constant encouragement and invaluable help of Philippa Windsor Liscombe. William Powell Wilkins, a direct descendant of the architect, generously made available the results of his own researches as well as the drawings, paintings and documents remaining with the family. I had the benefit of discussing Wilkins's architecture with Sir John Summerson, Professor P. Murray, Dr J. M. Crook, Dr D. J. Watkin and Mr J. Harris. The Earls of Falmouth and Rosebery, Sir John Summerson and Professor H. M. Colvin kindly allowed me to examine material in their possession. I am indebted to Mr B. Caven for most kindly translating from the Latin the letters written by Wilkins in fulfilment of the statute of the Worts Travelling Bachelorship.

I also wish to thank the Librarians and assistants in the Cambridge City Library, Cambridge University Library and the libraries of Corpus Christi, Downing, Gonville and Caius, King's and Trinity Colleges, Cambridge; the Manuscripts Department of the British Library, the India Office Library, the National Gallery, London, Reading University Library, the Royal Academy of Arts, the Royal Society, the Society of Antiquaries of London and University College, London; and the Archivists of Cambridge University, the Church Commissioners, the Corporation of London, the Counties of Dorset, Huntingdon and Norfolk and Yarmouth Borough. My researches were further facilitated at the Department of Greek and Roman Antiquities and the Director's Office of the British Museum, the National Monuments Record, the Public Record Office, the

Royal Commission on the Ancient and Historical Monuments of Scotland, the Drawings Collection of the Royal Institute of British Architects, St George's Hospital, London, Sir John Soane's Museum and the York Museum.

I am most grateful to the following for permission to reproduce drawings, photographs and plans from their collections: the Earls of Falmouth and Rosebery, Sir John Summerson, Captain P. J. B. Drury-Lowe, Mr R. Gurney, Mr R. Hill, Mr W. P. Wilkins, the Vicar and Churchwardens of Sherborne Abbey, the Masters and Fellows of Corpus Christi, Downing, Gonville and Caius and Trinity Colleges, and the Provost and Fellows of King's College, Cambridge; the Bath Library, the Cambridge University Library, the Avery Library and the Phoenix Collection in the Rare Book and Manuscript Library of Columbia University, *Country Life*, the Director of the India Office Library and Records, the National Library of Ireland, the National Monuments Record, the National Monuments Record of Scotland, the Norfolk County Library, the Castle Museum, Norwich, Nottinghamshire County Library and Nottingham University, the Public Record Office, the Royal Academy of Arts, the Royal Institute of British Architects, Sir John Soane's Museum, Tulane University, University College, London and the Yale Center for British Art, Paul Mellon Collection.

ABBREVIATIONS

B.M.	British Museum
C.U.L.	Cambridge University Library
Ch.C.	Church Commissioners
C.C.C.	Corpus Christi College, Cambridge
D.C.	Downing College, Cambridge
I.O.L.	India Office Library
K.C.	King's College, Cambridge
N.G.	National Gallery, London
N.L.I.	National Library of Ireland
N.M.R.	National Monuments Record
N.N.R.O.	Norfolk and Norwich Record Office
P.R.O.	Public Record Office
R.A.	Royal Academy of Arts
R.C.H.M.	Royal Commission on the Ancient and Historical Monuments of England
R.C.H.M.S.	Royal Commission on the Ancient and Historical Monuments of Scotland
R.I.B.A.	Royal Institute of British Architects, Drawings Collection
S.A.	Society of Antiquaries of London
S.D.	Society of Dilettanti
S.M.	Sir John Soane's Museum
T.C.	Trinity College, Cambridge
U.C.L.	University College, London
W.P.W.	W. P. Wilkins Collection
Y.A.	Yarmouth Borough Archive
Y.B.A.	Yale Center for British Art, Paul Mellon Collection
Y.P.S.	Yorkshire Philosophical Society

INTRODUCTION
'The best educated classic'

'At his residence, Lensfield, in the Town of Cambridge, on his sixty-first birthday, William Wilkins, Esq., M.A. F.S.A., a Royal Academician and Professor in Architecture in the Royal Academy.'[1]

Thus began the appreciative obituary published in the *Gentleman's Magazine*, some weeks after William Wilkins's death on 31 August 1839. It was one of a number about the Regency architect who, despite the fact that his work has passed out of favour, designed at least two public buildings that are among the most famous and well loved in England, for the screen of King's College, Cambridge and the National Gallery in Trafalgar Square, London have come to represent the national heritage and to be popularly associated with learning and the arts (Pls. 1 and 2).

The obituarist, apart from praising Wilkins's architecture and scholarship, gave a vignette of the man that adds reality to those facets of his personality discernible in his writings and the scant remains of his private papers. Much of his correspondence, all his notes and the diary of his Greek tour have been lost. That circumstance necessarily limits the understanding of his character, and to indulge in speculation might be unjust to him or fanciful. The loss of his papers and many of his designs also hampers study of his work, especially since a number of commissions, particularly those on a small scale, must be unrecorded (one, possibly, being the addition to Brooke Hall, Norfolk in 1830).[2]

The obituarist remembered Wilkins as 'tall and muscular, to appearance strongly framed but lately much altered by illness. In Society he was cheerful, and his conversation displayed a mind stored

I

with various information' and, quoting from *The Athenaeum* obituary, agreed that he was 'a lover of the arts, which he encouraged to the extent of his means. In all the relations of private life, he was most amiable; and these combined high qualities of head and heart obtained for him the friendship of men in the highest walks of literature and fame.' Even more telling is the last paragraph of the obituary printed in the *Civil Engineer and Architect's Journal*:

> In his private character, Mr. Wilkins was a most amiable and honourable man, warm in temper, but kind hearted, affable, generous and liberal, without the slightest tinge of that ostentation which sometimes renders pecuniary liberality little better than pride and self-worship. Unlike his predecessor in the office at the Academy [Professor of Architecture, Sir John Soane], he was not given to make any parade of public donations, but his liberality was prompted by sincere benevolence, and placed beyond the suspicion of any unworthy motive. We have heard anecdotes of his kindness and generosity, that reflect the highest honour upon his memory, and prove him to have been, what is infinitely superior to his highest title as a scholar or an artist, a truely noble-minded and worthy man.

The physical description is borne out in the portrait of Wilkins and family painted by A. E. Chalon in their fashionable London home at 36 Weymouth Street in 1824 (Pl. 4).[3] Dressed in Caroline costume, perhaps to signify his pleasure in theatricals as much as his historical taste in art, Wilkins is seated beside his pretty wife, Alicia, with their three children, Henry Robert, Alicia and William Bushby (born in 1813, 1817 and 1822), posed about them. In the background is part of his large library and collection of paintings, with a copy of Raphael's 'Transfiguration' hung prominently. Such powers of perception that Chalon commanded seem to have been concentrated upon his patron. Wilkins appears alert, proud and even a trifle pompous, characteristics which, together with a lively wit, are to be found in his writings and extant correspondence. He was also loyal and possessed of a kindly disposition, especially towards less fortunate fellow artists, as evident in a letter fired off sometime in 1827 at Leonard Horner, Warden of University College, London:

Any decent drawing, or one worthy of the occasion you mention would occupy a young artist 14 days. I do not know any artist above the rank of a street sweeper that would consent to work for 18d a day! To talk of giving a young artist a Guinea for a drawing is paltrey [sic]. Such a proposition would disgrace even Mr Savings-banks [possibly a reference to Henry Bankes, M.P., who begrudged public expenditure on the arts].[4]

Later John Cotman wrote to his wife on 31 December 1833 about his application for the post of drawing master at King's College, London (which he secured), 'I have obtained a testimonial from Wilkins, R.A., the architect. He acknowledges his school-fellowship with me, and my *honourable conduct through life*, and my high character as an artist.'[5] The little that can be glimpsed of the Wilkins family life suggests that it was a close and affectionate one, as shown by the letters William Bushby wrote home when touring Europe. A delightful sample occurs in one sent from Rome on 21 September 1836 to cheer his father, depressed by professional reverses and afflicted by gout: 'the form of the Dome of St Peter's reminded me exactly of the London University'.[6]

Present in Chalon's depiction of Wilkins's gaze and countenance is more than a hint of the determination which had brought about his rise from a comfortable but modest background to wealth and esteem, confirmed by the three major Cambridge commissions upon which he was then working. In recognition of the success of one, Trinity College New Court, the Seniors later commissioned a bust from his friend, E. H. Baily, finished in 1830, which reinforces the impression of the strength and magnetism of Wilkins's personality (Frontispiece). Clearly this was a man of decision, the characteristics of whose work were deliberately chosen and not the result of chance or default.

As the obituarist remarked, Wilkins's mind and personality won him entrance into the ranks of that educated high society in Britain which exerted such an important influence on the national taste and patronage in his lifetime. He quickly became a respected member of the antiquarian group at Cambridge, among whom was Lord George Gordon, 4th Earl of Aberdeen, who merits particular attention not only as a friend and literary collaborator but because his correspondence and diaries as a young man help to re-create the intellectual background and experiences that set Wilkins's mind. As early as 1801 Wilkins was received into the Society of Antiquaries and, eight years later, into the Society of Dilettanti, thus mixing with the leading men of taste such as Sir Alexander Baring, Sir George Beaumont, Thomas Hope, Richard Payne Knight, Sir Thomas Lawrence, Charles Long (later Baron Farnborough), the Marquis of Lansdowne, Frederick Robinson (later Lord Goderich and Earl of Ripon), and the Earl of Stafford.

A brief outline of the careers of three, Aberdeen, Long and Robinson, is enlightening. Each graduated from Cambridge and entered politics, the young earl after a tour of Europe, Greece and Asia Minor, and eventually held senior appointments in government. Long was chairman of the Committee for the Inspection of National Monuments which, under its later sobriquet, the Committee of Taste, conducted most of the major official architectural competitions until the one for the Houses of Parliament in 1835, and whose members included Aberdeen, Baring, Knight and Lawrence. Apart from forming a fine collection of paintings and writing *Remarks on the Improvements in London* (1826), Long was a fellow of the Antiquaries and of the Royal Society, as were Aberdeen and Wilkins, a trustee of the British Museum and one of the first deputy presidents of the British Institution. Aberdeen occupied the same position before being elected president in 1825, and also presided over the Antiquaries between 1812 and 1846 and was a power in the Society of Dilettanti. Aberdeen, too, was a collector, though mainly of antique sculpture and coins, and was a trustee of the British Museum with Baring, Beaumont, Knight, Lansdowne, Lawrence and Stafford, and later, in company with most of these, on the Board of Trustees of the National Gallery, often acting as chairman of both bodies. Those honours were extended to Robinson who, as Chancellor or in the popular parlance 'Prosperity Robinson', channelled public funds into the erection of the new British Museum, the acquisition of the Angerstein Collection for the nation, and the housing of the National Gallery and Royal Academy in Trafalgar Square, a scheme brought to architectural fruition by Wilkins between 1832 and 1838. Acquaintance with such men as these advanced Wilkins's career, and some of his patrons came from the Antiquaries and Dilettanti though, clearly, they respected and valued his proven ability. And, as his acceptance of progressive ideas in the last years of his life testifies, Wilkins was not a place-seeker who attached himself to a particular political or social group in the hope of reward.

Wilkins was one of the most able antiquaries of the period, whose study of Greek and Gothic design was the source of a series of admirable publications and of the scholarly detailing of his revivalist architecture. The two were interdependent. Throughout his career he expended almost the same energy on his writings as on his architecture, and to effect, for, as the obituarist of the *Gentleman's Magazine* wrote, the former placed him 'amongst the most accomplished scholars of the architectural school; whilst the restoration of the mutilated Greek inscriptions relating to the public edifices of Athens bear ample testimony to the depth and extent of his scholarship'. In fact his translation of the so-called 'Athenian Inscription', retrieved by Richard Chandler in 1765, was consulted by some of those Germans who wrested the mantle of Greek scholarship from their English fellows in the second quarter of the nineteenth century. From the outset of his career Wilkins's publications provided the means of displaying, in the words of the obituarist of the Royal Society, 'a profound knowledge of the principles both of Grecian and Gothic architecture' and 'led to very extensive professional engagements, particularly in the University of Cambridge'.[7]

Neat in composition and learned and refined in articulation, his style caught the tenor of Regency taste and vied in critical regard with the styles of Soane, Nash, Smirke and Wyatville – until, at least, the disastrous commission for the combined National Gallery and Royal Academy. The lamentable conditions imposed on Wilkins by the Government for this commission threw into excessive relief his linear rather than plastic idea of design and laid him bare to severe censure in the press. Misguidedly he attempted to counter his critics through the same medium but only succeeded in presenting himself as an arrogant and dogmatic Greek Revivalist, as illustrated by a review in the *Gentleman's Magazine* of his rejected Greek Doric columnar design for the Duke of York's Monument, exhibited at the Academy in 1835: 'Alas! for Wren and Palladio, and Vitruvius, ancients and moderns your fame is fast waning; it will vanish with the National Gallery. Mr Wilkins has built a column; Trajan's pillar is thrown into shade. No more shall the graceful structures of Rome claim our attention.'[8] The critique also reflects the emergence of those changes in English taste that spelled doom for Wilkins's work: a renewed appreciation of Roman and Renaissance architecture, a growing preference for rich articulation and bold massing, and the decline of the Greek Revival in favour of a more full-blooded Gothicism than he wished to adopt. Indeed as early as March 1833 'E.I.C.' in the *Gentleman's Magazine* had arraigned the design for the National Gallery, 'the naked frigidity of Downing College' and 'the square posts which supply the place of columns in the pure Grecian of St. George's Hospital', among other examples of the 'miscalled Greek structures of the day', when supporting the case for the 'beauties and the merits of Pointed architecture' – quite forgetting Wilkins's competence in the Gothic.[9]

Wilkins's reputation revived temporarily following his retirement in 1837 and his death. In 1838 a correspondent wrote in the *Civil Engineer and Architect's Journal* that his 'fame will require no blazon from us; the integrity, taste and science which he has brought into his professional practice are evinced in so many ways and always so much to his honour that we look to his long enjoyment of his retreat with equal hope and pleasure'.[10] Nine years later the critic, James Elmes, stated in the same journal that Wilkins had been 'perhaps the best educated classic that has honoured the profession of architecture since Sir Christopher Wren'.[11] But he considered that Wilkins lacked 'the architect's greatest qualities, invention and freedom from pedantry', thus identifying him with those 'modern Greeks' whom he had castigated in his lectures on architecture, delivered in 1819–21, for copying 'the very fractions of lines and profiles instead of composing in the same spirit' as the ancient Greeks.[12] Worse, he stigmatised Wilkins's buildings as monotonous: 'so much Greek, so much *cold* was the practice of William Wilkins – for no liberty would he give or take, no line or member would he use, for which he could not find a precedent in some ancient Greek building'. While Wilkins was to receive fairer treatment from that unrepentant foe of revivalism, James Fergusson, in his *History of the Modern Styles of Architecture* (1862), Elmes's article, sweeping as it was, signalled his banishment to limbo for the remainder of the century.

The first rehabilitation of his reputation came in A. E. Richardson's pioneering study of English Classicism, *Monumental Classic Architecture in Great Britain and Ireland*, published in 1914.[13] He thought Wilkins to have been the most 'learned exponent' of the Greek Revival, being 'an accomplished draughtsman and archaeologist of considerable reputation', if lacking the 'elastic mind' and 'requisite power of adaptation essential to a first class designer' for, while his mouldings and ornaments were 'invariably beautiful, and well selected for the purposes they serve', he was not a 'strong man' as a monumental architect. At that time he did not take much account of the manifold difficulties Wilkins faced in his major commissions but, in the discussion that followed Bereford-Pite's lecture on his work at the R.I.B.A. in December 1932, Richardson assessed Wilkins as 'a great architect', particularly commending the beauty of the proportioning of the pilasters on the façade (Pl. 3), the use of cast iron girders in the large lecture theatres and the sheathing with copper of the iron cramps in the portico of University College.[14] Most recently H. M. Colvin has written in the second edition of his *Dictionary of British Architects* (1978) that in his handling of the Greek Orders Wilkins 'showed more scholarship than Nash or Burton, and more sensibility than Smirke or Burn'. He has also pointed out that Wilkins's Neo-Gothic has not been much studied, and applauded the King's screen as an 'ingenious and effective architectural impropriety'.

Wilkins was indeed as fascinated by mediaeval architecture and as active in its revival as in the Greek. In 1823 he told the Master of Trinity College, Cambridge, that the Gothic was his 'forte', and in 1827 presented an elevation of King's screen to the Royal Academy as his diploma piece.[15] His earliest antiquarian studies had centred upon East Anglian Gothic and, while an undergraduate at Gonville and Caius College, he completed a detailed survey of King's College Chapel. The number of his Neo-Gothic designs, both executed and unexecuted, almost equals those in the Greek style and earned him as many encomiums. He was respected as a restorer and arbiter of Gothic architecture, being consulted, for instance, as late as 1833 by the Rector of Exeter College, Oxford about H. J. Underwood's proposed alterations and offered 'our best thanks for the essential Services lately rendered us by your inspection and observations of certain designs for the front of the College...the improvements which you were kind enough to suggest, have been adopted by unanimous consent'.[16] Three of the architects who passed through his office, B. Ferrey, G. F. Jones and J. H. Stevens, worked mainly in the Gothic style.[17] Fergusson thought that Wilkins had been 'probably the first who really aspired to pre-eminence in both styles' even if 'the feelings of his heart...were towards the pure Greek'.[18]

Wilkins's aspirations took the form of accurate though not exact imitations of Greek and Gothic architecture. He did not seek to be original in the modern sense – on one occasion he remarked 'we are all plagiarists more or less; there is nothing new under the sun' – but rather to adapt his models sympathetically to the contemporary scene.[19] The 'beauty of ancient architecture' was not to be imitated, he wrote in 1831, quoting from Aberdeen's *Inquiry into the Principles of Beauty in Grecian Architecture* (1822), 'with the timid and servile hand of the copyist, but...transferred to our soil, preserving, at the same time, a due regard to the changes of customs and manners, and to the differences of our climate, and to the condition of modern society'.[20] The process touched upon in that last phrase did not strike his generation as illogical or unfeasible and, in his case, was achieved by first selecting a model or models appropriate to the setting and purpose and then by adjusting those to the specifications of each commission. Though a circumscribed approach, the results were striking and neither impractical nor without variety. The main façades of his three Neo-Greek colleges differ in articulation, com-position and visual effect and, moreover, the last reveals a relaxation of his youthful purism, for the portico of University College is topped by a Neo-Renaissance dome. His was a reasoned as much as a scholarly revival which surely explains the indulgence shown by Fergusson to his work and especially to University College: 'If it were desired to make a building both monumental and ornamental, it would not be easy to do it at less cost, either in money or convenience.'[21] Keenly interested in the application of structural technology, Wilkins used cast iron extensively and kept abreast of progressive thinking on such utilitarian building types as the prison and hospital. The plans of his Neo-Gothic country houses were, relatively, as functional as those for his institutional buildings. He was diligent in providing the required accommodation with least extra-vagance either of space or expenditure, being among the first regularly to employ a quantity surveyor.

Wilkins's Janus-like posture, authoritarian and modernist, is apparent in replies to two questions about the optimum design for a theatre posed to him at the 1832 Select Committee on Dramatic Literature. He thought the best form as a semi-circle, as had been developed by the ancients, but, in pointing out the differences of environment, continued, 'I think it should be constructed of more permanent materials. If you could have a theatre of iron or a stage of iron you would have a perfect theatre.'[22]

Wilkins's interpretation of the Classical and mediaeval styles was novel when measured against those of his immediate predecessors. In the designs for Downing College, 1805, he produced the earliest consistent 'pure' Greek Revival. He eschewed the two predominating strands that had previously characterised the English Neo-Classical School: eclecticism and French rationalism, and set an example that influenced among others F. Bedford, D. Burton, J. P. Gandy (Gandy-Deering), H. W. Inwood, J. Sanders and the young Charles Barry. To a degree he also anticipated the direction taken by the Synthetic Classicists when he combined the Roman and Renaissance dome with the Greek Orders at University College, which was likened to that masterpiece of English architecture, St Paul's Cathedral, and said to honour England – praise more lavish than that accorded to Smirke's nearby British Museum. In the Gothic he staked out a new path by adopting a less Picturesque composition and also by basing his designs on the most appropriate historical sources. He modelled his houses upon the Tudor manor, and his additions at Cambridge on the adjacent Tudor buildings. The result was neither as dramatic nor as influential as his Neo-Greek style, though he instigated a more studious Neo-Tudor mode, imitated in Scotland by W. Burn, echoed in the work of Gandy-Deering and developed in that of H. Hutchinson, T. Rickman, Wyatville and Barry. At Cambridge Wilkins fostered the association between the Gothic style and university architecture that lasted into the twentieth century and spread beyond the shores of Britain. Moreover, Corpus Christi and King's Colleges gave him the opportunity to unite mediaeval ornament with mediaeval structural forms, a union which was to be a cardinal principle in A. W. N. Pugin's rigorous Gothic polemics. What is more, King's College scored a major critical success, one reviewer even writing that it would, when completed, 'present a pile of buildings unrivalled in this kingdom, and scarcely equalled by any Gothic edifices in Europe'.[23]

Yet there can be no gainsaying that Wilkins's talents as a designer were restricted. Unlike his greatest contemporaries, Soane and the German K. F. Schinkel (who realised Wilkins's Greek ideal with a brilliance and imagination he lacked), he either would not or could not conceive of architecture that transmuted historical authority. However, such an attitude found more favour in his period, since antiquarian study was accorded an essential rôle in the arts of design, as G. F. Waagen, Director of the National Gallery in Berlin, indicated in his brief biography of Wilkins, noting that apart from the translation of Vitruvius, he had undertaken

> the direction and editing of those splendid works on the Monuments of Ancient Greek Architecture, published by the celebrated Dilettanti Society, which has now existed above one hundred years, and has so astonishingly contributed to diffuse a knowledge of genuine Greek architecture, and to give to all the architects of Europe the means of acquiring the most profound acquaintance with the principles of art.[24]

The Regency men of taste tended to place greater value upon the studious emulation of historical art and architecture than had their predecessors. An amusing illustration can be found in a letter William Gell wrote to Aberdeen on 1 December 1806 about the choice of sculptor to carve a monument to William Pitt, Aberdeen's guardian, at Cambridge. Having heard that Nollekens and not Flaxman was to be commissioned, he asked Aberdeen to send 'some certain poison by return of post as I am determined not to survive such a misfortune. Of all the artists of England none but Flaxman have any taste for other Statues, than Gold laced coats & long flapped waistcoats – Flaxman has really done all that could be done to acquire Classical taste & real *Greek* knowledge – '[25]

    This emphasis was to be found in the contemporary moves to improve the education offered by the Royal Academy through a renewed stress on copying celebrated models of historical painting, sculpture and architecture; and there was a continuing intercourse between the members of learned societies and the Academy, which Constable called a 'house of so much intellect', typified by Wilkins.[26] The members of those fraternities, some such as Knight, Hope or Fuseli with reservations, agreed upon the importance of assembling collections, either in the form of originals or copies and engravings, which they trusted would inspire high art, good design (and consequently commercial reward) and social enlightenment.[27] The museum was the most exemplary cultural institution of the period.

In his preface to *Specimens of Gothic Architecture* (1824), E. J. Willson wrote lines which elucidate the antiquarian disposition:

> The use of ancient Architecture; either Grecian or *Gothic*, may not inaptly be compared to that of dead languages...and in employing them we must be guided by original examples. The rules of construction are fixed in both: and the proportions and ornaments of Architecture require to be thoroughly studied, and strictly followed, no less than the metres and phrases of the classic tongues.[28]

But Willson unwittingly exposed its chief limitation, namely the elevation of imitation over invention. However, it was a view of design which persisted, in various guises, through the nineteenth century. As its earliest expression in that period, the Greek Revival, with which Wilkins became particularly associated, was the first of the copyist styles to be labelled with the stigma of creative failure. Nevertheless, it dominated English architecture for at least three decades, surviving longer in Scotland, Germany and the United States, where one of Wilkins's former assistants, James Gallier, enjoyed success with the style into the 1850s. Indeed it spanned almost the same period of time as had the Palladian and Adam styles, which was remarkable given its fewer sources and stricter maxims. Nor can its failures, some of which Wilkins indirectly acknowledged in his writings, be accounted worse than those of the Gothic Revival, which became the predominant style in the Victorian era. The later Gothic Revivalists, apart from exploiting the nationalist and religious sensibilities aroused by the Romantic movement, learned from the rigidity of their Attic predecessors and, given the more sculptural quality of their models, were able to respond to the preference for plasticity and decoration that emerged in England during the 1830s, partly in reaction to the severity of Neo-Greek design. That change was also appreciated by the second generation of Greek Revivalists who, like Barry, G. Basevi, C. R. Cockerell and H. L. Elmes, turned to the more ornate Roman and Renaissance styles, though neither they, nor the 'Goths', could dispense with antiquarian study.

With the hindsight of the triumph of the functionalist idea of design, antiquarianism, and especially its manifestation in the Greek Revival, may be considered antipathetic to creativity. Yet to William Wilkins it was essential to the attainment of architectural beauty and the expression of his profound reverence for and intuitive understanding of those historical periods which had absorbed and delighted him from his youth.

I

Beginnings

William Wilkins was born on 31 August 1778 in the parish of St Giles, Norwich, the eldest son of an ambitious and self-taught architect, William Wilkins senior. His father was determined to rise above his craftsman background, which had been, nonetheless, distinguished. His ancestors, Chrysostom and John Wilkins, had executed plaster-work in some of the finest of the churches built in London under the 1711 Act, including St Anne, Limehouse, St John, Horselydown, St Mary Le Strand, St Mary Woolnoth and St Michael Cornhill; Chrysostom had been Wren's third and last plasterer.[1] William's grandfather had established a solid trade as a plasterer centred on Norwich and had worked on the Octagon Chapel of the cathedral, the Assembly House, the Churchman's House and the ceiling of the main staircase of Blickling Hall. With his son he had formed a partnership, offering, on 6 November 1773 in the *Norwich Mercury*, to provide estimated designs and sections of rooms. Two years later William's father completed his first recorded architectural design, a mausoleum commissioned by Thomas Wale of Shelford, Cambridgeshire, although he was still described as a 'plaisterer' in the lease of ground from St Benedicts, Norwich, recorded in the Great Hospital Minute book. In 1780, to further his professional and social standing, Wilkins senior removed his family to Cambridge, later building houses in Newmarket and Queen's Roads.[2]

At this time Wilkins senior became agent to the 1st Viscount Newark, from 1806 Earl Manvers, and it is likely that one of the first two architectural designs William exhibited at the Royal Academy in 1799, entitled 'Design for improving the seat of a nobleman in

Nottinghamshire', was a project for alterations at Thoresby Hall, the seat of Lord Manvers (where his father was building a bridge), and for which he ordered Tudor style chimneys from the Coade Stone Company in 1819.[3] William's younger brother, George (1786–1865), received a number of appointments in the Church of England under the patronage of Lord Manvers, one as vicar of St Mary's, Nottingham from 1817, in which office he was able to secure for his brother the commission for a new church, St Paul's, built in the city under the 1818 Act.

More valuable was Wilkins senior's association with Humphry Repton with whom he collaborated from circa 1785 to 1796. The informal partnership with Repton gave him a professional reputation and earned him sufficient income to invest in the then profitable theatre business. In 1799 he bought the lease of the Theatre Royal, Norwich and thereupon submitted a scheme for improvements to the proprietors, writing that the theatre was 'justly considered as the first nursery for Actors in the Kingdom', but its fame was tarnished by poor facilities, 'the Entrances and Avenues being so ill contrived that only one person can approach the Lobby, a Lady must be separated from the Arm of her Protector both on entering and leaving' and the ensuing scrum was often spiced with unwelcome drama: 'it is really otherwise impossible that Ladies can reach their carriages without danger of spoiling their Dresses and being squeezed perhaps between Doorkeepers, Porters and prostitutes who are forcing their way without regard to Beauty or Dress'.[4] Wilkins senior persuaded Repton to rewrite a comedy for production at the theatre, presented as *Odd Whims*, and dedicated to a Norfolk patron, William Windham, M.P.[5]

Wilkins senior assisted Repton in the improvement of a series of houses including Babworth, Bracondale, Brandersbury, Hailing Grove, Langley, Little Green, Northrepps, Rivenhall and Welbeck, predominantly in the 'Gothick' style.[6] Through Repton he came by several commissions: for extensions at Locko Park (Nottinghamshire, 1803), and Prestwold, Leicestershire, circa 1805, both in a Neo-Greek style, the former having a fashionable unbased Doric colonnade probably inspired by William's sojourn in Greece (Pl. 5); for the design and erection of Donington, Leicestershire, 1790–1800 (Pl. 6), for the 2nd Earl of Moira; for Stanfield, Norfolk, circa 1792, for the Reverend George Preston; and for The Cottage, a small house adjoining Northrepps, which belonged to Bartlett Gurney, a member of the influential Norfolk banking family and related to Hudson Gurney who was to become one of William's dearest friends.[7] Other works may have stemmed from the association with Repton: two lodges and cottages for Edward Foley of Stoke Edith, Herefordshire, in 1792; stables for Captain G. S. Legh of High Legh Hall, Cheshire, 1795–7; a Gothic lodge for the 4th Earl Fitzwilliam of Milton Hall, Northamptonshire, circa 1800; and lodges for Sir Henry Harpur, Bt, of Calke Abbey, Derbyshire in 1804.

Their partnership was successful and amicable, Repton being content to commit his shy son, John Adey, to Wilkins's tutorship. After the dissolution of the partnership Repton passed on at least one commission to the Wilkins father and son, that for the enlargement of Pentillie, Cornwall in 1809; in 1807 William had influenced the Building Committee of East India College at Haileybury to engage Repton to landscape the grounds of his Greek Ionic buildings.

Repton was generous in his references to Wilkins senior, writing of Bracondale near Norwich, altered in about 1795 for Philip Martineau, 'it would not be difficult for the inventive genius of my friend Mr Wilkins to depart from all quadrangular ideas, bow windows and other hackneyed forms and adapt a building for this situation which fronts only towards the most favourable points...'.[8] In truth, Wilkins's style was a flimsy Neo-Gothic, barely more convincing than that of his contemporaries, except perhaps in the Elizabethan Tudor of Stanfield Hall, despite Repton's belief that Donington was one of the 'most correct specimens of true Gothic recently built', vying with the alterations James Wyatt made to Sheffield Place and Nacton.[9] But then, Repton, no doubt fairly, claimed to have influenced Wilkins, recalling 'the same degree of elevation may be obtained by building the cellars above the ground, and afterwards raising earth over them, as I advised at DONINGTON and BLAIZE CASTLE', a procedure which was to prove useful to William when he altered Grange Park.[10]

Not all concurred with Repton's judgement and Soane later bracketed Wilkins senior with Batty Langley. Though he applied the pointed arch and a species of Gothic moulding consistently, his style was not a significant departure from those 'quadrangular ideas' Repton castigated, and Wilkins seems to have refrained from the emphatic Picturesque irregularity of plan and profile propounded by

Repton, who, perhaps for this reason, entered into partnership with Nash in 1796.

For his part, Wilkins thought highly of Repton's taste and reputation. In May 1794, for instance, he wrote to William Windham about the progress of repairs he was making to the east part of Felbrigg House, Norfolk, suggesting in a postscript further improvements. He had sent drawings of these to Repton for his opinion, which, he ventured, 'should it coincide with mine will be extremely flattering to me and will probably have some weight in your determination to the plan submitted to you'.[11]

Later Wilkins participated in Windham's political campaign and was accepted into his clique. And, an essential asset in that period, he was befriended by other influential patrons like Lord Howard for whom, he wrote, he had built a lighthouse at Orford Ness.[12] His patrons surely contributed to his being elected to the Society of Antiquaries in 1796. Apart from social introductions, Wilkins was qualified for membership by virtue of his study of mediaeval architecture in East Anglia, dating back to at least 1780, when he had surveyed Norwich Cathedral with a Mr Sanders.[13] Subsequent research had provided material for a paper entitled 'An Essay towards a History of the Venta Icenorum of the Romans and of Norwich Castle' read in 1795 to the Antiquaries. In this he criticised the new gaol John Soane had constructed against the walls of Norwich Castle, begetting a resentment which Soane nursed right up to 1826 and the occasion of William's election as a Royal Academician, which he tried to frustrate. In 1798 Wilkins senior read to the society 'A Description of the Church of Melbourne in Derbyshire', researched while he was working at Donington, and, in 1807, the more scholarly 'Account of the Cathedral Church of Norwich'. This last was associated with a further study of the cathedral made between 1798 and 1800 which the Antiquaries intended to publish in their series of illustrated books on British cathedrals. John Repton executed a number of fine elevations to accompany Wilkins's commentary.

These writings enhanced Wilkins senior's professional career. In 1795 he was asked to extend the Master's Lodge at Gonville and Caius College and in 1798 to undertake the first of three repairs to the exterior of King's College Chapel, the others being carried out by him in 1802 and 1811.[14] He was consulted upon other important restorations in East Anglia, beginning with Norwich Castle in 1792, reversing the destructive rôle he had played a year before as adviser and contractor in the demolition of six of the ancient gates of Norwich: Bishopgate, Brazen Door, Pockthorpe Gate, St Benedict's, St Giles' and St Stephen's Gates.[15] In 1803 he restored the choir and re-roofed the Chapter House of Southwell Minster and, in 1806, repaired the roof of Norwich Cathedral, partially damaged by fire in 1801, and refurbished the exterior and interior. 'In 1806', John Britton wrote in *The History and Antiquities of the See and Cathedral Church of Norwich* (1816), 'nearly the whole Church was repaired, the stone roof washed over with a light colour, and many improvements made in the appearance of the interior, under the direction of the late Mr. Wilkins, architect.'

In 1812, probably aided by William, Wilkins restored St Ethelbert's Gate, Norwich.[16] William might also have assisted in the renovation of St Nicholas, Great Yarmouth. Between 1803 and 1810 Wilkins reconstructed the spire, re-roofed the nave and restored the south side and west end at the direction of a Committee of Trustees appointed under an Act of Parliament.[17] The committee was chaired by Sir Edward Lacon, Bt, who, a decade afterwards, expedited the erection of the Nelson Column at Great Yarmouth, built to William's design.

The Great Yarmouth commission, as much else in Wilkins senior's career, established a good basis for his son's practice. Yet, the most valuable example that he set was a reverence for learning, of which, G. K. Blyth wrote in the *Norwich Guide* of 1842, he had 'received but little' when young.[18] Wilkins became interested in disciplines outside his immediate activities and apparently educated himself quite widely. He studied astronomy, owning a telescope and corresponding with the Reverend Samuel Vince, later Plumian Professor of Astronomy and a Fellow of Gonville and Caius College. He entered William at Norwich Grammar School and so encouraged his natural abilities that in 1796 he won Dr Gostlin's Scholarship to Gonville and Caius College. While at school William frequented the studio of (Sir) William Beechey, who, he recalled in a typically witty letter written to Hudson Gurney on 15 February 1839:

> died in his 86th year in the arms of a family whose constant care was to make his old life a scene of joy and happiness and well did they succeed... [He] knew little of pain and

a strong constitution enabled him to go almost daily to his painting room in Henrietta Street from Hampstead and return to dinner except when a casual invitation held out to him the hope of an additional pint of madeira beyond the one to which he was restricted. He was a friend of my earliest recollection, daily after School hours I used to resort to his painting room...[I was] placed opposite...a chubby cast of a dirty cupid making eyes, and noses at which others made mouths – I was under the guidance of the muse of drawing in the person of the pretty Phillis Jessup – another Mary of Buttermere – but with a happier fate – First his pupil, afterwards his wife.[19]

Here was one source for the crisply defined style of William's beautiful mature architectural drawings.

William went up to Gonville and Caius in the Michaelmas term and read mathematics, graduating 6th Wrangler (sixth in the university class lists) in 1800. No doubt his success depended upon that consistent application to work which characterised his subsequent career; in reply to a question about the number of buildings he had executed at Cambridge, he was to say that 'it was possible to do a great deal by method'.[20] He was a devoted scholar, who preferred study to any other pursuit. While many of his contemporaries sowed their oats, William pored over Classical texts, marking in that mien of concentration which lent such authority to his features in later years, and patiently measured and drew King's College Chapel. He may have compiled the series of elevations, sections and details of the chapel at the time when his father was supervising repairs to the water spouts in 1798.[21] The first of these eleven drawings uses the west door to frame an explanatory inscription, while the quality of the remainder and his attention to the principles of the chapel's construction are exemplified in the fifth, an east–west section (Pls. 7 and 8).

In 1800, qualified by such studies, which anticipated the endeavours of A. C. Pugin and E. J. Willson, William was introduced into the Society of Antiquaries as 'a gentleman conversant in the History of the Antiquities of Great Britain and especially in the ancient architecture of this Kingdom'.[22] Sponsored by two Cambridge scholars, the Reverend Thomas Kerrich, librarian to the university,

1797–1817, and Sir Busick Harwood, professor of anatomy and a member of the embryo Downing College, and by Craven Ord, the vice-president of the society, William was elected on Thursday, 4 December 1800, the occasion when his future rival, Robert Smirke, was presented. In turn, this honour contributed to William winning the Worts Travelling Bachelorship in 1801 that financed the extensive tour from Naples and Paestum to Sicily, Greece and Asia Minor upon which the majority of his later antiquarian work was based.

Before he left England in July 1801, however, William was more of a mediaeval antiquary, though surely acqainted with at least some of those undergraduates and graduates who shared Robert Wood's desire to tread in the footsteps of Homer.[23] A number were as much adventurous travellers as serious scholars of Greek literature and art which, furthermore, seldom monopolised their antiquarian pursuits. Three, Edward Dodwell (1767–1832), Sir William Gell (1777–1836) and Robert Walpole (1781–1856), later turned their attention to Roman art and architecture; with Sir William Drummond, Walpole wrote *Herculanesia, or Archaeological and Philological Dissertations, containing a manuscript found among the ruins of Herculaneum* (1810), while Dodwell and Gell (who also published books on Roman architecture) took up residence in Italy, where both died.[24] They were the products of a new phase of Classical learning in England, excited by the prospect of rediscovering the remains and the spirit of ancient Greek art and civilisation.

Among the most outstanding Graecophils of William's period at Cambridge were Edward Daniel Clarke (1769–1882), Gell who graduated from Emmanuel College before migrating to Jesus in 1804, Dodwell and Walpole of Trinity, and Thomas Smart Hughes (1786–1847) who, in 1807, won the Sir William Browne Medal for a Greek ode apostrophising the former Prime Minister, William Pitt, guardian of that other celebrated Graecophil and graduate of St John's, Lord George Gordon (Hamilton-Gordon from 1818), 4th Earl of Aberdeen (1784–1860). Aberdeen, incidentally, went up to St John's from another breeding ground of Graecophils, Harrow School. There he had been preceded by Lord Elgin (1766–1841), whose admiration for Greek art made him either its greatest preserver or ravager, and joined by Henry Drummond (1786–1860), later to commission William to transform his house, Grange Park, into a quasi-Greek temple.

Perhaps the central figure in that somewhat disparate group – for their areas of interest differed quite widely – was Robert Walpole, editor of *Memoirs relating to European and Asiatic Turkey: edited from manuscript journals* (1817) and *Travels in Various Countries of the East: being a continuation of memoirs relating to European and Asiatic Turkey* (1820). As well as culling material from most of his Cambridge contemporaries and from military topographers, such as Colonel William Leake (1777–1860), he published writings by earlier Varsity antiquaries, including John Sibthorpe (1758–96) who, like James Dallaway (1763–1824), hailed from Oxford.[25]

Yet, so far as the young Cambridge Graecophils were concerned, their chief local heroes were John Tweddell (1769–99), Clarke and John Bacon Sawrey Morritt (1772–1843). Tweddell, a fellow of Trinity, whose Latin and Greek prize essays were published in 1793 as *Prolusiones Juveniles* – possibly the inspiration for the title of William's last book on Classical architecture, *Prolusiones Architectonicae* (1837) – left for Greece in 1795. He died at Athens and his grave in the so-called Temple of Theseus immediately joined the list of sites on the itinerary of English visitors; Byron afterwards had it marked by a block of marble from the Parthenon and cut with an inscription written by Walpole. Clarke graduated from Jesus and began his tour in 1799. During this he uncovered and removed a caryatid from the Inner Propylaea at Eleusis, which he denominated Ceres and presented to the Public Library at Cambridge (now Fitzwilliam Museum, no. 91) before publishing details of it in a short book with three engravings by Flaxman.[26] He sold the coins he had collected to Richard Payne Knight and the manuscript record of his tour, curiously, to Oxford University. He had used it to write the six volumes of his *Travels in Various Countries of Europe, Asia and Africa* (1810–22), which contributed to his being elected librarian to the University of Cambridge in 1817. Morritt of St John's headed east in 1794 with Dallaway and G. Wilbrahim (1741–1813) and helped to direct more English antiquaries, including Gell and Aberdeen, to a consideration of the thorny problem of the site of Homeric Troy with his *Vindication of Homer* (1798) and *Additional Remarks on the Topography of Troy* (1800).

These three men and William's contemporaries spurred on another wave of Cambridge travellers including Byron and his companion, John Hobhouse, the Hon. F. S. N. Douglas, John Palmer, J. N. Fazakerly and Henry Gally Knight (1786–1846). Knight, a Trinity man, who traversed Egypt, Greece and Palestine between 1810 and 1811, typified the catholicity of the Cambridge antiquaries since he went on to publish two useful books on post-Classical and mediaeval continental architecture, *An Architectural Tour in Normandy* (1836), and *The Ecclesiastical Architecture of Italy from Constantine to the Fifteenth Century* (1841). He reversed the direction from Gothic to Greek taken by William and Aberdeen.

Aberdeen's interest in Gothic architecture was stimulated by his friendship with George Downing Whittington (1781–1807), also up at St John's and later to take holy orders (he was to baptise Aberdeen's first child), and to be a means of Aberdeen meeting William. Whittington, like William, was intrigued by the most contentious current issue within the ranks of the Antiquaries, the origin of Gothic architecture.[27] In the paper on the Prior's Chapel, Ely, which William submitted to the society in the form of a letter addressed to the secretary, William bowed to the conventional wisdom that the Gothic style had originated in England with the intersection of Norman arcading which formed the characteristic pointed arch.[28] This opinion had been expressed by James Bentham in *The History and Antiquities of the Conventical and Cathedral Church of Ely* (Cambridge, 1771), and reiterated by John Milner in *The History, Civil and Ecclesiatical, and Survey of the Antiquities of Winchester* (Winchester, 1798). In his essay William speculated that 'Perhaps the result of a more particular Enquiry into the Differences subsisting between the *Norman* and *Gothic styles*, might satisfy us that we need not go to Palestine or Germany for authority to account for the origin of the latter.' If anything, he was more concerned with the inadequacy of the term 'pointed style', writing that it

> has been indiscriminately called *Saracenic* and *Gothic* without much foundation for either appellation, and as nothing perfectly satisfactory has been discovered to justify any determinate one for it, it may be as well to allow it to pass under its adopted Gothic provided we mean to distinguish it from the *Saxon* and *Norman*, of the latter of which it may possibly be a refinement.

Hoping to clarify such confusion, he proposed that three architectural features be compared in order to distinguish Gothic from Norman architecture: arch construction, window articulation and pier formation.

Whittington and Aberdeen arrived at an entirely different conclusion about the origin of the style over the course of the next six years. They rejected the chauvinistic argument in favour of one first proposed by a member of John Evelyn's circle in the seventeenth century; interestingly, Aberdeen's friend, Richard Payne Knight, voiced a similar conclusion in his *An Analytical Inquiry into the Principles of Taste* (1805).[29] In the preface which Aberdeen wrote to *An Historical Survey of the Ecclesiastical Antiquities of France; with a view to illustrate the rise and progress of Gothic architecture in Europe*, published as the posthumous work of Whittington in 1809, he stated that his friend had returned from a tour of France and Italy in 1803 intending to refute 'an hypothesis maintained by several writers and supported by the Society of Antiquaries, that the styles called Gothic, really originated in this island, and ought therefore in the future to receive the denomination of English architecture'.

Whittington had discussed his ideas with Aberdeen while he was assembling the material for his book. In a letter postmarked 8 September 1804 Whittington told Aberdeen that he believed the Gothic style to have been inspired by Eastern architecture because it had appeared in Western Europe immediately after the first crusade. He also declared that it had been perfected originally in France, and he informed Aberdeen that he was planning to write a book with 'copious notes' to be entitled 'The Antiquities of Foreign Churches considered with a view to illustrate the History of Gothic Architecture'.[30] By April of the next year he had changed the title to 'A History of Gothic Architecture in France, comprising the particular histories, dates & descriptions of several of the most remarkable churches in that country and containing a comparison between them and the contemporary edifices in England/buildings of England of the same period'.[31] Whittington was not alone among Cambridge mediaevalists in his interest in the continental Gothic style. Between May and June 1809 Thomas Kerrich wrote a series of papers which were published in *Archaeologia*, the Antiquaries' journal, in 1812 as 'Some Observations on the Gothic Buildings Abroad, Particularly those of Italy, and on Gothic Architecture in General'. In company with Aberdeen, Whittington, William and many antiquaries of their generation, Kerrich was dissatisfied with the contemporary terminology employed to describe Gothic architecture and rejected the idea that the pointed arch was its major constituent.

Whittington mentioned his studies in most of the extant letters he addressed to Aberdeen up to his untimely death in the spring of 1807, an event that ended a correspondence which is fascinating as an insight upon the antiquarian alumnae. An amusing extract may be found in the letter he wrote from Wimpole in 21 August 1805. He and Lord Royston, who also died prematurely, were employed in 'converting Lady Hardwicke to what she calls "Lord Aberdeen's intolerant admiration of Grecian Columnes [sic]" & as we have already exploded pillasters [sic] & blown up Soane [who had made additions to the house] I think we are getting on very well'.[32] Still, Whittington's first love appears to have been mediaeval architecture. York 'Cathedral', he wrote to Aberdeen on 20 December 1806, was admirable for 'its general stateliness and extent...though I must always consider the high-pointed Gothic of the 13th Century to be preferred before all others'.[33]

Within a year Whittington was dead and it was Aberdeen who prepared his incomplete notes for publication with the blessing of his family. Whittington's executor, Henry Raikes, warned Aberdeen that the papers were in a very imperfect state and that 'the materials are scanty, confused & disjointed; the hasty look I was able to give them made me aware it will require considerable time & labour to form them with a regular shape....'.[34] By the end of August Aberdeen had completed the preface and the first chapter, the former being, according to Raikes, 'so particularly useful in preparing the reader for the Work'.[35] This was a finer testimony of their friendship than the memorial tablet executed by Westmacott for St John's College, to the cost of which Aberdeen contributed. In the preface, Aberdeen claimed that Whittington had demonstrated 'the prior excellence of the French style' and also the deficiency of the term Gothic. Moreover, he supported Whittington's thesis that 'the origin of the Gothic style notwithstanding the occasional imitation of a corrupt and degraded species of Roman architecture is sufficiently indicated by the lofty and slender proportions, by the minute parts, and the fantastic ornaments of Oriental taste'.

By the summer of 1809, however, Aberdeen's attention was to be concentrated upon the study of Greek architecture, collaborating with William Wilkins on the compilation of *The Civil Architecture of Vitruvius*, a labour of love inspired by their respective tours of Greece and Asia Minor.

II
Antiquaries abroad

The award of the Worts Travelling Bachelorship in 1801 was a most significant event in William Wilkins's development. Through it he gathered the material for the majority of his publications and the inspiration for his most celebrated designs. The choice of Greece and Asia Minor could have been determined as much by a desire to extend the scholarly literature on ancient Greek architecture as by the disturbed political situation in France and Italy. Another factor might have been the very challenge of the difficulties that faced the traveller, vividly summarised in the letter Gell wrote to Aberdeen in October 1804 about a projected tour of the Morea: 'If the people don't kill me outright, I shall have I flatter myself – a most copious topographical knowledge of the country before the winter is over.'[1] Wilkins may have learned of such exigencies from the 2nd Earl of Moira, whose father, John Rawdon, had been one of the first English travellers in the Levant in the late 1730s.

The tour, beginning with sojourns in Naples and Sicily, was a courageous decision for a young man of little worldly experience and, notwithstanding the financial success then enjoyed by his father, Wilkins needed the annual grant of £100 to compensate for the want of those diplomatic introductions that were to be available to Aberdeen who, under the aegis of William Pitt, accompanied Sir William Drummond on an embassy to Constantinople.

The statute of the Bachelorship bequeathed by William Worts in 1709, a graduate of Catharine Hall, suited Wilkins's purpose of assembling new and timely archaeological information with which he planned to launch his career. In return for a pension of £100 for three years he was to write monthly letters in Latin to the Vice-Chancellor of the university, describing the 'religion, learning, laws, politics, customs, manners, and rarities, natural and artificial, which they shall find worth observing in the countries through which they pass'.[2] The Scholarship was open to Bachelors of Arts nominated by the colleges on a rotating basis, but the university records do not show whether Gonville and Caius College was entitled to present a candidate in 1801.

Wilkins left England some time after 24 June 1801, the date of his first letter to the Vice-Chancellor written on board ship at Portsmouth.[3] In this enthusiastic communication he reported that, through the aid of an anonymous nobleman, probably the 2nd Earl of Moira to whom he dedicated *The Antiquities of Magna Graecia* in 1807, he was about to sail to the Mediterranean in H.M.S. *Malta*, formerly the French ship-of-the-line, *Guillaume Tell*, eighty guns, captured off Malta on 30 March 1799.[4] Villeneuve's flagship at the Battle of Aboukir, she had been refitted for Mediterranean service, but this cruise was cancelled and the ship remained in home waters as the Spithead guardship from the summer of 1801 to the autumn of 1802. How Wilkins reached Italy remains, therefore, a mystery.

In that first letter written aboard the *Malta* Wilkins was brimming with expectation and literary flourish. After expressing gratitude for the award he regretted that hostilities in Europe had frustrated his 'most eager endeavours'. He continued:

> For when I earnestly desired to visit and explore the islands of the Mediterranean and the famous cities of Greece, and moreover the regions of Asia Minor, the remarkable kindness of a certain great nobleman provided for me to make my journey in a ship which was indeed almost the sole survivor of the French fleet driven ashore in Egypt, which had not 'at that time' fallen into the victorious hands of the British. But at last the warlike valour of our countrymen and their seamanship triumphed gloriously over her, too; and she is speedily to return to those seas in which she, and the allied ships, sadly and reluctantly struck, the French flag, in defeat, to our heroes.
>
> In this ship, then, I hope, I am very soon to visit those lands in which the relics of the Ancient arts and sciences

thrill the traveller; in which, if anywhere, traces of the most exquisite writings and most hallowed monuments of Antiquity still exist. When I have wandered through these lands, I shall certainly not lack material in which to work with both advantage and pleasure; nor, I trust, from which I may be able to bring away what even my University may not deem unworthy of notice.

If then anything of this sort cross my path, I undertake to effect all that a sedulous performance can achieve. So that I shall have demonstrated at least that, if nothing else, I was in no way wanting in either willingness or industry; and that I have never for a moment lost sight of that association which exists between myself and this famous home of learning and scholarship.

Wilkins's itinerary can be reconstructed from the three remaining letters written to the Vice-Chancellor, references listed from a lost diary, the contents of his publications and three gouaches signed by the Italian painter, Agostino Aglio. Wilkins apparently engaged Aglio as draughtsman at Rome in 1801, where the artist returned in 1802; according to one tradition, Wilkins invited Aglio to come to England in December 1803 as drawing master at Gonville and Caius College.[5] The Aglio gouaches depict the Bay of Naples and two scenes made near Syracuse, one perhaps including Wilkins seated sketching in the foreground (Pl. 9), and come from a series used to illustrate *The Antiquities of Magna Graecia*, the first fruits of the tour.[6] Of Wilkins's extant letters to the Vice-Chancellor, the second was despatched from Syracuse on 1 March 1802, the third from Malta on 5 August 1802, and the fourth from Smyrna on 8 April 1803. His diary was seen by Walkley and said to include entries written at Naples, Paestum, Selinus, Segesta, Athens, Sunium, Rhamnus, Eleusis, Olympia and Aegina. Most of these centres are referred to by Wilkins in *Magna Graecia*, while in *Atheniensia, or Remarks on the Topography and Buildings in Athens* (1816), in two articles submitted to Robert Walpole's publications in 1817 and 1820, and lastly in *Prolusiones Architectonicae or Essays on Subjects connected with Grecian and Roman Architecture* (1837) he concentrated upon Athenian architecture.

Naturally, Wilkins included numerous expressions of gratitude in his letters and, given their relative brevity, many generalities. Still, the letters evinced his eager idealism and his real pleasure in antiquarian study, and deserve full quotation as rare evidence of his youthful character. That written from Syracuse contained his response to the massive proportions of the Sicilian Greek Doric temples and also his desire for the preservation of such antiquities:

There really is no place, worthy Sir, from which I should more like some remembrance of myself to reach your famous seat of ancient scholarship and true abode of more modern science, than from an island made famous by the repute not only of its fine art but also of a more austere discipline. This is the place where Pindar celebrated in noble verse both the virtues of his friend Hiero and the portents of the fiery mountain; and where Plato sought to turn the mind of a tyrant from every kind of cruelty and brutality to pursuits and habits more worthy of a man, by the weighty precepts of Philosophy. Nay more, in this very City the famous mathematician, Archimedes, embarked on those fortunate courses of Science, through which he paved the way to discoveries, some of them more servic-eable to the life of man, others more adapted to exercise and amuse the intellect.

I tarried a while, therefore, in a City such as this is; and hope I may be allowed to give a short account of some of the most precious monuments of Antiquity; an account not wholly unworthy of your ears, learned Sir; or which at least may show my mind to be both inclined to 'things of ancient praise and art', and also not forgetful of my Alma Mater.

Accordingly, among those relics of Antiquity which particularly strike the mind of the traveller with awe, the Temple of Minerva especially presents itself to the admiration of the beholders, either because the passage of the years has spared it more, or because M. T. Cicero has praised it so much in the famous and often repeated speeches against Verres.

This famous temple rises from the middle of the island once called Ortygia. Its columns are 40 in number, of the

Doric order, and fluted. Two of them, which stood in the Pronaos, were of such a girth that four men with extended arms could hardly [or, not even hardly] grasp hands [about it]. These columns, which it is still possible to see in the west wall of the Church, are said to be fashioned from a single stone. But they have this peculiarity, that they overtop the other columns of the same temple by more than 18 inches of our measurement. If you consider this circumstance, indeed, and the fact that much of the work around them does not smack so much of that fine and polished genius of the ancient craftsmen, one may conjecture, if one likes, that these two were added by some later hand, to complete the number of the rest.

Be that as it may, this must have been a temple of the most elegant character, and cost a vast amount of labour; and what still exists today is wonderfully consistent with that antiquity which, in comparison with the other temples of this Island, it confidently claims for itself. To be sure absolutely nothing has remained to this day of the paintings mentioned by Cicero and the doors that both glittered with gold and ivory, and were most ingeniously decorated with carvings of the head of Medusa. But an over-officious piety has also disfigured some parts, in transforming the seat of an Hellenic diety into a Christian church. I am not indeed one who wants to assail with reproaches an undertaking of this sort, however directed; since I am well aware that that same officiousness which has disfigured some buildings has actually rescued others from the sport of centuries and the ravages of barbarians. The Temple of Olympian Jove [at Agrigento] affords striking testimony, for only 2 columns in all remain of it, and they indeed are shorn of bases and capitals. Further, I have not been so fortunate as to find any part at all of the Temple of Diana [probably one of the eight temples erected at Selinus], of which also Cicero has made mention: although there are not wanting those who would say that two columns of this Temple, too, have survived – 'hedged about', I imagine, 'on all sides (like the Tomb of Archimedes, searched for by the Man of Arpinum,) and clothed with briars and thorns'. [See Cicero, *Tusc. Disp.* v. 23].

Clearly the actual sight of the buildings and scenes about which he had read profoundly fired his imagination. And in the third letter his feelings of awe at visiting the Plain of Marathon and the remains of Plataea stimulated speculations on political liberty, which he went on to associate with British democracy. No less typical of his generation are those sentences laced with poetic melancholy:

I am not unaware, learned Sir, how insignificant is the information that can be comprehended in a short paper; and how feeble and inadequate will be my account of places which have of necessity to be visited to be properly understood.

Certainly I should like again to render myself agreeable to you and to my Alma Mater, the University, in order to show my gratitude. Meanwhile I may advise you, lest this gift may seem to have been entrusted to some lazy and undeserving person, that I have collected a wealth of examples of those relics of the Ancient Arts which are less well-known than their value and worth deserve. If God permits me to return to my household gods, yea, and to the bosom of the University, these may be published in a book. If, then I bring this undertaking to a happy conclusion, it will, I hope, be my warranty that I never spared myself, either by reason of idleness or fear of sea-voyaging [or, fear of the sea and journeying], from making use of every advantage offered by foreign parts, for my own education or for the amusement of others.

Having thoroughly examined and explored whatever survived of ancient art at Athens, I betook myself to other places in Greece, noted in the minds of posterity by reason of some famous deed. I resolved that above all I must visit the Plain of Marathon; that Plain, indeed, upon which true patriotism, and hatred of tyranny and foreign domination, produced the richest and most enduring fruits of valour. But I turned a little aside from the road, to look at the stone-quarries of Pentelicus. Assuredly, these should most certainly not be neglected by an Architect; because it is from that stone, almost comparable to even the marble of Paros, that the most beautiful buildings at Athens, as well as the fame of Ceres at Eleusis, are constructed, in all their elegance and majesty.

The site of the battlefield conforms today, too, to the accounts of ancient historians. The rather higher ground occupied by the small warlike bands of Greece; the swamps among which the unwarlike Persians were over-whelmed; brought before my eyes the action surely worthiest to be remembered by all [or, for ever].

But, indeed, the pleasure with which the recollection of former times thrills the heart, little by little disappears, when the appearance of things shows itself from all directions a cheerless one. Before reaching Thebes, I had to traverse Mount Parnes. How great was the grief that seized upon my mind, that such exquisite Muses, struck dumb by the sloth and disdain of the Turks, have so long been silent. Next, Thebes itself, what little of it still exists, has scarcely anything else to show other than those arrogant and spiritless enemies of literature, unmindful alike of their own and of others' freedom.

What did Plataea itself suggest to the mind of the traveller other than the ghost of former – but vanished – glory? What can he think of more desirable, than the vain prayer of Liberty, and her companion and attendant, Learning, may be renewed in a land, a climate, a soil, a genius once the happiest?

But what is the point of writing more? These, and other memorials of days gone-by, turn the mind more keenly and more vividly to one's Fatherland, which, by the glory of its useful sciences, if not of its refined studies; by the trophies set up by land and sea for so many generations, now; by its righteous zeal for freedom, finally, and its true love for the native soil; rivals the fame of that ancient Greece, and offers an example to the Greece of today.

And so, whilst I am wandering in these lands, I appreciate most fully the force of what the Poet, with marvellous pathos [or, sympathy], writes about his hero,

who is wandering far from his own dear island,
'Wishing to see even the smoke arising
> from his land,
> he yearns for death.'

Athens impressed Wilkins most, not least as the last resting place of John Tweddell. As he was to tell the 1816 Select Committe on the Elgin Marbles, he studied the monuments with 'Stuart's book in my hand, and some drawings of my own', being 'amazingly struck' with Stuart's 'great precision and accuracy'. The letter, posted from Smyrna in April 1803 prior to his journey home to England, dwelt fervently on the famed sites and sages of the ancient city:

> As I continued my travels, worthy Sir, a wider field of opportunity opened out before me, for commending myself to my Alma Mater, the University, both in respect of gratitude and ready willingness. At the outset, Sicily held me enthralled, as I gazed with attentive eyes on the region made famous by the poems of Pindar, and by the vigilance of Archimedes himself [Archimedes's defence works at Syracuse]. Most recently, indeed, I was the guest of Greece, the nurse and perfectress of those Arts which contribute to the education and betterment of mankind; yea, the guest of famous Athens, of all cities the most praiseworthy of learning, and almost for valour. What a spring of joy flooded my deepest feelings, when it fell to me to see afar the cliff of Sunium, the relics of the bastions of the Piraeus, the proud bulk of the Temples, and finally the very Acropolis itself! With what greedy eyes I scanned everything! With what tireless feet I traced out the coastline, the harbour, the City, the temples of the gods, the monuments of the heroes, and the Argora, Pnyx and Areopagus. When the virtues of Aristides and Phocion thrilled my memory, and the lofty poetry of the tragedies and delightfully composed character-drawing virtually rang in my ears; when the philosophy of Socrates, the most perfect that the powers of the human mind could rise to, occurred to my mind; I felt I was being carried out of myself and was present in ages long, long past, talking with the supreme philosophers and the greatest men, and

experiencing in the depths of my heart those powerful masters of mood.

I was permitted to do more than just gaze upon 'things of ancient praise [or, worth]', and recall to mind the names of men long dead, and pay my due of respect and grief, with love and veneration, to the foreign individuals renowned for wisdom and virtue. I entered the Temple of Theseus [Hephaestus]. Yet neither the magnificence of the Temple itself (however little the passage of years has impaired its marvellous beauty and natural forces damaged the majesty of its columns); nor the sheen of its marble, nor the skill of the craftsmen took such a hold of mind and eye as did the tomb in which the bones of Tweddell lie at rest.

For indeed that fine young man, the great ornament of our Athens, who had mentally drunk deep of whatever Greece had left of the beautiful and sublime; and who, in the vigour and quickness of his genius had almost equalled the grace and charm of the Greek poets; met his end in this City. Undoubtedly he died an untimely death, if you consider his age and the hopes of whatever there is of learning and elegance had placed in him, on the basis of studies auspiciously begun. Yet it was timely enough, if one may measure the scan of a man's life in terms of the most happy progress in learning and virtue. In that, most patriotic citizen of his Country, he died among foreigners; in that a man most disposed towards the tender affections, he died far from friends and family; the fate by which he perished was a sad one. But you could not call wholly unhappy the death of one who, fired with a passion for ancient studies and having in particular sedulously cultivated Greek literature, breathed his last in Athens itself and on the very banks of the Ilissus.

Yea, most distinguished young man, may you accept the regrets [or, longing] of a traveller, who has undergone the same training as yourself (but with what inferior talents!); and is entering upon the same career (but at how great a distance behind!). May the undying memory of you kindle in the minds of young men at *our* Athens an equal love of literature and an equal assiduity in its pursuit!

The profound admiration for Athenian architecture that courses through this letter conflicts with an accusation made in 1819 by George Basevi, one of John Soane's protegés. Writing from Rome on 18 January, Basevi told the no doubt delighted Soane that Wilkins had 'only spent four days in Athens' according to 'Mr. Lusieri and Mr. Fauvel, the French Consul', using this snippet of uncorroborated gossip to enlarge upon his disparagement of the interpretation of the meaning of the inscriptions on Hadrian's Arch that Wilkins had published in *Atheniensia*.[7] The accusation seems to be unfounded since, in evidence to the Elgin Marbles Select Committee, Wilkins implied that he had stayed there throughout the summer of 1802 measuring 'a great many' of the monuments studied by Stuart, while in a footnote on page 129 of *Atheniensia* he recalled: 'During the time I resided at Athens, Lord Elgin excavated' the caryatid portico 'and discovered several steps leading down to a doorway in the south wall of the Pandroseum'.

A decade earlier another member of the Soane circle, the architect Robert Mylne, had cast aspersions on William's scholarship, either in deference to his mentor's resentment towards the Wilkins family or, as likely, because he had failed to complete a book projected in 1758 and to be entitled 'The Antiquities of Sicily'. Mylne suggested that *Magna Graecia* was cribbed from books by Antonini and Pigonati.[8] Given Wilkins's extensive acknowledgement of source material in *Magna Graecia*, beginning with the best recent study of the Greek temples, Thomas Major's *Ruins of Paestum* (1768), and including those by Delagardette, Denon, Paoli, Piranesi and Winckelmann (as edited by Carlo Fea), it would appear that he set little store by Antonini or Pigonati.

Wilkins began work on *Magna Graecia* immediately after returning to Cambridge in the summer of 1803, fortified by election to a fellowship at Gonville and Caius which was announced on 4 August (terminated when he married in 1811) and in 1804 by his appointment as Master of the Perse School which lasted until 1806. He received further financial support from the subscribers to *Magna Graecia* who included many of the artistic profession: Edmund Aiken, George Byfield, Mrs Damer, John Foster, Henry Howard, Robert Mylne, John Nash, John Plaw, William Porden and Humphry Repton; the Cambridge fraternity: Aberdeen, Clarke, the Hon. J. Cust, Dr Davy (Master of Gonville and Caius College), Gell, Harwood, the Reverend T. Kenrick (whose son, John, was to be a founding member of the Yorkshire Philosophical Society for which Wilkins was to design a museum in 1827), Whittington and Robert Woodhouse (Senior Wrangler in 1795, a Fellow of Gonville and Caius until his marriage to Wilkins's sister, Harriet, and subsequently, by virtue of his work on calculus, Lucasian Professor of Mathematics between 1820 and 1822, when he replaced the deceased Vince as Plumian Professor of Astronomy and Experimental Philosophy); the learned and antiquarian London circles: Sir Jacob Astley (an early Paestum enthusiast), the Reverend Edward Balme, Sir Joseph Banks (President of the Royal Society), the Earl of Camden, the Reverend Chetwynd Eustace, Robert Fellows, four members of the Gurney family, Thomas Hope, the 3rd Marquis of Lansdowne (whose collection of antique statuary vied with those assembled by Towneley and Weddell) and Ichabod Wright; and present or future patrons: Lord Elgin, F. F. Foljambe, Manvers, Moira and Viscount Primrose (later 4th Earl of Rosebery).

Magna Graecia was printed at Cambridge in 1807, having received the Vice-Chancellor's imprimatur in the winter of 1806, and soon became an acknowledged work of scholarship, alluded to by Colonel Leake as one of those books which had publicised 'the knowledge of the genuine architecture of the Greeks'.[9] It was modelled upon the first three volumes of James Stuart and Nicholas Revett's *Antiquities of Athens* (the second was edited by William Newton and the third by Willey Revely) and comprised a series of chapters relating the history and modern state of the main Greek sites in Sicily and Italy, with full bibliographical information, especially with reference to the relevant ancient literature, and illustrated by sixty-two plates, forty-seven of which were excellently drawn (but not uniformly correct by modern archaeological standards) elevations, excellent sections and details of the celebrated antiquities, engraved by I. Ieakes, W. Lowry, T. Medland, S. Porter and J. Roffe from drawings by Aglio and Wilkins. Part of the manuscript and the original illustrations, minus plates 17, 20 and 21 from chapter 3, and those from the appendix, were presented to the R.I.B.A. in 1874 by M. D. Wyatt. The chapters on Syracuse, Agrigento, Selinus, Segesta and Posidonia or Paestum were prefaced by a more lengthy introduction in which Wilkins attempted a short history of the development of Greek architecture. Therein he first advanced two propositions that were to be examined more fully in *The Civil Architecture of Vitruvius*

(1813 and 1817) and *Prolusiones*, namely the inaccuracy of some of the information about Greek temples contained in modern editions of the Treatise of Vitruvius, and the influence of the Temple of Jerusalem upon Greek architecture. The latter was taken from Sir Isaac Newton's *Chronology* (Cambridge, 1728) and John Wood's *The Origin of Building, or the Plagiarism of the Heathens Detected* (1741).

Magna Graecia contained many references to Pausanias, whose Baedeker-like travelogues were to be of particular use to Wilkins in the composition of *Atheniensia*. This was a fundamental source and one used extensively by Gell who, in 1810, published *The Itinerary of Greece, with a commentary on Pausanias and Strabo and an account of the monuments of antiquity at present existing in that country; compiled in the years 1801, 1802, 1805, 1806, etc.* In the appendix to *Magna Graecia* Wilkins acknowledged the inspiration of Gell who had assiduously undertaken 'a minute investigation of the whole of the Peloponnesus, and particularly...the scenes of important events in the annals of Grecian History'.

Gell and Hudson Gurney were certainly links between Wilkins and Aberdeen, though it seems to have been Whittington who brought them together. Apart from their antiquarian pursuits, Wilkins, Whittington and Aberdeen were almost bound to cross one another's paths due to their mutual interest in the theatre. On the strength of his success at Norwich, Wilkins's father had taken the lease on the Cambridge Theatre, and Whittington might have referred to a performance by Miss Baillie there in a letter to Aberdeen dated St John's College, 9 October 1805.[10] Two weeks later he again touched on theatrical matters, but then mentioned that he would solicit Hayter's opinion of one of the Temples of Paestum, about which Wilkins was currently writing.[11] On 25 November Whittington reported Wilkins's view of the probable age of the walls of Paestum.[12] At that time Aberdeen had just finished fitting up a theatre at Bentley Priory, Middlesex, the seat of his first father-in-law, Lord Abercorn; amusingly, Aberdeen had written to Pitt to ask whether his appearance in a play at Stanmore could damage his reputation as a budding politician.[13] Thus Aberdeen's direct reference to Wilkins in a letter addressed to Whittington, dated 26 July 1806, comes as no surprise: 'If Mr. Wilkins is in Cambridge pray ask him if he has received a letter from me [with] a plan for the theatre at the Priory – Pray tell him also that I beg a thousand pardons for troubling him about the Temple at Phigilia, but that his plan is perfectly correct and that there are 15 columns in length.'[14] This illuminates a passage in the Farington diary for 15 December 1810 when Lawrence told him that 'Lord Abercorn had employed Wilkins, the Architect, at Stanmore Priory, but was not satisified with his manner of proceeding and proposing to build a theatre there. He intends to employ Robert Smirke.'[15]

Aberdeen admired Wilkins's scholarship and evidently consulted him on Greek archaeology as he did Payne Knight on ancient literature and coinage. Almost certainly he invited Wilkins to join the Athenian Society which he had helped to found after his return from Greece in 1804, exclusive to those who had visited Athens; another of its promoters was Walpole, who wrote from Malta on 10 April 1807: 'No more members for the Athenian Society for some time – Indeed it cannot be safe, even after peace should be made, to travel in Turkey – considering the exasperated state of mind in which the Turks will continue towards the English and the Russians.'[16]

The experiences and observations recorded by Aberdeen in the diaries of his tour are partial compensation to the historian for the loss of Wilkins's diaries, and surely fostered the understanding between the two which culminated in their co-operation in the compilation of *The Civil Architecture*. In 1802 when he ventured across the Channel Aberdeen was already a serious Classical scholar, remarkably widely read, and corresponding with Payne Knight (a frequent visitor to Stanmore, as was Sir Thomas Lawrence).[17]

Aberdeen's companions were Hudson Gurney, who apparently left the party in France, and, from Naples, Sir William Drummond, the recently appointed Ambassador to the Supreme Porte, an accomplished Classical scholar and a fellow of the Royal Society, Miss Fenwick, Lord Brooke, Aberdeen's brother Robert Gordon, a Mr Findlay, and the French artist, Preaux (or Preaulx), who had worked for Tweddell.[18] The party left London for Dover and Calais on 19 November 1802, having delayed their departure on the advice of Pitt.[19]

Aberdeen kept a fairly consistent account of his journeys and impressions, in France especially assembling a large quantity of statistical information. At Paris he was entertained by the notabilities, as an intimate of the illustrious Pitt, conversing with Buonaparte for about a quarter of an hour when attending a military review, and spending many of his evenings at the theatres, by which he was not greatly impressed.[20] He visited the studios of two painters and sculptors, the latter unnamed:

> of the Painters I did not think much; one was the master of David [Vien], an extraordinary old man of eighty five, who has just finished a series of designs for the Life of Cupid, in which there is much merit; but although in England we have Painting far superior to these (Vincent and Vien) yet David, Girard, and Prud'hon stand unrivalled.[21]

The French artists, he wrote, 'with the avowed protection of the Government, and the most admirable specimens in the world, as models,...bid fair to bring Painting and Sculpture to a height of perfection far beyond what has ever been witnessed in Modern Europe'.[22] Aberdeen was expressing a commonly held opinion on the supposed ills of English art which was articulated more publicly by such theorists as Prince Hoare, and also by Wilkins in the last decade of his life. Later Aberdeen mused in his Greek diary on the poverty of patronage in England:

> this may in some measure arise from the people of England being divided into two classes the occupations of each of which, are in some degree incompatible with great attention to the Arts. The great body of the wealth of England is commercial, and men who are continually employed in trafic [sic] cannot be supposed to bestow much time on the cultivation of what is called Taste.[23]

Aberdeen's comments on the works of art in Paris were hardly more than *aide-mémoires*, and reflect conventional taste. For example, he wrote, 'It would take up a volume if I were to describe the pictures' in the Louvre, 'for they are all originals, and almost all fine paintings'.[24] Of the

> Statue Gallery I can say but little for it beggars description. – it is however a Gallery divided into several parts decorated with the greatest possible taste and filled with antique statues; the Greater part of which are the best that have come down to us, among which I need only mention

The Apollo Belvedere, The Venus of the Capitol, and d'Arles, The Läocöon, the dying Gladiator ec ec.[25]

The Elgin Marbles did little to shake that opinion.

As to architecture, he preferred buildings in a Classical style, but not exclusively, admiring St Denis, Versailles, the Petit Trianon and the chapel of the Invalides. Of Paris he wrote, 'I must merely observe that of architecture there is nothing really beautiful, but the well known [east] façade of the Louvre and the Portico of the Pantheon.' Of Soufflot's portico he wrote, 'when viewed as unconnected with the building to which it is attached', it was absolutely perfect. 'I am told it is precisely that of St. Peters upon a reduced scale...the eye is delighted beyond measure at the purity and elegance displayed throughout, and at the decided triumph of classical taste over the Gothic and unatural [sic] portals of Amiens and Notre Dame crowded with saints angels and non descript monsters.'[26] What he disliked in the Gothic style was its excess of detail, even if he could appreciate its magnificence of spatial volume and decoration.

On quitting Paris, saddened by the loss of his dog, Tag, en route, Aberdeen travelled by way of Lyons, Avignon, Aix and Nice to Genoa. In Avignon he searched for relics of Petrarch with but little success and pondered on that favourite theme of his contemporaries, the tenuous survival of culture

> at a time when Europe was immersed in profound ignor-
> ance,...the lamp of science feebly, yet here only shed its
> rays...where now little else but the marks of ruin and
> desolation are to be discerned, once was fixed the seat of
> empire, and papal magnificence, the Traveller must be
> possessed of but little feeling who can leave Avignon
> without mingled emotion of pleasure and regret.[27]

From Genoa he journeyed to Pisa and Florence, in his opinion the most beautiful city he had seen and where he responded enthusiastically to the sculpture of Donatello, Gian da Bologna and Cellini, and thence to Cortona and Rome.[28] Unfortunately his reactions at Rome are absent from the remaining volumes of his diary.

The narrative continues with his departure from Naples on 15 March 1803, bound for Constantinople aboard the frigate *Medusa* with Sir William Drummond. They sailed via Malta, where he discussed the strategic position with Admiral Lord Keith and the Ambassador, Sir Alexander Ball, and Melos, arriving at the Piraeus on 17 April. Between the 18th and 21st of that month Aberdeen met Fauvel, the French consul, visited the famous antiquities, made a pilgrimage to the Theseum, and determined to excavate the Pnyx. The brevity of his account might indicate that he committed fuller notes to a separate book, since lost, and he was always pressed for time.

Standing atop the Acropolis, Aberdeen 'saw devastation committed which is indeed continual' – ironic in view of his own activities as a collector, nicely illustrated by two later references: on 16 July, 'I caused some excavation to be made and got two inscriptions and some coins [at] Alexandria Troas. We cd. not get my inscription on board [the brig *Hannah*] – it cost 20£ to get it half a mile', and a month later when he was at Patmos, 'I expected to have been able to procure mss and scarce books from their library but notwithstanding I offered a great sum it was not possible. They have a great many Mss the oldest of which I should take to be of the 13th century and very valuable printed books Editiones principax Aristophanes. 2 Aristotle.'[29] Among his best acquisitions was a beautiful head of Hermes, bought by the British Museum after his death.[30] Yet he was aware of the significance of such relics to the modern Greek, who though 'ignorant of arts and arms while gazing at the works of his forefathers, experiences a sort of tumultuous exhaltation and breaks out in lamentations over his country'.[31] He appears to have been more interested in the fate of the modern Greeks than was Wilkins, although neither joined the Greek Committee.[32]

Aberdeen had to cut short his first stay at Athens in order to accompany Drummond to Constantinople. There he observed attentively the architectural and social curiosities of the Turkish capital and the beauty of the surrounding country. He was struck by the glorious interior of Santa Sophia and fascinated, as elsewhere, by examples of arch construction; on 23 May he rode 'to the aqueduct of Justinian. The pointed and round arches are there intermixed. It is a great architectural curiosity as it is by far the earliest specimen of the pointed arch known.'[33]

Between times he sketched in the mundane vicissitudes encountered by contemporary travellers, as on 23 June, 'walked along the

Bosphorus. Killed another scorpion in my Bath', or 10 August at Scio, 'The women are extremely free in their manners. We were invited at several places to stay the night', or again three days later at Ephesus, where he picked his way through the ruins with the aid of Spon's *Voyage d'Italie, de Dalmatie, de Grèce, et du Levant* (Lyons, 1678), the modern village was 'composed of about a dozen cabins so filthy that we could not enter one of them. We could find nothing to eat and it was with great difficulty we got our fish boiled. We laid down in our clothes but I did not close my eyes during the night.'[34]

On 2 July, supplied with the necessary firmans, he sailed from Constantinople to the Troad, with Gordon and Preaux. The Troad was one of Aberdeen's major goals, and a subject of discussion with Knight before he left England. The Lawrence Correspondence at the Royal Academy has a letter from Knight to Aberdeen dated 1 March 1802, ending, 'Do not however let me be supposed to favour Mr Bryant's wild hypothesis of the whole Trojan war being one of these Allegorical tales';[35] later, in Greece, Aberdeen was to jot down points under the heading of 'Notes concerning the credibility of Homer's relation of the seige of Troy', and, on 9 July 1803 near Bunarbashi, to fault J. B. Lechevalier's map of the area. In 1796 Jacob Bryant had published *A Dissertation Concerning the War of Troy...as described by Homer, shewing that no such expedition was ever undertaken, and that no such city of Phrygia existed*, written in response to Lechevalier's argument presented in a paper read at two sessions of the Royal Society in Edinburgh during March 1791, printed that year as *Description of the Plain of Troy*, that the ancient city of Troy lay south west of the river Scamander and not in the Roman ruins of Alexandria Troas.[36] These speculations had prompted J. B. S. Morritt and R. Chandler to enter the lists and later stimulated a clutch of the Cambridge fraternity, first E. D. Clarke and then Gell, to visit the supposed site of Troy south of the modern village of Bunarbashi, respectively in 1799 and 1801. Gell presented his ideas in *The Topography of Troy and its Vicinity* (1804), based on a stay of less than a week, which led Lord Byron to dub him 'rapid Gell' in 1816.

Thus the diary entries describing the visit to the presumed site of Troy were more detailed than was customary for Aberdeen, if no less easy to decipher.[37] His party arrived on 6 July opposite the so-called tomb of Antilochus, near the presumed fort of Herakles, and passed through the Sigeum to modern Kumkali, visiting the 'tombs' of Achilles and Patroclus. Aberdeen failed to find the 'tomb' of Ilos or to determine precisely the ancient course of the river Scamander, and returned to the ship via the 'tomb' of Penelus the Boetian (perhaps the tumulus near modern Basik). Next morning the party went to 'Halileli' (possibly Hisarlik, the true site of Troy discovered by Schliemann from 1871) and 'Thiblack' (probably modern Chiplak, also near the actual site) before crossing the Plain to test the temperatures of the supposed sources of the Scamander near Bunarbashi. The discovery that these were the same confounded part of Gell's interpretation of the topography. Over the next three days they again traversed the Plain, slept at Bunarbashi and followed the rivers Scamander and Simois in the company of the Bey and an escort of one hundred mounted attendants.

Parting with Gordon and a tearful Preaux, Aberdeen returned to Athens, arriving there on 30 August. The following day he met Lusieri, Elgin's agent, and set in hand the excavation of the Pnyx. Before work began he made a day's excursion to the church at Daphni. He regarded the celebrated mosaics as an illustration of the decline of the arts from Grecian excellence, though better than those at Santa Sophia. On 1 September he bought an inscription from the Athenian Disdar, copied others – many such are in the diaries together with ground-plans and free-hand sketches – superintended the digging at the Pnyx and supped with Fauvel. The excavations continued until the 5th when he wrote, 'I finished my excavating of the tribune of the Pnyx which is perfectly restored and opened a tomb', adding about a conversation with one of the workmen, 'The poor Greek when I told him Ld Elgin was in prison in a palace said he wd rather be free than a slave in luxury.'[38] The tomb, situated on the site of what he supposed to be the ancient village of Ilissus, might have been the one he described in a lengthy letter to Clarke, dated 22 July 1807, which was published as an appendix to Clarke's *Greek Marbles* (1809).[39]

Leaving Athens for a second time Aberdeen went to Aegina, measuring the remains of the Temple of Aphaia 'with the greatest attention' and tracing a ground-plan into his diary, and rode to Epidaurus, Corinth and Mycenae.[40] Mycenae he visited twice to study the Treasury of Atreus and the Lion Gate which he described in some detail, being convinced of their great antiquity and intrigued by resemblances to Egyptian design.[41] Between these expeditions he went to Argos and thereafter travelled to Sparta which he reached on 12 November, employing twelve men to excavate what he surmised to be the tomb of Leonidas. Three days later at 'Amyclae' (the modern Slavochori) he uncovered two curious bas-reliefs depicting 'articles appertaining to the toilette of a woman' which were to be the subject of a paper and an associated letter in Walpole's books, and were also mentioned in correspondence with Knight.[42] These were shipped to England together with the coins and antiquities he had purchased on his journeyings and some arrived at Chatham on 16 December 1808 aboard H.M.S. *Standard*.[43] Passing through a number of lesser centres, including 'Mesene', where he conducted further excavations, Aberdeen came to Olympia on 3 December, from where he travelled to Corfu and Pola, ultimately arriving at Venice on 15 February 1804, prior to his return to England.

Aberdeen set down ideas for future literary efforts, as, doubtless, did Wilkins in his lost diaries. In the volume relating the tour from Athens to Corfu, Aberdeen devoted some eleven pages to preparatory notes headed 'Observations on the Architecture of the Ancients', mainly concerned with the influence of materials on Greek design. The tour stimulated thought about the history and evolution of Greek architecture, so that he, like Wilkins, determined to bring to light its original principles and forms.

Yet his first published work differed markedly from Wilkins's scholarly *Magna Graecia*. It was a critique of recent books on the topography of Troy, chiefly of the one written by Gell, and printed in the July 1805 issue of the *Edinburgh Review*.[44] Letters between Sir William Drummond, Knight and Whittington in the Aberdeen Correspondence in the British Museum prove that it was written jointly by the young earl and Drummond, who was a close friend of the editor, Francis Jeffrey, but it appeared anonymously. Drummond wrote to Aberdeen from Lord Melville's house at Twickenham in August 1805: 'I am quite confident of being right about the battle between the Scamander and Achilles having taken place above the junction, provided always, as I have expressly said, that the maps of Chevalier and Morritt be correct.'[45] Drummond went on to detail other facts supporting their analysis, doubtless replying to the letter Knight had sent him from Downton on 10 August and which he forwarded to Aberdeen. 'You and Lord Aberdeen – have been very sharp upon poor Gell: but if he has any sharpness in him – which he does appear to have, he may retaliate with Interest.'[46] Knight then picked out errors in their critique, especially their apparent acceptance of the validity of the Homeric account: 'Your acute scepticism might have indulged itself in some suspicion of the Integrity of the Text, as well as of the Accuracy of the Topographers.'

In fact, Aberdeen and Drummond had noted that the text was open to question, not least because Homer had possessed 'the most brilliant and inventive imagination that ever existed'.[47] Their critical analysis of the deficiencies of the proposed topographies was reasonable, although they offered no new interpretation beyond confirming that Troy had probably existed in the area mapped by Gell. They concentrated upon the topographer's response to three problems, the supposed sites of the Greek camp, the city and the course of the Scamander, drawing upon the Homeric text and Aberdeen's observations. Their basic criticism was the propensity of Lechevalier, Morritt and Gell to apply preconceived theories to the topography around the modern village of Bunarbashi. Thus local tumuli were identified wantonly with the tombs of the Homeric heroes, particularly by Gell whose 'good luck in making discoveries can only be equalled by his sagacity in seeking for them'.[48] Attracted by a heap of stones, probably created by land clearance, Gell thought that he had found an earth mound mentioned by Homer, and he had even had the temerity to claim that he had identified the marsh where Ulysses had slept some three thousand years before. Conversely the topographers had ignored the text when it suited them: 'We shall leave it to the travellers to explain, how Homer's great, broad, deep and divine Scamander has dwindled into the little brook of Bournabaschi [sic].'[49] Nor did their surmise that Troy had been situated in the environs of the modern and elevated village accord with Homer's description of the city built on a plain. In such a vein the review moved to a climax, the authors writing that they could not

> help being astounded, that he [Gell] should have collected the materials of his book – that he should have observed, read, reasoned, described and drawn, in three short winter days, more than we, sluggish children of the North, should have expected to have done in as many months. But Mr.

Gell did all this and much more. He went through the common duties of an English morning toilette, brushed his teeth every day...performed his ablutions with a scrupulousness worthy of a musselman...drank his Muscatel white wine; took angles; made a map.[50]

Finally Aberdeen and Drummond, little wonder anonymously, trusted that the future topographer of Troy

will not dream of what he is to discover before he goes there, like M. Chevalier, that he will not forget to make his map on the spot, like Mr. Morritt; and that he will not do everything in a hurry like Mr. Gell: we believe we need not caution him not to drink of the warm spring of Bournabaschi, without a thought of Homer in his mind.[51]

Obviously the Cambridge Graecophils were less an homogeneous group exclusively dedicated to the revival of Greek art, than a bevy of critical and competitive scholars. They delighted in sniping at each other, as two letters Whittington wrote to Aberdeen in 1805 show.[52] In the first, dated 27 January, Whittington terminated a discussion of the historical evidences of Christianity with doggerel about Clarke:

I sing of a tutor renowned
who went roving and roaming for knowledge
and gathered it all the world round
and brought it in *boxes* to College

Clarke has certainly been exposing himself by giving one of Dr. Gell's lectures at Jesus to his pupils. I intend to add a sting to the whole – a verse on the excellence of friendship and constancy exemplified by Davy one moment singing out Clarke's praises in the Senate House as Vice Chancellor & then singing a most abusive song against him & saying it is the best in the world –

In the second, written on 3 August, he detected plagiarism on the part of Walpole. Nonetheless, the disputes were not taken too seriously as Gell later exchanged jovial letters with Aberdeen, though he probably knew who had written the *Edinburgh Review* piece. On 1 December 1806 he wrote to Aberdeen about the choice of sculptor to execute the monument to Pitt which was to be erected at

Cambridge, beginning, 'My dear Ld Aberdeen, grand Duke of Athens Cousin of Theseus & intimate friend of Pericles', and, on the occasion of his election as a Scottish Representative Peer, addressed him as 'My dear Pericles'.[53] In 1809 Aberdeen seemingly suggested that he and Knight join Gell upon what might have been the germ of the Dilettanti expedition to Ionia, to be superintended by the Committee of Publication, to which Wilkins had just been elected.[54] Knight replied from Downton on 15 July 1809 that he

> should like extremely to be a partner in an Olympian Adventure, under the auspices of Gell, if we could be sure of proper protection from *any* Government: but in the present state of Europe there is none that can give it; for if Napoleone is successful on the Danube, the Turkish Empire is parcell'd out and disposed of, so that the Peloponnesus will be in his possession before we can get a spade put into the Banks of the Alpheus.

He advised delaying the expedition for a few months and continued:

> There cannot be a better person than Gell for such an undertaking, as he will unite the Activity of an Agent to the zeal of a Friend and the Principles of a Gentleman: but unless the constituted Authorities of the country are favourable ponderous Objects cannot be remov'd even should they be discovered, and all that are discovered probably will be ponderous.

He also expressed his surprise that he had not heard of any increase in Aberdeen's family, 'but hope to hear of a young Solon or Pericles appearing auspiciously with the arrival of the Grecian Treasures'.[55]

On one issue of taste the Cambridge Graecophils were able to concur, namely the choice of style to be adopted for the latest addition to the architecture at their seat of learning, Downing College. Their success was reported to Aberdeen by Whittington in one of his regular news letters on Cambridge life, dated 8 September 1805: 'Wilkins is to build the College after his Athenian model, he has been formally advised of this, which is the only satisfaction I have received on the subject of fatal Decree.'[56] The hopeful exhibition by Wilkins of his designs for the south and entrance fronts of the college at the 1805 Royal Academy might have helped to achieve the crowning of his young head with the wreath of laurel (Pl. 10).

III
Temples of learning

The fellowship at Gonville and Caius College enhanced Wilkins's standing among the Graecophils and, judging by Whittington's letter of 8 September 1805, he had been favoured as the architect to realise their taste in the commission, supposedly reserved for James Wyatt, for the new college to be erected under the bequest of Sir George Downing.[1] Some, perhaps, had influenced the Master of Downing, Francis Annesley, to forward Wyatt's previously accepted plans to Thomas Hope. Hope responded with *Observations on the Plans and Elevations designed by J. Wyatt, Architect, for Downing College, Cambridge*, published 24 February 1804, in which he argued for the substitution of a Neo-Greek design and significantly referred to Wilkins, who had 'lately brought home, and soon intends to publish designs of a Greek temple [Minerva, Syracuse], in the cella of which Doric columns rise on distinct bases'.

Hope effectively reopened the commission by contrasting Wyatt's old-fashioned Roman Neo-Classicism with the prospect of an 'unique' and 'noble edifice' articulated with the Greek Doric Order, distinguished by strongly projected porticoes and elevated on a stylobate. Thus Hope envisaged elements of Wilkins's plan. However, it would be mistaken to attribute either the form or the selection of Wilkins's design to Hope, since the initial outcome of his intervention was the instigation of a limited competition between Wyatt and George Byfield.[2] This did not produce a plan that satisfied the college authorities so that, in 1805, they considered unsolicited designs from William Porden, Francis Sandys, Lewis Wyatt and Wilkins. Furthermore Wilkins did not follow Hope's proposals in

46

detail, which in any case enshrined his own taste, choosing the Ionic as the predominant Order and pioneering the campus plan. Also, in addition to his reputation in Cambridge, Wilkins enjoyed the support of one of the senior academic staff attached to Downing College, Sir Busick Harwood, who had sponsored his election to the Society of Antiquaries.

Ultimately, Wilkins officially secured the commission in March 1806 because he supplied the best design in the new taste and one which appeared to be the most functional. The College Committee selected it after consulting three men, S. P. Cockerell, George Dance junior and James Lewis who, though favourable to the Greek style, were experienced institutional architects. They deemed that Wilkins's design combined 'more advantages than that of Mr. Lewis Wyatt and is therefore as we are unanimously of the Opinion to be preferred as on the whole fit and proper' and that 'the general decorations possess more grandeur, simplicity and classical effect than those of Mr. Lewis Wyatt'.[3] Only two features were censured, the insufficient projection of the 'magnificent portico at the Entrance for the Propylea' and the 'winding subterraneous passage of 140 ft in length' leading from the kitchens to the hall. (In fact the kitchens adjoined the buttery which was attached to the west side of the hall.)

That the young Wilkins possessed both competence and initiative is confirmed by his prising contemporaneously the East India College commission from the Company Surveyor, Henry Holland. In October 1804 the College Committee had decided to erect a new college at Haileybury to replace temporary accommodation in Hertford Castle, for the improvement of which Holland had prepared designs.[4] The committee drew up a loose specification for a new building, but Holland was slow to respond, to the annoyance of the Principal, Dr Henley. He was a graduate of Queens' College, Cambridge and an Antiquary, who probably knew Wilkins and sent him a copy of that specification, since, apparently uninvited by the committee, Wilkins submitted a plan estimated at £34,171, which was received on 13 November 1805.[5] The project accompanied a letter addressed to Henley, with whom Wilkins continued to correspond over the course of the ensuing commission. His estimate turned out to be £7,000 lower than that eventually sent in by Holland on 11 December. In the meantime Wilkins had prepared a revised estimate and tender, guaranteed by his father and brother, Henry, which amounted to

£40,000 for the entire work; this reached the committee on 10 December. The members were so impressed by the economy and rationality of Wilkins's scheme that they ignored Holland's attempt to discredit him by stressing the similarity between the designs and those for Downing, for the minutes include a letter from James Wyatt, 'addressing his intention of furnishing Mr. Holland with the Drawings of Downing College'. Having Holland's justifiable ire in mind, the committee went to the trouble of listing the reasons for their selection, of which the most telling were the provision of twice the student accommodation within almost the same space as in Holland's plan, a common room for the staff next to the hall, a larger chapel, a division in the library affording a section for lectures, better 'Collegiate conveniences', two spaces thirty-seven feet in length for additional buildings, a lower estimate and, lastly, because his scheme appeared to be 'the best contrived, most convenient and formed in the best taste'.[6] Wilkins triumphantly showed an elevation at the 1806 Academy Exhibition.

A key to the functional and aesthetic qualities of these two almost contemporary designs was his adoption of the 'campus' plan, a unique solution which was probably inspired by both Classical and Gothic sources, combining the antique forum and the mediaeval collegiate quadrangle (Pls. 11 and 12) (Thomas Jefferson's University of Virginia was not begun until 1817).[7] This form allowed Wilkins to separate the various facilities required by the institutions within a unified and regular composition and to concentrate the ornamental architecture on the visible external façades, at Downing to the north and south and at Haileybury on the south front facing the London Road. Moreover, at Haileybury the arrangement enabled Wilkins to sub-divide the side ranges into blocks – accommodating students and staff as at Downing – so as to counteract the potentially awkward effect of the rising ground and to place the entrance to one side (Pl. 13). In both designs Wilkins situated the main facilities in one structure which was to be the most ornamented, the chapel and library on the south side at Downing, and the chapel, library, hall and committee room on the southerly front of the East India College.

At Downing this structure, unfortunately not executed, was to have been articulated with tapered Greek windows, engaged Erechtheum Ionic columns and two pairs of six and four column porticoes of the same Order (Pl. 14). The six column porticoes were placed centrally on each front and the four column ones at either side, literally creating a mirror image of those on the inner façades of the hall and Master's Lodge which respectively terminated the two accommodation ranges. The centre building was to have been further linked with the side ranges by a continuous stylobate. The design for the interior was less felicitous, the spatial division being unequal and the decoration, apart from the columnar screen in the chapel, sparse (Pl. 15).

At Haileybury Wilkins inserted two four column Ionic porticoes between the main building and side ranges, which stand in the same plane as the façade and so recall Chambers's 'Palladian' bridges at Somerset House. The porticoes formed covered passages between the kitchens and the hall on the west side and the chapel and Principal's Lodge on the east side; in April 1806 Wilkins had reversed the position of the two ranges on his ground-plan, as illustrated in a drawing dated 30 June 1807 at the Soane Museum (Pl. 11).[8] This produced a more distinct movement towards the central portico that began with the engaged anta porticoes at either end of the main front, modelled upon the Choragic Monument of Thrasyllus at Athens, as were the entrances in the quadrangle. That monument became one of his favourite sources and, much as *Magna Graecia* contained the first statement of archaeological subjects expanded in later publications, so the campus designs for Downing and East India Colleges displayed much of his Neo-Greek architectural vocabulary.

In these designs Wilkins presented a new approach to the Greek Revival. First, he imitated features from the monumental Athenian antiquities, as in the pleasing interpretation of the Erechtheum at Downing in the Master's Lodge and hall (Pl. 16). Second, he attempted to adapt their scale harmoniously to the proportions of the modern structure. Third, he gave the Greek Orders their proper dominance and divested them of those elements of the post-Renaissance Classical tradition, such as the raised basement and attic storey, that were still retained by Thomas Harrison, the most advanced practitioner of the style among his immediate predecessors, whose Chester Castle was being built between 1785 and 1822. The one element that Wilkins took from the English classical inheritance was the Neo-Palladian tripartite division of main fronts. Fourth, he rejected pedantic antiquarianism, being prepared to adjust his sources to contemporary purposes, exemplified by the entrance gateway he designed for Downing. This comprised a portico modelled on the Athenian Propylaea in which the flanking buildings were regularised and transformed into a porter's lodge and lecture theatre (Pl. 17). Even at this early stage, Wilkins was not averse to the use of new materials, dictating on Working Drawing no. 19 in the first volume at the college that the 'Propylea' be roofed with 'artificial Stone' tiles.

Of the two schemes, Downing was the most original but, sadly, the college finances were less secure than those of the East India Company, resulting in the abandonment of the 'Propylea' and chapel and library building. Building operations were delayed at Cambridge until 27 November 1806 when it was resolved to begin digging the foundations of the east range, completed by 17 May 1807, when the first stone was laid amid considerable ceremony. On the next day the College Committee ordered Wilkins to 'proceed with all convenient expedition' to build the lodges for the Master and the professor of medicine, and the intervening accommodation block. Their funds were insufficient to undertake the erection of the architectural nucleus, the chapel and library building, and delayed the partial completion of the east range until 1813. This restricted programme was nearly disrupted by Christian, the professor of law, demanding that his lodge at the centre of the west side be built at the same time as that for Harwood, the professor of medicine.

Haileybury presented a different problem. Wilkins had to justify his appointment as architect to the College Committee, who were nagged by a disgruntled Holland until his death in 1807. On 11 March 1806, two months after the completion of the plans and Working Drawings, the committee were alarmed to discover a 'great variation' between Wilkins's confident estimates and the 'detailed and general Abstract of the Several costs of the different buildings' as computed by their surveyor, Rowles. Eight days later the receipt was minuted of an estimate for £48,630 from F. Stone of Norwich which was attested by another Norfolk tradesman acquainted with the Wilkins family, John de Carle, together with a letter from Holland reminding the committee that Wilkin's lower estimate had been a telling factor in their choice. Wilkins was called in and interrogated about the accuracy of his estimate and the means by which the disparities could be resolved. He defended his calculations, arguing that Rowles had miscalculated the quantity and cost of the brickwork and asked that the estimates be examined by an independent umpire. Nothing daunted, he maintained that, if his designs were implemented, the college would be 'partially habitable' in three years and complete in four. His determination swayed the committee, since they then discussed the financing of building operations, accepted the estimates submitted by Stone with an additional sum to offset the inflated cost of bricks, and agreed a contract figure of £50,855, being persuaded finally by the offer of William's father and brother, 'who are architects', to stand security.

Wilkins pressed ahead with the building programme, arranging that the joiners' work be undertaken away from the site for greater speed and economy. He was worried by the prospect of Holland, still the Company Surveyor, being allowed to inspect the work during construction, writing on 6 April: 'The Committee are very well aware that the preference with which they honoured my plans, exacted the jealously of Mr. Holland and they have had recent proof, in Mr. Holland's last letter to the Committee, that he has used every exertion to put a misconstruction upon my intentions and to lower me in their opinion.' He asked to be allowed to perform the contract 'undisturbed by continual objections' and reiterated his analysis of the disparities between the estimates. The date of Holland's survey was set for 6 June, but his death spared Wilkins from that critical eye and, on 11 August, he wrote optimistically from Gonville and Caius College about Holland's successor, S. P. Cockerell.

His optimism was not disappointed. Cockerell wrote to the committee on 20 August that he had the satisfaction to state 'the Works already executed are performed in a sound and proper manner and the Bricks, Stones and Timber of excellent Quality'. He approved Wilkins's distribution of the smaller contracts, such as the joinery in hand at Bury St Edmunds, 'in order to avoid the inconvenience of frequent combinations occasioned by the great number of workmen assembled on the same spot'. Subsequently he supported Wilkins when the committee queried parts of the contract, and he commended the building programme. However, when he wrote his first full report on 18 May 1807, Cockerell proposed a number of improvements to Wilkins's designs concerned with the structural strength, fire security, drainage and decoration. Under the last he persuaded the committee to assent to the addition of ornament on the entrance and on the interiors of the chapel, library and hall.[9]

The main buildings were largely completed in 1809, only minor features being added in that year which were contracted to William's brother, Henry.[10] This was the year, too, in which Humphry Repton turned the surrounding heathland into an ideal setting for the college, which became the subject of popular engravings.[11]

Despite the initial problems over the estimate and the fact that the cost of the college rose to £56,118. 3s. 6d., Wilkins became established as the Company Surveyor. He was responsible for the enlargement of their Military Seminary at Addiscombe near Croydon and co-operated with the ailing Cockerell on the major alterations to East India House in Leadenhall Street, London, between 1825 and 1830.[12] Both were important commissions, involving an expenditure of £21,397 for Addiscombe and in excess of £40,000 for East India House, though the latter work had been begun by Cockerell, who retired in 1824 following the failure of the foundations under the addition at the south west corner. Wilkins repaired these, completed the fitting up of the Book Office, including a 'Fireproof and Iron cased Strong Room with proper Iron Safes, Closets and Racks', and added an accounting room on the third floor of the old building.[13] Wilkins was solely responsible for the installation of fire-engines and water tanks on the roof 'with the hydraulic apparatus leading from there to the interior' (an idea borrowed from his old foe, Holland, who had placed water tanks on the roof of his Drury Lane Theatre). The work was finished some time after 1830, though Wilkins was spending at least one day a week at East India House in the early months of 1833.[14] At Addiscombe he had added a dining-hall next to Vanbrugh's house, 1702–3, joined at right angles with barracks for one hundred and fifty cadets, class rooms and offices, which were placed either side of an extant chapel. The brick buildings were merely articulated with pilasters and cornices, as illustrated in H. T. Vibart's *Addiscombe. Its Heroes and Men of Note*, published in 1894 some thirty years after the closure of the Seminary. Besides the Corinthian scagliola columns and pilasters in the hall, the interiors were very sparse, in line with the resolutions passed by the directors on 7 September 1825 wherein each cadet was to be allowed only 'a space of nine feet by six feet for his bed'.

Perhaps the Haileybury commission was also to prove a benefaction to Wilkins's private life, for Alicia Carnac Murphy of Ravendale in

Lincolnshire, whom he courted and married in 1811, was related to one of the directors of the company, whose son, Colonel Carnac, was to become a regular visitor to their third and last London home at 36 Weymouth Street.[15] Alicia was a devoted wife and, as her account books show, she shared her husband's pleasure in entertaining. She bore Wilkins three children, two boys, William and Henry, who both took holy orders, Henry after a brief career as an architect, and a daughter, Alicia, who married the Reverend William Kingsley, a friend of Ruskin.

Meanwhile the Downing commission stagnated. The committee had to borrow £27,000 to finance the continuation of the construction programme after successfully petitioning the Court of Chancery in December 1817 for 'altering the Plan of the Buildings Borrowing Money to carry on the West side thereof in four years'.[16] This sum was also intended to cover other work 'essential to the occupation of the buildings' such as an entrance lodge, drains, railings and walls. The college could only afford to finish the west side and, mindful of their dilemma, Wilkins sent his designs to a number of contractors and engaged the services of a Mr Benjamin Broadbridge to check their estimates against the new volume of Working Drawings. Such steps assured the completion of the domestic facilities and gave the college its single monumental interior, for the hall is now rather impressive, following the removal of the partition which formerly divided off the Combination Room, being ringed by scagliola pilasters and engaged coupled Ionic columns, supplied by Coade, interspersed with tapered openings and panels.[17]

Seeking to swell the college funds and to shave off excess expenditure, Wilkins had also submitted a scheme for a housing development to be built north of the college and had drawn two simpler versions of the 'Propylea', each subsequently bound into the main volume of Working Drawings. The housing scheme, no. 107 inscribed 'Plan for the Improvement of the Estate belonging to Downing College', is signed by Wilkins and dated 1817, while the other drawings, nos. 95 and 96, can be associated with the 'alterations' to the design of the north side of the college mentioned in the Minute Book for 24 January 1818. Of the alternative 'Propylea', no. 95 dispenses with the side buildings and no. 96 follows the original but on a reduced scale. In no. 107 the original 'Propylea' is advanced some feet ahead of the northern blocks of the college (though not as far as in no. 91, another ground-plan, where it is linked to terraces by quadrant walls), flanked by pairs of detached houses and a terrace to the west and faces up a long street of terraced houses leading to Downing Street and two smaller terraces linking Tennis Court Road and Regent Street; the drawing has a flap with an alternate layout for the longer street including two rows of trees (Pl. 18). In 1822 Wilkins sold the western part of his garden at nearby Lensfield for the erection of Annesly Place.[18]

Another drawing, possibly made at this period, might be the elevation in the Avery Collection at Columbia University which has been identified as a design for the hall (Pl. 19).[19] It shows a nine bay structure with a central four column Ionic portico and coupled pilasters at either end but no side portico. Given the absence of this essential feature of Wilkins's conception of the design of the college, it is more likely that the elevation represents a revised and cheaper version of the chapel and library block, or a preliminary design for the Freemasons' Hall, Bath, 1817 (see Pl. 47), as the three figures in the niches could depict Faith, Hope and Charity, the Masonic symbols.

By 1822 this second spate of building was finished and Wilkins's last contact with the college occurred on 14 April 1823 when he negotiated on behalf of Corpus Christi College in order to secure the use of the main drain which crossed their property. Yet to the credit of Downing College, successive College Committees voted to retain the idea of realising Wilkins's admirable design and, up to 1873, the committee resolved to complete the east side according to his plans. However, the later additions to the college buildings, largely by Sir Herbert Baker, compare but poorly with the 'ruins' of Wilkins's Temple of Learning.

Standing in the broad campus and contemplating the nicely proportioned and neatly composed east and west ranges, it is possible to imagine the sensitive balance between enclosed space and open vistas, smooth surfaces and sharply defined details which Wilkins had envisaged a year after his return from Greece. But there are signs of the limitations of his learned and mathematical approach to design. Though C. R. Cockerell's description of the buildings as 'a string of sausages' was carping, their height is perhaps too low for the breadth of the quadrangle. Wilkins had mastered the process of translating the images of ancient architecture in two dimensions but was less secure in the handling of spatially related masses. The scholarly if elegant revivalism of the hall, rather than the freer Classicism of the north end of the west range, was to be the keynote of his architecture. Charles Barry later told J. A. Wolfe that a visit to the college had turned him against the Greek style.[20]

IV

'The true proportions of that noble architecture'[1]

At Cambridge and Haileybury Wilkins had been able to advance a strict Greek Revival architecture without too much difficulty, but, in the series of other commissions he received in those early years of his career, he had to dilute his purist principles to accord with earlier structures or traditions. On the strength of the triumphs of 1806 Wilkins was asked by Foljambe to add a fashionable Doric portico to his house at Osberton, Nottinghamshire. In 1807 he won the competition for Nelson's Pillar in Dublin, honouring a fellow alumunus of Norwich School. A year later he was engaged to refurbish the Lower Assembly Rooms at Bath and called in soon after by Aberdeen's friend, Henry Drummond, to transform Grange Park into a Doric temple.

These valuable commissions broadened his professional reputation, yet either he did not compete for or he failed to capture the more important commission for Covent Garden Theatre, London, the award of which, in 1809, surely helped to win for his rival, Robert Smirke, a place in the triumvirate of the profession, the 'Attached Architects', joining Nash and Soane. Wilkins, in company with Soane, S. P. Cockerell and two more obscure figures, Cavendish and Simmonds, criticised the façade of Smirke's design, probably on the grounds that the portico was overborne by the cubic superstructure of the auditorium.[2] Smirke's success may also have prompted Wilkins's removal from Cambridge when he took up residence at 30 Bedford Place in London, the centre of events.

Foljambe consulted Wilkins late in 1805 or early in the next year, since the alterations to Osberton were finished by 1808, when

56

they were published, as was Donington, in the second volume of Richardson's prestigious *New Vitruvius Britannicus*.[3] Foljambe faced Wilkins with a difficult task, to marry a full scale and carefully detailed Doric portico, derived from the Theseum and Parthenon, with an elegant and simple late-eighteenth-century country house of moderate dimensions, or, in metaphorical terms, to harmonise Attic austerity with late Georgian refinement.

Wilkins tried to resolve the problem by aligning the cornice of his portico with that of the house (Pl. 20). Unfortunately, this left the entablature of the portico, accentuated by its archaeological detailing, to depend heavily over the three central windows of the main façade. Choosing not to compromise the accuracy of his archaeologically inspired revivalism by reducing the elevation of the portico, as George Dance junior, for example, had done at Stratton Park, Hampshire in 1803, Wilkins could not help but produce a disharmonious aesthetic effect, an ancient thoroughbred dominating a contemporary hybrid. Still, a worse effect might have resulted if he had superimposed a Doric entablature to which the portico would have been joined.

He redecorated the library and hall, installing an organ in the gallery of the staircase which was framed by two columns, apparently of the Ionic Order. According to Richardson, he made other more practical improvements which included the construction of an office wing on the right side of the portico, so that the house became 'a very convenient family residence, possessing also extensive accommodation for visitors'.

Wilkins sustained his rapid professional success by winning the commission for Nelson's Pillar in Dublin at the close of 1807, the first memorial erected to the beloved national hero; 'The death of Nelson', wrote Wilkins's friend, Robert Southey, 'was felt in England as something more than a public calamity: men started at the intelligence, and turned pale, as if they had heard of the death of a dear friend.'[4] Within ten days of receipt of the official despatches describing the Battle of Trafalgar the aldermen and merchants of Dublin had agreed upon the 'expediency of some speedy and practicable measure to compliment the memory of Lord Nelson'.[5] A committee was appointed on 28 November, the members of whom pledged over £1,000. By 12 December the fund had reached £3,827 and the commission was advertised.

Wilkins seized the opportunity and submitted a design comprising a Greek Doric column raised on a plinth and capped by a capital and abacus supporting a Roman galley (Pl. 21). This neatly synthesised the Greek form with the traditional Classical column and elements of the Roman *columna rostrata*.[6] The new taste was melded with the appropriate convention; it preceded Percier's Trajanic column in the Place Vendôme, Paris, by three years and indicates the different allegiance in taste for public architecture between the warring nations. The relative novelty of the design obviously appealed to the Dublin committee since they launched a further appeal to execute the 'highly beautiful and approved plan', estimated without 'Emblem or Sculpture' at nearly £5,000. That sum was donated by 14 February 1808, the anniversary of the Battle of Cape St Vincent and the day upon which the foundation stone was laid by the Governor General at the centre of Sackville Street, thus bringing the Greek taste into Dublin, in the presence of a body of Irish peers, civic and military dignitaries, the Provost and Fellows of Trinity College, detachments from the local Horse and Foot Yeomanry, Sea Fencibles and Marine School boys 'in three divisions, preceded by the marine boat, manned'.[7]

However, the committee could not afford the galley and Wilkins had to substitute an indifferent statue of Nelson by Thomas Kirk, R.H.A., as the crowning ornament, for which the committee apologised in the pamphlet they distributed in 1811. Noting that the local architect, Francis Johnston, had 'afforded the necessary assistance' during the construction of the 'beautiful column', they nevertheless complimented Wilkins on his unabating 'zeal and kindness' and regretted their inability to execute his design 'precisely as he had given it'. Despite the weak statue, less impressive than those he was to commission for the Yarmouth Column, the slender form of the pillar became a distinctive and renowned landmark, and its viewing platform on the abacus rewarded the determined visitor with superb vistas across the city and its chief buildings to Dublin Bay and the Wicklow Hills.

In 1808 the proprietors of the Lower Assembly Rooms in Bath decided to improve the property in the hope of reviving their ailing business. Aware of the new architectural fashion, they sought out Wilkins, and his modish restyling of the exterior brought his name to the attention of the *beau monde*. He clothed the main entrance with a rather squat portico which earned it the sobriquet, 'Paestum', though it was surely modelled upon the Theseum and Parthenon (Pl. 22).[8] Since the Rooms were rebuilt between 1823 and 1825 by G. A. Underwood it seems likely that the attic was a later addition. What might be attributed to Wilkins with reasonable certainty, despite the disappearance of the designs he exhibited at the Royal Academy in 1808 and 1809, are the Doric entablature that bound the unequal main and subsidiary fronts, and the small antis Doric portico and the tapered windows on the latter. After his marriage Wilkins added an antis portico to his Cambridge house, Lensfield, which led the editors of the R.C.H.M. study of Cambridge to describe it as the 'most important of the local houses' (Pl. 23).[9] Some time before 1828 he built another such portico on one side of Kingweston, Somerset, for his friend, William Dickinson (Pl. 24).[10] Despite the ensuing changes in popular taste, as late as 1864 G. N. Wright admired the six column Doric portico of the Lower Assembly Rooms in his *New Bath Guide*.[11]

The Rooms were reopened on 1 November 1810, some months after Wilkins had completed his most striking adaptation of the Greek ideal, Grange Park, Hampshire. One letter from Wilkins to Aberdeen shows that building operations were under way in 1809, though these might have commenced during 1808, the year in which Drummond married. Wilkins exhibited two designs of the Grange at the 1809 Royal Academy which tends to confirm this dating.

Wilkins transformed Samwell's seventeenth-century brick house into an almost unique temple-like structure at a cost of some £30,000.[12] It is only equalled by Sir Charles Monck's Belsay Hall, Northumberland, 1810–17, in which Gell and the architect, John Dobson, each had a hand, more memorable perhaps for its cella hall than its antis Doric portico and ashlar façade; and by the copy (excepting the Ionic Order of the portico) that William Burn transported to chilly Angus when he built Camperdown near Dundee, 1824–6. Sir Nikolaus Pevsner has described the Grange as 'sensational' and as one of the first 'determined credos' of the Revival.[13] The Grange is superbly, dramatically revivalist when compared with Smirke's 'Graeco-cubic' country house style (epitomised by Normanby Park, Lincolnshire, 1821), the more conventional houses of Dobson and Archibald Simpson or the graceless version of Wilkins's stunning display of archaeology perpetrated by

James Knowles at Silverton Park, Devon, 1839–45. More than a
hint of the portico composition of the Grange can be discerned in
the most magnificent building of the British Greek Revival: H. L.
Elmes's St George's Hall, Liverpool, begun in 1842, which also has
a massive portico, one column in depth, though of the Corinthian
Order, covering all but two bays of the main front, and projected
colonnades on the side façades. A distant echo of the Grange portico
composition may also be found in the City Hall, New Orleans,
1845–50, designed by James Gallier senior, Wilkins's clerk of works
at Huntingdon, 1826–8 and, more directly, in William Strickland's
contemporary State Capitol at Nashville, Tennessee.[14]

Given Drummond's determination to 'out-Pericles' his neighbour,
Sir Francis Baring of Stratton Park, Wilkins could proceed along
more radical lines. To preserve the effect of the massive scale of the
fifth-century Greek Doric Order he rearranged the four storeys of the
old house and masked its brick with Roman cement. The level of the
surrounding ground was raised to that of the ground floor, absorbing
the semi-basement into a terrace or stylobate. In his first designs
Wilkins defined the perimeter of this terrace by six square plinths (Pls.
25 and 26), probably modelled on the ancient tombs that he had seen
in Sicily, but which could be read as archaeologically chastened
versions of Soane's celebrated funerary motif.[15] The ground and first
floors occupied the height of the Doric Order while the third storey
was fitted into the entablature, illuminated on the subsidiary fronts
by small square windows doing service as metopes, the ground floor
having Wilkins's preferred tapered openings. Thereby, Wilkins could
give full play to the six column Doric portico, which even included
the proper articulation of the triglyphs at the corners of the
entablature, and encompassed all but two bays of the east façade of
the old house, with its pediment rising clear of the structure.

During the early stages of the rebuilding Wilkins decided to project
the portico further forward by inserting one column on either side
so that it commanded the main façade when seen frontally; this
arrangement countered two criticisms often levelled subsequently at
the Greek Revival, namely insufficient weight and chiaroscuro.
C. R. Cockerell remarked after a visit to Grange Park in May 1823,
'The depth of the portico gives a density to the shade which is most
happy & assists the clear expression & ever just & satisfactory effect
of the cols & their entablature.' And it was he who, after his first visit

in January 1823, best described the extraordinary conviction of Wilkins's bold archaeological design: 'nothing can be finer...more classical or like the finest Poussino...its elevation on terraces gives it that which is essential to the effect of Grecian arche. & which no modern imitations possess'.[16]

The monumental proportions of the portico were carried on to the side fronts by pilasters and projected Thrasyllan anta porticoes, that on the north serving as the entrance (Pl. 27). A similar composition, but with columnar side porticoes, had been published in 1801 by Robert Mitchell, but it is more likely that Wilkins conceived the idea from his study of the Erechtheum and the Choragic Monument of Thrasyllus. The strong projection of the anta porticoes imparted a powerful plastic quality to the side elevations to weld the main portico into the whole. The main and side fronts in a sense represented the two poles of Wilkins's revivalist architecture, arch-aeological yet also rational. R. Ackermann thought 'the classical alterations...leave scarcely any trace of the original design. It is highly creditable to the taste and judgement of Mr. Wilkins, that he could thus introduce these improvements without raising the original building.'[17] However, by 1862 James Fergusson dismissed the alterations as inappropriate to country house architecture and castigated the porticoes as immensely expensive 'without in the smallest degree increasing either its comfort or convenience'.[18]

Yet the porticoes satisfied Drummond's demands and were placed so as not to disrupt Samwell's layout, and when his family outgrew the accommodation Drummond added to rather than rebuilt the house, though he employed Smirke and Cockerell. The main portico fronted part of the drawing-room and a bedroom and dressing-room, the anta porticoes the hall and saloon, and the pilasters on the west side the staircase and part of the library and offices. Nor was the superb portico copied exactly from any one source, although it is probable that the predominant inspiration, as for the earlier works, was the Theseum, a building which Wilkins described in *Atheniensia* as 'one of the noblest remains of ancient magnificence'.[19]

The transformation marked the achievement of Wilkins's maturity as a designer. Thereafter his use of Greek, and also Gothic, models was more assured and flexible, as can be seen in four unexecuted Greek projects dating from the next decade.

In 1814 Wilkins submitted two slightly different Neo-Greek

designs to Lord Rosebery, who rejected both in favour of the Gothic Revival house that was erected at Dalmeny.[20] In one design the main façade comprises an imposing six column Corinthian portico fronting the body of the house, flanked by short wings of three bays articulated with pilasters (Pl. 28). These wings are terminated by projecting porticoes that imitate the Thrasyllan Monument in their side elevations, excepting the addition of square podia in the attic, as used at Grange Park. These projections neatly turn the corners of the side façades, amply fenestrated and intended to exploit the fine vistas over the Firth of Forth. In the second design, a related elevation, for the main front, Wilkins raised the height of the Corinthian portico above the level of the entablature of the house and Thrasyllan projections, omitting the incised panels from their antae (Pl. 29). Both designs anticipate Archibald Simpson's Strathcathrow House, Angus, 1827.

The other two projects, one not attributed previously to Wilkins, display the same reasoned application of scholarship. Probably the earliest was that for a mausoleum or pavilion, commissioned in 1815 by Richard Colt Hoare for an unspecified site at Stourhead (Pl. 30).[21] The drawing, exhibited at the Academy in 1817, illustrates the beauty of his renderings. The precise detailing and dramatic shadow cast by the portico reveal Wilkins's passion for the incisive and massive qualities of fifth-century Greek architecture. For this less functional design he experimented with various themes having Greek associations – a 'Greek cross' plan and the enlarged central inter-columniation of the portico of the Athenian Propylaea. The choice of this portico could have been motivated by his keen disappointment at the failure of the Downing authorities to finance the construction of the entrance 'Propylea'. In addition, the side porticoes were copied from the cella entrances of Greek temples and their secondary importance signified by the superimposition of a pedimented attic over the main axis.

The last project, now at the R.I.B.A., is an undated scheme for a monumental country house, possibly drawn for Lord Elgin (Pl. 31); the grand scale precludes its identification with the unexecuted design, exhibited at the 1808 Academy, for a villa to be built in North Berwick and commissioned in 1808 by Sir Hew Hamilton, a subscriber to *Magna Graecia*.[22] The elevation, like that for Stourhead, is strongly shaded. If it is Wilkins's design for Lord Elgin, it must have been undertaken between 1822 and 1824. Cockerell, who was asked to submit a design in 1824, learned that Elgin had been 'amazingly bitten with the University Club', executed in 1822 by Wilkins in collaboration with J. P. Gandy.[23]

The design has many of Wilkins's favourite Greek themes, but handled with a greater appreciation of three dimensional composition than present in his previous works. A six column Ionic portico was to be projected one column in depth from single bay framing sections, each flanked by Ionic colonnades and pavilions articulated with coupled pilasters, tapered windows and squat podia reminiscent of those intended for the terraced stylobate of Grange Park. Mindful of the problem of maintaining both the dominance of the portico and the unity of the whole, Wilkins rejected the idea of elevating the main portico in favour of a stepped attic placed above and behind its pediment, and, indicative of a further development away from his youthful style, an open dome at the hub of the building decorated with the wreaths employed at the Grange. (The dome, with its anta peristyle, anticipates that projected in an early scheme for St George's Hospital which Wilkins or an assistant might have drawn in 1826 (Pl. 32). In the same year he also won the competition for University College, London, with a design that included a more conventional Renaissance dome constructed above and behind a Greek portico. At one stage during the work on University College he proposed using semi-circular porticoes of the type that appear on the side façades of the R.I.B.A. design, a theme he had first utilised in his winning project for the Army Monument in 1817.) The superimposed central structure and the related contrast between the main façades look back to the Stourhead design and it is likely that the plan of the house comprised an enlarged Greek cross set into a square.

Yet this more diversified composition might have lacked the impact achieved so superbly at Grange Park, and Wilkins was at his best when he limited the number of archaeological motifs in his architecture, for then he most perfectly fulfilled his authoritarian concept of design.

V

The Civil Architecture of Vitruvius

During the transformation of Grange Park Wilkins corresponded frequently with Lord Aberdeen upon two matters, the translation of four books of Vitruvius's Treatise and the redecoration of Argyll House, Aberdeen's London home.

Published in 1813 and 1817 (though dated 1812 on the title-page) as *The Civil Architecture of Vitruvius*, Wilkins's translation was prefaced by an introduction entitled 'An Historical View of the Rise and Progress of Architecture amongst the Greeks', anonymously written by Aberdeen to whom the book was handsomely dedicated. The reason for Aberdeen's anonymity remains uncertain, but one reviewer detected the style of two authors, writing in the *Quarterly Review* of 1819 that the 'Introduction was from the pen of another person' and displayed 'no common acquaintance with Greek and Latin authors, set forth in a language at once perspicuous and polished'.[1] The truth of this surmise was to be proven when Aberdeen wrote in the Advertisement of his *Inquiry into the Principles of Beauty in Grecian Architecture* (1822), an expanded version of the Introduction, that the 'substance of the following pages was prefixed, as an Introduction to Wilkins's translation of Vitruvius, published January 1812'.

The project fulfilled their desire to propagate an appreciation of the rules and qualities of Greek architecture, Wilkins endeavouring to clarify the inaccuracies contained in previous printed editions of the Treatise and Aberdeen to expound its aesthetic beauty and history. Both regarded fifth-century Athenian architecture as peerless. 'Athens', Wilkins declared in the dedication, 'in her progress towards the most exalted stage of her brilliant career, produced, under the direction of Pericles, monuments which, as they have never been equalled, may be justly considered as affording to the followers of the science unerring principles for their guidance', while Aberdeen wrote in the *Inquiry* that the name of Athens 'can scarcely be pronounced without emotion'.[2]

The major part, undertaken by Wilkins, was the translation of the more controversial books of the Treatise, numbers 3 to 6. Explaining his purpose in the Advertisement, he opined that the first editors, being ignorant of Greek architecture, had 'searched for illustrations of their author amongst the edifices of Rome; expecting, with some degree of probability, that the principles he promulgates would be found to prevail in the buildings of the country which gave him birth'. An examination of the various 'readings and interpolations may not be thought uninteresting', however, since the treatise was the only one surviving from ancient times on the 'science of architecture' despite 'the corruptions [with] which the early editors have loaded it. Former translators, in following the text of the printed editions, have propagated these errors, which, in many instances, are wholly subversive of the principles of architecture our author intended to inculcate.' Wilkins felt qualified to attempt the task because of his 'acquaintance with the remains of ancient art in Greece and in Ionia, obtained by studying upon the spot the principles of their construction'. He had decided to concentrate on books 3 to 6 because the textual errors 'apply almost exclusively to those parts of the author which relate to the civil architecture of the ancients'. The translation was divided into four sections which followed the order of the books, omitting the introduction to each. It was illustrated by forty-one engravings executed by W. Lowry which included fine plates delineating the Greek Orders.

The Introduction by Aberdeen comprised a review of the theories about the Beautiful, the Picturesque and the Sublime in relation to Greek architecture, and a history of its development, necessary, he wrote on page xv, because the original Treatise, while 'full of varied learning, remarkable for ingenuity, science, and acuteness, will not however, afford any succinct view of the progress of architecture'.

Wilkins sent Aberdeen drafts of his translations of some of the more problematical passages; no doubt he was asked to comment on the contents of the Introduction. Four of Wilkins's letters remain in the

Aberdeen Correspondence at the British Museum together with a draft for chapter 10 of section 4, 'Of the Houses of the Greeks'.[3] This subject appeared in the third of the letters, dated 10 October 1809, which commenced with a report on the progress of the redecoration of Argyll House. Turning to Vitruvius's account of Greek domestic design given in the sixth book, Wilkins wrote:

> My observations upon the palace of Ulysses were thrown together in so vague a manner that you could have made very little out from them; besides which I had committed an introductory sheet in which I set out with observing that it was not to be expected that Homer's account would accurately apply to the individual Palace of Ulysses; but that the plan of Greek houses of his age was present to him when he found it necessary to mention any parts of it. Because it was essential that his description should be recognised by the Greeks to whom the poem was recited. I am putting this in better form and will then send them for your inspection when you can reject whatever interferes with your observations upon the Homeric architecture.

He then reviewed the meaning of sundry descriptive terms such as 'oudos' and 'tholos' in the *Odyssey* and other ancient texts, and mentioned that he had related 'to our Cambridge Philologists my idea of the Thebes of the Odyssey which they have thought not an improbable one and I have engaged Blomfield [E. V. Blomfield (1788–1816) who was to graduate from Gonville and Caius in 1811], whom you may know by fame, to consider the subject'. Returning to the meaning of 'tholos', he continued, 'The sketch here given might certainly be the prototype of a monopteral temple whose roof Vitruvius calls tholos – The monopteral Temple had no walls but only columns disposed in a circle with a conical roof over them.' In the margin Wilkins drew a circular roofed building supported by four large posts on the circumference, with a central post inserted into the upper millstone turned by two oxen. The roof is conical and secured by a thick rope to which are attached stones that hang below the eaves. Under the drawing Wilkins appended a passage from the *Iliad* xx. 496.

Earlier, in August, Wilkins and Aberdeen were corresponding on the proper translation of a passage in part 8 of the second chapter of book 3 in which Vitruvius made reference to an octastyle hypaethral Temple of Jupiter (Zeus) Olympius. Wilkins had touched on the difficulties concerning this on the third page of the introduction to *Magna Graecia*, where he had proposed that the word 'octastylos' had been interpolated in the manuscripts of the Treatise. He wrote to Aberdeen from Bedford Place on 23 and 25 August, testing, at great length, the relevant passages in Vitruvius against references in Pausanias. The nub of his argument comes towards the end of the second letter:

> I now feel disposed to let the reading stand as it is in all the Mss (excepting [that] which inserts the *et*) 'sed Athenis octastylos in templo Jovis Olympii' – The various readings of *in templo Jovis Olympii* and *in templo Olympio* will not affect the passage.
> The temple to which Vitruvius alludes in his proem which was finished by Cossutius *400* years afterwards must have been founded about 600 years before Christ and Hadrian's Temple must have been built in some interval between 117 and 138 A.D. Might not the latter have been built upon the site of the old or within the ancient ιερον or sacred inclosure?

After quoting another excerpt from Pausanias, he finished: 'I shall be much obliged to you if you will have the goodness to give me your opinion of the passage as soon as possible as I wish to get it immediately prepared for printing. Pray address me at the Grange Alresford Hants.'

Whether influenced by Aberdeen or not, Wilkins changed his mind, as is clear from the footnote to the translation in section 1. He had decided to omit 'altogether the word *Jovis*: the change of *et* to *in* is scarcely worthy of attention. For *octastylosin* I propose reading *in asty Jovis*; the passage will then read as follows: Sed Athenis in asty Jovis Templo Olympio.' This differs from the Latin text in Granger's standard modern edition of the Treatise, 'sed Athenis octastylos et templo Olympio'; however, Wilkins's rendering of the complete sentence as 'There is no temple of this description at Rome, but there is one at Athens, within the city, dedicated to Jupiter Olympius which is Octastyle' tallies with Granger's, 'Of this there is no example at Rome; but there is the octastyle at Athens, in the Olympian Temple.'[4]

Wilkins's translation, if not the footnote, helped to clarify Vitruvius's original meaning, and compared well with the ambiguous version given by William Newton (1735-90), whose two volume translation was published in 1771 and 1791. Newton had written, 'Of this there is no example in Rome, but such is at Athens, the octastyle temple, and that of Jupiter Olympius.'[5] In his translation and accompanying footnote Newton had synthesised the two most popular interpretations, between which James Stuart vacillated in the first two volumes of the *Antiquities of Athens* published in 1762 and 1787. In the first Stuart decided that the passage referred to a Temple of Jupiter at Olympius, while in the second he plumped for the existence of two hypaethral temples at Athens, an octastyle temple and a temple dedicated to Jupiter Olympius.[6] The veracity of Wilkins's translation was proved by the excavations conducted by F. C. Penrose in 1883, 1885 and 1886, which revealed the foundations of an octastyle temple beneath that completed during the rule of Hadrian.

Wilkins, conscientious as ever, examined all the manuscripts of the Treatise available in London. In a footnote on page 68 he stated that he had consulted 'five MSS copies', almost certainly the Cottonian and Harleian texts in the British Museum and, probably, also the Arundel manuscript then in the possession of the Royal Society; elsewhere Wilkins referred to the major printed editions, including those by Barbaro, De Laet, Elzevir, Galiani, Palladio, Perrault and Newton.[7] Newton, by comparison, wrote that he had 'made use of the printed editions of Barbaro, De Laet and Galiani; and when occasion required of sundry manuscripts'.[8] Nor had Newton the advantage of Wilkins's extensive first-hand study of Greek architecture. And an anonymous reviewer of a later translation of the Treatise went so far as to assert that no scholar had checked the manuscript texts for possible errors 'until Mr. Wilkins, [who] from his early studies of classical literature and his intimate acquaintance with the rich treasures of Grecian art, united the qualities necessary to a translator and illustrator of this treatise'.[9]

Such a painstaking programme enabled Wilkins to elucidate

Vitruvius's description of the principles and details of Greek architecture, and especially those passages in the third chapter of book 3 concerning the refinements introduced to counteract visual distortions. He provided a valuable interpretation of the meaning of the term 'scamilli impares'. In a lengthy footnote he concluded that the 'rule for making an addition to the stylobate' had been prompted by the desire to 'counteract the supposed imperfections of vision'. He further stated:

> The image formed by the rays which pass through a convex lens from a straight line is not, like the object, straight, but somewhat curved; and is in fact part of a conic section. In a like manner the image of a straight line, formed upon the retina, is curved, whether the line be vertical or horizontal. Owing to this defect of vision, if it may be so called, it might appear that the line of the stylobate would form a curved image; and be what Vitruvius terms, alveolated; that is, hollowed like the bed of a channel. Hence if we wish it to appear perfectly horizontal, we must make it rise in the centre and fall gradually towards the extremities... In rearing the columns upon a stylobate thus constructed, we must have recourse to some expedient for placing them so that their axes may be perpendicular to the horizon. This object may be effected by the use of scamilli impares, or small plinths formed like wedges; placing them with the lower end towards the centre of the building.[10]

But he questioned whether such refinements had been actually employed by the Greeks and mistakenly suggested that the principle demanded that the line of the epistylium (architrave) be concave 'towards the middle point', being above eye-level.

However, he had described the scamilli clearly (noting that Gibbs had misused them in the portico of St Martin-in-the-Fields) and may well have inspired the more detailed examination of the geometrical subtleties in Greek architecture undertaken by Penrose and Pennethorne; and Wilkins had arrived at an explanation of 'entasis' two years before C. R. Cockerell claimed to have discovered its use at Athens, writing on page 39 of section 1, 'In fact, the entasis, like the addition of the stylobate, was intended to correct want of bulk in the middle, which columns were supposed to have, if the shafts were made to diminish in a straight line from the bottom to the top.'[11]

F. C. Penrose quoted from Wilkins's translation in the third chapter of his book, *An Investigation of the Principles of Athenian Architecture* (1851), in preference to that published in 1826 by Joseph Gwilt.[12] As he wrote, in the first of two footnotes relating to these,

> Wilkins's translation is preferable to the others in our language, on account of his clearly explaining the word 'adjectio' as a rise above the straight line joining the ends of the stylobate; he fully recognises the meaning of Vitruvius, and attempts to explain the philosophy of it, by reference to the *structure of the eye*, and to the tendency of his author to reduce everything to the guidance of general principles – and he adds, 'this great refinement, suggested by physical knowledge, does not appear to have entered into the execution of the works of the ancients'.[13]

The last sentence was presumably included because Penrose agreed that the refinements were not universally employed by the Greek architects. The second footnote was more critical, containing a paraphase of Wilkins's erroneous proposal that the epistylium should have a concave curvature.[14] Penrose also quoted Wilkins's translation of passages from part 4 and part 13 of the fifth chapter of book 3 on the inclination of the axes of the columns and the face of the entablature.[15] In the footnotes to these passages Penrose further questioned the validity of Vitruvius's assertions, indirectly complimenting the caution expressed by Wilkins.

Wilkins's translation was also praised by other contemporary archaeologists including W. Kinnard (or Kinnaird), who produced a new edition of the *Antiquities of Athens* between 1825 and 1830. The second volume had as a frontispiece an engraving of Allan Ramsay's portrait of Revett dedicated to Wilkins.[16]

No less an admirer was Aberdeen, who was happy to consign the majority of his research on Greek architecture to the Introduction to *The Civil Architecture*, and, regarding his London house, to entrust its renovation to Wilkins upon the death in 1808 of Joseph Bonomi.[17] 'Before I left town', Wilkins wrote in a typically considerate letter, the one dated London, 10 October 1809, 'I went to Argyl [sic] house', where he found the walls of the salon and staircase too damp for painting "'til next summer'. Amid a miscellany of detailed comments on the decorations such as whether the Erechtheum Ionic columns in the salon were to be of alabaster, he reported that, 'Boileau assured me when I last saw him that the frize [sic] for the Salon was nearly completed; and that he had frequently gone to Lord Elgin's to study the Character of the figures.' Here was one of the first instances of the imitation of the Parthenon Marbles, and, at this time, Wilkins may also have persuaded another friend, Samuel Rogers, to install a copy of part of the frieze on the staircase of his house in St James's.[18]

A week or so later he sent another letter in which the mention of 'Reviewers' could refer to the publication of either Whittington's *Historical Survey* or Wilkins's essay on early English Renaissance architecture in *Vestusta Monumenta* for 1809 entitled 'Observations on the Porta Honoris of Caius College, Cambridge', in which he associated the introduction of the style into England with the design of the gate. As a pioneering study, he might be forgiven the mistaken attribution to John of Padua, though, as a graduate of the college, it is odd that he did not assign it to Caius, as is now generally accepted. He had been at 'Argyl house yesterday' after returning from Bath, and thought that Aberdeen should be able to 'inhabit it in the early part of February'. The remainder tells of his trouble to find the best fixtures and right colour schemes for the rooms. He asked for a reply to be sent to Gonville and Caius College. The alterations were completed well before 28 September 1812, when Knight was dismayed that Aberdeen contemplated the sale of the house.[19]

Working from notes in his Commonplace Book, Aberdeen had striven to finish the Introduction when his political responsibilities allowed. 'On examining the inscription as given in Chandler', he wrote to Wilkins in July 1810,

> I decidedly am of the opinion that you are right about δρδβ οτα[?]. But what is of much more consequence I have convinced Knight that you are right – Those only who know how difficult it is to stagger Knight in any Hypothesis he has once adopted will be able to appreciate this triumph. He means when he reprints his book to acknowledge his error. The great press of Business in the House of Lords, occasions me to advance but slowly.

However, it is always in view – when do you come to Town.[20]

In 1806 Aberdeen had been elected a Scottish Representative Peer in the Tory interest and within a year Robert Walpole asked him to send news of his activities, 'Whether you are totally literary or totally political.'[21] The Order of the Thistle was bestowed upon him in 1808 and a year later he was entrusted with the task of moving the Address to the Prince Regent in the Lords. His career began in earnest after he was appointed Ambassador Extraordinary and Minister Plenipotentiary to the Emperor of Austria in 1813, but his dilettanti activities were not severely curtailed until he became Secretary of War in 1834, when he resigned from the presidency of the British Institution. After the defeat of the Tories under Peel in 1846 he relinquished the presidency of the Antiquaries in order to consolidate the Party, of which he was chosen Leader in 1851, forming a new administration in 1852 that governed until defeated on 23 January 1855 over the conduct of the Crimean War. He published no antiquarian writings after 1822 when he revised the Introduction to *The Civil Architecture* for publication as the *Inquiry*. Appropriately, in view of his abiding interest in Greek art, this was published again in 1860, the year of his death.

The Introduction had been the partial realisation of the history of Greek architecture which Aberdeen had planned on his tour. In notes headed 'Observations on the Architecture of the Ancients' he had questioned Vitruvius's contention that the triglyphs had been nailed to the transverse beams of the early wooden temples, suggesting instead that the ends of the beams were notched to prevent splitting.[22] As Wilkins wrote in the Advertisement, 'The introduction is selected from materials for a much more extensive work, which the author has wanted leisure to arrange and complete.' It took precedence over other schemes which Aberdeen contemplated after his return from Greece. One, contained in a volume of miscellaneous notes dating from about 1806, concerned the geography and towns of Attica, while others, reflecting his taste for ancient coins and medals, were worked up as 'On the Mines of Laurium – Gold and Silver Coinage of the Athenians – Revenue of Attica', an article written with Walpole for the *Memoirs* of 1817.[23] The Introduction allowed Aberdeen to exploit his wide reading of the Classical authors and especially of Pausanias,

Strabo and Homer, about the historical and archaeological interpretation of whose poetry he had already exchanged letters and opinions with Richard Payne Knight.

Sharing a taste for numismatics and philology, Aberdeen accepted Knight as something of a mentor in matters of scholarship and connoisseurship. In 1808 they considered the joint purchase of coins from a Sicilian collector by the name of Astuto through the dealer, Bonelli.[24] Earlier Aberdeen had consulted Knight about a number of paintings he contemplated buying from Lord Radstock. Writing on 23 February 1807, Radstock expressed surprise at having received a letter from Aberdeen, 'After the unpleasant & mortifying visit I had the misfortune to experience on Monday last from Mr. Knight.'[25] According to Radstock, Knight presumed to act as Aberdeen's agent and to dictate the price he should ask for various pictures. Radstock would only show his paintings to Aberdeen again 'provided you come to my house unaccompanied with any person whatever: – each day confirming me in the opinion that the fewer amateurs I admit to my collection the better'. Meantime, Knight was not in the least chastened by the episode, notifying Aberdeen about other paintings then on the market in London and how to best the dealers, adding, 'I had in my youth some dealings with Gentlemen Jockeys, & thought their professional morals rather lax; but they are quite rigid compared with those of Gentlemen Picture Dealers.'[26] The cost of refurbishing his dilapidated estate at Haddo in Aberdeenshire prevented Aberdeen from purchasing any pictures from Radstock and forced him to consider the sale of some of his coins in 1810.[27] Nonetheless he continued to tour the sale rooms with, amongst others, Sir Uvedale Price, and he loaned six paintings to exhibitions at the British Institution between 1815 and 1830.[28]

On questions of scholarship Knight was of more positive assistance. For example, on 18 September 1805, he replied to Aberdeen's enquiry about the translation of a passage from Homer in which some scholars had claimed to find a reference to arch construction, continuing that the arch was not generally used until the 'time of Augustus' since the massive arches of the Cloaca Maxima 'upon which so much stress has been laid' had been built by Agrippa, as demonstrated by Edward King in *Munimenta Antiqua* (1796).[29] Aberdeen adopted Knight's thesis when he came to write the Introduction, although he did not regard the arch as a beautiful form: 'perhaps we may doubt whether a very material addition has been made to the ornamental architecture of the Greeks by its introduction'.[30]

The 'grand Duke of Athens' was more of a Graecophil than Knight, or possibly even than Wilkins, and always, in the final analysis, arrived at his own conclusions. Thus, while he declared in the *Inquiry* that the need for further critical studies of Homer's texts had been 'rendered nearly superfluous...by the learned and successful labours of my friend Mr. Knight; who, in the edition of the Homeric poems which he has recently published, has attempted to restore them to their ancient and primitive state', amplifying references in the Introduction, Aberdeen had, in that earlier work, refuted Knight's proposition that columns had been fluted originally to hold spears.[31] Knight based his assumption upon a reading of Homer's description of the hall of the Palace of Odysseus, as he informed Aberdeen in a letter dated 25 November 1809.[32] Again, in the Introduction, Aberdeen disagreed with Knight's idea that 'the villas and country houses of the ancients were quite irregular in appearance, and adapted to local areas'.[33] If, he reasoned, Hadrian's villa displayed a variety of 'form and situation' there was 'no reason to imagine that the generality of their country residences were not in their exterior perfectly simple and regular'. Referring to descriptions in Vitruvius and Pliny, he continued, in a sentence that militates against over-emphasis of the influence of the Picturesque in the Greek Revival, 'the ancients never possessed any knowledge, or just perception of those qualities of external objects which are called Picturesque'.[34] Nor did Aberdeen wholly accept Knight's subjective concept of aesthetic response, and was exchanging letters with Price, who occupied opposing ground, at the time when Knight wrote in October 1810,

> Corresponding associations are so necessary to produce a sense of the Delicacy of picturesque Beauty that not very clever Men but the most learned & refined judges of imitative Art, as far as it has been employ'd upon Forms, have never acquired it. Such was the late Charles Towneley; and if there needed any further proof of the Fallacy of Price's system of it belonging to a distinct class of objects, this would be sufficient.[35]

In seeking to explain the 'unanimous' admiration for Greek architecture, Aberdeen brought the theories of both his friends to bear, writing at the beginning of the Introduction 'that the pleasure which is derived from surveying the ancient models of Grecian architecture is incalculably heightened by ideas connected with learning, with science and art', but also that 'their buildings possessed qualities which effect us independently of all these associations and which, even without them, fail not to produce in us sentiments of admiration and feelings of delight'.[36] Essentially those qualities were simplicity and regularity based upon 'propriety and deduced from the just ordinance of nature', as Wilkins wrote at the end of chapter 2, section 2, 'approving only of what could be supported by arguments founded upon the basis of truth and reason'.

Turning to the development of Greek architecture, Aberdeen expanded upon the account in *Magna Graecia*, to which he referred, and it is unthinkable that he did not consult Wilkins. He set aside Laugier's version of the Vitruvian theory of the natural origins of the Greek temple, stating that the earliest human habitations were probably in caves and not in proto-templar wooden structures, although he admitted that later Greek articulation 'bore a striking testimony to the early use of that timber in which the country abounded'.[37] More significant, in his belief, was the influence of Egyptian and Middle Eastern architecture, a source overlooked by Vitruvius despite the fact that Homer's poetry proved 'the prior advances made in the arts of design by the inhabitants of the coast of Syria and of Egypt'.[38] Archaic Greek architecture displayed a 'stiff columnar style, which, from remotest antiquity, prevailed on the banks of the Nile'.[39] Succeeding generations of architects had evolved a style characterised by 'propriety, elegance and grandeur', especially in the temple or the 'house' of the Gods; therefore, Aberdeen examined the probable form of the Homeric mansion in some detail before analysing the evolution of the temple and the Orders.[40] Once established as a type in the Doric style, temple design had progressed from such examples as that of Jupiter Panhellenius (Aphaia) at Aegina, which he believed, incorrectly, to be one of the oldest (in the *Inquiry* he claimed that the sculpture discovered there by C. R. Cockerell and his companions was later than the structure), to the Parthenon which he described as 'the most perfect... production of Grecian art' and attributed solely to Ictinus.[41] Again parting company with Knight, and Spon and Sir George Wheler, (author of *A Journey into Greece* (1682)), he asserted, rightly, that its sculpture was executed contemporaneously. He thought that the Ionic and Corinthian Orders had largely superceded the Doric after the completion of the Parthenon. These he discussed briefly and, having offered suggestions for an improved method of dating temples, dismissed Vitruvius's anthropomorphic explanation of their origins and also Winckelmann's statement that the Corinthian had been invented before the Phidian period.[42] Not unnaturally 'Athenian' Aberdeen judged post-Periclean developments as inferior, and it was his opinion that the Roman conquest of Greece heralded the decline of architectural design. To him, the Roman Doric, or Tuscan, was 'debased' while the Composite was a 'barbarous mixture'.[43] Worse, the Romans had polluted the Greek style by adopting the arch, which he considered to have originated in the cheap, functional architecture of the East, writing, 'few will deny that its abuse has perpetuated a greater corruption of style, and a more truly vitiated taste, than would probably have been witnessed had it never existed'.[44]

On that melancholy note Aberdeen ended the Introduction. In the *Inquiry* he extended his historical account of Classical architecture to embrace the Renaissance. Unfortunately, he opined, architects had then 'looked for instruction to the monuments with which they were surrounded', that is to the Roman and not the Greek.[45] The finest, among whom he numbered not only Bramante, Michelangelo and Palladio but also Bernini, might 'perhaps fairly challenge a comparison with the boasted production of the Augustan age. It is not however, to be expected that their compositions should be free from those imperfections which are to be found in the models from whence they derived their knowledge, and on what their taste was formed.'[46] By contrast the contemporary architect could study 'the precious remains of Grecian art' which scholars had 'accurately measured and delineated'.[47] Indeed, Aberdeen seemed to anticipate a new and purer Renaissance provided that the modern architect eschewed 'timid' and 'servile' copying (an injunction first made in the Introduction and possibly inspired by comments in Knight's *Analytical Inquiry*) and transferred the beauties of Greek design 'to our soil, preserving at the same time a due regard to the changes of customs and manners to the differences of our climate and to the conditions of modern society'.[48] But he offered little practical advice on the resolution of such inherently contradictory aims beyond the proposal that the architect should emulate the 'spirit and genius by which it was originally planned and directed'.

The revision of the Treatise was important to the achievement of that aim, not least, in the view of Aberdeen, because Vitruvius had confused some of the principles and rules of Greek architecture. In the Introduction he had noted that Vitruvius's 'professions' to having authority had persuaded succeeding generations of architects that 'his leading principles and precepts would be conformable to the practice of the Greeks'.[49] Vitruvius possessed a 'mind replete with notions in a high degree fanciful and visionary, and influenced by a strong bias towards metaphysical distinction and refinement' to which Aberdeen attributed his anthropomorphic theories on the origin of the Orders – ridiculed in 1809 by the German scholar, Alois Hirt (1759–1839), and later by Wilkins in *Atheniensia* – and his ideas on harmonic proportions.[50] These had spawned

> the laboured dissertations on the unintelligible connection between architecture and music and the institution of that scale of harmonic proportions which has exercised the ingenuity of the learned to so little purpose, down to the present day; and which has led one of the most able commentators [B. Galliani] to state that he considered the deficiency of musical knowledge as the great cause of the inferiority of modern architecture.[51]

In the *Inquiry* Aberdeen further indicted Vitruvius for contributing to the mistaken interpretation of Classical art during the Renaissance, suggesting that his analogy between members of architecture and the human frame might have induced Michelangelo to assert that anatomical knowledge was indispensable to the artist; he condemned Michelangelo's 'ostentatious display of anatomical science as a sculptor', a phrase that helps to explain his evidence to the Select Committee on the Elgin Marbles.[52]

Later Wilkins too directly criticised Vitruvius. When, in March 1826, he submitted his designs to the Council of University College, London, he appended an explanatory statement, including a section on the composition of the main portico, in which he faulted 'Vitruvius and his commentators' for misleading 'modern architects' into accepting that the proportion to be observed between the diameter of the columns and the distance they are placed asunder may be assumed almost *ad libitum*. On the contrary all the best examples of antiquity prove where the number of columns in porticoes were increased from four to ten the proportionate interval between them was gradually lessened. For example in the Corinthian and Ionic orders a portico of four columns has the intervals between the columns equal to three times the diameter of the columns.[53]

He was to be most condemnatory in the letter he addressed to the editor of *The Athenaeum* on 16 February 1833, when angered by the opposition to the façade line he had selected for the combined National Gallery and Royal Academy building, 'it would have been better for modern architecture that the work of Vitruvius had never reached us; the errors it has propagated are numerous, and so rooted, that it will require the greatest efforts to eradicate them'.[54] In the next sentence Wilkins recalled the fundamental inspiration that had guided the preparation of *The Civil Architecture*, declaring that a 'system founded on the pure basis of Grecian excellence must and will finally prevail'. While that sentence should be read in the context of the history of the commission and the attacks of the Gothicists (A. W. N. Pugin placed a drawing of the façade of the National Gallery and Royal Academy at the top of the satirical engraving which served as the frontispiece for the 1841 edition of *Contrasts*), it suggests that *The Civil Architecture* ultimately possessed a polemic purpose. Aberdeen, too, in the *Inquiry* had emphasised the creative rôle of archaeological research, writing that, since accurate examples of Greek architecture had been published, 'these exquisite remains should form the chief study of the architect who aspires to permanent reputation; other modes are transitory and uncertain, but the essential qualities of Grecian excellence, as they are founded on reason, and are consistent with fitness and propriety will ever continue to deserve his first care'.[55]

The Civil Architecture augmented Wilkins's reputation as a scholar. In 1814 he was appointed editor of the Society of Dilettanti's publications and his book was cited in the testimonial for his election to the Royal Society in 1831.[56] And first news of the preparation of the book and then notice of its impending publication appear to have contributed to Aberdeen's election as president of the Society of Antiquaries in 1812. It could not have consoled him for the death that year of his beloved first wife, Lady Catherine Hamilton, for whom he wore mourning till the day of his own passing.

On 18 December 1809 (Sir) Thomas Lawrence had written to tell Aberdeen that his portrait was nearly finished, adding a paragraph headed 'secret'. In this he suggested that however important were Aberdeen's political duties

> they will never be wholly disunited from Pursuits of Learning, and enquiry into the records of past Ages – Are you so wholly occupied with the researches of highest Antiquity, as to be *indifferent* to those of the Country in which we live? and would you object, to fill the Chair of the Society of Antiquaries. It is now most unworthily occupied [by the Earl of Leicester], and the shameful neglect of its duties is a source of the greatest discontent, with the most active part in [the] Society.[57]

Lawrence believed that this group was powerful enough to secure Aberdeen's election, though he was not a member, being admitted on 11 November 1811. But, in his reply to Lawrence, penned on 23 December 1809 at Haddo House, Aberdeen was less certain of his chances of success, though not of his qualifications. The office was 'honourable' and as such to be desired.

> Its duties do not appear to be very formidable, and they are probably not incompatible with other pursuits. Of their proper discharge, I entertain no fear myself, and any such on the part of the Society would be groundless...but neither that circumstance nor any other will make me submit to *briquer* the nomination, or to encounter the harassing difficulties necessary in gaining their *most sweet voices*...The widsom of the whole project, as far as I am concerned depends on the probability of success. Have you duly weighed this?[58]

The matter could not long remain a secret and on 30 November 1810 Knight wrote to Aberdeen regretting that he had not been apprised of the negotiations because he could have stopped Sir Henry Englefield from putting forward his name for the presidency. He was not enthusiastic about the office:

> The Society is so numerous, promiscuous & thoroughly Gothicised, that I fear it will be impossible to turn its Attention to objects of real taste and elegance, or employ its funds on their cultivation and promotion. I have so long despaired of it that I have not attended or interfered for many years except one, when I exerted myself to prevent the Engraving of the Rosetta stone going into the World with a Latin Inscription too barbarous to be Intelligible out of England; & then the Committee altered one which I substituted to it, corrected by Dr. Parr; &, without consulting me or the doctor, changed titulum (which they took in its Gothic or heraldic sense) to inscriptinion, thereby making it very crude and bald, though not absolutely barbarous.[59]

Aberdeen did not stand in the first election of 1811, won by Englefield, who defeated the Reverend Anthony Hamilton but was debarred from taking office, being a Roman Catholic. Seizing the opportunity, Lawrence again approached Aberdeen, who wrote on 7 October that he would accept the presidency since 'so many respectable members of the Society have, unsolicited by me, expressed their wishes in my favour'.[60]

Finally, Aberdeen was elected with the aid of Lawrence and surely Wilkins and Knight who, on 28 May 1812, congratulated him upon his 'elegant Introduction [Aberdeen had sent him a final draft for comment]; of the general Form & substance of which I have nothing to say but in commendation'.[61] By way of repaying his support, Aberdeen successfully nominated Knight as his deputy.[62] He also smoothed Lawrence's path into the Society of Dilettanti. Lawrence was to be elected secretary in 1822, although the day to day duties were executed by Wilkins, who, on 6 June 1830, was presented with a silver inkstand engraved with an inscription recording, 'The unanimous and grateful thanks of the Society...for his kind and constant zeal in promoting the high objects of the Society of Dilettanti and for his effective services in voluntarily discharging, on every occasion, the arduous duties of Secretary.'[63]

VI

The Gothic mode

While Wilkins was preparing *The Civil Architecture*, his father suffered a gradual deterioration of health. Wilkins senior referred to a 'recent attack' in a letter of 13 November 1809 to the trustees superintending the renovation of Great Yarmouth church. So, it would seem, William assumed increasing responsibility for both the theatrical business and architectural practice before his father died in 1815.

William inherited the lease of the Theatre Royal in Norwich and the tenancy of the theatres at Cambridge, Bury St Edmunds, Colchester, Great Yarmouth, Ipswich and King's Lynn. The circuit had prospered, the income rising from £600 in 1800 to more than £1,150 in 1825, sufficient to finance the remodelling of the theatres at Colchester in 1810, Cambridge in 1814, Yarmouth in 1817, Bury in 1818 and Norwich in 1819 and 1826.[1] The profit also enabled Wilkins to begin assembling what was to become a large collection of Old Masters – of a quality by contemporary standards of connoisseurship to be noted by G. F. Waagen, Director of the Berlin National Gallery – porcelain and Flemish stained glass which he acquired from J. C. Hampp of Norwich and later gave to Corpus Christi College, most of which was sold in 1920 and subsequently bequeathed to King's College for installation in the chapel.[2] One of his first acquisitions might have been the 'Parmegiano' 'Holy Family', which he sold in 1838, and which had been bought anonymously at a sale at Hermon's in 1814.[3] He may have been thinking of starting a collection as early as 1811, for William invited Farington to look at three paintings attributed to Salvator Rosa belonging to Dr Thoner, the Dean of Norwich, perhaps with a view to purchase.[4]

81

But, in 1811, William was doubtless more absorbed with his courtship of Alicia. His brother, George, was also in love and took the unusual step for a clergyman of eloping to Gretna Green. This unconventional manoeuvre secured the hand of Amelia Auriol, daughter of Dr Hay-Drummond who was uncle of the Earl of Kinnoul and the vicar under whom George served as curate at Plumstead. The match was to his advantage since he was later inducted vicar of Lexington in 1813, of Lowdham in 1815 and in 1819 of the prosperous parish of St Mary's, Nottingham. William was also on the move but within the capital, settling his wife in 11 New Cavendish Street where their first child, Henry, was born.

Of greater importance to his career, William had, in 1811, the opportunity of gaining practical experience in the Gothic style at Pentillie Castle in Cornwall. The commission to enlarge the castle for the Coryton family came to the Wilkinses through Humphry Repton, who, in 1809, had visited Pentillie with his son, George, when travelling to view Endsleigh in Devon.[5] They prepared a *Red Book* with proposals for the landscaping of the beautiful site atop 'Mount Carmel' above the upper estuary of the Tamar but left the architectural work in Cornwall to the Wilkinses. While on that trip the Reptons also called upon Edward Boscawen, 4th Viscount Falmouth, who engaged them to prepare plans for the improvement of his seat, Tregothnan, commanding the Claudian undulations of the banks of the River Fal near Truro. However, their proposals for the enlargement of the existing seventeenth-century house did not satisfy the fastidious Falmouth who, in 1815, turned to William, already at work on a new house in the Gothic style, Dalmeny, for another member of the Dilettanti, the 4th Earl of Rosebery. Yet another Dilettanti, the 5th Earl of Dunmore, commissioned William's last Gothic Revival country house, Dunmore, Stirlingshire in 1820.

Features of the additions to Pentillie bespeak the collaboration of William and his father (Pl. 33). While the battlements, unarchaeological fenestration, central position of the tower with tall arches on the new south front, and the octagonal entrance hall compared with Donington, the stronger projection of the entrance porch and thicker dimensions of the tower turrets suggest William's participation; interestingly, the placing of the entrance porch to one side anticipated the form adopted at Dalmeny and Dunmore. His hand can also be detected in the decoration of the library situated below the tower, which has a screen of two columns taken from the Order on the Choragic Monument of Lysicrates, and the installation of medieval glass in the hall. Nonetheless, the external articulation lacked the more accurate Tudor detailing and greater substance of Dalmeny, Tregothnan and Dunmore. And the only features that William was to retain from his father's architectural vocabulary were the inclusion of towers on the main fronts and, internally, the contiguous position of living-rooms linked by corridors to the entrance halls, staircases and offices.

In 1810, just before the commencement of the alterations at Pentillie, William had advertised his renewed interest in Gothic architecture by exhibiting two of his drawings of King's College Chapel at the Academy. In 1813 he sent all the drawings he had made of the chapel to the Antiquaries. On 25 February Aberdeen, in the chair, read a letter from William dated 25 January in which he regretted that his 'professional pursuits' had prevented him from preparing the drawings for publication upon 'a Plan somewhat similar to that which has been adopted by the Society...in their splendid Publications of our English Cathedrals' and requesting that 'they may be submitted to the inspection' of the members.[6] Presumably these were exhibited since he was accorded a vote of thanks.

His first major independent commission in the Gothic style came in 1814 when Lord Rosebery was forced to vacate the ancient family seat, Barnbougle Castle, situated on the southern bank of the Firth of Forth.[7] Family tradition holds that the decision to build a new house on adjacent higher ground was pressed upon the unwilling nobleman when, partaking of dinner one evening, he discovered that he was seated in a foot of Firth water. Chastened, he ordered designs from Wilkins and also Jeffry Wyatt, by whom there remain drawings at Dalmeny signed and dated 1814, which are similar in plan and include octagonal traceried turrets not unlike those that articulate the executed building. Wilkins submitted Greek and Gothic designs, the latter being selected by Rosebery.

Rosebery chose well, for Wilkins's Gothic design was something new. The most recent historian of North British Gothic Revival architecture, James Macaulay, has remarked upon 'Dalmeny's revolutionary principles in design and planning'. Macaulay has shown how Dalmeny effected a change of taste in Scotland, sustained in the 1820s by William Burn who imitated its compact form and neat Neo-Tudor decoration, most directly at Carstairs House, Lanarkshire, 1821 and Ratho Park, Midlothian, 1824.[8]

The revolution in design consisted of the adaptation of the Tudor manor house, specifically from examples like that dating from about 1520 at East Barsham in Norfolk (in a state of picturesque ruin when J. A. Repton published four engravings of it in *Vetusta Monumenta* (1811), pls. 24–7), and the adoption of a regular composition (Pl. 34). Wilkins considerably improved upon his father's rather feeble efforts at a Tudor Revival, and exhibited a greater consistency in its application than did his contemporaries. He also eschewed the mixture of secular and ecclesiastical mediaeval sources practised most obviously by James Wyatt at Fonthill Abbey, Wiltshire from 1795 and at Ashridge from 1808 to 1813 (completed by Jeffry Wyatt) and John Nash at Ravensworth Castle, County Durham from 1808, as well as the synthesis of Classical and quasi-mediaeval elements popularised in Scotland by Robert Morris and the Adam brothers. (Robert Adam had prepared a scheme for re-building Barnbougle Castle upon a large triangular plan.) The composition of Dalmeny, the pattern for Wilkins's two later houses, marked a departure from the emphatic irregularity employed by the adherents to the Picturesque. Even his fellow Graecophil, Smirke, had diversified the symmetrical massing of his two most celebrated Neo-Gothic mansions, Lowther and Eastnor Castles, begun respectively in 1805 and 1810, by the addition of numerous and prominent towers and turrets. By contrast the towers and turrets of Dalmeny rather reinforce the compactness and squareness of the house. This is particularly true of the façade which overlooks the Firth of Forth (Pl. 35). It has a centralised tripartite composition worthy of a Palladian house formed by the central tower and the flanking gabled projections or pavilions which are framed by traceried turrets closely modelled upon the one that ornaments the Parsonage House at Great Snoring in Norfolk. In the original design the pavilions had projected more than the central turret. Less regular is the entrance front, the composition of which clearly derives from that of East Barsham with the position of the porch and turreted projection reversed. Thus the house as built, an elevation for which was exhibited at the 1817 Academy, displays something of a dichotomy between the two fronts, which Cockerell noted in his diary, among other criticisms and a sketch plan, following a visit he made with Lord Elgin in August 1822.[9] The contrast between the fronts probably also resulted from Wilkins's experimentation with the style, reflected in his use of Coade stone for the chimneys and traceried panels and turrets; the turrets were installed in 1815 by nine craftsmen and proved to be satisfactory despite the appearance of a crack in one three years later.[10] Wilkins did not employ the material in his later houses except for the scagliola columns and pilasters that ornamented the library at Dunmore.[11]

The revolution in planning also expressed Wilkins's liking for regularity. The ground-plan of Dalmeny is virtually an open 'E', chosen to provide a commodious and convenient layout, as illustrated in one of the presentation drawings, showing the penultimate stage in the development of the plan before he reduced the staircase to two flights ascending the walls abutting the court and private apartments and made lesser changes to the internal layout, mainly on the first floor (Pl. 36). The library, drawing-room, billiard room and dining-room open into each other along the Forth front, reminiscent of the Tudor gallery, and are served by a corridor, which links the entrance and stair-hall to the domestic offices in the opposite wing, and from which a covered passage leads to the private apartments. The main rooms, on average measuring 36 by 24 feet, are large enough to befit gentle living but sufficiently small to be warm in winter, of particular importance in Scotland. The system was recast at Tregothnan to accommodate the shell of the original house and reworked for Dunmore. At Dunmore the plan was more obviously quadrangular, having the wings joined by a continuous corridor or enclosed cloister with a dining-room, library and drawing-room along the main front (Pl. 37). The entrance hall was polygonal, perhaps taken from that in Nash's Luscombe Castle, 1800, as was the dairy in the servant's court, though Wilkins had used the form as a pantry at East India College and as the boudoir at Dalmeny. The addition at Tregothnan contained a stair-hall communicating on the ground floor with a billiard room and a library giving into a ballroom, with the corridor set at ninety degrees to the entrance, off which lay the drawing-rooms and dining-room, and which led to the offices in the old house (see figure). The family bedrooms in each case lay above the main apartments. The compact and practical nature of these plans prompted Fergusson to comment that Wilkins's Neo-Gothic houses afforded 'far more accommodation for the same expense, with

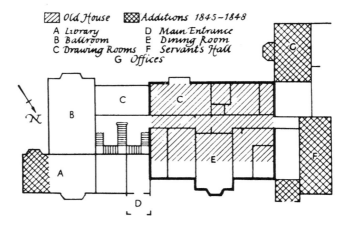

infinitely more appropriateness and convenience' than Grange Park.[12]

Convenience possibly also determined Wilkins to limit the Neo-Gothic articulation of the interiors to the stair-hall and to execute the other rooms in a plain Neo-Classical style; the Regency doyen of British country house design, J. P. Neale, wrote that the main rooms at Dalmeny 'were calculated more for comfort and convenience than show'. Another factor was Wilkins's appreciation that the historical style had to be adapted to contemporary life. Certainly he avoided the rather stagey wood and stucco versions of Gothic decoration to be found in, say Nash's Ravensworth Castle, and the thin tracery in the stair-halls at Tregothnan and Dunmore shows his distaste for excess. The Dalmeny stair-hall has a more substantial wooden hammer-beam ceiling, complemented by the nearby Flemish mediaeval stained glass, which he installed in the pointed windows of the corridor to the advantage of the Neo-Tudor stucco fan vault.

The distinctive character of Wilkins's Gothicism was not lost on his contemporaries. Neale, for one, wrote in the second volume of the first series of his *Views of the Seats of Noblemen* (1819) that Dalmeny 'presents an example of the splendid and much decorated style in use during the reign of James IV of Scotland'. In the first volume he reported that Tregothnan 'has recently been erected...in the style and agreeably to the taste displayed in the reign of Henry VII; in the construction, the architect it must be admitted, has made a very choice selection of the most perfect examples extant', and in the third volume of the second series (1826) that Dunmore 'was erected after a very correct design...in the Tudor style'. These comments match the judgement of the members of the committee (among them Hope) appointed to examine the plans submitted in the competition for the new Theatre Royal, Drury Lane, who declared in 1811 of Wilkins's Neo-Greek design, since lost and rejected in favour of one by Benjamin Wyatt, that it bore 'full testimony to the depth of his research amongst the specimens of antiquity, and the success with which he has cultivated his natural genius, and adapted the great examples, which he has personally viewed, to produce a design of erudition, simplicity and magnificence'.[13]

A measure of the appeal of his Neo-Gothic domestic style was the Tregothnan commission, for there he took over from the highly regarded Repton family partnership. Humphry and his son George had submitted a *Red Book* and separate elevations for rebuilding the old house as early as 1811 (Pl. 38). Two elevations, now at Tregothnan, are similar to those in the *Red Book* and are distinguished by an extended and irregular ground-plan and a number of towers; two smaller elevations with as many towers are also preserved at Tregothnan but may be by another architect.[14] The former were executed by George who wrote to Falmouth from Eastbourne Castle on 16 August 1811 requesting payment of one hundred guineas 'for Designs and fair Drawing of the alteration of your house'. In his letter George recommended an 'irregularity of outline which scorned all affected symmetry' in emulation of 'the commanding Towers of Windsor, of Warwick, of Belvoir, of Kenelworth [sic], [which] carry the mind back to former times to prove that their possessors could boast of what wealth alone can seldom look back upon – a Grandfather'.

Lord Falmouth did not share George Repton's taste or, perhaps, appreciate his allusion since the scheme was abandoned. In 1815 he corresponded with Wilkins who sent four elevations, seven ground-plans and three variant plans for the porch and first floor during the course of the year; there also remain two designs for the internal decoration, one for a vaulted hall and a second in a plain Classical style for the ballroom. These were more compact and less complicated than those of Repton, who had envisaged a house of two storeys with ten bays and five towers. Obviously Repton planned to demolish the old house, whereas Wilkins was happy to accept Falmouth's decision to convert the original house into offices, thereby preserving the Cromwellian plasterwork in a room now used as a study, and to 'gothicise' its exterior.

Wilkins, as ever, was amenable to his patron, a man evidently given to changes of mind, for two of the proposed ground-plans have incisions to take flaps with further suggested alterations. On 9 November 1815 he wrote to Lord Falmouth from London about one of his plans:

> The alteration proposed by myself and the removal of the porch as suggested by your Lordship have never been well considered (at least by reference to a plan) as to what must be the necessary arrangement above. I have therefore sent a sketch of both, which tend to throw a little light upon the subject – If the porch be removed we cannot get a W.C. below stairs – It must be remembered that in this case we shall be obliged to give some more finished Character to the old building. My accounts from Cambridge describe my Sister as nearly the same – our former Physician (the Master of Caius College who has abandoned the practice of Physic) has promised to visit her, I will immediately set out for Cornwall. The delay is not less pleasing to me than it can be to your Lordship as the long journey in Winter is what I very much dread, I fear it will be Monday before I can quit London.

Eventually the porch was retained and its presence in the wash drawing of the main front, preserved at Tregothnan, indicates that the four elevations and accompanying plans bound into a volume were drawn at the end of the year (Pl. 39). The ground-plan in the bound volume represents a penultimate stage in the lengthy process of decision, which began with two plans notable for their Neo-Classical style, having an apsidal ended ante-room and large double-return staircase – the form ultimately used in the addition but with Neo-Gothic cast iron balusters (Pl. 40).

Wilkins's desire to create a regulated exterior, unified by repeated projections and towers, would have been realised had the scheme in the bound volume been constructed. For, despite the strong chiaroscuro used in the wash elevations, each façade consists of symmetrical sections integrated into the whole by continuous mouldings and grouped about the elevated staircase tower, which recalls that at East Barsham and also the one James Wyatt built at Ashridge.

Unfortunately Wilkins's neat Tudor scheme, appropriately given a fortified character by the bastion in the wash elevation of the house as seen from the garden (Pl. 41), was compromised by yet more alterations. Falmouth decided to add a ballroom ending in a polygonal projection facing the river – Gothic on the exterior but masked with a Palladian opening on the interior – pencilled in on the ground-plan. It necessitated moving part of the drawing-room into the space occupied by the ante-room in the bound volume plan. The addition, as a whole, was contracted, apart from the staircase tower which was widened and pierced by more windows to compensate for the loss of a large window absorbed by the re-positioning of the porch. Thus Britton and Brayley found the completed house to be 'much diversified'. The appearance of Picturesque irregularity exceeded Wilkins's original intentions, though he had exhibited an elevation of his extension to the house at the 1817 Academy. It was much augmented by the towers added by Lewis Vulliamy between 1842 and 1846 at the junction between the old and new houses on the entrance front and to the office wing, and by the extension he built on to the library (Pl. 42).

At Dunmore, Wilkins finally brought his ideas on the domestic Gothic Revival to fruition.[15] Sadly the house was demolished in 1972 (Pl. 43). His design, exhibited at the 1821 Academy, was built almost as planned apart from some minor deletions on the garden façade (Pl. 44). This and the main front were virtually symmetrical in composition and bound together by continuous battlements and mouldings. Even the irregular entrance façade was ordered by the insistent horizontal and vertical accents, though the junction with the subsidiary section was abrupt. The traceried panels were banished and the projections fewer, but in their place Wilkins emphasised the substance of the granite walls. The austere exteriors and bastioned terrace yielded an impression that seems less revivalist than actually historical. However, there is no denying Wilkins's artistic restraint and apparent distaste for visual display which soon rendered his style unfashionable.

VII
Dilettanti

During the building of Dalmeny and Tregothnan Wilkins was invited to edit the material gathered by the 1811–13 Dilettanti Society expedition to Greece and Ionia. The majority of this appeared in the *Unedited Antiquities of Attica* (1817), but a proportion was committed to a revised edition of the *Antiquities of Ionia*, published in five parts from 1820.

At a meeting of the Ionian Committee held in 1814 and attended by the Earls of Aberdeen and Hardwicke, Viscount Morpeth, the Lords Northwick and Selsey, Englefield (the secretary of the committee), Gell, Hope, Knight, Lawrence, Benjamin West and Roger Wilbrahim, Wilkins opined that the printing of the findings of the expedition 'would be surpassed by no architectural publication extant and equalled only by the second volume of the Antiquities of Athens', which, as he recalled, had been supported by the society.[1] He spurred their enthusiasm by warning them of the jealous competition that could be expected from the French scholars. On a motion from Englefield, the committee agreed to finance what was to be the *Unedited Antiquities* by raising the membership subscription of the society.

Wilkins's ardour was rewarded with the responsibility for the publication, which was only fair since he had advised Gell in 1811 'as to the monuments to be examined', perhaps in collaboration with Aberdeen, who had drawn up the detailed instructions.[2]

His appointment was appropriate on another level, given the intent of *The Civil Architecture*. For, as Wilkins wrote in the introduction to the first volume of the new edition of the *Antiquities of Ionia* (published in 1820 with the second volume), one of the purposes of the expedition had been 'the correction of errors which had arisen [in the original work by Chandler and Revett (1769)] from the imperfect knowledge of Greek architecture'.

The editing, a voluntary task, coincided with the period when Wilkins's reputation as an architect and scholar reached a new peak. In 1816 he was called before the Select Committee on the Elgin Marbles, his evidence being among the longest given, and *Atheniensia* was also published in that year. More importantly, in 1817, he won the commission for the Army Monument, alas unexecuted, which might have been the richest architectural prize of his generation, since £200,000 had been allocated to it by the Liverpool Government, twice the sum assigned to the Navy Monument commission awarded to Robert Smirke. That year Wilkins moved his home and office to a new and larger property, 36 Weymouth Street off Portland Place, near the proposed site of the Army Monument opposite what is now Park Terrace.

The selection of Wilkins's design for the Army Monument was almost certainly clinched by Knight and Aberdeen, who were leading members of the 'Committee of Taste' appointed by the Treasury to oversee the competition under the chairmanship of the Paymaster-General, Long.

The success of two Antiquaries in the National Monuments competition and the Neo-Greek style of their respective submissions also marked a high point in the influence of dilettanti upon contemporary English taste. The Greek Revival had been nurtured through the archaeological expeditions and publications supported by the Society of Dilettanti, encouraged by their patronage and that of members of the Antiquaries (some of whom, Wilkins included, were laying the foundations of the archaeological Gothic Revival through a similar process of scholarship). In addition they had an effect upon commercial design and on more ephemeral fashions such as dress and furniture through the activities of men like Thomas Hope. By 1816 and the acquisition of the Elgin Marbles, the Greek style had become the national style to a considerable extent, as reflected in the preface of the Report of the Parliamentary Select Committee on the Marbles: 'no country can be better adapted than our own to afford an honourable asylum to these monuments of the Schools of *Phidias*, and of the administration of *Pericles*'.

Many of the dilettanti realised the hollowness of that high-sounding sentence, especially with regard to the patronage of British art, and were trying to improve the situation. In 1805 a diverse group had established the British Institution to promote British painting by holding exhibitions and offering prizes, to the distaste of the Academicians; but their attempts in 1810 to obtain a grant from the Government for the patronage of British artists failed.[3] Among their number were a host of Antiquaries and Dilettanti, including Abercorn, Aberdeen, Beaumont, Alexander Baring, Arthur Champernowne, Hope, Knight, Lysons, Lord Spencer and the Earl of Stafford, Aberdeen's predecessor as president of the Institution. Wilkins was a supporter and lent some of his paintings to the Old Master exhibitions organised by the Institution after 1813 with the aim of providing exemplars to British artists and thereby of raising the standard of native art. And Beaumont and another supporter, the Reverend Holwell Carr, made important bequests of paintings to the National Collection, originally formed in 1824 by the purchase of the pictures acquired by J. J. Angerstein. It was a case of the dilettanti trying to bolster what they saw as the dilatory efforts of the Royal Academy, which explains the sharp note its council received from Lord Egremont, a member of the Institution, on 2 August 1816, communicating his inability to lend Claude's 'Landscape with Jacob and Laban' to the recently founded School of Painting: 'I am very glad to find that the Academy are going to take the direction of the Arts into their own hands.'[4] The failings of the Academy and the expansion of the most famous of the antiquarian institutions, the British Museum, led Knight to bequeath his superb collection of antiquities and drawings to the Museum, rather than to the Academy as he had originally intended.[5]

However, a number of individuals within the Academy recognised the need for reform and concurred with the dilettanti in setting great store by the beneficial effect of the availability of collections of historical art. Their want in the Academy had been bewailed by Prince Hoare, Secretary of Foreign Correspondence 1799–1835, and (Sir) Martin Arthur Shee, president 1830–50, who had commended the foundation of the British Institution and wished to improve patronage in England. In collaboration with Francis Chantrey, Flaxman (professor of sculpture 1810–26), Fuseli (keeper 1804–25), Henry Howard (secretary 1811–47 and professor of painting

1830–47), William Marchant, Smirke, Richard Westmacott (professor of sculpture 1827–56) and John Yenn (treasurer 1796–1820), they forwarded the creation of the School of Painting in 1816, the improvement of the library (adding most to the stock of archaeological books) and the enlargement of the collection of casts and antique statuary with the aid of the Prince Regent; Wilkins was made an Inspector of the Library and Casts in 1836.[6] They were to press the Government into providing larger quarters in the new National Gallery building overlooking Trafalgar Square.

These reforms in the teaching facilities were inspired not only by Sir Joshua Reynolds but also by James Barry who, in 1797, had printed *A Letter to the Dilettanti Society respecting the obtention of certain matters essentially necessary for the improvement of PUBLIC TASTE, and for accomplishing the original views of the ROYAL ACADEMY of GREAT BRITAIN*. Significantly Barry had addressed the *Letter* to the society because he believed that its members were 'possessed of all the advantages of education and foreign travel, [and] can want no information from me respecting the importance, nature, and extent, of that collection of exemplars and materials of information and study, so absolutely necessary for advancing and perfecting the arts of Painting and Sculpture in a National Academy'.[7] He, and those Academicians who took up his cause, appear to have interpreted the academic principles rather more rigidly or literally than their predecessors, in a way that corresponded with the attitudes of the dilettanti who, as has been proposed, placed a new importance on scholarship and accuracy of imitation. The artistic fraternity was closely associated with the Societies of Antiquaries and Dilettanti.[8] Hoare was elected to the Antiquaries in 1815, following not only Wilkins but also Beechey, S. P. Cockerell, George Dance, James Gandon, Farington, Ozias Humphrey, H. W. Inwood, Lawrence, Smirke, West and Westmacott. In the Society of Dilettanti, Shee succeeded Lawrence as Painter to the Society, whose membership also included J. P. Gandy, C. R. Cockerell, Westmacott and, of course, Wilkins. Conversely, it should be remembered that the official appointments in the Royal Academy encompassed professors of ancient history and literature and an Antiquary, this post being held by Lysons 1818–19 (a vice-president of the Antiquaries) and Englefield 1821–6; Smirke was treasurer of the Academy from 1820 to 1850.[9]

While it would be erroneous to overstate the existence of a harmony of attitudes, most believed that the removal of the Parthenon sculptures by Elgin would achieve his intention of accomplishing 'something beneficial to the fine arts in Great Britain'.[10] Lawrence informed the Select Committee that the collection would 'be a very essential benefit to the arts of this country' and invaluable to the development of a School of Historical Painting, while Flaxman declared, 'I think works of such importance could not remain in the country without improving the public taste and taste of the artist.' Even the critic, William Hazlitt, who thought that the Marbles offered the best rebuttal to Reynolds's academism, considered that their arrival in England could effect the 'commencement of real art'. The conviction that such collections would exert an elevating influence on education and society grew during the century. Certainly, the assumption that antiquarian study was fundamental to the improvement of architectural design coloured the opening statement of the 1814 Report of the Ionian Committee: 'The improvement of Architecture is the principal object of . . . the Society of Dilettanti, already known to the world by the former publication of two magnificent volumes on the Antiquities of Ionia.'

The expedition was in large measure a Cambridge affair, conducted by William Gell, based on an itinerary worked out by Wilkins and organised by Aberdeen, who probably procured essential travel documents through his diplomatic contacts, as he was later to do for the expeditions made by Robert Fellows to Xanthos in 1838 and Charles Tatham to Egypt in 1842, both under the auspices of the British Museum.[11]

Despite the sarcasm of his *Edinburgh Review* article Aberdeen reposed full confidence in Gell as an experienced traveller and, in 1810, Gell had dedicated *The Itinerary of Greece* to him. Perhaps Wilkins and Aberdeen were asked to prepare the programme for the expedition to forestall Gell's fascination with the picturesque and anecdotal, which he displayed in the preface of that book:

> for when the classic traveller is satisfied with the simplicity of the Heroic ages in the mountains of Arcadia, where a single brass kettle is frequently the only utensil in a family and he descends in the course of an hour into the plain, and, drinking coffee in a cup set with rubies, realises the

splended visions of the Arabian Nights in the Court of the
Pacha of Tripolizza.

The *Itinerary* was a precursor of the modern guide book, as had been
The Geography and Antiquities of Ithaca which Gell wrote with Dodwell
in 1807, the year he was elected to the Dilettanti, and so were his
later volumes on the region: *The Itinerary of the Morea* (1817),
dedicated to Harriet, wife of Sir William Drummond, and *The
Itinerary of Greece* (1827), dedicated to a travelling companion, the
Honourable Richard Keppel Craven. The last was published after
Gell's election to the Royal Academy of Berlin, a further example
of the contemporary marriage between art and archaeology. In it
he alluded to that bond by describing the work of Stuart as 'of
most essential service to the arts', continuing in the vein of Wilkins,
'by first showing to the world, how very unlike the architecture of
the Greeks is that which has disfigured the cities of northern Europe
under the name of Grecian. It is probable that in time the science
will be gradually diffused, and that in another century the grandeur
and unity of Grecian architecture may reappear'.[12]

Actually Gell's interests were, by then, turned towards Roman
architecture, largely because between 1820 and his death at Naples
in 1836 he lived in Italy. He published *The Topography of Rome and
its Vicinity* in 1834, at intervals conducting luminaries like Sir Walter
Scott around the ruins. His house at Naples, called the Villa Gellia
by the locals, was decorated with Pompeian and Etruscan motifs,
inspired by research completed in 1814 when chamberlain to the
Princess Caroline of Wales on her notorious tour of Italy, and
described in *Pompeiana. The Topography, Edificies, and Ornaments of
Pompeii* (1817 and 1819). It was dedicated to Englefield and written
with J. P. Gandy, with additional help from C. R. Cockerell and
Richard Hey Sharp, whom Wilkins succeeded as architect to the
Yorkshire Philosophical Society.

Gandy and another budding architect, Francis Bedford, accompanied Gell on the 1811 expedition as draughtsmen. Gandy had
won the Silver Medal of the Royal Academy in 1806 and attained
a post at the Barrack Office, but little is known of Bedford before
1811.[13] Both benefited professionally, Bedford perhaps most since he
completed six churches in London for the Church Commissioners
during the 1820s, though those four in the Greek style hardly

emulated the 'grandeur and unity' Gell admired in ancient architecture.

The party sailed from England at the end of 1811, arriving at Zante (then a British possession) early in the new year. Thence they journeyed to Athens where they encountered difficulty in obtaining a passage to Smyrna, which decided them to excavate at Eleusis, the source of some of the most valuable material to be published in the *Unedited Antiquities*. At Eleusis Bedford drew a detailed reconstruction of the 'Propylea' (Inner Propylaea) and Gandy one of the Temple of Ceres (Demeter); on page 31 of the text Wilkins noted that Vitruvius had wrongly attributed the temple to Ictinus. Once in Turkey they studied the Temple of Juno (Hera) at Samos, the Temple of Apollo at Didyma near Miletus, the antiquities at Halicarnassus, Cnidus, Patara, Myra, Antiphellus (plague prevented them from visiting Laodicea and Hierapolis), Aphrodisias and the Temple of Diana (Artemis) Leucophryne at Magnesia. Returning to Athens, they unearthed what they called the Thoricus (probably the Demeter Thoricus which in ancient times had been reassembled at Athens) and made tours to Rhamnus, excavating the Temple of Nemesis and discovering a temple presumed to have been dedicated to Themis, and to Sunium, measuring the Temple of Poseidon.[14]

In the *Unedited Antiquities* the first five chapters were devoted to Eleusis, the sixth and seventh to Rhamnus, the eighth to Sunium and the ninth to the Athenian Thoricus. The survey of Eleusis drawn by Gell and the illustrations executed by Bedford and Gandy were engraved by Armstrong, Coke, Porter, Walker and Roffe.

The remaining material was set aside for the new edition of the *Antiquities of Ionia*, sanctioned by the Committee of Publication in 1819 at Wilkins's suggestion. Its quantity decided Wilkins merely to revise the original two volumes, mainly confined to the illustrations, and to present the new information in two additional volumes, carrying respectively forty-two and sixty-three plates. Volume III, mostly on Samos, was delayed until 1840, while the rest had to be further sub-divided into volumes IV (1881) and V (1915).

Wilkins was too busy, and latterly ill, to complete more than the descriptions for the plates and the editing of volume III, the general articles being written by W. R. Hamilton. But a letter from Lawrence in the W. P. Wilkins collection dated 26 May 1826 underscores his importance to the enterprise: 'The Committee of Publications meet here at Twelve tomorrow, but will you oblige me by your visit at half past Ten, or at farthest Eleven oclock? You are so essential to the business of this meeting.' Publication was also delayed because the French archaeologist, Huyot, and later T. L. Donaldson, had observed that the centre intercolumniation of the Temple of Diana at Magnesia was wider than drawn by Gandy. Wilkins was loath to change the plates and amend the relevant passages, writing to the committee in 1838 that it was 'only a hypothesis based on Vitruvius', continuing:

> Cockerell would say, 'look at Sardis', but there was no proof that the columns at Sardis were in their original position. Donaldson, Cockerell, Dick, Huyot have visited the spot with early notions so deeply impressed that Bramah's hydraulic machine would never be able to root them out, and they will die in the belief that the central interval of temples is enlarged, whereas I contend that such a notion has arisen for a similar kind of enlargement in the Propylea that was introduced for a very obvious reason.

(In the last phrase he was referring to the Athenian Propylaea which had a central carriageway leading on to the Acropolis.) In a second letter he protested, 'But really Leake and Cockerell persist with such pertinacity in ancient dicta that they seem rather to contend for victory at the expense of plain sense and truth.' In the end the engravings were altered, much to Gandy's ire.

Wilkins had nearly finished the third part before his death in August 1839, but in the preceding January, weary of the project, he had written to the committee:

> All matters connected with the fourth volume had better be deferred for the present, only remember that if long delayed I shall become, as I have hitherto been with the third volume, out of love with it. The present is a favourable moment for proceeding. If I get young and lively again I may turn my back on Myra and close the doors of its sepulchres.

On 2 February 1840, the society learned that it was printed 'except five or six pages which had been delayed in consequence of the lamented death of their late member Mr. Wilkins, and which was now in progress under the superintendence of Colonel Leake and Mr. Deering'.[15]

Two decades before, Wilkins's enthusiasm for Greek archaeology was undiminished and, as well as the books for the society, he was preparing the 'observations made during a residence at Athens in the year 1802' for publication as *Atheniensia*. Dedicated to Henry Pelham, Duke of Newcastle, its contents had been intended originally for Walpole's *Memoirs*. In the Advertisement Wilkins remarked that he had postponed publication since he did not wish his comments on the Parthenon sculptures to 'be construed into an attempt to deprecate their worth'.[16] His real aim had been to supplement though not to duplicate the work of Stuart and Revett and of Lord Elgin's agents, whose operations 'within, and around the ruins of the Acropolis' he had witnessed. [17] Although he knew that Elgin was unlikely to publish the drawings of the Parthenon executed at that time, he understood that the 'particulars so desirable to the amateurs and professors of architecure, are, however, likely to be amply supplied through the exertions of Mr [Charles] Robert Cockerell, a gentleman in every way qualified for the undertaking, and to whom the arts are chiefly indebted for the discovery of the Phigaleian marbles, recently purchased by the British Government'.[18] This generous praise – characteristic of Wilkins before his professional and bodily decline – was eventually realised in part by Cockerell in his study of the two pediments printed by the British Museum in 1830.[19] At that time Wilkins subscribed to the fourth supplemental volume of *The Antiquities of Athens*, published in 1830 with contributions by Cockerell. In the third chapter of *Atheniensia* he also alluded to Cockerell's explanation of the large central intercolumniation of the Athenian Propylaea as a carriageway.

In his book Wilkins carved out new areas of study by combining an historical account of Greek architecture with a translation of the inscription describing the construction of the Erechtheum (discovered by Chandler in 1765 and subsequently deposited in the British Museum) and a topography based upon the tours of Pausanias. He had prepared the translation of the inscription for Walpole's *Memoirs*, which contained as well a long article by his acquaintance, Edward Hawkins (from 1826 Keeper of the Antiquities at the British Museum), on the topography of Athens.[20] Wilkins took issue with parts of the interpretation of the inscription and the description of the temple which Chandler had published in *Inscriptiones Antiquae* (1774) and *Travels in Asia Minor and Greece*, I and II (1775 and 1776), and which had been favoured in the second volume of the *Antiquities of Athens* (1787). On pages 141-2 of *Atheniensia* Wilkins argued that the Erechtheum – he believed the name applied to the whole building – was a double, and not a triple, temple, in which the east cella had been dedicated to Minerva Polias and the western rooms had served as the Pandroseum. He seems to have imparted this idea to Clarke, who had endorsed it without acknowledgement in his *Travels*, III (1814), p. 499. It was accepted by the majority of scholars writing on the subject in the 1820s and 1830s including Inwood, Kinnard and Leake, and, on the continent, Raoul-Rochette, Tétaz and Beulé. One exception was E. J. Burrow (1785–1861), a Cambridge man who had migrated to Oxford, author of *The Elgin Marbles, with an abridged historical and topographical account of Athens* (1817). Wilkins criticised Burrow's commentary on the inscription, temple and Athenian topography generally in a letter published in October 1817 first in the *Literary Gazette* and then in the *Gentleman's Magazine*.

The first chapter of *Atheniensia*, 'On the Origin of Greek Architecture', covered much the same ground as Aberdeen's Introduction to *The Civil Architecture* and extended Wilkins's own account in *Magna Graecia*. He began by emphasising the pre-eminence of Greek culture in the history of European civilisation and argued that a distinct style of Greek architecture had arisen after the Homeric age, more precisely between 863 and 821 B.C., being a new version of the structural systems constructed with wood and stone in Syria and Egypt. The invention of the column he traced to Egypt but surmised that the Doric Order and the entablature owed their origins respectively to the Syrians and Phoenicians. He dated the beginnings of Hellenic architecture to approximately 968 B.C. when the Corinthians had colonised Sicily; the development of Greek architecture had been retarded by the Trojan War. The Greeks had introduced fluting, the Ionic and Corinthian Orders and the tympanum for sculpture. In discussing the Orders, Wilkins could not resist a lunge at Vitruvius, ridiculing his anthropomorphic theories as the 'offspring of a mind addicted to the practice of tracing invention to an imaginary source'.[21] Nevertheless he gave credence to Vitruvius's statements that the Ionic capital, in its earliest form, as Wilkins believed on the Temple of Juno at Samos, had been inspired by the spiral horn of Ammonian Jupiter and that Callimachus had created the Corinthian Order.[22]

As to natural origins of ancient design, Wilkins thought that the tapered shape of the column derived from the 'bundles of reeds, which the Nile copiously supplied, bound together at intervals'.[23] Possibly recalling the disagreement between Aberdeen and Knight about the source of fluting, he noted the similarity between the Greek words for reeds and flutes. Contrary to Vitruvius, Wilkins was inclined to believe literary accounts of the appearance in ancient paintings of rustic buildings with reed bundles supporting pediments. To Wilkins the tapering form of the reed also explained the diminution of the Classical column from the bottom to the top.

The acceptance of a correspondence between natural forms and Greek design was a commonplace attitude, but Wilkins was more specific than most of his contemporaries.[24] In the glossary to *The Civil Architecture* he had described the echinus as a 'member of the Doric capital, so called from its resemblance to the echinus or large vase, in which drinking cups were washed. The form of the vase might be suggested by the echinus marinus, divested of its spines, and placed with the open part outwards.' This kind of interpretation had been hazarded by Thomas Hope in *On the Art of Gardening* (1808), and was to be extended considerably by H. W. Inwood, who praised Wilkins's translation of the Athenian Inscription in his *Erechtheion* (1827). In *Of the Resources of Design in the Architecture of Greece, Egypt and other Countries* (1834), Inwood wrote: 'The plants on all sides surrounding...gave details of the enrichments so that' the Greek temple 'stood in beautiful harmony with the surrounding scenery'. J. Pennethorne, however, in *The Geometry and Optics of Ancient Architecture* (1878), concluded that 'in Greece we lose all trace of nature in the designs and the columns, as well as the ornaments, are purely intellectual works of geometry', continuing in a manner that echoed Wilkins's idea of the revival of Greek architecture, 'dependent for their beauty upon accurate proportions, true mathematical curves...upon great precision in the execution of every detail'.[25]

The remaining chapters of *Atheniensia*, 'On the Plan of Athens', 'On the Acropolis', 'On the Buildings of the City' and 'On the Athenian Inscription' (illustrated by a map of Athens and a plan and elevations of the Erechtheum) had a didactic purpose. In the last he sought to clarify that account of ancient construction, while in the first three he tried to establish the roll call of original Greek buildings 'in order that the defects which may be thought imputable to some of the works with which this interesting city was at various intervals embellished, may not attach to the purer style of the Greeks'.[26] To achieve this he turned to ancient literature and inscriptions. However, he expanded his list to include the 'principal remains' so that it embraced the Stadium of Herodes-Atticus, the Temples of Theseus and Jupiter Olympius, the Agora Gate, the Tower of the Winds, the Theatre of Herodes, the Monument of Philopappus, the Arch and 'Pantheon' of Hadrian, the Choragic Monuments of Thrasyllus and Lysicrates and, naturally, the buildings on the Acropolis.

If his topography is rudimentary by modern standards, containing confusions such as the description of Hadrian's Library as the 'Pantheon', a number of his conclusions were cited in later archaeological books. In the third edition of *The Antiquities of Athens* published in 1849, he was commended as the first 'to suggest that on the extensive platform [of the Temple of Jupiter] stood the Hieron, or Sanctuary common to all the gods, built by the orders of Hadrian'.[27] The edition contained numerous other laudatory references to *Atheniensia* and to *The Civil Architecture* including the following: 'Mr. Wilkins has made proof of admirable scholarship in his examination of one of the most singular and instructive among the remaining inscriptions of antiquity [Erechtheum Inscription]' and, in quoting from his description of the Erechtheum, 'Mr. Wilkins, to whom this work has been already much indebted, and whose close and critical observation is quite otherwise than the vague and discursive manner of Pausanias, made this Temple the object of long and successful examination.'[28] Some months before his death Wilkins had the gratification of receiving tangible recognition of his work on Athenian topography in the form of a letter from the Reverend Christopher Wordsworth, Master of Trinity College, Cambridge, dated 3 February 1839, now owned by W. P. Wilkins: 'in consequence of the light which your researches have thrown upon' Athenian topography he felt 'it not merely a pleasure but a duty to render by all means in my power the justice which is due to the person who was the first to communicate to the world that information...which has been confirmed by subsequent investigation'.

However, Wilkins was not infallible. In trying to separate ancient from modern Athens, or Hadrianopolis, he advanced a disputable interpretation of the inscriptions incised into either side of Hadrian's Arch. He translated that on the south east front as, 'What you see is the city of Hadrian, and not that of Theseus', and that on the north west front as, 'What you see is Athens, the ancient city of Theseus.'[29] He queried the view adopted by Spon and Wheler and, less definitely, by Stuart, that these referred to the areas lying behind the inscriptions. Instead Wilkins, like Chandler whose translation in *Inscriptiones* he altered slightly, thought that the inscriptions denoted those areas viewed by the spectator through the arch, which conflicts with the usual modern opinion that the arch marked the limit of the ancient city. Thus on reading the inscription on the south east side, according to Wilkins, he would have looked towards 'the greater part of the modern town. . .lying in the plain on the north-east side of the citadel, whilst the Acropolis is on the left, without the field of view'.[30] Basevi seized upon this in the letter he wrote to Soane from Rome in 1819, and was one of the reasons he gave for dismissing *Atheniensia* as 'the greatest mass of absurdities ever given to the public'.[31] Incidentally, both Edward Hawkins in his essay on the topography of Athens in Walpole's *Memoirs* and Colonel Leake in *The Topography of Athens with Some Remarks on its Antiquities* (1821) argued that the arch represented a boundary and that the inscriptions indicated those areas lying behind each.

Leake also disagreed with Wilkins about the route of the Panathenaic procession and the subject matter of the pediments of the Parthenon, though the last was in reference to Wilkins's essay published in Walpole's *Travels* (1820) and entitled 'On the Sculptures of the Parthenon'. In it Wilkins reasoned, unlike Spon and Wheler and E. Q. Visconti, that the subject of the west pediment was the contest of Neptune and Minerva (Poseidon and Athena). His basis for this was ancient literature and the similarities existing between its iconography and that on a vase excavated by Sandford Graham in a cemetry on the north side of the city and later acquired by Clarke who, in 1816, had advised Wilkins on the type of stones used in the construction of the buildings on the Acropolis.[32] He therefore believed rightly that the birth of Minerva was depicted on the eastern pediment above the main entrance. He gave less space to more effective arguments, some based on first-hand observation, such as his having seen a fragment showing an olive trunk in the pedimental sculpture taken from the west end by Lord Elgin, the fact that Nointels's drawings, made before the explosion in 1687, clearly showed the scene of the birth of Minerva on the eastern pediment, the reference in Plutarch (*Vit. Numa* 14) to golden shields having been removed by Lachares from the eastern portico, of which traces still remained, or that the Erechtheum entrances were placed on the east and north sides.

Leake, who later joined Cockerell to form a kind of scholarly opposition to Wilkins, complimented the description of the Stoa in *Atheniensia* in his own *Topography* and, in its introduction, echoed the emphasis Wilkins and Aberdeen had laid on the stimulus of functional necessity and the significance of experimental development in the creation of the Greek style of architecture. Also he shared their desire for the emulation of the 'genuine architecture of the Greeks'.

Another of the bones of contention that divided Wilkins from Leake and Cockerell was touched upon in *Atheniensia*. Amplifying passages in *Magna Graecia* and *The Civil Architecture*, Wilkins reiterated that the Parthenon had not been a hypaethral temple, that is with the cella open to the sky, but had been roofed in wood. Without naming them, he correctly stated that they, together with Stuart, had misconstrued Vitruvius's description of the type by supposing that the opening had been supported on columns in the cella, of which they claimed to have found the remains. Unfortunately, Wilkins weakened his valid surmise by denying that columns had existed in the cella, because he had found no trace of their bases and the fragments of columns he saw were unfluted, too thin and too short to have been original and were, therefore, probably later insertions. He also noted that Walpole had received a memorandum from Fauvel ('a French artist of great merit, who devoted many years to the study of Grecian architecture and sculpture at Athens') to the effect that the internal columns 'were of the lower Greek empire'.[33]

Though he drew upon his own direct observation in that instance, the text of *Atheniensia* betrays Wilkins's wary approach to visual evidence. He relied much more upon ancient literature, and this might explain his failure to discover the site of the Temple of Athena Nike. Nor did he elaborate on his discovery of remains of polychromatic decoration on the Propylaea. He wrote

upon minute inspection of several fragments of the two
pediments found among the ruins, it was discovered that
some members of the cornice were gilt, and on others an
enrichment was painted, with a reddish ochre: in one
instance, the form of the echinus was slightly sculptured
for the purpose of assisting the effect of painting. This mode
of decoration is not uncommonly met with in Grecian
buildings.[34]

He also remarked upon the presence of similar traces on the cornice
of the Theseum and on the pedimental sculpture of the Parthenon,
but assumed that the colour was only a ground for gilding. He left
the issue to be elucidated by others, and most painstakingly by Jacob
Hittorf (1792–1867) in *L'Architecture polychrome chez les Grecs* (Paris,
1831).[35] Wilkins was one of those who associated Greek art with
purity, in the chromatic as well as the compositional sense, being
more imbued with the taste of the late-eighteenth-century connoisseur
than was Gell, who wrote in *Pompeiana* 'that no nation ever exhibited
a greater passion for gaudy colours, with which, in the absence of
the rarer marbles [the Greeks] covered the surface of the beautiful
pentelic'.[36]

Wilkins's reliance upon evidence in Classical literature lay behind
his observations on the Parthenon Marbles in *Atheniensia* and was
specified in two sentences from his essay on the pedimental sculpture:
'however estimable they appear in the eyes of modern criticism, they
excited no strong sensation in the mind of the writer [Pausanias]
accustomed to the contemplation of works of higher pretensions.
What a vast idea of the excellence of Grecian sculpture is conveyed
by admitting the existence of such transcendent specimens of the
art!'[37] Earlier, giving evidence at the Elgin Marbles Select Committee, he cited Pausanias, Aristotle and Plutarch to support his belief
that Phidias has never 'worked in Marble', his statues being executed
in 'ivory and brass'. These authorities led him to presume that
Phidias had been merely the 'director and inspector', though he had
'made the designs of the sculpture'. He considered that 'the very
mistaken notion' that Phidias had cut the sculptures on the Parthenon
had given them an inflated 'value in the eyes of a great many people'.
Modern scholarship has tended to confirm his conclusions about

Phidias's part in the creation of the frieze, if not of the pediments, and much of the finest Greek sculpture had verily vanished.[38]

Quite apart from his interpretation of literary evidence, Wilkins continued to admire the refined idealisation and polished surface of the Hellenistic and even Roman sculptures which his generation had been taught to regard as the exemplars of the Classical Greek style. This was less apparent in his comments on the aesthetic quality of the various types of sculpture – justifiably he spoke of the 'very many degrees of merit' between 'the extremely fine' tympanum figures and some 'extremely indifferent' sections of the frieze, with the metopes at the intermediary level – than in his declaration that there were

> certainly very many things in the collection of the Louvre very far superior to the generality of the Elgin Marbles. I think in the kingdom we have some much finer statues than in the Elgin Collection: I think the Venus of the Townley Collection [presented to the British Museum in 1805] is one of the finest statues in the world, and the Hercules in the Lansdowne Collection is equally fine.

In this part of his evidence he affirmed that he had 'very lately visited Rome', a tantalising statement as there is no extant record of that continental journey and his views upon the Vatican and Capitoline Collections especially – let alone the architecture – would be of great interest.

The description of the pedimental sculpture in *Atheniensia* as 'vigorous' and displaying 'extravagant action' suggests an uneasiness with the vitality and naturalism of their style, of which much was made by many critics and artists. More objective were his remarks that the frieze showed a 'neglect of execution' in some parts if also a 'laudable economy' due to its internal position, and that the architectural framework had posed considerable problems for the sculptors:

> The groupes [sic] in the pediments, and the figures in the metopae might indeed be viewed from a distance more than sufficient to obviate the disadvantage arising from the foreshortening occasioned by the proximity of a spectator to the building: but the loss of the minutiae of execution

must have been the necessary consequence of this distant inspection; nor could a vigorous effect be produced without extravagant action in the composition, and a disproportionate relief in the details of execution.[39]

For this reason he did not believe that the Marbles were 'fit models for imitation' for free-standing sculpture though he allowed that they would afford 'a very fine school of study' where 'a sculptor should be called on to ornament an architectural building'.

Academically rather than imaginatively inclined, and ponderous in expression, his statements were misunderstood by some contemporaries including Farington, who wrote in his diary that Wilkins had 'exhibited great presumption and self-sufficiency'.[40] He neglected Wilkins's unequivocal declaration to the Select Committee that the value of the Elgin Collection was of the highest order and that he had considered it 'of very great importance' that the collection should be acquired for the nation. Maybe Farington read arrogance into Wilkins's explanation of why he had delayed publication of *Atheniensia*: 'I did not wish that my views should influence the disposal of the Marbles in any way, and I have only now recently put it into the hands of the Printer, in the expectation that this question would be settled before the book would appear in print.'

Wilkins defended Elgin, unlike Knight and, of the Cambridge circle, Clarke, Dodwell, Douglas, Hobhouse and the elder Tweddell.[41] He commended the earl for having saved the Marbles, first at the Select Committee and more forcefully in *Atheniensia*:

I am far from going in the clamour which has been unjustly raised against Lord Elgin, by some recent travellers. As I resided in Athens whilst the collection now in England was removing, I can venture to say that the absence of what was actually taken down from the Parthenon will scarcely be felt. Had the Erechtheum been suffered to remain untouched His Lordship might have escaped well grounded censure [a reference to the removal of one of the caryatids from what Wilkins called the 'Porch of the Maidens']. The advantages, however, that we may confidently expect to derive from the possession of the collection are of too great a magnitude to permit us long to regret the loss the originals have sustained.[42]

Later, in the essay on the Parthenon sculpture, he blamed the depredation of the Acropolis upon the local inhabitants who had taken pieces 'in the expectation of selling...to some of the English lately in Athens [such as Aberdeen and Clarke], who purchased every fragment with great avidity and thus contributed to the destruction of the monuments of Athenian antiquity'.[43] It was Wilkins who, on 1 May 1831, seconded Hamilton's abortive nomination of Elgin to the membership of the Society of Dilettanti.[44] Elgin declined, remembering the obstructive attitude of the society towards his efforts to publish engravings of the Marbles and to transfer them to public ownership. That had been largely engineered by Payne Knight, who directed the society's funds to the publication of the first volume of the *Specimens of Ancient Sculpture* (1809), further stretched by the Ionian expedition and the printing of the *Unedited Antiquities*.

Wilkins's support of Elgin, no less than his evidence, shows that, despite his admiration for Knight's scholarship, he took an independent stand, and the same can be demonstrated for Aberdeen. It would seem that they only wholly agreed with Knight on one point, that Phidias had acted as superintendent, Wilkins including a sentence to this effect in *Atheniensia* taken from Knight's introduction to the first volume of the *Specimens*.[45] Neither for one moment entertained Knight's ridiculous initial surmise that the pedimental sculpture had been cut during the Hadrianic period. Admittedly they, like Knight, were disappointed by the damaged surface of the Marbles and somewhat perplexed by their naturalism, but they could not follow him in judging the Phigaleian Marbles to be superior. Again, despite their reservations about the quality of the major figures, neither was anywhere near as churlish as Knight in their utterances to the Select Committee. Aberdeen, for example, ascribed them to 'the very highest class of art', and, together with Wilkins and other witnesses such as Flaxman and Chantrey, only moderated his plaudits when invited to compare the Marbles with such celebrated pieces as the Apollo Belvedere. 'By this term, however,' he continued, on the same tack as Wilkins, 'I beg to be understood only as expressing a very high degree of excellence, and not as, in strict language, comparing them with the most perfect specimens of art on the continent or even in the Country.' Aberdeen, too, seems to have rather admired Elgin's acumen in exploiting his official position and the favourable political situation to rescue the sculptures from piecemeal destruction by 'the frequency of travellers going to that country, and from the continuous endeavours of the French Government to obtain possession of them'.

Aberdeen had been one of the first to learn of Knight's immediate reactions to the Marbles. In July 1807 Knight wrote to Aberdeen from Soho Square:

> I have just been seeing Lord Elgin's things with Mr. Hamilton, and should eagerly embrace the oppurtunity [sic] of seeing them with you; . . . The preserved Fragments of the Frieze are interesting; but I do not think the Workers of them deserve any better Title than common *Stone hewers* of the Age of Phidias; and doubt not of your being of the same opinion, when you come to compare them with some of the specimens of the real works of the great Artists of that Age in the Townlian [sic] collection. The difference is as great as between an Altar piece of Titian and a pannel [sic] by Ribera.[46]

This extraordinary lapse in his powers of perception is perhaps explicable on the grounds of personal animosity towards Elgin. How different is the communication Aberdeen received from Englefield on 24 August 1807: 'Since you left town I have seen Lrd Elgin's Marbles. I am I own quite astonished both at their number & beauty. As I probably shall never see Athens I am obliged to him for his depredations. I envy more & more you who have seen those glorious remains.'[47]

On 26 May 1808 Knight thanked Aberdeen 'for the references to Pausanias: but I have no thoughts at present of publically discussing the Question, or expressing any opinion concerning it. Phidias certainly did not acquire celebrity by his Works in Marble, & the Passages are some of them distinct enough to discriminate satisfactorily between what was done under his Direction & what was finished by his Hand.'[48] Here was the germ of the paragraph in the first volume of *Specimens* quoted by Wilkins and might be Knight's first admission that the sculptural decoration was probably coeval with the construction of the Parthenon. But he was loth to swallow his pride because he had expressed such forcible opinions so openly. Thus in three letters, written in the summer of 1812 following a tour of Scotland when he had visited Aberdeen (at Haddo), Lord

Dunmore, W. R. Hamilton and Samuel Rogers, Knight continued to try to justify his position by applauding Byron's scathing attacks on Elgin and earnestly recommending the purchase of the marbles unearthed at Aegina and Phigaleia in 1811.[49]

In the last letter on the issue remaining in the Aberdeen Correspondence, dated 16 January 1816, he again pleaded the superior merits of the Phigaleian sculpture that had been bought for the British Museum in 1815.

> The Relief is much higher, the details more finish'd, and the style much less archaic than those of the internal frieze of the Parthenon;...the draperies being remarkably light and luxuriant; and the limbs and Bodies among the most supple and fleshy extant...They being sufficiently entire to be restored and employ'd as Fixtures or Furniture, which scarcely any of Lord Elgin's are.[50]

Yet when he appeared before the Select Committee that March he qualified his praise of the Phigaleian frieze, as much else in his evidence, probably heeding the conclusions reached by Aberdeen and his friend, Wilkins. He admitted the weakness of his attribution of the pedimental sculpture to the Hadrianic era, possibly influenced by Aberdeen who, at the Select Committee, dismissed Spon's identification of a statue on the west pediment as a portrait of Hadrian. Knight's acknowledgement that the metopes were of the 'first class of high relief' and the frieze of the 'first class of low relief' smacks of Wilkins, though Knight still believed the collection as a whole to be in the 'second rank' because 'their surface is gone mostly'. He also said that his estimate of their monetary value, £25,000, was too low and that 'in bringing them away' Elgin was 'entitled to the gratitude of the country'. Nor should it be forgotten that Knight had served from 1814 with Aberdeen as a trustee of the British Museum and, in 1815, had agreed that the Government should purchase the collection.

VIII
National monuments and private commissions

The chief subject in Knight's letter of 16 January 1816 was the deliberations of the Committee of Taste about the proposed national monuments to commemorate the victory of British arms in the Napoleonic Wars. He wanted Aberdeen to join the committee, doubtless to consolidate his own influence which, as events proved, was not to be as important as he might have wished. Whether through Knight's intervention or not, Aberdeen was invited to become a member on 25 March 1816.[1]

Of those deliberations Knight informed Aberdeen that

> the general Inclination seems to be for an arch; though it is difficult to find a proper place for it. I should prefer a Church to any other kind of Building; as I hate all those obtrusive Structures, which when employed to adorn a place in the Country, are properly named by the proprietors *Folly*; and if we must have an Arch it must at all Events [act] as a gate to the Town. If we can have two, one naval & one military, the two Ends of the new Strand Bridge are admirably adapted; & the whole would undoubtedly be the finest structure in this world.

He calculated the cost of the arches at £800,000 and hoped that the government would vote another £100,000 to relieve bridge traffic of tolls. As to the church, he considered that the 'Centre of the great circus in the Regents Park would be an admirable site for a church upon a simple Plan something like the Pantheon at Rome'. He thought it would require about one million pounds and ten years to execute, but feared 'that we shall at last produce a Folly more fine than magnificent'. He ended on a more humorous note, gleefully relating the Reverend Holwell Carr's account of the bad state of the pictures in the Louvre which made him 'less regret the not having seen them prior to their dispersion & more regret their ever having fallen into the hands of such Barbarians'.

The arch and church schemes were discarded since the winning designs, those submitted by Wilkins and Smirke, fell within Knight's genus 'Folly'. But current gossip, recorded by Farington on 9 June 1817, was that Knight still exercised a commanding vote as Samuel Lysons opined 'that not Lord Aberdeen but *Payne Knight* got the Waterloo Monument for Wilkins and Gandy...they having been employed by the Dilettanti Society on other matters'.[2] Earlier Farington had summarized a conversation with Gandy who 'spoke of having, in combination with Wilkins, the Architect, made a design for the National Monument to the Battle of *Waterloo*, which had been approved by the Committee appointed by the Govt....He said He *proposed* the design to Wilkins.'[3]

The collaboration of Gandy with Wilkins might at first appear rather incongruous in view of the fact that his brother, J. M. Gandy, was Soane's personal assistant. But they had worked together on the *Unedited Antiquities* and the *Antiquities of Ionia*, and, beginning with the Army Monument scheme, Wilkins was prepared to call on Gandy to assist him in the 1820s when his time was at a premium. In return, he appears to have expedited his young friend's election as an Associate of the Royal Academy in 1826 and to the Society of Dilettanti in 1830, honours not accorded to Francis Bedford. Reading between the lines of a letter John Constable wrote to C. R. Leslie on 28 December 1831, Gandy nagged Wilkins to support his candidature for election to the ranks of the Academicians, unsuccessful until 1838; and a month later Constable gave Leslie a report of the previous vote which includes a vignette of Gandy's character that casts doubt on his claim to have proposed the design of the Army Monument: 'he must see that his *only* superiority (cunning) is not a metal of weight in a house of so much intellect'.[4]

Gandy's contribution cannot be conjectured since the design has been lost and the descriptions of it in the press are cursory. The most helpful is in the 1817 *Gentleman's Magazine*: 'an ornamental tower of three orders of columns around the base of which is a circular colonnade which resembles one of the most admired remains of antiquity, the Temple of Sibyls Tivoli'.[5] The author of an unidentified newspaper article pasted into Wilkins's book of press cuttings discerned 'in the form, proportions, ornaments, a more than ordinary share of architectural erudition and resource'. The catalogue for the 1826 Academy Exhibition, where a model and design (to which the article might refer) were shown, stated that 'the Tower of Waterloo' would rise 280 feet.

The design envisaged a more massive and plastic structure than Wilkins had attempted before and marked the beginning of a relaxation of the strict Greek Revivalism of his early career. The shape would have exploited the intended site at the Regent's Park end of Portland Place, matching the curved façades of Nash's incomplete Park Terrace begun in 1812. Indeed the design might have influenced Nash's composition for the portico of All Soul's, Langham Place, 1822, which can be traced back to one of the grandest specimen designs he had submitted to the Church Commissioners in 1818.[6] Smirke also selected a geometrical form for his Naval Monument, 'a plain octagonal structure 45 feet in diameter at the base raised upon a magnificent flight of steps surmounted with a naval coronet'.[7] He was peeved that the Army Monument was allocated twice the sum granted for his part of the commission, complaining to Farington that he 'very much disapproved the design of *Wilkins* and *Gandy* for the *Waterloo Monument* as being in bad taste' and that it could not 'be executed for £200,000, the sum allowed, such is the quantity of ornament'.[8]

The importance of the national monuments commission can be gauged from the fact that it attracted more than sixty competitors, among them, almost certainly, Thomas Harrison, whose splendid 'National Building to record by painting and sculpture the Victories of the Marquis of Wellington and other commanders by sea and land during the present war', exhibited at the Royal Academy in 1814, was not unlike an aggrandised version of the unexecuted library and chapel block Wilkins had planned for Downing College.[9] The monuments were the architectural prizes of their generation and, given the difference in projected cost, the award of the Army Monument would have confirmed Wilkins as the leading architect of the Greek Revival. But the commission was riven from him when Lord Liverpool's Tory Administration was forced to abandon it, being confronted by a worsening economic recession that was an outcome of the war. Earlier, in 1816, flushed with the victory of Waterloo and roused by the oratory of the Foreign Secretary, Viscount Castlereagh, Parliament had voted £500,000 for a single monument to the naval and military forces.[10] Castlereagh had propounded a memorial of national cultural significance wherein 'painting, sculpture and Architecture' were to have been united, perhaps inspired by John Opie's idea for a 'Naval Pantheon', described in a letter addressed to the editor of the *True Briton* in 1806.[11] Sadly, the Royal Academicians had refused to help in the judgement of the competition, apparently fearing accusations of favouritism, so that Castlereagh lost interest and the project was restricted to architecture, divided into two commissions, and the budget reduced to £300,000. At the time of the competition Benjamin West tried to resuscitate the concept of a commemorative Pantheon of British culture 60 feet square at its base and 150 feet high, constructed

> out of the spoils of victory, diminishing as it rises, the centre to be an equestrian group to the Duke of Wellington, under which 'Waterloo' should be inscribed; the four angles to contain tablets of record and statues of generals. The interior to be a place of deposit for preserving the powers of the pen, the pencil, the other gems from perishing; all the ornaments of the building to be of metal and to be illustrative of victory.[12]

Smirke, too, had contemplated a composite monument, closer to Knight's proposal, comprising, 'Two simple obelisks connected by a Church or Chapel in the form of an ancient Temple – the Parthenon for instance', dedicated to the 'God of Peace'.[13]

In vain, that and his actual submission, together with the Wilkins and Gandy monument design, fell victim to Government austerity. The exhibition at the 1826 Academy of their scheme was surely meant to remind Parliament of its obligation to carry out its decision of nine years' standing. A formal letter in the W. P. Wilkins collection, signed by Wellington on 27 February 1821, might signify justifiable pressure on the Iron Duke by Wilkins; Wellington presented his compliments, 'and will on his return to town a few days hence, avail himself of Mr. Wilkins's permission to call upon him'. By then the noble rhetoric was as mute as the corpses on the field of Waterloo or beneath the waters of Trafalgar Bay.

Wilkins was denied the national patronage he most surely coveted.

As to a monument to British valour he had to be satisfied with the privately funded commission for the Nelson Column, Great Yarmouth, begun in 1815 and finished in 1817 (Pl. 45). Like the commission for the Freemasons' Hall, Bath, 1817–18, erected under the patronage of the Duke of Sussex, it enhanced his reputation but, like the additions he made to Keswick Hall, Norfolk in 1817 for his friend and banker, Hudson Gurney, was only of local significance. As Preston wrote in the *Picture of Yarmouth* (1819), the column eclipsed 'every other modern piece of architecture in the neighbourhood'.[14] Through it Wilkins probably won election to the Norwich Society of Arts in 1818, joining his friend, Shee, who had been elected in 1817; two others of his circle, Beechey and John Cotman, became members before he resigned in 1828.[15]

The Yarmouth commission also served to remind Wilkins of the dilapidated state of the theatre he leased in the town, which had been built by Fulcher of Ipswich.[16] On 15 June 1816, while the column was rising in the centre of the fashionable race-course, he presented a renovation programme to the shareholders estimated to cost £1,500. The capital was to be raised by selling transferable tickets to local families, among them, doubtless, some who had subscribed to the column fund. He intended to increase the height of the existing walls, fix a new slate roof, refurbish the interior and renew the stage machinery. However, on 18 August 1817, he had to report that structural faults had been revealed by the stripping out of the old interior which made a complete reconstruction more economical. Although this necessitated a further sale of tickets at £70 each, the shareholders endorsed his policy on 21 August and the work was, apparently, executed.

Wilkins must have been gratified by the commission to honour his fellow East Anglian on home ground. Nelson, born at Burnham Thorpe Rectory, had landed first at Yarmouth after the battles of the Nile and Copenhagen. In his biography of the Admiral, Wilkins's friend, Robert Southey, dwelt on the second homecoming when Nelson had disembarked in bad weather and straightway visited 'the men who had been wounded in the late battle, that victory which had added new glory to the name of Nelson, and which was of more importance even than the battle of the Nile to the honour and strength of England'.[17] Bearing these events in mind, a committee of some fifty gentlemen from the county resolved to raise funds for a memorial on 20 October 1814. Within a short period £3,715 had been subscribed and when a formal meeting was called for 12 January 1815 in Norwich the committee had some £6,000 at their disposal. Here it was agreed to institute a competition for a 'column with appropriate ornament' to be erected in Aberdeen granite or Portland stone at Great Yarmouth, the best site for 'its future utility, as a sea mark, for the benefit of navigation'.[18] They also decided to establish their base of operations at Thetford which fostered the erroneous supposition that there were two competitions.[19]

The presence in Soane's Library of a copy of the advertisement published in *The Times* of 24 January 1815 and another of the committee's meeting in Norwich suggests he was one of the forty-four contestants. One documented competitor was the sculptor, Chantrey, who proposed that a statue 130 feet high be erected on a pier projecting 'far' into the sea, though he did not specify whether the statue was to be of Nelson, Victory or Britannia.[20] The figure was to be illuminated at night and supported on a 'pedestal made of the bows of vessels taken from the enemy'. However, the committee plumped for Wilkins's 'Athenian Doric column'.

The design was a taller version of the Dublin Pillar and, had the foundations not proved to be so expensive, it would have been 30 feet higher. As built, including the statuary, it stands only 10 feet higher than its prototype, rising 144 feet (one foot less than the Trafalgar Square Column by Railton, 1840–3) from a more substantial pedestal, in turn placed upon a terrace with steps at the centre of each side and diagonally projecting corner bastions. The pedestal is tapered and articulated with four porticoes surmounted by a deep entablature, each ornamented with four laurel wreaths in the frieze. Raised plaques above record Nelson's four victories, with Aboukir substituted for the Nile. The names of his respective flagships are chiselled on the sides of the abacus resting upon the capital of the column – Vanguard, Captain, Elephant and Victory. Formerly the abacus was a viewing platform, reached by 207 steps, lit by slits in the fluting and entered through a doorway cut into the pedestal under the Trafalgar portico.

The Yarmouth Column differs most from the Dublin Pillar in the arrangement and character of the statuary. It is crowned by six caryatids surrounding a stone post, together supporting a roof on which is placed a globe surmounted by an impressive statue of a

Minerva-like Britannia replete with staff, trident and copper olive branch, the larger scale of which is a successful impropriety. The figures were commissioned from the Coade Company in 1817.[21] The arrangement of the caryatids, displaying their copper laurel wreaths, once to the Yarmouth race-goers on the Denes Course below, but now to a dismal industrial estate, and the circular roof ornamented with six scrolls, represent an amalgam of themes from the caryatid portico of the Erechtheum and the Choragic Monument of Lysicrates. The caryatid peristyle was taken from Wilkins's unsuccessful project for the Wellington Testimonial, Dublin, 1815 (awarded to Smirke), although the scale of the caryatids and of the seated statue of Wellington or Victory would have been smaller in relation to its Greek Doric column. That design is preserved in the National Library of Ireland (Pl. 46). For the Yarmouth design, as at Dublin, Wilkins had originally wished to cap a taller column with a Roman galley – shown above the caryatids in a drawing by John Cotman – but the estimated cost of £7,500 was too great for the resources of the Yarmouth committee.[22] The revised design was exhibited at the Royal Academy in 1821.

Both he and the committee had hoped to finance the extra expense of the galley by obtaining a grant from Trinity House on the grounds that the column would aid navigation in the Yarmouth Roads. The design was dispatched to Trinity House on 7 September 1815 only to be rejected by the Court because 'if erected at Yarmouth, it could be of no very essential use to navigation as a sea mark, but if erected at Cromer, it might possibly become serviceable to navigation as a lighthouse'. Undeterred the committee continued unsucessfully to press for a grant, while the Court insisted that, to be of any use to Yarmouth, the column should rise at least 280 feet above sea level.

Wilkins revived the subject in his report on the site dated 10 January 1816 which was included in the pamphlet printed by the committee. It was addressed to a leading member, William Smith, also the local Member of Parliament, and is an affirmation of his habitual care. Wilkins had consulted the area Trinity House agent who, unlike his London masters, thought the column could be 'of essential service to the navigation of the coast' taken in conjunction with traditional sea-marks, and he had then engaged men to test the soil around Yarmouth. Beneath the bed of sand was a stratum of shingle 'of very considerable depth' and below that 'a bed of soft loam or clay, which the builders there call ouse', conditions that precluded the use of piles. Instead Wilkins proposed laying over 1,500 cubic feet of oak in planks on the shingle so as to form a level area 55 feet square for a brick foundation of nearly 85 rods. He calculated the cost at £1,952, too much for the committee, who asked him to find means of reducing expenditure, beyond the deletion of the galley. So, writing from 36 Weymouth Street on 14 March 1816, he concluded that the column should be shortened by 20 feet and 'a proportionate reduction made in the bulk'. On those foundations for over 160 years the Nelson Column has withstood the buffeting of North Sea gales, the shifting sands that surround it and the neglect of the local council.

Besides the admirals, generals and local worthies who gathered at the ceremony of the laying of the foundation stone of the column – when Wilkins read an address, 'which cannot fail to be admired by those for whom polished and classical Latinity possess any charm', fittingly in the amphitheatral depression caused by the excavation – were a group of seventy Freemasons.[23] And when the Fraternity decided to build a new hall at Bath in 1817 Wilkins was their chosen architect (Pl. 47). The hall was opened on 4 August 1818 by the Duke of Sussex who was Grand Master of the United Grand Lodge of England. (Incidentally, by his annulled morganatic marriage to Lady Augusta Murray, he had been brother-in-law to the Earl of Dunmore; from 1809 the Earl of Moira was guardian of the son of the alliance.) Although no records remain of his having been a Mason, Wilkins was described as 'our Brother William Wilkins' on the plaque installed in the hall.

The portico of the Freemasons' Hall combines the Erechtheum Ionic Order with the antis form. It is topped with a plain pediment, intended to have been decorated with sculptures representing the Masonic symbols of Faith, Hope and Charity. Of chaste appearance, the portico is framed by pilastered ashlar sections of the same height pierced by tapered windows and raised on a stylobate to distinguish the building from the surrounding domestic architecture. The portico is ornamental, the entrances being in each of the lower flanking wings. Despite his later strictures on the Renaissance style – Rogers recorded his saying that he had the 'greatest contempt' for Palladio – Wilkins rusticated the arched openings on the side walls to lend the hall a hint of sixteenth-century Italian architecture.[24]

The interior was as practical as the exterior was finely proportioned. Rooms on the ground floor were reserved for 'Masonic purposes', while the hall above, 50 by 30 feet, could be used by the Freemasons or let for entertainments. This had seating on three sides, with a semi-circular platform and organ gallery on the east side, and was top-lit by two circular lanterns on high glazed drums from which hung glass chandeliers. The hall was highly praised in the *Bath Herald* of 9 August 1817, much to the delight of the local Masons, who had a medal struck of the façade on 18 September 1819 to coincide with the Bath Masonic Festival.

The influence of the Italian Renaissance can also be discerned at Keswick Hall in the additions Wilkins made to the existing house in 1817, namely the Venetian opening in the staircase tower, the window frames on the bow and the balustrading with which the tower and parts of the refurbished house were ornamented (Pl. 48).[25] The influence of the English Renaissance, too, can be seen in the fluted chimney stacks. Five years later Wilkins sent an impressive scheme for a house in the Jacobean style to Edward Lombe, which can be considered in the context of the Keswick commission.

The house was to have been built at Bylaugh in Norfolk under a complicated provision in the will of Sir John Lombe, Bart, of Great Melton.[26] Lombe might well have been responsible for the choice of the impure English Renaissance as the model since, when sufficient funds finally became available in 1848 to build the house, he asked Alfred Ainger, Charles Barry junior and Robert Richardson Banks to prepare designs in the same style; the house, called Bylaugh Hall, was built by the latter partnership. However, Wilkins had shown an interest in the English Renaissance as early as 1809 when he wrote the essay on the Porta Honoris of Gonville and Caius College for *Vetusta Monumenta*. The polygonal dome capping the Porta Honoris was a source for the corner turrets of the central raised staircase hall in his designs for Bylaugh. He was also friendly with Jeffry Wyatt who, between circa 1806 and 1813, refurbished two of the most famous English Renaissance houses, Longleat, Somerset and Wollaton Hall, Nottinghamshire, which were to provide sources for the major revivers of the style, Charles Barry and Anthony Salvin.[27] Wilkins's designs anticipated that phase of nineteenth-century historicism by almost two decades and derived from Wollaton. This is especially obvious in the beautifully rendered elevation showing the north and east sides of the proposed house in a landscaped setting, whereon the projecting corner pavilions are ornamented with strap-work gables (Pl. 49). The designs, now at the P.R.O., are not entirely uniform, there being a variant elevation with straight façades and a two storey portico slightly projected from the centre bays (Pl. 50). With certain consequent changes in dimensions, the layout of the rooms and internal decoration are similar. The nucleus is a large double-return staircase backed by the servants' stairs and surrounded on three sides by corridors communicating with the entrance hall, the main rooms and the servants' wing (Pl. 51). The dining- and drawing-rooms, separated by an ante-room, open along the south façade to recreate the effect of the Tudor and Jacobean gallery, as was the case in his Neo-Gothic houses. Both the interior and exterior show Wilkins refining his historical pattern and the variant elevation suggests that he had studied the architecture of Inigo Jones. Its portico resembles the loggia of the Queen's House, Greenwich, which he surely recognised as the progenitor of a new and more Classical fashion in English architecture. Although Wilkins exhibited one of the designs at the 1828 Royal Academy, he chose not to capitalise upon his early entry into this new field, possibly because he wished to uphold the purer classicism of the Greek Revival as it came under ever sharper attack from the 'Goths' and Synthetic Classicists.

To return to Keswick Hall, Wilkins had written to Hudson Gurney on 12 July 1817 while overlooking the work at Dalmeny, giving him much good advice on the trials of building and setting out an estimate for all the work Gurney wished to have done at Keswick, which amounted to £8,321. 9s. 6d.[28] The old house at Keswick was seven bays in length, four in depth and two storeys in height (Pl. 48). To it Wilkins added the pivotal staircase tower and a three sided block with a projecting bow rising the height of the house and flanked by lower one bay side pieces which have tapered Greek windows. He unified the old with the new by facing both with white brick, aligning the fenestration and mouldings, and making an intelligent use of anta, free standing and engaged. The former provided verandahs either side of the original house and were joined by an entablature to those coupled and engaged on the projected central section of the old house to which he added a pediment. The decoration was no more pronounced internally, and only one room seems to have been given scagliola pilasters.

The success of the anta formula led Wilkins to adopt it in the design of a new theatre at Bury St Edmunds. The plans were placed before the Corporation towards the end of 1818, probably about 6 November when he informed the authorities that he had purchased a site in Westgate Street for £200, a part of which had been resold for pasture.[29] In return for the closure of the old theatre in Market Cross, which had been reconstructed to designs by Robert Adam in 1780, and for the use of the box fronts, seats, traps, stage machinery and wings, he undertook to build 'a theatre of ample dimensions and elegance corresponding to the other buildings of the place'.

The new Bury St Edmunds theatre was one of Wilkins's most delightful designs, which, fortunately, was restored in 1966 (Pl. 52). A felicitous effect is created by contrasting full and half-width anta, or more exactly pilasters, carrying a plain Doric entablature, and by piercing the centre section and lower wings with large arched openings. The arch motif was repeated in the middle of the brick attic above the entrance to heighten the effect of the pyramidal massing created by its low gable or pediment. The classicism of the auditorium is more delicate (Pl. 53). Slender cast iron columns support the main tier of boxes, which have simple antique decoration. When opened on 11 October 1819 the walls were covered with French paper patterned with cupids on a blue ground. A report from a local newspaper in Wilkins's press cutting book applauded the 'dignity and beauty of perfect simplicity, chastening every ornament . . . visible in combination and in unity with the elegance of both the entire design and execution'. It was also functional, as the theatre seats in excess of six hundred people.

Financially it was not so successful. Costs escalated from £4,000 to £5,000 and insufficient share capital was forthcoming. Wilkins had undertaken to buy fourteen £100 shares himself but failed to persuade the Corporation to acquire another twenty. Thus he was forced into complicated arrangements with the shareholders, which retrieved the immediate debt, but left him vulnerable to loss when the box-office returns fell disastrously in the next decade.

IX

Alma Mater

Wilkins had not ceased to work in Cambridge, still attempting to realise more of his Downing scheme and, during the 1820s, he was to contribute to the great renewal of the university as architect of additions to three of the colleges. This new phase of endeavour may have begun in 1815, there being a Neo-Tudor elevation at Gonville and Caius College traditionally associated with the plans he was asked to prepare about that time for the reconstruction of the Perse and Legge Buildings, which were not executed (Pl. 54).[1] The drawing may be a copy of Wilkins's design for the rendering is unusually sharp, but the detailing, and particularly the decorative panels, correspond with his contemporary work at Dalmeny, though the window tracery is more ornate.

In 1816 he fitted out three rooms for the temporary exhibition of the newly bequeathed Fitzwilliam Collection in the Perse School.[2] Special cases were installed in two rooms on the ground floor for storing the books and prints, while one above was prepared for the hanging of pictures; in 1820 Wilkins, hoping for the commission, showed a design, since lost, at the Royal Academy for a new museum. In 1818 he spanned the Cam, at the request of King's College Congregation, by gently curving what was basically a Greek Ionic architrave across the river, upon a site selected in consultation with a member of the Rennie family, one of whom, John, designed Waterloo Bridge. Of pleasing proportions, the bridge possesses a modest elegance of design (Pl. 55).[3] Meanwhile, in about 1814 and doubtless in collaboration with his ageing father, he had rebuilt the theatre on the Newmarket Road, replacing a wooden structure: 'Too

long', he rhymed at its opening, 'our shapeless Theatre of wood /
A just reproach to taste and judgement stood.' Built of brick in a plain
Neo-Classical style its most interesting feature was the auditorium,
the fronts of the boxes being 'painted in arabesque' and the
proscenium supported by 'four Giallo Antiquo marble pilasters' said
to be 'really simple and magnificent'. The proscenium arch was
decorated with a gilt frieze depicting Apollo and Minerva visiting
the Muses.[4] Here Wilkins relished entertaining his university friends.

He was engaged in 1819 to refurbish the interior of Great St
Mary's, the university church. The alterations are described in an
article taken from an unidentified newspaper in his book of press
cuttings and illustrated in an etching by Storer. The galleries over
the aisles, where sat the Bachelors of Arts and undergraduates, were
'partly built up and covered with Roman Cement, and the sides
facing the pit [in the nave and seating the Masters of Arts and
fellows]...decorated with beautiful ornaments of the same material'
and 'considerably enlarged by their extension and junction to the
new west gallery; which has been erected in place of the old organ
loft'. The 'Father Smith' organ was re-installed above the west
gallery and the loft faced with a Roman cement 'screen of Gothic
arches supporting circular panels'. The gallery stood on three
pointed arches of stone, the side ones partly filled with blank tracery,
and was 'richly ornamented with cement-work, representing panels
enclosing diamond figures, in the centre of each of which is placed
a rose. Beneath these panels a most chaste and elegant antique
moulding runs along the whole length of the gallery.' The patterns
had been chosen by Wilkins and the moulds made by a Mr Brown
under the direction of 'the celebrated artist', Francis Bernasconi, who
had, the reporter recalled, decorated a temple at Claremont and part
of Windsor Castle – he might also have mentioned the staircase
towers of Wyatt's Ashridge and the Elliots' Taymouth Castle.[5]
Though the reporter's suggestion that Wilkins had recreated 'some
of the choicest beauties of gothic architecture' may seem fulsome, the
alterations were sympathetic and practical.

The commission was necessitated by the considerable and relatively
sudden growth in undergraduate enrolment that followed the cessa-
tion of hostilities with France. The university and college authorities
were spurred to embark upon a series of new building programmes
not only by that factor and the need to house and thereby discipline

the undergraduates, but also, as far as they were concerned, by the prevailing low rates of interest. The members of the Building Committee at Corpus Christi placed the economic argument first in their list of reasons for rebuilding the college. Other, more idealistic motives were invoked by Wordsworth in the circular letter he sent to potential subscribers to the Trinity fund. They would 'have the satisfaction of contributing to an undertaking intimately connected with the advancement of Religion and Learning', ideals which were close to Wilkins's heart.[6] He was invited to design a new court for Trinity as early as 1821 but financial and aesthetic problems delayed the decision to proceed until 1823.

In the interim he had submitted a design to the University Observatory competition in 1822, during the preparation of which he had consulted John Rennie.[7] He had to be content with the second prize of fifty guineas, losing to John Meade, who paid him the compliment of copying his still unexecuted Downing 'Propylea' for the portico. More tangible compensation came in the form of the invitation to virtually recreate Corpus Christi College, and triumph in the competition for the equally comprehensive additions to King's. His Neo-Tudor designs for these set the fashion for collegiate architecture at Cambridge, as reflected in the similar style of Thomas Rickman and Henry Hutchinson's St John's College, 1825, a commission that Wilkins narrowly lost.[8] They fronted their new quadrangle with a cloistered screen and central gatehouse, possibly inspired by his 1823 design for King's screen.

At the audit of 1822 the Corpus Christi Building Committee led by the new Master, Dr John Lamb, and the Reverend Thomas Shelford, a fellow and a student of Gothic architecture, went straight to Wilkins, 'a celebrated architect, for a plan and estimate of a new building with a front towards Trumpington Street'.[9] The Provost and Fellows of King's preferred an open competition.[10] They announced their decision in favour of Wilkins (who used the motto Pentalpha) on 25 March 1823, placing Inman and Lapidge second and third, and better known architects in limbo, notably Charles Barry, Decimus Burton, T. L. Donaldson, the partnership of Rickman and Hutchinson, and Lewis Vulliamy. These and the other ten unsuccessful competitors were dissatisfied with the result and mounted an exhibition of their designs in London where they distributed a short pamphlet, a copy of which Soane garnered.[11] But

Wilkins's designs were investigated and praised in June 1823 by two seasoned architects, John Nash and Jeffry Wyatt, and, in 1829, no less an authority in matters of construction than Sir Robert Smirke complimented Wilkins on the appearance and structure of the roof of the hall after thorough inspection; Wilkins did not return the compliment as far as Nash was concerned, finding in Burton's favour when asked to adjudicate a dispute between the two architects over the erection of Chester Terrace, London in 1825.[12] The suspicion of favouritism attaching to the King's commission might explain Wordsworth contacting in the spring of 1823 Hudson Gurney, William Treese (the Master of Downing), William Jenner (secretary of the Church Commissioners) and the Provost and Fellows of King's about the competence of Wilkins. Gurney testified that Keswick Hall had been 'most capitally executed'.[13]

The lack of dissension about his appointment as architect of Corpus Christi, the absence of those financial and aesthetic problems attending his work at King's and Trinity (and elsewhere), and the chance to plan a virtually complete new college led Wilkins to single it out in a letter to the Bursar as his best work up to 1828:

> I feel much obliged by your kind communication and I will thank you to express to the Master and fellows my most grateful acknowledgements on the occasion to which you allude, and for their most kind and liberal conduct throughout the whole of the period during which I have had the happiness of being employed by them.
>
> No circumstance in my professional pursuits has ever afforded me more gratification than the creation of Corpus Christi College. I consider the buildings upon the whole as the most complete and satisfactory of any I have yet had the opportunity of erecting and it is with great pride that I hear on all sides, with scarcely any exception expressions of approbation.
>
> Perhaps you will have the goodness to favour me with a short inscription to be cut upon the wall of the Entrance behind the gates. Although I am anxious for the record I am desirous that it should not be of an obtrusive character.
>
> I shall feel highly gratified by the permission to place

my arms, as the College architect, in any situation approved by the Society.

I have now to request that the Society will allow me to present as an heirloom to the Lodge, the beautiful portrait of the present Master, painted for this purpose by my friend Sir William Beechey. It is a fine picture, extremely like and an example of beautiful colouring.[14]

Wilkins's estimation contrasts with C. Oswald's judgement that the college was his least successful work in Cambridge, and, setting aside the stylistic similarities with his other college extensions, also casts doubt on the attribution of the best elements to 'the architectural knowledge and taste of Mr. Shelford' made by the doyen of Cambridge architectural history, Willis.[15] Nonetheless, Shelford was the most active member of the Building Committee, and Wilkins corresponded with him on the progress of building, as for example in one letter preserved at the college, dated 19 November 1828, concerning an error made by the contractor, Phipps, in laying the foundation.

So Corpus Christi can be used to gauge Wilkins's aspirations. Paramount was his respect for mediaeval architecture. Though the Tudor Master's Gallery and chapel had to be demolished, he preserved the Old Court excepting the Master's Lodge and hall (which he retained as the new kitchens), unlike James Essex, who, in a design dated 1773, had projected its entire destruction. Having saved part of the ancient court, Wilkins set about creating a modern collegiate entity clothed in a Neo-Gothic fabric modelled on the major mediaeval monuments of Cambridge (Pl. 56). The New Court at Corpus Christi is a compact and simplified version of the traditional quadrangle geared to a small budget: the total expenditure, including the renovation of some of the older buildings, amounted to some hundreds over £60,000, compared with £50,444 for Trinity and £101,021 for King's.

The relative lowness of these figures indicates his second priority, economy of plan and articulation. He concentrated the accommodation for the fellows and undergraduates in the battlemented block fronting Trumpington Street, the new façade being set back to widen the street (Pl. 57).[16] Through the turreted gateway, akin to Trinity Great Gate, appears the more richly ornamented chapel, traditionally the heart of college life, separated from the Master's Lodge on the right and sets, or undergraduate rooms, on the left by turrets adapted from King's Chapel (Pl. 58). The battlements of the flanking buildings rise towards the traceried turrets of the chapel and its west window is larger and richer than those on either hand. Further elevation is imparted by the pinnacled niches and the change from a flat balustrade over the porch to the angled one above the window, which is contrasted with the steeper pitch of the roof behind. Having imprinted that ordered impression upon the mind of the beholder, Wilkins allowed himself a less regular, if not truly Picturesque, composition for the hall and library ranges, on the left and right sides of the entrance. These are clearly differentiated, though both are of two storeys, the upper ones being taller. The hall is buttressed, pierced by high five light windows and ornamented with a projecting bay, again like that on the Trinity College hall or the King's Hall at Christ Church, Oxford and Crosby Hall, London; the last was probably also the source of the hammer-beam ceiling (Pl. 59). The library has a flat façade with broader five light windows providing ample illumination for the display of the valuable collection of books and manuscripts owned by the college. Both the hall and library stop one bay short of the chapel range, the junctions being marked by plain turrets and turned by angled projections – on the hall side giving access to the Old Court. The projecting bay of the hall and the arched doorway into the sets below the library were placed at their own centres, and not those of the whole range, to draw the mass towards the three storeyed Trumpington block. Before the unsympathetic addition of sets above that and the library the spatial effect would have been more satisfactory.

But it would be wrong to disregard the aesthetic consequences of Wilkins's deferential and practical aims. Viewed cursorily, Corpus Christi and his later college additions are blandly attractive, quite convincingly Tudor and harmonious with their surroundings, but, examined in detail, they appear somewhat brittle and, in parts, disjointed. The façades, due to the play of the linear mouldings against the ashlar walls, can seem more like a series of screens than compositions of solid blocks. The corners of the Corpus Christi quadrangle are awkward. On the one hand Wilkins sought to bond the different elevations by repeating the motifs of turret and battlement but on the other he altered the level of the mouldings and the articulation of the windows in such a manner as to make the transitions abrupt. This weakness is less apparent at Trinity where he was only required to provide undergraduate accommodation. But at King's the links between the screen and chapel and the new fellows' building, and between the Combination Room and library are staccato (Pl. 60). And the whole range of new buildings opposite the chapel breaks up into a succession of curiously disparate runs in which the turrets act as divisions rather than caesurae, though not deserving Cockerell's censure: 'narrow Huddled ill contrived ill conceived. the whole system is conceived in a servile spirit of imitation & that of a limited period.'[17]

Cockerell ignored Wilkins's real achievement there and at Corpus Christi and Trinity, the preservation of the mediaeval Cambridge architectural tradition. Conversely Nash and Wyatt saw 'great merit' in the King's additions which convinced them 'that the author is much experienced in Gothic Architecture', while Pevsner has written that at King's Wilkins 'designed with gusto. The scale is right, the heights are right, the execution is substantial – not mean, like so much neo-Gothic work – and the detail is by no means dull.'[18] His style might be described as an attempt at a 'survival', that is a continuation more than a revival.

The halls and libraries at King's and Corpus Christi combine mediaeval structural and ornamental forms (in advance of Pugin's strictures on the proper revival of Gothic architecture) and are convincingly historical, but also functional. The fusion of ancient form and modern use is nicely illustrated in the library of Corpus Christi where the traceried panels of the book cases lead the eye up to the decorated corbels from which spring the ornamented ribs of the ceiling (Pl. 61). Most splendid is the King's hall when the afternoon light filters through the lanterns and elevated windows and where only the sharp detailing of the entrance screen betrays the late date of its construction (Pl. 62).

The traceried panels on the hall screen at King's, as all the ornamental motifs, were copied directly from identifiable sources. A realist, Wilkins knew that the mediaeval mason tradition was defunct, as Ruskin was to find during the execution of the Oxford Museum in 1854, and he substituted a system of taking moulds from selected mediaeval models which the masons were set to copy. The Working Drawings of the colleges are liberally strewn with instructions, like that for the Trumpington Street front of Corpus Christi, no. 11: 'Observe particularly the Contractor is to produce a plaster cast for all the sculptures and carved work, from some building to be approved by the architect of the College before it is executed.' Or that for the exterior of King's hall, no. 43: 'The pinnacles terminating the buttresses of the Bay window to be similar in form (but less in proportion) to those on the summits of the Chapel buttresses.'

This procedure was also an aspect of Wilkins's wish to render the additions unobtrusive. His buildings have settled in their environment with age and, in the case of the inner façades of Trinity New Court, with the growth of creepers. King's screen has become, seemingly, one of the most characteristic features of mediaeval Cambridge, and indeed approximates to what had been envisaged in the Memorandum or 'Will' of 1448 establishing the college. The articulation of windows, battlements and pinnacles and the thicker block of the tripartite central gatehouse are sufficiently bold to create a distinctive entity, but also sufficiently modest to allow the chapel its full grandeur, from which nearly all the elements of the screen are derived. The screen is more imaginative and sympathetic than the two storey accommodation block James Wyatt had proposed in 1795.[19]

The King's commission was the last Wilkins received at Cambridge and manifests the extent to which his style was governed by the budget, being more decorated and strongly defined than the first Tudor designs for Trinity. The invitation to submit drawings for the New Court at Trinity (also called Speaker's and King's Court since the Speaker of the House of Commons laid its foundation stone on 12 August 1823, the sovereign's birthday) came in 1821. Here it was that he first confronted the main problem to be encountered in each of the commissions, that of marrying the old with the new which, at Trinity, comprised both mediaeval and classical architecture, the last in the form of Wren's superb and highly sophisticated library.

To a degree Wilkins brought that forlorn task upon himself for, when he despatched his original designs, including two ground-plans, with a letter to Wordsworth in May 1821, he proposed the present site in favour of one at Scholar's Green. His reasoning was, as so often, based upon an appreciation of economic necessity. The erection of the court on the ground next to the library and Nevile's Court would be cheaper, even allowing for the expenditure of some £400 on the demolition of old buildings on the site, and 'the interiors may be of very simple architecture and only *one* exterior need assume a character of genuine importance'.[20] Materials from the old buildings might be sold to pay for a new brew-house and stables, while 'the buildings of Nevile's Court facing the Brew house Court, may be made to assume a consistent character; but this front must be cemented because of the various kinds of materials used in the exterior'. After commenting on possible variations in the ground floor, he estimated that 120 sets could be fitted into three storeys and an attic lit by dormer windows concealed by a battlemented parapet akin to the 'manner adopted in the buildings first executed for Downing College'. This was 'the extent of the accommodation that can be obtained at present, with due regard for salubrity and the ventilation of the building; but when the premises on the left of the College gate of entrance fall into hand, 32 sets of Rooms may be obtained in the way shown by the Plan No. 1'. The second plan included a lecture room off the kitchen court behind the quadrangle which has Neo-Gothic features on three sides (Pl. 63). Finally, Wilkins proposed that the work be financed by increasing rents on local property owned by the college and referred to the low rates on borrowed capital, currently about 4 per cent.

The six elevations he sent with the letter were less persuasive, judging from those four remaining at the college. Three are best described as Graeco-Palladian designs, exemplified by that numbered 5 (Pl. 64). The tripartite composition, rusticated basement and arched entrance hall recall the English Palladian pattern, but the severe articulation matches the end and rear façades of the west range at Downing. No. 6 transposes the basic composition into the Neo-Tudor mode, even more symmetrical than his contemporary Gothic country houses (Pl. 65). Each might have been acceptable as individual structures but suffer greatly when set against Wren's library. Moreover, Wilkins ignored the entrance line marked out by the celebrated Lime Avenue which the Seniors of the college wished to retain. This he excused in his letter, writing that 'the style demands a rigid observance of the parts'.

Having offered the Seniors a choice, both his and their inclinations seem to have moved towards the Gothic. He wrote from Weymouth Street on 6 June 1821, enclosing another elevation of the 'proposed elongation of the Library Building, supposing the Monastic style to be adopted'.[21] That elevation has since disappeared, unless it be no. 6.

Apart from the thorny problem of matching the addition to Wren's Library, the Seniors were indeed beset by financial constraints. In February 1822 Wilkins wrote of having received 'intelligence' of opposition to 'building the entire quadrangle'.[22] Ever accommodating, he proposed that only two sides be built with a 'battlemented wall with a gateway in it on the East side', a kind of embryo King's screen. There the matter rested till 1823 when Wilkins prepared an enriched Tudor Gothic design with three blocks forming a quadrangle alongside Nevile's Court, and only one gateway to the west, now aligned to the Lime Avenue. Between May 1823 and the winter of 1825 this scheme was substantially erected.

An elevation for the Backs façade as built remains at the R.I.B.A., perhaps that exhibited at the Royal Academy in 1823 (Pl. 66).[23] Unlike the squat proportions of the 1821 Gothic design this façade has marked vertical movement, mainly created by the oriel windows. It is separated from Wren's Library by a two storey battlemented structure of two bays in width. A more distinct break is supplied by the turrets astride the gateway. The entrance archway has ceiling tracery taken from the vestibule of Henry VII's Chapel at Westminster Abbey and sets the ornamental pattern for the quadrangle. The interior of the New Court is decorated with Tudor hood moulds over the windows of the ground floor and has the turrets and gables of the façade, now capped by chimney-like pinnacles, which Wilkins used extensively at King's. On the side abutting Nevile's Court, turrets frame two gabled projections, ornamented with large square-headed Tudor windows that flank a recessed and arcaded section communicating between the courts (Pl. 67). The turrets together with a low screen at the east end serve to regularise its unequal length. The projections are matched on the other side of the quadrangle by one that spans the whole centre, which has two unfilled niches echoing a single one above the arcade to Nevile's Court. The effect of contrasting composition and repeated articulation is now masked by the large tree flourishing in the middle of the court. Lastly, the gateway leading to Trinity Lane is also turreted and, with the continuous mouldings and battlements, completes the sense of cohesion within the quadrangle.

The interior of New Court, however, suffers from the substitution of Roman cement for stone. More successful aesthetically are the cast iron window frames which, with iron chimneys (both used at Corpus Christi and King's), Wilkins had recommended for economy's sake in a letter dated only 10 December. The Seniors refused to use cast iron for the chimneys and hoped to achieve other savings by reducing the thickness of the internal turrets. Persuaded by Wilkins's offer to pay half the cost, a sum of £71. 7s., they eventually agreed to the planned dimensions, and also to the completion of the greater majority of the intended ornamentation including the remodelling of the obverse side of Nevile's Court. Leaving aside all other considerations, the New Court was functional. Professor Trevelyan wrote in 1946 that its great merit 'was that it comfortably housed so many undergraduates'.[24]

Wilkins's task at King's was no less daunting. He had to deal with another magnificent classically styled building, and his beloved chapel. Equally troublesome was the site which forced him to group the large volume of requisite accommodation in a line of buildings opposite the chapel, as shown in his original ground-plan numbered 62 in the series of designs in the College Archive; the position of the library was subsequently changed at the behest of Nash and Wyatt (Pl. 68). He was also unable to execute his scheme for the re-positioning of King's Lane nearer to Catharine Hall, to provide more accommodation for the college, due to the refusal of a Mr Cory to sell Canterbury House for a reasonable price.[25] Nor could the college afford to clothe the centrally placed Gibbs Building in the Neo-Gothic skin Wilkins had projected (though it is not indicated in K.C. no. 62).

Wilkins had no qualms about altering Gibbs's offering to the architecture of Cambridge, probably regarding the Tudor style of the chapel and the less distinguished Old Court (sold in 1829 and demolished in 1835 to make way for the University Library) as justification. He thrice exhibited his original scheme at the Royal Academy, that in 1827 probably being the signed elevation numbered 59 in the College Archive (Pl. 69).[26] In this the Neo-Tudor style of the new accommodation range and hall courses over Gibbs's English Baroque towards the west end of the chapel, bound together by a fountain in the Decorated style at the centre of the quadrangle. In all likelihood he deemed Gibbs's work to be doubly corrupt, having its roots in Vitruvian lore and some of its inspiration in the continental Baroque. Evidently his taste was shared by the Provost and Fellows since they rejected a number of Neo-Classical designs and, at their first meeting after Wilkins's appointment, agreed to 'Gothicise' the Gibbs Building once the hall and flanking blocks were completed.[27] Their judgement was confirmed by Nash and Wyatt who, in their report, described the proposed transformation as essential to the 'unity and thereby the magnificence of the Quadrangle' and even suggested the insertion of an 'open cloyster of sufficient heighth [sic]' between the chapel and Gibbs Building 'so as to give the impression of the three sides of the Quadrangle being united'.[28] It is more likely that the Congregation abandoned this part of the plan, and the fountain and fan vaulted cloisters behind the screen, on financial rather than aesthetic grounds. Before Wilkins presented an elevation of the screen to the Royal Academy in 1827 as his diploma piece (now sadly dilapidated), it must have been apparent that his original estimate of £73,000 was inadequate (Pl. 70).

The looser linkage between the old and new buildings as executed is possibly more attractive for, in designing the new range, Wilkins acknowledged the impossibility of competing with the chapel. (The experience may account for his decision at York to adopt the Greek style for the Yorkshire Philosophical Society Museum in deference to the quality of local mediaeval architecture.) Where the chapel is elevated and continuous in both planes, Wilkins's façades are low, differentiated and independently centralised. The range opposite the chapel is divided into three parts and both the whole and the parts have central emphases, since the hall can be read as a broad portico for the accommodation blocks on either side.

More irregular is the composition of the second group of buildings which are set back from the line of the hall range (Pl. 71). Here Wilkins made a curious aside in the Classical style by fitting a Thrasyllan window on to the Combination Room at the west end of the hall range, probably to tie in with the parallel rear façade of the Gibbs Building. This second group contains the library and Provost's Lodge, but its insertion cuts into the symmetrical arrangement of the two gables above the Combination Room. Thus the range appears to be an afterthought rather than an integral part, which is unfortunate for, as individual buildings, the library and, more particularly, the Provost's Lodge are architecturally commendable. The compact massing of the lodge is a more sturdy version of Wilkins's Tudor domestic style.

The confused character of this section can be attributed largely to Nash and Wyatt who insisted that the library be moved 'as close as convenience will allow to the Provost's Lodge' and occupy the position reserved for a cloister linking the lodge to the new range. (Between 1934 and 1935 the ground floor of the library was opened up and arcaded to provide access into Webb's Court, again to the detriment of Wilkins's conception.) Further, the lodge may not represent Wilkins's first idea as the report also refers to a preferred alternative elevation. The other changes they suggested were effected, namely, the deletion of the ornamental gables on the screen (moved to the sides of the gatehouse) and the niches with which Wilkins had intended to grace the façade of the hall.

Those weaknesses that exist in Wilkins's scheme are more than compensated for by the screen, which is one of his finest creations. Even at the design stage Nash and Wyatt appreciated its 'great merit' as being in 'sufficient unison with the Chapel – the perforate Cloysters will in a picturesque manner show the interior of the Quadrangle without injuring its privacy and cannot fail of being a beautiful object to the Town'. They were also much taken with the 'picturesque' lanterns atop the hall.

Understandably, Wilkins was buoyant at this time. On 22 April 1825, and perhaps as a result of his contact with John Nash whose Haymarket Theatre in London had been constructed during 1821, he persuaded the proprietors of the Norwich Theatre Royal to rebuild it upon a new site.[29] J. Stacey in *A Topographical and Historical Account of the City and County of Norwich* (1819) probably disclosed a telling reason for Wilkins's decision, writing that though the old theatre was a 'very handsome building, with good Scenery and decorations' it was only 'tolerably ventilated'. Wilkins judged that the cost would be offset by the sale of the old materials and of thirty 'silver' (permanent family) tickets, and by a capital defrayment of £500 on the old stage traps and machinery. He produced the plan at a later meeting of the proprietors and won their unanimous acceptance.

The new theatre was neatly dressed up in the Classical style with two Greek Doric colonnades, one before the manager's accommodation and lobby, and the other spanning the pedimented projections containing the box-office and staircase to the pit, themselves forming the lowest stage of the pyramidal composition fronting the auditorium (Pl. 72). A ground-plan drawn up by Robert Kitton in 1847 and preserved at the N.N.R.O. shows the clever arrangement Wilkins made for the sale of tickets and access to the various levels of seating in the large rectangular auditorium, the most direct being into the dress circle through a lobby on the left side of the central box-office; on the right were stairs ascending to the upper boxes and others descending to the pit (Pl. 73). More capacious was the stage and its attendant accommodation with the dressing-rooms above. G. K. Blyth in his *Norwich Guide* of 1842 admired the 'chaste character' and 'handsome' Classical embellishments of the auditorium and thought that the seating equalled the 'metropolitan theatres', comfort and convenience having 'evidently been the study of the architect'.

Wilkins also studied the local goodwill, as can be deduced from a letter to the editor of the *Norwich Mercury*, dated Weymouth Street, 26 February 1826, inviting him to dine in London when, if given time, the writer would 'endeavour to get two or three unusual men to meet you'.[30] The theatre was opened with a flourish on 25 March 1826, as glowingly reported in the *Norwich Mercury* of 1 April. Some 150 guests were shown the scenery, 'introduced to the stage by their courteous entertainer' and regaled with a 'cold collation' in the scene room 'rendered more refreshing by exhilerating draughts of sparkling champagne'. The reception raised £150 which was distributed amongst the local poor. At the first performance, given on Monday, 27 March, Mr Osbaldiston took the leading rôles in 'The School for Scandal' and 'Youth, Love and Folly'.[31]

Back at Cambridge, however, Wilkins's plans for the completion of the King's commission were baulked by Mr Cory, and the litigation dragged on until 1870. The experience exasperated Wilkins and he sought some relief, as increasingly he was to do, by recourse to the pen and the press. A lengthy article in his press cutting book headed 'Architectural Improvements in Cambridge', addressed to the editor of the *Cambridge Chronicle* and printed in two parts on 3 and 10 November 1826, and a signed letter about the Bull Inn (next to Catharine Hall) also published in the *Chronicle* on 21 March 1828, may be the 'communications I had published in the Cambridge papers, relating to the projected improvements in the University [made by a Syndicate in 1824], and pointing out objections to the method pursued for carrying them into effect', mentioned in the first of his two pamphlets on the University Library competition, *A Letter to the Members of the Senate*, dated 9 February 1831.[32] In it he queried whether his comments on the Bull Inn had offended some Cambridge figures and been a reason for the adverse reception of his designs for the University Library by the Syndicate.

The theme of the *Cambridge Chronicle* article was the inadequacy of the conduct of individual commissions at Cambridge. Four obstacles hindered redevelopment. First, a separate Syndicate was appointed for each commission, which had 'never been instructed to proceed upon a system nor to prepare a synopsis of what is desirable to be effected upon any plan of *general* improvement'. Second, developments were so dogged by the exorbitant cost of land, leases and compensation that he asked with perspicacity, 'Does not improvement stop where the possession of private property or a long lease begin?' Third, the Syndicate members were selected on their status within the university and were 'not, nor cannot be, from the habits of life, men of business – nor fit to cope with the more worldly-minded'. Fourth, there were too many members, and, to highlight his point, Wilkins quoted Pepys's aphorism that the more the councillors the greater the confusion.

He then turned to the long drawn out discussions about the erection of a new museum for the Fitzwilliam Collection.[33] In 1824 the Perse School required the rooms which he had fitted up for the collection, though a Syndicate had been formed as early as 1818 to handle the prospective commission. By 1824 the members were contemplating building the museum on a site next to the Senate House which entailed the demolition of part of Gonville and Caius College, and in July one of the local Members of Parliament, W. J. Bankes, a graduate of Trinity, had published a scheme exactly modelled on the Parthenon. Much as Wilkins venerated the original, its proportions would be 'out of harmony with the neighbouring buildings' and would overpower 'the minute and delicate architecture of the Senate House...which all concur in admiring as one of the greatest embellishments of the University'. It would also be excessively expensive, estimated at £60,000, some £20,000 above the limit set by the Syndicate and, as such, 'wholly incommensurate with the expenditure, when it is known that the portion of the London University about to be built for the present purposes, comprehending a range of libraries and museums, 430 feet in length and 50 feet in width, of considerable extent, with a splendid architectural front, is contracted for at less cost'. And the form of the Parthenon precluded the installation of proper side and top lighting.

From these comments it is possible to surmise that Wilkins entered a more conventional design for the eventual competition in 1835, described by his acquaintance, Romilly, as 'vastly heavy'.[34] Few of the Syndicate voted for it and the commission fell to an old adversary and a member of the new breed of Synthetic Classicists, Basevi. The eclipse must have wounded Wilkins in view of his previous association with the collection. Furthermore, he had played a part in ensuring the establishment of a new museum by warning the university authorities in the article, and indubitably in conversation as a member of the Senate, of the 'fatal tendency of their apparent apathy on the subject of the Fitzwilliam Collection'. He was concerned about the fire risk at the Perse School and the absence of additional bequests since with 'few exceptions, the pictures of this collection are not of a high class of paintings, and they are principally valuable as forming a nucleus of a gallery...Nothing has more contributed to the increase of the National Gallery, than the pledge of the Government, to the immediate constitution of a proper receptacle for those invaluable objects.'

Returning to his main theme Wilkins lamented the inferior and jumbled character of the architecture of the main thoroughfare of the town. Visitors entering the central area of the university were confronted by the shambles of the 'Sun Hotel, and have before us the narrow path of St. John's Lane! We must either turn into the one, or creep through the other unless St. John's will obligingly consent to set back the front of the College, in order to enable us to reach the gorge which terminates in – Bridge Street!!' Such was the 'incapability' of the town he had called 'our Athens' when travelling in Greece that the best termination for its main street was the Senate House, a fine but uncommanding building. In this regard Wilkins regretted that Gonville and Caius College lacked funds to erect a new façade 15 to 20 feet back from its present line and he offered, coyly, to supply a more extensive but 'equally handsome' version of his Corpus Christi building for about £20,000 – a change realised some decades later by Alfred Waterhouse in a High Victorian Gothic style. He did not dissemble in declaring that his work at Corpus Christi and King's Colleges had opened up Trumpington Street to great advantage.

The preliminary step would be the appointment of a Syndicate – presumably on his improved model – with responsibility for the enhancement of Trumpington Street from the London Road to the Senate House. Its immediate task should be the securing of an Act of Parliament to remove the dilapidated house on the north side beyond Pembroke College, promote the plan to withdraw the façade of St Botolph's, align the house alongside King's and demolish the premises next to the Bull Inn. Then it should co-operate with the members of Corpus Christi Building Committee, who were prepared to help the work of improvement by repeating Wilkins's Trumpington Street façade along Bene't Street, north of the Old Court, at the expiry of leases, and by renovating the houses on the south side of the college to 'contribute to the general effect, by what the painters would call repose and contrast'.

Those objectives achieved, the Syndicate should turn its attention to the embellishment of the outlying areas and colleges, especially Emmanuel and Christ's. These ought to magnify the 'grandeur and extent' of the university and it was 'scarcely possible to conceive the importance the University would derive if these Colleges were connected with her handsome buildings, by a succession of objects placed in communication, beginning with St. Botolph's Church and ending in St. Andrew's Street, in front of Emmanuel College'.

Wilkins knew only too well that the senior members of the university would reject his proposals as financially impracticable. Therefore he tossed out some economic carrots, such as the demolition of unsightly buildings opposite the south wall of St Botolph's Churchyard to provide a site for a profitable housing scheme. He hoped that Pembroke would construct at the intersection of Pembroke Lane and Trumpington Street 'a building corresponding to the [Wren] Chapel, and applied to the purposes of the College Library', to 'extend her line of front, and make the whole symmetrical'. The offensive cattle market at the other end of Pembroke Lane could be removed at the same time. Thereafter better access should be created to Trinity and Clare Colleges and to the Senate House, while the contraction of the burial grounds of the central churches would offer further opportunities for speculative redevelopment.

Wilkins hoped that one of the 'great' buildings to be erected in this outer area would be the University Library, preferably in the Botanic Garden behind Corpus Christi College. Here he raised another topical subject, for a Syndicate was to be constituted for that purpose in May 1829. In his words the old library was 'a reproach to the University'.

Wilkins failed even more dismally in that competition which, as will be shown, exemplified the ills outlined in his first letter. Whether the cursory rejection of his design owed anything to his outspokenness is highly debatable, not least because his revivalist styles were becoming outmoded and because he was architect to a potential rival to the Cambridge tradition, the non-sectarian University College, London. The 'Cambridge system' of 'logic' which he had described to Gurney in 1817 acted upon his own fortunes at his Alma Mater: 'Whereas common experience proves that all who dabble in brick and mortar begin and end this operation with sensations totally dissimilar.'[35]

X

Institutional architecture

'Considering Gothic architecture to be my *forte*', Wilkins had written to the Reverend Christopher Wordsworth on 8 May 1823, 'I am very desirous of executing a Gothic church; if His Majesty's Commissioners could be prevailed upon to confide the execution of one to my superintendence...if you feel no objection to mention the circumstances to your brother Commissioners it might procure me the opportunity of which I am so desirous.'[1]

Wilkins wished to extend his practice in this field of institutional design, recognising that ecclesiastical architecture was central to the development of the Gothic Revival and that, thanks to the so-called Million Pound Act of 1818, the Church through its Commissioners had once again become a significant patron. Ecclesiastical commissions were more numerous than those offered by the national and local governments, or by the charitable and private foundations which, however, even beyond the 1860s, financed the construction of the newer institutions, the hospital and the educational establishment.

But the entreaty failed despite the fact that Wordsworth had tutored Charles Manners Sutton, son of the Archbishop of Canterbury who had been Bishop of Norwich 1792–1805. The design of a church for Bothamsell, Nottinghamshire, commissioned by the Duke of Newcastle and exhibited by Wilkins at the Academy in 1817 was not executed. Since lost, and probably in the Greek style, it is not to be confused with the Neo-Gothic structure dedicated to St Peter and St Mary.[2] Thus the only example of Wilkins's expertise in the ecclesiastical Gothic Revival appears in the elevation for the

Trumpington Street façade of Corpus Christi, showing the front of St Botolph's 'redesigned' (Pl. 57).[3] The massing and use of turrets to mark the nave and side aisles, but not the battlementing, may have been inspired by St Peter Mancroft, Norwich, though the turrets recall those on King's Chapel. The angled buttresses and turrets, the gradation of the openings and mouldings recreate the solid, vertical movement of mediaeval ecclesiastical architecture, particularly when compared with a Gothic Commissioners' church, such as Nash's St Mary Haggerstone, London, 1822. Clearly Wilkins shared A. W. N. Pugin's loathing for those flimsy parodies of Gothic which passed muster until as late as the third decade of the nineteenth century.

Had St Botolph's been altered according to Wilkins's design, then he might have suffered less at the hands of the Victorian 'Goths'. In any case it would have mitigated the impression left by his only executed church, St Paul's, Nottingham, built for the Commissioners between 1821 and 1822 in a Neo-Greek style, that he belonged wholly with the pagan Classicists (Pl. 74). In his letter to Wordsworth, Wilkins made no mention of St Paul's. He owed the commission largely to the good offices of his brother, George, who was vicar of the 'mother' church, St Mary's, Nottingham, under the patronage of Lord Manvers. George had petitioned the Bishop of Nottingham for a new church on 15 August 1821.[4] He was concerned that the Anglican churches could not accommodate anything approaching the current population of the city which amounted to some thirty thousand souls, and disturbed by the fact that at least ten thousand were attending the local Dissenting Houses. With the Bishop's blessing he forwarded a request to Jenner at the Church Commissioners for a grant towards building a church to seat two thousand. Before the end of the year he had received a grant and acquired a site at the top of the rising ground of Broad Street. Judging by the fact that Wilkins exhibited a design entitled 'New Church, Nottingham' at that year's Academy, George may have asked William for a design before he corresponded officially with the Bishop. The documents remaining at the Church Commissioners give no indication as to who was responsible for the choice of the Greek style, though William could have selected it as appropriate to the surrounding architecture.

For the front, Wilkins designed a four-columned Doric portico based upon the Athenian Propylaea flanked by ashlar walls and framed by pilasters. The portico was capped by a steeple comprising a square podium, an octagonal Doric peristyle, the shape of which was inspired by the Tower of Winds, and a raised cupola and lantern adapted from the Choragic Monument of Lysicrates. The façade was nicely distinguished from adjoining domestic buildings by low curtain walls, containing doorways, as had been the case with the Freemasons' Hall. The most successful features were the steeple and its coupling with the portico. The steeple, an economic and inventive reworking of the eighteenth-century English type and the Inwood's St Pancras Church, was less awkward than the amalgams formulated by Smirke, for example, at St Mary's Wyndham Place, or Soane at Holy Trinity, Marylebone. By compacting the historical sources Wilkins made the steeple seem less like a tower, and thus created a better relationship between it and the portico and less of an offence against the Greek canon. Again, he showed himself to be more flexible than in his earlier career by blending ancient motifs with the national tradition of Classically styled Protestant church architecture. A measure of its contemporary success is indicated by Smirke's having copied it almost exactly for the Newcastle family at Markham St Clinton Chapel in 1832; its Greek cross plan also relates to Wilkins's unexecuted design for Stourhead (see Pl. 30).

The interior of St Paul's, measuring 104 by 62 feet, was less well proportioned than the exterior. Photographs taken just before its demolition in 1926 show a wide rectangular nave with eight unfluted Corinthian columns of Mansfield stone, 22½ feet high, dividing off the aisles (Pl. 75). The capitals were rather too large for their height since the columns stood on a low wall. Pilasters flanked a plain altar, the central arch on the west wall, the corners of the staircase projections at the west end and the robing room and vestry at the east end. Galleries, 13 feet in depth and reached from the side doors, were later removed. The broad dimensions of the interior and the large side windows, if not the austere articulation, looked back to Wren's City churches but typified the Commissioners' bald interpretation of the Protestant preaching hall.

The church was built at remarkable speed, without detriment to the structure, by the contractor, Spicer Crowe, who was employed at Keswick Hall and Trinity College. The final cost of £12,775. 5s. 7d. included the digging of deeper foundations than had been envisaged, part being used as a water storage tank, and was £1,251 below the estimate. St Paul's seated 1,850 persons, and the ratio of cost to seating capacity compared well with, say, Francis Bedford's St George, Camberwell, 1822-4, accommodating nearly two thousand, but built for £16,700. Moreover, parts of St George were likened in the *Gentleman's Magazine* to a 'common dwelling house'.[5]

By contrast, St Paul's was acclaimed in the *Nottingham Journal* for 26 October 1822 as a 'beautiful building...and for massive grandeur and fine effect nothing can be happier than that which is now executed'. The correspondent was equally taken with the elevation of the side aisles to the level of the tops of the pews in the nave, 'thus enabling all the persons the better to see and hear the Minister; having this advantage, also, that however full the church may be, every column is distinctly visible in every part, its base being fixed upon the solid masonry which forms the enclosure around the pews in the body of the church'. The raised aisles had been commended by the Commissioners' surveyor, Edward Mawley, but inconvenienced George who, possibly fussed by the presence of the Primate at the service of consecration on 21 October 1822, wrote to Jenner six days later that

> Though the morning of Thursday was fine, yet when the Gallery and aisles of the Church were filled the Archbishop had not light enough at the altar to read – and without respect to what I experienced in the pulpit, that although the sun was shining it was with difficulty that I could read although my sermon was written in unnaturally large and clear characters.[6]

On 4 November he pleaded for 'four additional windows to the new church'. In vain, and he seems to have exaggerated the problem since there is no mention of it in the reports of the ceremony.

Few of the Commissioners' churches fared so well in the press. Returning to St George, Camberwell, the reviewer in the *Gentleman's Magazine* gave an account all too typical of those Neo-Greek churches financed by the First Parliamentary Grant: 'To the western part of the building is attached a portico of six fluted columns of the Grecian Doric Order, sustaining an architectural frieze and cornice of a doubtful order and insignificant proportions...It is naked and empty, with the air of a conventicle ill suited to the dignity of the Established Church.'[7] Another report from the same magazine on St Mary's, Wyndham Place, London, 1821-2, was more summary in reference to its ornamentation: 'The public have a right to better things from eminent architects, and the public taste demands a protection from the insult which such absurdities offer to it.'[8]

The architect was Smirke, who, as one of the three 'Attached Architects', had been invited to submit specimen designs to the Church Commissioners in 1818.[9] It was he who had aphorised the aims held out for these churches in the chilling phrase 'economy, character and durability'. Though his specimen designs, handled in his 'Graeco-cubic' style, were perhaps preferable to the attempts made by Soane and Nash to recreate the seventeenth- and eighteenth-century traditions of ecclesiastical architecture, the Neo-Greek churches he built for the Commissioners were as disappointing as were theirs, being, like the majority of those executed under the first two Parliamentary Grants, gaunt in proportion and scanty in ornament. What had appeared to present an opportunity to uphold the tradition of Protestant church building in England became something of an architectural flop, mainly because the Commissioners placed greatest emphasis on economy – a sign of the waxing impact of utilitarian considerations upon nineteenth-century architecture – and on these grounds sanctioned many poor designs, by which the prestige of the Greek Revival was degraded. The churches erected under the First Grant were predominantly in that style – twenty-two out of thirty-three – and many of those built in London were criticised adversely in such influential journals as the *Gentleman's Magazine*. Only two out of ninety-four were built in the Greek style under the Second Grant.[10]

Wilkins was distressed by the enterprise, later writing in his trenchant pamphlet, *A Letter to Lord Viscount Goderich on the Patronage of the Arts by the English Government* (1832), that 'All regard to propriety and unity of design has been disregarded by the Church Commissioners, whose sole object seems to have been directed to vary the means of acquiring a certain quantum of accommodation for a given sum...'[11] He was dismayed by the engagement of untried architects 'who were left without employment when the casual demand for their services ceased'. The Commissioners had muffed the chance to enhance national architecture because apart from 'some very creditable exceptions from the general run of design,...in the great majority, especially in those which are called Gothic, we find the architectural character of every age and no age at all combined'.

Sad it was that Wilkins did so little for the Commissioners since he was adept at satisfying the dual aims of economy and dignity, exploiting his command of mathematics to adjust the nature and scale of his historical sources to the specifications – and the purses – of his clients. Those accomplishments were evident in the design of the United University Club in Suffolk Street, London, 1822 (Pl. 76), almost certainly completed with the aid of Gandy who, according to John Britton, was made a member 'in compliment for the skill and zeal he manifested in his professional capacity'. [12] Ackermann considered it to be entirely by Wilkins and admired 'its general arrangement of parts as well as unity in the general design'.[13]

The site was confined, squeezed between Suffolk Street and Pall Mall East, measuring 106 by 53 feet, with a section 24 by 12 feet reserved for a light-well serving the building on the east side. Within it Wilkins fitted quite extensive and varied accommodation: a coffee room, bar, committee room and dining-room on the ground floor with a saloon, ante-room, library, reading room and five drawing-rooms on the first floor, with twenty-two rooms for the members and staff above. The building cost £16,800, the furnishings £5,500 and the architect's fee and the clerk of works' salary £1,100, totalling £23,400.

With or without Gandy, Wilkins gave the club a building that complemented its reputation for excellent cuisine. Sir John Summerson has written that it presented clubland with 'its sense of architectural consequence'.[14] The entrance front on Suffolk Street had a single storey portico of two Doric columns set between coupled antae supporting a balustrade which registered harmoniously against the plain stucco façades of Nash's adjacent development. On the more important Pall Mall side Wilkins engaged a pedimented portico on the first storey imitated from the Erechtheum, above which was a parapet. Together with the rustication, fenestration of the piano nobile and the balustrade of the Suffolk Street façade, the parapet lent an Italianate appearance to the club that anticipated the style developed for this building type at the Athenaeum and, more especially, by Barry at the Travellers' (for which Wilkins submitted an unsuccessful design in 1828), both of 1829.[15]

The interior won Britton's unqualified approval, being, he wrote, executed 'in a tasteful and scientific style'. The entrance led into a hall rising through the first storey. The illusion of space was magnified by a large mirror opposite the main door and by the green scagliola columns that formed a screen to the double-return staircase, upon which played tinted light filtering through a coffered ceiling pierced with coloured glass. The handrails of the staircase were of gilded bronze and the walls decorated with casts from the Panatheniac frieze, which elicited Britton's comment that the interior held 'much to please the eye and gratify the judgement'. To the right lay the coffee room, decked out with six yellow scagliola columns, and beyond it a small bar communicating with the corridor, lit from the light-well along the rear wall, which led to the committee room. The dining-room was on the left side of the hall and also linked with the corridor and a staircase to the kitchens in the basement. Above, the saloon was said by Britton to be 'rich, but simple and chaste in colour and form' and the library in a 'handsome style, the colouring neat and pleasing and all the architectural details in harmony with the general design'.

In this decade Wilkins produced schemes for those increasingly important institutions, the prison and the hospital, which showed an acquaintance with progressive thinking about their optimum design. Those for the Norfolk County Gaol and St George's Hospital, London, reflected the moderately reforming attitudes embraced by a number within his social and dilettanti circles, many of whom sat as Justices of the Peace or upon the boards of charitable foundations, such as the London hospitals. Though few wholeheartedly supported the Reform movement, a good number acknowledged the need for more enlightened government, and the intermingling of antiquarianism and liberalism can be detected in the selection of books reviewed, for example, in the 1806 *Edinburgh Review* – like the *Gentleman's Magazine* a favourite journal of dilettanti – which ranged from J. Gillies's *The History of the World from the Reign of Alexander to that of Augustus* to J. Lancaster's *Outline of a Plan for Educating Ten Thousand Poor Children, by Establishing Schools in Country Towns and Villages; and for Uniting Works of Industry with Useful Knowledge*. Payne Knight, for one, questioned the lasting effectiveness of the repressive policies of the post-war Tory administration in at least three letters written to Aberdeen in 1819 at the time of the 'Peterloo' tragedy.[16] In the first he rejoiced that in Shropshire the 'Reformers' concentrated upon the

> Mills and Markets; and when Corn is plenty they remain quietly at work in their coalpits. In the Year of scarcity I was however obliged in conjunction with a Brother

Magistrate to order a Charge of Cavalry against them, which they sustained most sturdily...but after many hard Blows and Cuts were overpowered, their Leaders taken and transported, without any loss of life.

He mistrusted Draconian measures because he thought the chief agitator, Henry Hunt, 'too base, foolish and contemptible to be capable of importance' and believed rioters were best countered by depriving them of publicity. The Government should offer 'beer *after* a meeting to those who would toss Hunt or his cronies in a blanket', since ninety per cent of those who attended were 'idle and indifferent spectators' drawn as to 'a Fair or Wake, only for Amusement'. However, writing on 1 November he cautioned Aberdeen that 'if the Measure [the Sedition Bill] announced be Carried into effect, I shall feel it prudent, in common with many others, to convert some of my Capital into foreign stock', adding, 'If let alone the Ferment will subside of itself.' He had no patience with the plan to enlarge the army since the newly armed conscripts could become the instrument of a revolution. He reiterated his misgivings in another letter dated 16 November, wherein he pointed to the participation of the French army in the Revolution. But, evidently in answer to one of Aberdeen's replies, he agreed that the rebels sought to divest the rich of their property rather than attain suffrage, continuing, 'but that red Coats, leathern caps, & Muskets will damp their Appetites, or give them a different direction, by supplying them with the means of gratifying them, is to me as incredible as Metamorphosis in Ovid'. While Aberdeen retained his Tory principles, later opposing the disestablishment of the Scottish church, Wilkins seems to have been impressed by the liberal theories of his day, taking cognisance of Bentham's ideas upon contemporary social issues, one outcome of which was the founding of University College, London.

The plan of the gaol which Wilkins built at Norwich in 1822 bears the stamp of Bentham's thinking, for the Norfolk County Gaol had a radial form comparable with his Panopticon model. Another source, surely considered by both, was the reproduction of the plan of the half completed Maison de Force at Ghent, 1771–5, in John Howard's celebrated book, *The State of Prisons in England and Wales* (1777); Wilkins probably also read his *Account of the Principal Lazarettos* (1789).[17] Closer at hand, the categorisation, and separation of prisoners into single cells with centralised supervision and a higher standard of sanitation had been implemented in East Anglia by William Blackburn for the Ipswich Gaol in the first decade of the nineteenth century and later by George Byfield for that at Bury in 1816. The Ipswich Gaol comprised a Greek cross plan central building with four radial cell blocks attached at the intersections, and the layout had been adapted by Byfield. Interestingly, Wilkins altered the Bury Gaol in about 1819, collaborating with the Governor, John Orridge, and it was used as a standard of comparison with Wilkins's design for the Norfolk Gaol by the members of the Committee for Improving the Castle Hill and the Courts of Justice.[18]

Late in 1819 or early in 1820 the Visiting Justices at Norwich organised a competition for a new prison and two new courts, the former to replace Soane's goal of 1789–93. Erected alongside the Norman Keep, the chief remains of the ancient castle, it had offended the sensibilities of Wilkins senior who had exhibited drawings of the castle at the Academy in 1786 (no. 589) and 1787 (no. 612) and repaired it in 1792. His criticisms were published in a paper presented to the Society of Antiquaries in 1795, entitled 'An Essay towards a History of the Venta Icenorum of the Romans, and of Norwich Castle'. This gave rise to an episode in William's life that belongs in the context of the Norwich commission.

Soane was to defend his work in *Memoirs of the Professional Life of an Architect, 1768–1835* (1835). In it he described Wilkins senior as 'an able stuccatore' who, like Batty Langley, 'had acquired some facility in drawing, and a smattering of Gothic lore, fancying himself an Architect, felt much disappointed at not having been entrusted with the alterations and additions to the Castle, and gave vent to his feelings' in 'unfounded criticisms'.[19] He quoted Wilkins's criticism that the gaol had bereaved the castle 'of its ancient beauty, under pretence of giving more internal convenience for the accommodation of its miserable tenants', and those lines from Milton's *Paradise Lost* which Wilkins had inserted into his paper, beginning, 'A dungeon horrible on all sides round' and ending, 'Regions of sorrow, doleful shades, where peace / And rest can never dwell' (book I, lines 61–6). In a subsequent passage Soane asserted archly that he had believed the paper to have been written by the son and, on these grounds, excused his spiteful action in having distributed copies among the members of the Royal Academy at the time of William's successful candidature for membership on 10 February 1826. It was a curious manoeuvre, expecially as he had let pass William's election as an Associate in November 1823, though he could have voted against him in the ballots for Academicians held in 1824 and 1825.[20] But Soane overplayed his hand in 1826, perhaps assuring William of the place vacated by the death of George Dance, if William's letter to Soane of 13 February is anything to go by. He had heard with 'inexpressible surprise, of an attempt by you to prejudice my election into the Royal Academy friday last' William

> could not have believed, but upon the authenticity of the source whence I derive my information, that any man of common feelings could be found, capable of entertaining hostility...after the interval of 11 years which intervened since his death – Still less that he should transfer that hostility to a son who could not have participated in the alleged offence as he was only 15 years old at the date of publication of the paragraph, at which you appear to have taken umbrage...[I regard] the attempt with pity!! for my deceased father's sake. However I very much regret that the Etiquette of the academy defeated your intentions – because the attempt to injure would have recoiled upon the aggressor, for it would have revived a subject, long since forgotten by all but yourself, which could only have reflected discredit upon the professional character of the individual so justly censored.

He intended to distribute copies of the relevant passages from his father's paper to show that he had 'exercised a sound and accurate judgement in his critique, [and] it shall add – that the building so justly stigmatised has been taken down after its condemnation by the great body of Norfolk Magistrates; and the son professionally employed to restore the ancient fabric and to make additions in the true spirit of the father's obvservations'. Then the Parthian shot: 'This hostility proceeds with a very ill grace from one whom I have endeavoured, on every occasion that presented itself, to defend against the censures so liberally bestowed upon his recent buildings in Westminster.'[21] Within a week William's temper had cooled but he maintained a superior tone with Soane, writing that the 'result of a more mature deliberation has been to convince me that my character has always been beyond impeachment, any vindication of it would be a matter of supererogation. The same observation applies to that of my late father.'[22] He was prepared to discontinue the skirmish 'unless in the event of further provocation'.

As to the commission, the prison population at Norwich had risen sharply between 1815 and 1820, reaching 245 inmates by 1821.[23] At the General Quarter Sessions in 1820 the committee was asked to approve Wilkins's plan, estimated at £45,000, but with the 'removal of the Courts to a Place below the Hill even more convenient than their present situation'. To the Visiting Justices his scheme was 'the only one, which after the most careful and minute examination...they would have decided it expedient to recommend as a good and sufficient Prison'. Happily they minuted their reasons in full, of which the most significant were his provision of

> ample means of classification and security for the safe custody of Prisoners...free circulation of air – of an Infirmary removed from the Body of the Prison – of a good supply of Water – of a space for exercise – of a Mill for labour – of Work Rooms for Employment – of a commodious Chapel in which Classification shall be preserved – of Day Rooms – of Solitary Cells – Baths – and Privies – and finally all those required in the construction of a Prison, which shall with the aid of good discipline answer the purpose of effecting a moral Reform among those who are under Confinement – thus at once satisfying the Law, accomplishing the ends of Justice, and benefiting Mankind at large by the diminution of Crime.

The radial plan 'admits of complete Inspection, upon which the Security of a Prison mainly depends...the Division of Prisoners into sixteen Classes...a separate sleeping Cell to each', spacious yards each with 'a separate Privy' and covered ways 'to protect Prisoners from the burning rays of the summer sun, and from the violence of the winter Rain, during the time allotted them for taking air, so essential to Health –'.

The layout of the gaol is illustrated in a large ground-plan, now at the Norwich Museum, signed by the County Surveyor, Francis Henry Stone, and dated June 1826 (Pl. 77). The categorisation of prisoners was achieved by the construction of three battlemented cell blocks, also containing 'Day' and work rooms, radiating from the central chapel and gaoler's quarters, and three more set nearer the hexagonal outer wall. Each block was divided in half with separate access to enclosed exercise yards. These were visible from the gaoler's quarters, much to the satisfaction of the Justices. Two other details are worthy of remark. The treadmill installed by Timothy Bramah was placed at the perimeter of the complex to give safe entry to the farmers who brought corn to be ground. In order to isolate outbreaks of gaol fever, the infirmary was located on the two upper floors of the ancient Keep, that building having been integrated with the prison so that two of its sides formed part of the outer wall. The lower floors of the Keep housed reception rooms and the solitary cells.

Nearly two years elapsed between the acceptance and the erection of Wilkins's plan. In the interim the committee toyed with less expensive alternatives, two by Wilkins and another based upon the brick prison at Bury, and, on 18 April 1821, they sacked their chairman, Robert Fellows, for promoting his own design. But the Justices stuck to the original scheme and on 17 April 1822 Parliament 'resolved, approved and confirmed' the Act to finance its construction. Contracts for the masonry, bricklaying and carpentry were signed on 17 July, and sureties of £2,500 each promised by J. Steward and by Wilkins's old friend, Hudson Gurney, assured the start of building.

The course of the work ran smoothly, the Visiting Justices reporting on 12 October 1822 that it was 'proceeding with regularity and Dispatch and we have no reason to doubt. . . will be concluded in a manner satisfactory to the County'. The only alteration they ordered, following the Epiphany Meeting of 1823, was the facing of the walls with granite and not Roman cement for reasons of security. This enhanced the fortified character of the gatehouse in which Tudor and Norman elements are combined to complement the Keep, the success of which has since been compromised by the insertion of a bay window, absent from Stone's plan (Pl. 78). The Shire House which contained the neatly disposed courts and offices, but having a dull Tudor-Gothic exterior, was completed first in the summer of 1824 (Pl. 79). The main work of the gaol on Castle Hill was concluded by Michaelmas 1825 and the gaoler in residence that autumn. A full account of the expenditure, amounting to £53,873. 7s. 11d., was made to the Epiphany meeting of 1826 in the final

Report of the Justices; Wilkins and his clerk of works together received £2,949.[24] Not only the Justices considered the goal conducive to 'efficient Prison Discipline', for as late as 1842 Blyth wrote that it was 'commodious, and well adapted for the health and regulation of the prisoners'. The Norwich Museum now occupies the site of Wilkins's gaol, girded by the old wall.

Wilkins retained the radial plan and the separation of prisoners in his design for the smaller Huntingdon Gaol, built 1826–8 north of the town in the Parish of Great Stukely. A watercolour perspective of the gaol, now preserved at Tulane University, New Orleans, with other drawings of the prison made by James Gallier senior in circa 1826, shows the original layout.[25] Flanking the entrance and turnkey's lodge were, on the left, the brewhouse and, on the right, the reception cell and bathroom, with the men's and women's infirmaries on the respective upper floors and accommodation for vagrants in attached buildings on either side. On the front to the Huntingdon to Ripton road the plain side blocks were nicely gathered about the rusticated entrance arch (Pl. 80). Behind the turnkey's lodge and at the centre of the complex was the gaoler's house and the chapel, also of two storeys. From these radiated four walls enclosing exercise yards for the debtors' and felons' prison blocks to each side and the bridewell and treadmills behind. The gaol could house some sixty-five prisoners including provision for fifteen women, the inmates being incarcerated in single cells placed on either side of a central hall in each of the blocks. Every cell had a metal basin and the gaol was well served with water closets; sanitary facilities almost comparable with those being installed at the new St George's Hospital, which Wilkins began in 1827.

Most contemporary hospitals were less hygienic than St George's; as much houses of death – and ill repute – as havens of healing. The gloomy statistics still prevailing were recorded by Charles Knight in *Cyclopaedia of London* (1851). The fundamental problem was the lack of sterile conditions which Lister did much to alleviate during his career at Wilkins's St George's. Despite a high rate of mortality, apparently partly attributable to the number of traffic accidents in the local area, St George's was advanced by current standards, embodying some of the recommendations of reformers like John Howard in the *Account* of 1789 and John Aitken in *Thoughts on Hospitals* (1801), which may also have been known to Wilkins's friends, Lords Falmouth, Rosebery and Manvers, who were among the benefactors.[26] Howard had advocated a rural site, a pavilion plan (the wards separated from the central building), a raised stone structure, large staircases, bathrooms, a piazza for 'airing' and wards of no more than eight patients. Aitken, who had participated in one of the first commissions of enquiry on hospital design, that for the Newcastle Infirmary, added to Howard's list the provision of isolation rooms for patients with dangerous diseases, cross ventilation in the wards, warm air heating and nurses' rooms, sculleries and water closets on each floor. Bentham's Panopticon also had some advocates, among them James Bevan in the scheme he presented to the House of Commons Committee on Hospital Design in 1814, and the Glasgow architect, William Stark, in his *Remarks on the Construction of Public Hospitals* published in 1810.

When he came to design St George's, Wilkins opted for an 'H' plan which was a compromise between the usual block plan and the pavilion (Pl. 81). The twenty-eight wards, containing on average fourteen beds each, were placed in the two wings, males in the south and females in the north, and amply fenestrated to provide cross ventilation. At that time the site was salubrious, adjacent to Hyde and Green Parks and abutting the rural parishes of Chelsea and Knightsbridge. Certainly, the environment was superior to that of Charing Cross, North London or Westminster Hospitals which were built in the same period, and a correspondent commenting in 1827 on the scheme to erect a hospital in Westminster thought it 'ludicrous to bring a lazerhouse of disease into the heart of the town'.[27] The wings of St George's were further separated into two halves by staircases which permitted some kind of isolation for patients with contagious diseases as well as affording communication between the three storeys and the service rooms in the central block. Each floor had water closets, probably to Joseph Bramah's design patented in 1778, and two hot water taps for movable baths, supplementing the two fixed baths in the basement, and linked to the internal heating system. The out-patients were kept to the ground floor in areas either side of the entrance hall, while the operating theatre and preparatory and post-operative wards lay on the top floor. The operating theatre also served as a lecture theatre and was situated above the board room and chapel, respectively on the ground and first floors. The theatre accommodated 150 and was 'well adapted for hearing' according to an article in *The Times* of 6 October 1830, which also remarked on the contiguous anatomical museum and the airiness of the hospital.

St George's compared well with the designs of Burton and A. Ainger for Charing Cross and the North London (later University College) Hospitals, 1832 and 1834, and, more particularly, with the Inwoods' Westminster, begun in 1827, which one historian has claimed 'crystallised' the modern concept of hospital design.[28] At Westminster the nineteen wards of ten beds each lay in the body of the hospital, a single block and so less well ventilated. The only marginal improvement was the more complete isolation of the combined operating and lecture theatre in a structure attached to the rear of the hospital. In the matter of sanitation Westminster was decidedly inferior. Although each ward had a water closet, these were only partitioned off with wooden screens and the receptacles joined to a single drain running through each floor. This resulted in obnoxious blockage which must have produced foul air; worse, the overflow emerged in the kitchens, which, as at St George's, were in the basement. There was one fixed bath in the basement in Westminster with hot water points on each floor supplied from a heating system designed by Timothy Bramah.

Beside that of basic hygiene, the Minutes of the Hospital Boards indicate the importance of two other criteria, utility and architectural dignity. For example, the Westminster Governors thought their hospital would 'answer the expectations of those who have at heart the comfort and welfare of the sick, but will also in an Architectural point of view prove a great ornament to the neighbourhood', while the final report of the Building Committee of St George's presented on 18 April 1834 states that 'the Governors are now possessed of a substantial Building of a size adequate to the increasing wants of this part of the Town – providing in the most effectual way for the accommodation and comforts of the sick poor, and affording every desirable facility for the prosecution of scientific research'.

St George's was inexpensive. The total cost, including the fittings, was some £50,000, just over the estimate, and the hospital furnished accommodation and ancilliary services for 400 patients.[29] Westminster provided comparable facilities for 190 patients at a cost of about £40,000. Wilkins also made fewer structural errors. The subsoil at both sites was unstable. Wilkins overcame the problem by infilling, costing £1,208, whereas the Inwoods spent more than £2,000 on concrete foundations to a depth of 4 feet. But they forgot to lay concrete under the lecture and operating theatre, necessitating extra expenditure and disrupting the hospital. Further, the walls of the building later expanded laterally and required the insertion of iron chain bonds. Wilkins's decision, which he 'strongly' recommended and upheld to the Governors on 26 August 1829, to substitute iron girders supplied by Bramah for wooden beams subsequently enabled a fourth floor to be added to his hospital. St George's still functions on Wilkins's basic design, while Charing Cross, Westminster and University College Hospitals have had to be rebuilt.

Given the Governors' sense of pride in their charitable endeavours, the exterior of St George's was and is impressive (Pl. 82). Whereas Westminster had a meagre covering of Neo-Gothic motifs (it is impossible to believe the apocryphal story that one applicant for a post at the hospital arrived late for his interview because he could not distinguish it from Westminster Abbey), Wilkins created a monumental Greek Revival structure that took full advantage of its open site.[30] He had entered designs for the Westminster competition, exhibited at the Academy in 1837, which one critic described as 'in the old English domestic style, the material red brick, with stone copings, and a tower with turreted angles above the principal entrance; it is a respectable example of the Tudor style, and would certainly have been better in the vicinity of Westminster Abbey, than the building which has been erected'.[31]

At St George's Wilkins eventually decided to adapt a single ancient theme, the Choragic Monument of Thrasyllus, to unify the three exposed sides. From it derived the antae of the raised main portico, the engaged porticoes on the wings and the façades to Knightsbridge and Grosvenor Place, as well as the articulation of the openings onto the staircases. The portico compositions on each front echo the Palladian arrangement, though less on the Knightsbridge façade where a two storey block was tacked on to the west side. The solution was economical and matched the Neo-Classical style of the nearby Apsley House by the Adam brothers. At one stage Wilkins had thought of using the Corinthian Order for the portico, but on reflection, informed the Board of Governors that he considered it 'necessary, in point of taste, that a different and more simple elevation should be adopted, having as much of novelty in it as is conformable and consistent with the principles of architecture of the style adopted'.[32]

The Corinthian portico appears on a design now at the R.I.B.A. which also shows a variation in the composition of the north side façade (Pl. 83).[33] The Knightsbridge façade has two additional bays and is of a continuous height. The central emphasis is less pronounced since the two inner projections are not joined by the attic and Thrasyllan openings of the executed building. The R.I.B.A. also has another design with floor plans for St George's formerly attributed to Wilkins which, however, displays a more severe style (Pl. 32).[34] The least characteristic features are the round headed openings in the basement and attic. Unsigned, the calligraphy of the explanatory inscriptions differs slightly from those on his signed drawings. Yet the monumental Doric portico and engaged columns are not foreign to his style, and the low dome raised on a squat drum recalls the grandest of his Neo-Greek country house designs, while the plan and arrangement of accommodation closely resemble the executed hospital. Nor are the drawings easily attributable to the other competitors excepting, perhaps, Burton out of J. P. Gandy, Cockerell, E. Hakewill and C. Tatham.

All came late to the commission for, in 1813, the Governors had asked James Wyatt, their Honorary Architect, to report on the condition of the existing building. This housed only 200 beds so that they were forced to reject over 600 sick poor each year. Wyatt drew up plans that he estimated would cost £39,000 to build. They found the figure too high so that not until 10 June 1825 did the Special General Court resolve to build a hospital of 350 beds, which their architect, now Lewis Wyatt, thought would cost about £50,000. He drew designs for which he was paid £50. By 16 December 1825 Wyatt had been all but passed over, and a list of competitors was compiled after the distribution of one hundred copies of the site plan. Financial problems delayed the selection of a design by another year. Wilkins was declared the winner on 15 December 1826 and his design shown to the King who was most complimentary. The Governors ordered the commencement of rebuilding on 2 March 1827.

The new hospital was erected in three stages to allow for the accumulation of funds and the continued use of the west wing of Isaac

Ware's old structure during the process. The first contract was agreed on 16 November under which the contractor, Martin, was to complete the central block for £15,986. Extras to the value of £2,966, 16s. od. were conceded on Wilkins's authority. A second contract was signed with Harrison in August 1829 for £12,300, with £1,000 allocated for the portico. An additional expenditure of £3,065. 17s. 6d. was incurred, some possibly for the portico, since the Hospital Minute Book records a contribution of £100 towards its completion by Wilkins. He intervened successfully again in 1831 'to express my conviction of the expediency of raising the lower building another story [sic] – otherwise the brick walls in the rear of the present hospital will be visible and hurt the general effect'.[35] The third contract for £10,251. 12s. 8d. was concluded with Read in September of that year and covered the north wing and the fitting up of the centre building. By early 1832 the new hospital was functioning and the architect George Wightwick was able to write that 'under the hand of the most accomplished physician [Wilkins]', it had 'acquired as great a renovation in "complement extern" as we desire its poor inmates to experience in bodily health'.[36]

Wightwick was one of those who greatly admired University College, London, the commission which brought Wilkins into closest contact with the chief social reformers of his era, including Henry Brougham and Jeremy Bentham, whose theories on education were to colour passages in the *Letter to Lord Viscount Goderich*. Bentham had long opposed the exclusive power of the Church of England in education and his criticisms were endorsed by, among others, two wealthy and influential London merchants, Isaac Lyon Goldsmid (elected to the Society of Antiquaries in March 1830) and John Smith, and a group of vociferous Hackney Baptists led by the Reverend F. A. Cox, who became Honorary Secretary to the Council of University College.[37] That they were outside 'the Pale' of established society had much to do with the opposition both in and out of Parliament to the Bill instituting the college, and prompted the speedy foundation of King's College, London as a rival Anglican stronghold, built alongside Somerset House by Smirke. Indeed its charter of incorporation came into effect in August 1829, four years before that for University College, and was championed by Wellington, with whom Wilkins was already at odds.

Another reason for opposition to the foundation of University College was its implied attack upon the deficiencies of Oxford and Cambridge. Its two most vocal apologists, Thomas Campbell and Lord Brougham, deplored the absence of adequate scientific education at those universities, among many other criticisms, though their own ideas might have been influenced by one of the Cambridge Graecophils, Charles Kelsall, who in *Phantasm of An University with Prolegomena* (1824) advocated a more practical curriculum to nurture 'great Statesmen, Orators, Ambassadors, Lawyers, Physicians, Surgeons, Painters, Sculptors, Architects, Agriculturalists'.[38] (From 1841 University College was to offer one of the first professional architectural courses in England, taught by T. L. Donaldson.) On 9 February 1825 *The Times* published an open letter written by Campbell to Brougham pleading for 'a great London University. Not a place for lecturing to people of both sexes (except as an appendage to the institution), but for effectively and multifariously teaching, examining, exercising and rewarding with honours in the liberal arts and sciences, the youth of our middling rich people between the age of fifteen or sixteen and twenty...' Brougham had already published *Observations on the Education of the People* in 1824 and was later to shepherd 'The London College Bill' successfully through Parliament.[39] Campbell had been inspired by his meetings in 1820 with professors of Bonn University, whom he had visited on behalf of Thomas Jefferson with a view to attracting scholars to the University of Virginia at Charlottesville.

In the open letter Campbell also alluded to the most appropriate design for such an institution, against which the eulogies of Wightwick and other commentators can be measured. 'All that would be necessary would be to have some porticos, and large halls independent of the Lecture-rooms to which they [the students] might resort for relaxation.' More imaginative was Cox who, at the first public meeting of the Proprietors on 4 June 1825, pictured the college as 'a palace for genius... where future Ciceros should record the influence of that excitement which Tully declares he felt at Athens, when he contemplated the porticoes where Socrates sat, and the laurel groves where Plato disputed'.

Britton, in the second volume of *The Public Buildings of London* (1828), considered that the design Wilkins exhibited at the Academy

in 1827, almost certainly represented by the elevation owned by
W. P. Wilkins (Pl. 84), would realise the aspirations of Cox and
others of like mind, promising to be

> one of the richest displays of Architecture in the Metro-
> polis...upon a scale that would alone render it a noble
> object...its splendid temple-like portico, with ten Corin-
> thian columns in front, rising above the general line of the
> façade, with its embellished flight of steps below, and a
> spacious dome, towering above, will impart to it an air of
> scenic beauty, that will render it one of our most original
> edifices.[40]

Viewing just that part of Wilkins's competition design which was
built, a revised version of the centre, Wightwick judged it to be only
surpassed by Wren's St Paul's Cathedral, while W. Hosking, Professor
of the Arts of Construction at King's College, London from 1840,
averred that it was, 'next to the dome of St. Paul's, the finest piece
of Graeco-Italian architecture which I have ever seen'. Leeds, noting
such extraordinarily laudatory comments, later remarked on the
'indirect testimony of Mr. Welby Pugin's Silence'.[41]

    No doubt Wilkins's candidature for election to the Royal Society
in 1831 was endorsed by those members of that august body who
served on the College Council – Brougham, Joseph Hume, the
Marquis of Lansdowne, the Duke of Norfolk, Lord John Russell,
William Tooke and the 'Pope' of Holland House, Aberdeen's old
haunt, John Wishaw.[42]

    The original design was Wilkins's grandest statement in the
Classical style and in the field of institutional architecture. Its
magnificence can be further appreciated by examining the engraving
of the floor plans and elevation distributed by the College Council
(Pl. 85). The accommodation is disposed on three sides of a broad
court, 356 by 280 feet, forming an 'E' plan that, in effect, synthesises
the campus with the mediaeval quadrangle. This was not entirely
his own creation since an 'E' plan with the Great Hall at the centre
seems to have been recommended in the specifications (of which no
copies remain) circulated among the competing architects, judging
by the ground-plan sent in by Gandy, preserved in the College
Archive, and by Cockerell's scheme now at the Victoria and Albert
Museum.[43] The teaching facilities are grouped in the central building

and in the adjoining part of the wings, with accommodation for students at either end of these. Wilkins translated the King's screen into the Greek vocabulary to isolate the college from Gower Street. 'The fourth side is formed by the Propylon', wrote a friend of Wilkins in an article from an unidentified newspaper in the press cutting book, 'and a low cloister connecting it with the main buildings...the Propylon...is a noble portico of the Doric order of architecture, having six columns in front nearly five feet in diameter'.[44] The anonymous author further reported that Wilkins envisaged the eventual creation of two quadrangles, each measuring 100 by 120 feet, behind the main block; these would have exploited the site, once intended for a residential square to be named after Lord Carmarthen, to its fullest capacity.[45]

But Wilkins was equally prepared for a contraction in the college building programme, since he concentrated the main accommodation in and the articulation on the central block. It contained the museums, libraries, a number of lecture rooms and the Great Hall, projected deep into the quadrangle and fronted by the imposing Corinthian portico raised upon an elaborate stepped basement, intended to be decorated, as the pediment, with sculpture by Westmacott. The Order was taken from the Temple of Jupiter Olympius at Athens and was to have been echoed in the four column porticoes terminating the wings onto Gower Street. Since this temple had been finished in Hadrian's reign, Wilkins may have thought it archaeologically consistent to augment the elevation of the main front by inserting a high basement below the portico, possibly inspired by that of Thomas Hamilton's High School, Edinburgh, designed in 1825, and a dome at the intersection of the hall and the central block. Domes, essentially Roman in form, were also to have graced the Thrasyllan porticoes at the centres of the side ranges. A compromise, it nevertheless enabled Wilkins to bend his style to the monumental requirements of large scale urban institutional buildings. He was aware of the incongruities, given his reputation as a purist, writing to the Governors that the 'four columned porticoes in front of the apartments of the Librarian and Secretary are attached to a part of the building intended for habitation and may therefore with perfect consistency have windows in the walls behind them, and in the rusticated basement below them'.

The passage comes in the persuasive explanatory report he

submitted with the original design. Alive to the ambitions of the Governors, he played upon the grandeur of his scheme:

> The Great Hall 80 feet by 65, is approached through a grand portico supported by a solid basement and approached by a double flight of steps. It opens to an octangular vestibule having on the right hand the Library, on the left the Museum and in front the Council Room. The Vestibule is the focus to which all the parts of the building intended for public inspection and for magnificence of these converge.
>
> The Longitudinal Section through the center of the principal public Rooms will convey some idea of the effect and of an interrupted suite of apartments extending 420 feet in length.
>
> There is no example in England of a portico with ten columns in front. It is for this reason that I have chosen as my prototype the magnificent Portico of the Olympeum at Athens, the proportions of which I have closely followed ...It...projects forward very considerably into the quadrangle, for the double purpose of avoiding the necessity for the introduction of windows behind the columns and to divest the portico of the commonplace appearance of being *an appliqué* to the main building.

At the same time he married splendour with economy, arguing, for example, that the Corinthian Order, though the most ornamental, was yet relatively cheaper than the others 'because the bulk of material employed is proportionally less'. He also remarked on the suitability of the large basements for leasing as wine vaults and anticipated the need to reduce expenditure, at least temporarily: 'The Doric Skreen in front of the Quadrangle and Propylaeum or gateway...not essential to the effect of completeness of the Design ...might be delayed as well as that of the sculpture in the pediment until the success of the Establishment has been placed beyond doubt.' No less intelligently he reminded them that he was fully qualified to undertake a 'subject so novel' and even questioned aspects of the specification prepared for the competitors by their Committee of Education in consultation with W. H. Playfair, who had completed and extended Adam's Edinburgh University. For instance, they had not included sufficient lecture rooms, whereas his plan was 'so formed that two or four Lecture rooms of the greatest capacity may be added at any time without any interruption to the business of the University'.

Wilkins had not been keen to respond to the invitation of the Council of University College to compete against Atkinson, Cockerell, Davies, J. P. Gandy and Wyatville following his experience at King's. The competition had been announced in August 1825, but Wilkins did not finally agree to participate until 1 November, on which day he wrote to Lord Auckland, one of the Governors and a member of the council, thanking him for an assurance that the competition would be judged objectively and be between 'men who bore the highest character in their profession'.[47]

Auckland and the members of the council were true to their word. Not only were the architects invited to submit explanatory reports so that their ideas should not be misconstrued but their plans were also subjected to a detailed comparative analysis. The accommodation provided by each architect and their estimates, where supplied, were compiled upon a large sheet divided into columns.[48] The architects were listed in alphabetical order down the left margin and the details of each design categorised under the following headings: 'Roof Extent, Area of Court, Total Area, Area Available, Hall, Library, Museum, Lecture Rooms, Examination Rooms, Residential Rooms', and the medical accommodation subdivided into 'Laboratories, Dissecting Rooms, Lecture Rooms, Museum', with 'Access' and the estimates down the right margin.

The analysis effectively narrowed the field to Wilkins and Gandy, their schemes having almost as much accommodation as the other architects supplied, but at considerably lower cost. Wilkins's design if built in brick with stone facings was estimated at £70,000 and that of Gandy at £75,000 with a brick façade or £85,000 with a stone front. Of the four other architects, Atkinson estimated his college at £104,360, Davies at £103,658, Wyatville at £250,000, while Cockerell gave no estimate but submitted one of the largest projects. Wilkins furnished two spacious halls, a Great Hall of 6,570 square feet and a Sub Hall of 2,604 square feet – compared with Gandy's single hall of 3,750 square feet – and two libraries, one of 6,608 square feet and a second of 2,884 square feet with a reading room, 24 by 16 feet, and a room for the librarian 16 feet square – as against

Gandy's two libraries each containing 4,250 square feet and two smaller rooms. Wilkins also assigned 512 square feet more to museum space than did Gandy and exceeded his provision of lecture theatres and rooms; indeed only Wyatville introduced more than Wilkins's twenty-six theatres and rooms, but then, his was the highest estimate. Similarly, Wilkins created the largest and most comprehensive medical facilities which the council had made a priority. Apart from allocating ample space, he isolated the department at the north east corner, as the Education Committee required. Gandy, whose provision for the faculty was almost as good, only envisaged a 'stable building' for the 'reception of subjects', compared with Wilkins's preparation room, 27 by 22 feet, linked by a staircase with the anatomical lecture theatre.

Before they reached a final decision, the council submitted the plans and estimates of Wilkins and Gandy to the scrutiny of C. H. Good, Surveyor to the Church Commissioners, a sensible but, in view of their non-sectarian constitution, ironic choice. The first report Good sent to Coates, secretary to the council, on 22 April 1826 indicated that their estimates were too low. However, he found in Wilkins's favour: £87,600 in brick with stone facings or £94,980 in Bath stone, compared with £91,800 or £102, 850 for Gandy on the same basis.[49] But two days later Good informed Coates that his estimate of Gandy's design had been calculated on inaccurate data and the rough figures '67,725' on the verso might represent an amended estimate. Yet the council was not swayed by figures alone and concluded that Wilkins's scheme had 'advantages in beauty and convenience of arrangement which entitle it to a preference over the other plans however great may be their attractions and points of recommendation'.[50]

Among these advantages, no doubt, were the student 'assembly rooms' introduced to prevent disorderly behaviour before lectures. 'There is one broad principle to be acted upon in the whole arrangement of the Plan', Playfair had written to J. A. Murray of the council, 'to remove all petty incitements to levity and disorder'.[51] The main block also had broad halls or 'cloisters' and 'ambulatories' to afford direct communication between the various faculty lecture rooms. For the teaching staff Wilkins provided office and preparation rooms next to the lecture theatres. The Great Library and Museum of Natural History were to have double ceilings and floors to ensure 'tranquility'. Other advantages were the toplighting in these and the lecture theatres, the use of two of the pillars in the former as drain-pipes and a system of hot air heating to dispense with noxious stoves. As importantly for the council's Building Committee, Wilkins showed willing to undertake the work in stages and to effect savings in materials, necessary in view of his extraordinarily optimistic estimate, still only £83,000 after second thoughts.

Wilkins had communicated this revised estimate in a letter dated 14 April, wherein he again offered to execute the college in stages. The Building Committee saw this procedure as an answer to their financial straits and advised the council to 'enter into contracts only for such parts as should be necessary for the first purposes of the Institution', beginning with the northern range, then the main building, including the portico and Great Hall, followed by the remainder of the main block and southern range and, if possible, the colonnade and 'Propylaeum'.[52] Nonetheless they also suggested

> to Mr. Wilkins the propriety of carrying the Colonnade in front of the north and south side of the square and of giving more light to the Vestibule by sacrificing the Lecture Room but little wanted in the dome and they lay before the Council his Estimate of Expense for the completion of the whole interior of the Square which being faced with Stone does not exceed £87,000.

That order did not suit Wilkins, and he wrote to the council on 24 April asking them to delay their decision on it until the receipt of the contractor's estimates, and those aside pressing 'strongly in favour of the Centre, the Council Room and Students Library being omitted, the sub-vestibule converted into a Council Room and a portion of the sub Hall into a Students Library'. Already fighting to preserve what he conceived as the aesthetic and functional nucleus, he also suggested that the council raise money by selling the land they owned on the other side of Gower Street for a housing development, continuing,

> the general design may be greatly improved by lessening the propylaeum, making it only a tetrastyle portico, and by the omission of the two four columned porticoes at the ends of the two wings. It would simplify the design and

give greater importance to the great portico. It would also be attended with a saving in expense. The two four columned porticoes are not so strictly in conformity with the rest as I could wish.

(Perhaps this led him to draw another elevation, a wash perspective owned by the college, of which an engraving was published by Leeds in 1838 and subsequently confused with his original design.[53] The 'Propylaeum' and colonnade are deleted and the articulation of the side ranges altered, though not as severely as he was forced to do after the receipt of the tenders in September. The ranges are terminated by semi-circular domed Corinthian porticoes based on the Temple of Vesta at Tivoli and the Choragic Monument of Lysicrates. The central porticoes have square turrets with octagonal lanterns in place of domes, derived respectively from the Monument of Thrasyllus and the Tower of Winds.)

Taken at his word, he was asked on 29 April if 'a further reduction in expense may not be made by narrowing the Hall and Portico to the extent of Eight instead of Ten columns'. This was the first in a long succession of requests that he pare down his design, which caused Wilkins to seek Gandy's aid. From as early as the winter of 1826 Gandy's name crops up regularly in the minutes and the nature of his position should be elucidated. Sometimes he acted in a menial capacity – superintending the execution of the Working Drawings – and sometimes as Wilkins's personal assistant. On 28 October 1827 Wilkins wrote to the Warden, Leonard Horner, about an alteration to the design and to deny implications of 'neglect on my part to my professional duties' and adding the postscript, 'I shall put the examination into Mr. Gandy's hands to arrange with Messrs Lee in order to save time.'[54] Three days later he wrote that the draft estimates for the accumulated alterations would be forwarded to 'Mr. Gandy to go through...It will take him a week or ten days to do so.' The arrangement caused some confusion and at the 57th session of the council in the first week of November 1827 he was asked to 'what degree they are to look to Mr. Gandy for efficient assistance, for Mr. Lee has stated that he does not consider himself bound to attend to the directions of Mr. Gandy, but solely to those of Mr. Wilkins'. Wilkins clarified the position at the next session on 10 November, tersely stating that 'the arrangement between himself and Mr. Gandy was entirely of a private nature, but that Mr. Gandy will be happy to afford every assistance in his power when he, Mr. Wilkins, is absent from town'. From this situation stemmed the erroneous idea that Gandy had collaborated upon the design of the college when, in fact, he was helping out the harassed Wilkins, already afflicted by gout. In 1832 Gandy was to witness Wilkins's will.

Gandy had been present at the 21st session of the council held on 19 September 1826, the day on which the tenders were opened and from which time Wilkins's troubles multiplied. Each one must have shocked those assembled for the lowest, sent in by Henry Lee, amounted to £107,767 and the highest, entered by George Harrison, to £128,904.[55] None of the eight tenders received included the ornamental stonework.

The worst fears of the council had been realised. Nevertheless one member, Lord Auckland, championed Wilkins because, as he wrote to Brougham on 2 October 1826, 'the excess of the tender above the estimate' was less than it first seemed, Wilkins having

> sacrificed nothing to gain applause by a low contract – he has almost been luxurious in his materials & excessive in the substance which he wishes to give the buildings – and he has been full in his specification inserting articles we should scarcely have criticised him for omitting – Chimney-pieces for instance to the amount of 200£ and Gravel walks upwards of 1000£ – Where the Church Commisioners would insist on a wall three bricks in thickness he has insisted on one of four bricks and his timbers are at least double the substance to be found, not in common buildings but in the new Churches. Upon these alone 6 or 7000£ might have been saved & no remark made and the same feeling I am told is to be traced in every part of the work.[56]

He agreed with Coates that the contract should be limited to the construction of the main building minus the Great Hall, followed by the side ranges, of which he drew a diagram, comparable to one made at about this time by Wilkins (Pl. 86). Ugly though this would be, the college could be opened for an expenditure, including books and furnishings, of some £90,000. He was glad to hear, though under this arrangement we could scarcely accept it, that Westmacott had expressed in conversation a strong wish to have committed to him the sculpture of the Portico – 'I should like it he said – I would do it for £2,500 or £2,000 if I could, and more than this I would take ten slaves' – This shows admiration of the buildings and a growing zeal in our favour.

His confidence in Wilkins never wavered, nor was he disappointed, assuring Brougham on 1 October 1828, 'You would have been out of yourself with admiration of the building which improves wonderfully as it gets an air of inhabitance. I know nothing more complete in arrangement or beautiful in design.'[57]

Auckland's earlier letter anticipated the business of the session on 11 November 1826 when the council decided to concentrate their inadequate funds upon the central block and pondered how to further curtail costs. Yet despite these uncertainties they drew up a contract for the excavations and work began on the site. A fortnight later they arrived at a loose arrangement with Wilkins to the effect that, for 5 per cent of the total, he would supply Working Drawings, superintend the building and check the contractors' accounts. They did not sign a contract with Lee until February 1827, being still undecided as to the best means of economising on the design of the central building.

The necessary savings were achieved by a process bordering on attrition. Wilkins was required to make numerous changes to the design and specification while executing the Working Drawings.[58] These show that most of the main accommodation had suffered diminution between November 1826 and the spring of 1827. For example, the Great Library and Museum of Natural History were altered from 118 by 56 feet to 117' 10" by 50 feet, and the Great Hall from 80 by 65 feet to 80 by 45 feet. Worse, Wilkins had to swallow a major revision which fundamentally altered his original conception when, on 16 May, the council agreed that 'it would be expedient to change the position of the Hall from the front to the rear of the building'. As constructed, the dome has more and the portico less prominence than Wilkins desired.

Minor irritations abounded throughout the commission, such as the delay in the delivery of cast iron beams supplied by Timothy

Bramah and Messrs Rottam and Hallam; the council also bridled at the expense of these contracts which Wilkins subsequently explained in a letter dated 10 March 1828 as the 'consequence of several precautionary addenda to the simple Cast Iron Girder & it includes the cost of trying their strength by means of Hydraulic apparatus'.[59]

A temporary respite came with the ceremony of laying the foundation stone which took place on 7 March 1827. It had been held up by frosty weather, which Wilkins feared would spoil the mortar, and by the indisposition during February of the Duke of Sussex. Wielding the mallet with which the foundation stone of St Paul's Cathedral had been laid, the Duke performed the ceremony amid considerable pomp, following a Latin oration by Wilkins. The mallet was lent by the Masonic Lodge of Antiquity to which the Duke belonged. Here was a measure of the esteem in which the design of the college was already held.

However, Wilkins's frustration increased through the middle of 1827 as the Building Committee kept instructing Horner to order new changes in the internal plan. Wilkins reprimanded Horner in a letter sent from Cambridge on 31 October, '*Every exertion* has been made by me to forward the business in hand. I again repeat that the London University has had more than its *due share* of my time & attention, but it is not by the *parade* of activity that great objects are accomplished.'[60] The session held on 5 November was the scene of an open row between Wilkins and his employers because he could produce only a gross account for the latest batch of alterations. Five days later they attacked him indirectly on the grounds that the clerk of works was 'deficient in energy' and regretted Wilkins's frequent absences from London.

Troublesome as ever, Horner then strove to supersede Wilkins in the direction of the contractors. Wilkins wrote to Brougham on 7 November reminding him that he had only agreed to compete once he had been assured that the council would respect his professional integrity. He further accused the council of reneging on his contract by

> placing me under the directions of an officer of the Council, and wholly destroying the authority I ought to exercise over the Contractor and all other persons engaged in the execution of the buildings. This proceeding, besides

being wholly novel, would if I were to comply with it, degrade me in the Station I claim to hold in the profession... [Horner has] already interfered in my department, in a manner wholly unusual, & extremely wounding to the *amour propre* of one who has been concerned in buildings of the greatest importance. In my last great work, King's College, the Provost & Fellows of *their own accord* before the buildings were begun, passed a resolution that no individual of the Society should interfere with the mode of constructing the buildings.[61]

Horner was not curbed and, among further interferences, instigated a vain move in December to alter the seating plans in the lecture theatres. On 8 February 1830 he unsuccessfully disputed the payment of Wilkins's 5 per cent fee.

The majority of the building was completed in 1828, being roofed in May. The portico was finished before 30 September when the Medical School was opened. Thereafter the college began to operate, though work on the dome did not cease until the spring of 1829 and the library and museums were not fitted up for a number of years. Classes were held in barely decorated rooms, the incomplete state of which is described in the final specification, as for example, 'Room Number One. *Contract*, to leave the walls without plaster & the floor without pavements – no door at the doorways into No. 2 and 3 – sashes and frames to all the windows that opened –'. Even the Great Hall lacked a ceiling. Fortunately, however, Wilkins had managed to obtain funds in June 1829 to raise the walls of its vestibule on three sides as a fire precaution.[62] These paid dividends by preventing the flames from a conflagration in the hall (rebuilt 1848–9 as the library by T. L. Donaldson) from spreading to the rest of the college.

The commission was a remarkable success despite the drastic curtailment of the original design. Thanks to his foresight and determination, Wilkins retrieved enough of it to provide the college with a magnificent and practical nucleus at a reasonable cost; the entire account of £85,809, which included non-architectural expenditure, was only £9,000 more than the Inwoods' nearby St Pancras Church erected nearly six years before. Wilkins achieved a fine balance between simplicity and monumentality which struck almost all his contemporaries as the consummation of their paradoxically historical and progressive attitude towards institutional architecture. A correspondent in *The Times* of 6 August 1828 declared that the bare bones of the initial design had 'no gaudy affectation of ornament or incongruous embellishment, defects which disfigure so many of the public buildings of the metropolis', but was a 'chaste and truly classic specimen of Grecian Architecture'.

XI

Preservation

In retrospect, the success of the University College commission, like that of St Paul's, did Wilkins a disservice. It lent further weight to the posthumous impression that he had been just a dogmatic Greek Revivalist. Actually Wilkins's appreciation of the Gothic continued to deepen at the end of the decade. He became involved in commissions which, quite as much as his Neo-Tudor colleges and houses, reflected his respect for mediaeval architecture.

For the first of these, the Yorkshire Philosophical Society Museum at York, he recommended a Greek style so as not to enter into a presumptuous competition with the glorious local mediaeval architecture. Early in 1827 the Reverend W. B. Vernon, president of the society, wrote to George Wilkins, now Rector of Wing, Buckinghamshire, seeking an introduction to William, whose 'architectural abilities and taste' he greatly admired.[1] The society wished to have a 'little advice' as to the most appropriate style for their proposed museum, considering that it was to be built

> on the Manor Shore, being part of the demesne of the old royal palace, the remains of which bound it on the one side, whilst the beautiful ruins of the St. Mary's Abbey terminate it on another, the boundaries being completed by the river and by the city wall and multiangular tower. The ruins of the Abbey will be placed with the grounds in the Society's hands.

Should, he asked, 'the style be Gothic, to be in keeping with the ruins, or should all comparison with the old architecture be avoided? A sketch of an elevation from your brother, whether Gothic or Grecian, of such a character as to be above contempt and yet not expensive, would be very valuable to us.' He thought that the building need be only one storey high and ornamented on the front, 'the other sides being flanked with plantations, and all the rooms not belonging to that front being lighted with skylights'. It should, however, 'admit hereafter of extension'. On the verso he appended a plan of the requisite amount of accommodation.

The society had been founded in 1822 after the discovery of fossilised bones of extinct species of animals in Kirkdale Cave.[2] By 1823 it had attracted 120 subscribers and amassed over 2,500 fossils, which were housed temporarily in the Wentworth and Rishworth Bank at York. In 1825 a Building Committee had been formed under the chairmanship of Vernon and the site described in his letter secured with the aid of Lord Grantham and the Chancellor of the Exchequer, the Right Honourable Frederick Robinson, later Lord Goderich, whom Wilkins was to seek as an ally in his attempts to improve English patronage. An initial design had been made by Richard Hey Sharp, the son of a local clergyman, who also completed a survey of the Abbey for the society.

The survey was associated with a study intended for publication by the Antiquaries and, at a meeting of the Philosophical Society on 3 December 1827, Vernon read the letter

> written by him to the Secretary of the Antiquarian [sic] Society communicating the proposal of the Council respecting the plan, and a letter from the Earl of Aberdeen, president of the Society, accepting the offer. Resolved that the Society of Antiquarians having agreed to the Proposal of the Council, and the plans and drawings referred to be communicated to them and that Mr. Sharp be remunerated for the same by the Society.[3]

The Abbey and the Minster loomed large in a letter Wilkins penned to Vernon on 29 June 1827. After excusing the tardy execution of his offer 'to furnish a plan for the new buildings' in the preceding April, he continued:

> A very great pressure of business, requiring constant and immediate attention, has prevented me from before send-

ing the sketch I offered for the design of your Museum. Even now I am compelled to confine it to an outline drawing [Pl. 87]. If, however, there should be a desire to carry the design into effect, I shall be most happy to send you working plans for the details of the architecture, upon the proper execution of the details the effect of Grecian architecture greatly depends...I am decidedly of the opinion that the architecture should be Grecian; you have such Gothic at York, that any design must appear trifling...I have again and again considered what you have stated with regard to the site; and I am convinced that, in *every* point of view, the style of architecture to be adopted in your museum *must* be Grecian; I cannot reconcile the notion of any other style, as to the locality or the purpose of the site...In the present instance, there is every security that the true proportions of that noble Architecture will be preserved; there is every security that the general effect will be fully obtained, which depends on the contour of mouldings, and light and shade arising from a strict attention to the mathematical sections of the ancient Architecture; for those sections and proportions have been studied and measured on classical ground,...[4]

The members of the society accepted his deferential solution, with the exception of the Earl of Carlisle (formerly Lord Morpeth) and Gally Knight who had written to Vernon from Firbeck Hall, Bawtry on 28 April, 'I confess my blood ran cold (perhaps you will say, more likely I goose-skinned) at the idea of placing a Greek or Roman building within the sanctuary of St. Mary's.'[5] Wilkins 'would never have suggested' it as 'the genius of the place is essentially Gothic'. He also favoured the style for its economy: a proper effect could be achieved by the application of cheap 'stone mullions and labels to the windows' – the very thing that Wilkins wished to avoid. Gally Knight was answered at the 1827 annual meeting of the society when it was agreed that a Neo-Gothic museum would be 'impracticable to execute, without at once offending good taste, and sacrificing the convenience of the Institution; and...that buildings of very different styles, Classical and Gothic, are seen mingled together in our Universities with an effect neither incongruous nor unpleasing'.[6]

Having won his point, Wilkins consented to 'give a plan and elevation for the Building; and also furnish drawings for the workmen, on condition that the details should be strictly attended to'.[7] He was protecting himself from interference from Sharp who was retained as the 'Architect whom the Sub-Committee have invited to attend the execution of it'.[8]

In place of Sharp's rather feeble design, a single storey building of seven bays with pilasters at each corner and framing the central entrance – hardly carrying the stamp of his three years in Greece, 1816–19 – Wilkins presented a finely proportioned ashlar structure of two storeys (Pl. 88).[9] The façade is defined by pilasters and an incisive cornice, and commanded by a Doric portico modelled upon the Athenian Propylaea that fronts a capacious, and functional, interior, with which the society was especially delighted. Either side of the entrance hall lie the Keepers's office and library and beyond it a lecture theatre seating 400 and surrounded on three sides by the exhibition rooms. Before subsequent extension, these rooms had 'an aggregate length of. . .not less than 300 feet lighted for the most part by skylights so that more than 500 feet of cases may be disposed longitudinally against the wall alone'.[10] The theatre, at the hub of the inverted 'T' plan, measures 54 by 35 feet, is ringed by Corinthian columns and top-lit by glazed ceiling coffers, originally having a system of shutters allowing the lecturer to adjust the light. At Wilkins's urging, a basement floor to contain a laboratory and eight smaller rooms was added to the initial plan.

The enthusiasm for Wilkins's design encouraged the society to accept an increase in the estimate from £3,000 to £5,650, over £1,600 above their funds. The 1829 Report states that the final cost was £6,868. 14s. 5¾d., of which Wilkins received £173. 5s. 0d., and an honorary membership. The society was in debt for over eighty years but, fortunately for Wilkins, the members treated their weak financial position in a cavalier manner, inspired by the rhetoric of Francis Cholmeley's speech delivered at the laying of the foundation stone by the society's first patron, the Archbishop of York, on 4 October 1827: 'The site of the Museum. . .will be handed down to posterity; and may the buildings which will rise upon their ruins exist to the remotest age, as a monument of the spirit and enterprise and love of service which characterised the nineteenth century.'[11] They had pressed ahead with building from late August 1827 so that the front and lecture theatre were finished by 20 January 1828, when a report in the *Yorkshire Gazette* lauded the portico as 'a chaste and beautiful specimen with a pure Greek Doric style of Architecture...built of an excellent freestone, obtained from a quarry on the estate of Sir John Johnstone Bt. at Hackness'. The writer was much taken with the theatre and its ingenious lighting. Funds evidently ran low soon after for the interior was still undecorated when the museum was opened on 5 January 1830 by Vernon, an event marred by inclement weather, which condemned the Honourable Edward Dundas to spend most of the day in a snow drift outside York, and by the refusal of the staunch Tories, the Archbishop and the Mayor of York, to attend in protest against the invitation of the local Whig Member of Parliament. The ceremony too was covered by the *Gazette*. Among the features of the building its reporter admired was the effect of the 'feeble' gaslighting upon the display of mediaeval sculpture from St Mary's in the Gothic Museum situated in the basement.

The preservation of the few sculptures removed from the ruins of the Abbey was wholly to Wilkins's antiquarian taste. Within his own field of expertise, he wished, where possible, to preserve ancient buildings in the functional as well as the aesthetic sense, as in the schemes he prepared for the preservation of the Keep at Norwich and of the Abbey Church of St Mary, Sherborne.

The demolition of Soane's gaol at Norwich in 1822 had disturbed the foundations and damaged the fabric of the Castle Keep, particularly on the east side. Wilkins had ensured its retention by strengthening the walls on the interior when fitting it out for the reception rooms, solitary confinement cells and infirmary of his new prison. In 1826 the Visiting Justices were persuaded – possibly by Wilkins – to order a report on the condition of the Keep from the County Surveyor, Francis Stone.[12] The report was passed on to Wilkins and their joint proposals, minuted at the Easter meeting of the Justices, clearly carried the imprint of Wilkins's thinking, one, for instance, requiring that 'the Mouldings and the other Members be executed after Models to be taken from the existing Remains'. Wilkins and Stone urged the entire rebuilding of the two centre compartments on the east side, using 'hard materials' faced with Bath stone. These were to be joined to the old structure by two 'Tiers of Timbers on strong Iron Bars, to be carried round its four sides within the Substance of the Walls and to serve as a Bond and support for the Whole'. Though they warned that 'serious ill consequences may reasonably be anticipated if the Repairs be deferred for any considerable time' their recommendations were shelved until 1834 when Anthony Salvin superintended a restoration programme that incorporated many of their proposals. By then the issue had become the property of the local antiquaries and papers by Gurney, Dawson Turner, Leake and the architects, Edward Blore and Thomas Rickman, remain in the Norfolk and Norwich Record Office.

Hudson Gurney corresponded with Wilkins about a short history he had written on the castle which was entitled *An Essay on the Antiquity of the Castle of Norwich* and received by the trustees of the British Museum at their meeting on 13 December 1834.[13] On 2 December Wilkins wrote to Gurney expressing the hope that it would be published. He noted a similarity between Castle Rising and Norwich Keep and suggested that its western arches were possibly taken from the local Roman 'templum cloacinae'.[14] He then made some observations on restoration in general, which, if obscure, indicate his realism and lack of humbug:

> Dawson Turner was not much out when he termed the restoration of one part an abomination – what is originally beautiful cannot suffer by restoration, witness Henry VII's Chapel and Whitehall to those who think the original design of Inigo Jones beautiful. Time has thrown a thick veil over the deformation of Norwich and if we remove this veil we must expect the natural result. The Castle is now a beautiful object...restore it to its pristine state and it becomes a shrine to enclose the relect [sic] – Let Mr. Turner console himself with this notion – It is a jewell in a deal box. What was never beautiful cannot be made so by restoration and hence the wish to retain it as it is – in its present state its ugliness is not obtrusive.

Wilkins was more impressed by the Norman and late mediaeval structure of St Mary, Sherborne. He was invited to write a report on the historic Abbey church by the vicar, the Reverend R. Lyon, and leading parishioners who, at a Vestry held in 1827, had resolved that he was the best qualified architect to advise on its restoration.[15] They wanted him to give a second opinion on a scheme previously submitted by a local architect, E. T. Percy, to shore up the tower.[16] Wilkins's *Report*, dated 20 September, was written in London but includes a letter from Brighton where he may have been recuperating from an attack of gout. His findings and recommendations, scrupulously explained and well illustrated by thirteen diagrams, sections and elevations, were printed in October 1828 and circulated within the parish.

> This edifice, built in an age when the knowledge of architecture and of construction was, perhaps, at its height, exhibits to the practised eye proofs of the exercise of both in no inconsiderable degree. Of the beauty of the Building it is unnecessary to speak; the excellence of the workmanship, the precautions observed to obtain stability, must be acknowleged by all competent judges of such works.

Thus Wilkins began his *Report*, surely especially admiring the splendid Perpendicular fan vaulting of the nave and choir which had been completed in the fifteenth century. He then sketched in the history of its construction.[17] He thought the basic fabric of the tower up to the floor of the belfry was Norman, and conjectured that the 'columns or piers of the Nave are of Norman origin'. The tower had been enlarged and the nave and choir rebuilt, being 'now masked by Gothic tracery [not using the more precise terminology established by Rickman in *An Attempt to Discriminate the Styles of Architecture in England* (1817)], in a manner nowhere else within my knowledge adopted, for the purpose of altering their original character, and making them in some degree to accord with the architecture of the reign of Henry the Seventh'. The fissures 'near the south-east and north-west angles' had 'existed prior to the construction of the Gothic Tower and, of course, were well known to the projectors of the later edifice, who seem to have adopted all necessary precautions to prevent the further progress of such dilapidations. In effecting this object, we cannot too much admire that nicety of skill which adapted the means to the ends proposed.' Those precautions included the installation of a large arch in the east wall of the south transept, the construction of the turret staircase independent of that wall to preserve its structural integrity and the placing of the weight of the tower on the arcade and gallery. But the hanging of heavy bells in the tower at some time in the sixteenth century had, in turn, worsened the extant fissures and fractured the north side of the tower, crushed the columns of the internal Norman arcade, damaged the ceiling of the crossing and the arch to the choir, and caused the tower to incline four inches towards the east. 'I see so many obvious signs of great intelligence in the construction of the Gothic Church, that I cannot be brought to admit of any consent or intention of the Architect that bells should be introduced in the Tower.'

The chief problem was to repair the tower at a reasonable cost without spoiling the historic fabric. In 1827 the crossing was disfigured by a temporary scaffold to shore up the gallery and arcade, and to guard against falling masonry. The primary consideration was the relief of the strain on the tower structure, either by the removal of the bells or by the transference of their weight from the east and west to the north and south walls. He thought the retention of the bells would be the perpetuation of an 'evil', adding, 'the durability of the Building [is] everything, and the bells as nothing!'. But, being a realist and, as he claimed, experienced in the restoration of parish churches, he knew that the parishioners would oppose their removal, especially as one had been given by Wolsey in about 1502. 'I have found, when I have been before consulted on the propriety of retaining bells, where the Building has suffered from the giant concussion they occasion, a very strong prejudice in the minds of the inhabitants against their removal.' Therefore, Wilkins advised that the weight of the bells be transferred to the north and south walls 'by the introduction of cast iron Girders; capable of sustaining nearly twice the weight'.[18] Two 32 foot girders would underpin the ancient timbers supporting the bells, which would be re-hung on a wooden truss placed over the old timbers and directly above the girders (Pl. 89). The north and south walls were to be strengthened by filling in the Norman arcade of the tower and by the addition of a new floor above it which would act as a brace, being connected to circular cast iron wall plates. Thereafter the shattered columns could be replaced and the upper part of the tower rendered secure.

For the girders he consulted Timothy Bramah, 'whose name', he punned, 'is a tower of strength on such occasions'. Bramah had supplied a diagram and an estimate for £240 which was printed as the first appendix of the *Report*, together with a letter suggesting that the girder be cast in 'two parts longitudinally, for added strength and ease of installation, like those he had made to support 'the large tower over the saloon window at Windsor Castle'. Were a slightly altered version of the 'University Girder' to be used, the Vestry would 'save £7 or £8'.

Wilkins's second major proposal was the bracing of the piers of the south transept with a substantial truss to be masked by a gallery with an ornamental front. He expressed 'great pleasure' in offering to furnish a design 'like the Stall-work in the Choir'.

There were a number of other necessary repairs. The timbers over the south transept ought to be replaced 'immediately and wholly'. All the choir buttresses needed repair and the spandrels of the interior vault, like those of the groined ceiling over the crossing, had to be filled up to the same level to introduce stability, using material removed from the tie beams of the choir ceiling at their junction with the walls to permit the circulation of air. The east wall of the north transept should be buttressed and an opening in the east wall of the adjoining old laundry sealed up and a new one made in a better position to increase resistance from north to south. The gutters ought to be relaid on a new base to replace the old sand which caused dampness, the wrought iron cramps in the stonework replaced by rustless cast iron and larger cast iron rain water pipes fitted with cistern heads matching the mouldings of the cornice. Lastly, a fourteen inch barrel drain, inserted below the foundations running from the 'little south portico' in the direction of Half Moon Street, should prevent further settlement which might invalidate any other work done to preserve the building.

In a letter to the vicar, dated 27 September 1828, the second of his replies to Lyon's queries about the *Report* (appendix 4), Wilkins estimated that the cost of its implementation would be £500. He also suggested an alternative, the erection of a campanile 'at the same expense, somewhere within the precincts, but removed from sight so as not to call for much attention to its architectural character', a solution adopted on the continent and formerly 'in this Kingdom. I have seen the original design for the Campanile, which was intended by the founder of King's College Chapel, to be erected on a spot west of the great door, where the intended foundations were laid, and may still be seen.'[19]

In truth, the parish could not afford to undertake his plan of restoration, although Wilkins generously offered 'at all times to give directions and sketches for carrying into effect the measures I have recommended, without further expense to the Churchwardens'. The Vestry was forced to accept Mr Percy's original plan for a wooden truss. Wilkins was paid £63. 3s. 6d. for his 'Survey and Report respecting the repairs of the Church including Travelling expenses'.

As for the projected renovations at Norwich, Wilkins was quite prepared to utilise modern materials and structural techniques to assure the conservation and continued use of the Abbey church, while endeavouring to maintain its historical integrity. In that letter of 27 September to the vicar Wilkins stressed the importance of the 'preservation of our national monuments' and at the end of the *Report* he described a procedure which anticipated the criteria of the most scrupulous Victorian restorers:

> In executing all works of repair or restoration; the utmost care should be taken to follow the original form in mouldings and ornaments...A *squeeze* in clay may be taken from the most perfect of these and a cast in plaster made from it. From authorities alone thus obtained the workmen employed should be compelled to copy. In the present enlightened age, some intelligent mind will always be found to direct the attention of the artisan to correct and classical examples for their imitation.[20]

XII

A temple of the arts

The award of the commission for the combined National Gallery and Royal Academy in 1832 should have been the culmination of Wilkins's career and not, as it became, the signal of its decline.[1] Thackeray, in a pithy sample of the criticism in the popular press, dubbed it 'a little gin shop of a building'.[2] Such sardonic sallies tarnished the renown of the Greek Revival by ascribing the weaknesses of the executed building almost entirely to the style and the architect, rather than to the parsimony of the Governments which Wilkins served.

Yet, beyond its potential prestige, the commission, with that already begun in 1823 for the British Museum, realised the ambitions of a broad group of progressive English artists and dilettanti who believed that native art and patronage would benefit by the improvement and greater availability of collections of works of art. Wilkins discussed these issues and the social significance of art and education in his fascinating *Letter to Lord Viscount Goderich*.

The pamphlet, dated 20 November 1831, might have been written, in part, to lay claim to the commission, since Goderich was a member of the 'Committee for the Superintendence of the National Gallery Pall Mall' with a clutch of fellow trustees of the British Museum who were close to Wilkins, notably Aberdeen, Beaumont, Long (now Lord Farnborough) and Lawrence. However, Wilkins did not finish the *Letter* until two months after the consideration by the trustees of the Gallery, meeting at Lord Dover's house on 16 September 1831, of his proposal to convert the old Royal Mews at the head of Whitehall into accommodation for both institutions and the Public Records.[3] In the *Letter* he recalled that the Whig Prime Minister, Lord Grey, whom he likened to that 'great statesman and economist', Necker, favoured the construction of a new building to house the National Collection as against its exhibition in the British Museum, enabling him 'to concentrate the public offices, and at the same time afford to the Royal Academy a greater degree of accommodation than they now possess in Somerset House' and 'for the more safe custody of the national collection of pictures'.[4] His decision to proceed with publication of the *Letter* early in 1832 indicates that he had still not been officially confirmed as architect.

The *Letter* reflects the mixture of altruism and ambition that motivated Wilkins. He was genuinely concerned about the distasteful contrast between England and 'every nation on the continent, whether free or despotic, [which] is engaged on the formation of galleries truly national', and, more specifically, with the lamentable condition of the temporary National Gallery at 100 Pall Mall, formerly J. J. Angerstein's house. It was 'ill calculated' for the display of the paintings which were

> subject at all times to the ravages of the elements. The principal room is above the Offices of the Keeper, where the accidental ignition of a chimney flue would subject the whole to immediate perdition; its little elevation in the midst of a neighbourhood of lofty houses has made it necessary to build the shafts of a most portentious height, and the adjoining premises having been pulled down to be rebuilt on a new plan, these lofty pieces of feeble brickwork left exposed to the assaults of the periodic gales frequently destructive to buildings and chimneys of more substantial construction.[5]

In more personal terms, the plan to rehouse both the National Collection and the Royal Academy, which though it dated back to 1824 had languished until 1831 largely due to a recession in the national economy, offered Wilkins a means of retrieving his reputation after the virtual ignoring of his design for the Cambridge University Library and the rejection of that for the Duke of York Monument.

In 1825 Nash had conceived a scheme for the development of the Charing Cross and St Martin's Lane area (soon to be known as

Trafalgar Square), published in 1826, that introduced a National Gallery on the site of the old Royal Mews and a new Academy modelled on the Parthenon opposite Smirke's Royal College of Physicians, 1822–4. In 1825 the Academicians appointed a committee at the suggestion of Shee and Flaxman 'to take into consideration what may be the wants of the Royal Academy in the event of the erection of a new building'.[6] Wilkins did not serve on it but surely knew of its deliberations through his friend, Wyatville, who, with Smirke, acted as architectural adviser. He could have learned of the private talks of the trustees of the National Collection from Aberdeen and Lawrence, apart from other contacts, and, as a supporter of the British Institution, had prior notice of the offer the Directors made in 1828 to donate £4,000 towards the erection of an extension to the Pall Mall Gallery. Earlier, on 12 February 1827, Wilkins perhaps tested the seriousness of the alternate proposal to install the National Collection in the British Museum by giving Benjamin West's 'The Banishment of Cleombrotus by Leonidas' to the trustees; this is not to belittle his generosity.[7] They passed the painting on to the trustees of the National Collection, in reality to themselves acting in a different capacity, thus suggesting a preference in official circles for a separate building.

Certainly Wilkins approached Aberdeen and a forceful young Whig Member of Parliament, Agar-Ellis (a trustee of the British Museum, later Lord Dover), to promote his scheme, as he related in the evidence he gave on the commission before the Select Committee on Arts and Manufactures in 1836. He averred that the suggestion to erect a building for both the Gallery and Academy 'originated with me' and that since 'the site was about to be converted into shops', he had taken 'the liberty of calling at Lord Dover's and Lord Aberdeen's'.[8] Dover had then communicated his idea to the Prime Minister, 'in consequence of which I had to wait on Lord Grey', whereupon he had prepared plans. (In subsequent evidence he remarked that Shee had later also urged Grey to appropriate part of 'the National Gallery to the Royal Academy'.) Among the letters owned by W. P. Wilkins is one from Lord Grey, dated 28 May 1833, thanking the architect for a copy of *Magna Graecia*.

Wilkins's version of the events preceding the acceptance of his design by the Government clearly exaggerates his contribution, since he had synthesised Nash's proposals. But, as at Downing College, he supplied a timely project which simultaneously appeared to answer the needs of the Gallery, already too large for the Pall Mall house by 1828, and the undertaking given by Goderich to rehouse the Royal Academy. In his evidence to the Select Committee, he also telescoped the process by which he was appointed and failed to explain that his initial design had envisaged merely a conversion of the Mews for the Gallery and Academy with, as a further sop to the tight-fisted Government, accommodation for the Public Records. That scheme had been sent straightway by its influential backers to the Treasury and thereafter to the specially instituted and so-called 'Committee of Noblemen and Gentlemen', which numbered other potential allies of his, Ridley Colbourne, Lords Duncannon and Lansdowne, Joseph Hume, Shee and Samuel Rogers (who became a trustee of the National Gallery in 1834). They approved his plan but considered that the estimated cost of the conversion of the Mews, £35,000, merited the construction of a new building and, not unnaturally, asked him to submit a revised design. Influenced by the 1828 Report of the Select Committee on Public Buildings which had demanded open competitions for official commissions, Cockerell and Nash were also invited to prepare designs.

Their drawings have disappeared but it is evident that Wilkins's submission was more economical.[9] As against Cockerell's projected building of 400 feet in length with the Gallery raised above shops and estimated at £60,000, Wilkins offered one 460 feet long and 50 wide, accommodating the Gallery in the west wing over the Public Records and the Academy in the east wing, all for £43,425, a sum which included his fee and that of a clerk of works, but not a heating system. It was to be built in brick with stone facings, ornamented at the centre by steps leading to a portico topped by a dome, and flanked by two shallow pavilions. Though the Committee found the façade to be 'too contracted and too insignificant' they knew that it stood the best chance of surviving the Commons for, while Peel carried the Tories in support of Whig policy on this matter, there was a strident minority which hoped that, when the plan was tabled on 17 July, 'they should not be called upon to erect palaces for the exhibition of works of the Fine Arts, when a famishing population was crying for bread'.[10] Wilkins, too, had the wit to seize the commission in the hope of persuading the Government to increase the grant at a later stage. Indeed he hoped to capture the commission to lay out Trafalgar Square with his temple of the arts as its crowning monument.

The official announcement of the project in July 1832 with Wilkins as architect won wide approval in the artistic fraternity. At the Academy Dinner held on the 24th Wilkins was accorded the honour of a toast proposed by the president, Shee.[11] Sadly Wilkins's reply was not recorded but it is likely that he voiced sentiments similar to those stated in the dedication of *Prolusiones Architectonicae* (1837). Therein he praised Grey for 'the stimulus given to the dormant state of the Fine Arts by the construction of a Royal Academy in conjunction with a National Gallery; the one to enshrine the precious remains of the departed genius, and the other to encourage the exertions of the present race in seeking to obtain a like degree of immortality'.

The dual building went far to satisfy Reynolds's dictum in the first Discourse of 1769 that the Academy should be 'a repository of the great examples of art'. That had become the goal of an active corps within the academy beginning with James Barry and was adopted by the Regency generation. In July 1797 Barry had published his *Letter to the Dilettanti Society* in which he argued that the formation of a national collection of art, including sculpture, would serve to foster native patronage and creative talent and quash 'the ill-founded, scurrilous aspersions of the climate, genius and capacity of the people of our islands' expressed, in his opinion, most unjustly by Winckelmann.[12] After sundry asides on the myth of the Venetian secret of painting and the failings of picture cleaners, he declared,

> I have long seen...that without some proper public collection of ancient art, to refer to occasionally, both our pupils and our public would be in the same bewildered situation so emphatically alluded to in the New Testament, of the people without guides, exposed to every imposture of 'Lo! here is Christ. Lo! there is Christ.' – This is Titian's manner – No, that was his manner.[13]

Prince Hoare advanced the argument more diplomatically by publishing detailed accounts of the superior facilities enjoyed by the institutions at Madrid, Milan, St Petersburg and Vienna in *Extracts from a Correspondence with the Academies of Vienna and St Petersburg* (1802) and *Academic Annals* (1805). But by 1813 he, too, was exasperated, writing in the first chapter of the second part of his *Epochs of the Arts including Hints on the Rise and Progress of Painting and Sculpture in Great Britain* that

> few degrees of inadequacy would be found to exceed those of the provision for study in the Royal Academy. . . Scanty in its supplies of Models and Plaster Casts; the latter crowded into so narrow a space, that it is difficult for the students even to obtain a proper view of them,. . . not a single original Picture is to be found in its Schools

while the library consisted of only 'a few translations from two classic authors'.[14] However, as has been noted, by 1813 the library had been improved and the cast collection was to be enlarged with the aid of the Prince Regent, though it was not exhibited properly until the completion of Wilkins's building. Similarly the adjacent position of the National Gallery was to greatly extend the facilities for the study of Old Master paintings afforded by the School of Painting from 1816.

In the *Letter* Wilkins wove the plea for the construction of an Academy and Gallery into a review of the state of the fine arts in England, echoing those other Regency reformers. The ideals which motivated them had been outlined by the first members of the British Institution at a Select Meeting on 18 June 1805. They were 'convinced that the pre-eminence, which the imitative arts attained in certain distinguished periods of ancient Greece and modern Italy, was produced, not by fortuitous circumstance, but by great and splendid patronage'.[15] The Fine Arts were entitled to

> respect and reward, not simply on account of the innocent and intellectual gratification which they afford, nor merely because they cultivate and civilize the human mind. In a country like our own, *they essentially and abundantly contribute to the national prosperity and resources*. It must be obvious that the present flourishing state of our manufactures and export trade, is greatly owing to the progress of the fine arts under His MAJESTY'S JUDICIOUS PATRONAGE; and that in hardware, cotton, and porcelain, and in every other article to which the industry and

attention of the British artisan has been applied, superior beauty of form, and refined elegance of ornament, have contributed to make our manufactures coveted throughout the world.

In his *Letter* Wilkins regretted the failure of the majority of the legislators and leaders of society to recognise the validity of such assertions. Indeed Wilkins's summation of the situation in 1831 was closer to that of Shee who, in *Rhymes on Art or the Remonstrance of a Painter* (1805), had written, 'All patriotic interest in the cultivation of British genius appears to be at an end.'[16] And in 1835 the Select Committee on Arts and Manufactures was to be called to investigate the inferior state of English design.

While millions had been lavished on palaces, Wilkins lamented – probably an euphemism for the Regent's Park scheme as well as a reference to Nash's notorious reconstruction of Buckingham House – but 'a few thousands have been refused to the annual augmentation of the national collection and the intellectual gratification of the people'.[17] Successive Governments had ignored the example set by the last three sovereigns in founding and fostering the Royal Academy and British Museum and, in the case of George IV, patronising contemporary artists and supporting the creation of a National Gallery. Their relative enlightenment had been confounded by the false economic attitudes of recent administrators who were in a position to provide the kind of substantial patronage unavailable to private individuals. The former were typified by men like the Duke of Wellington who had 'exercised an influence less beneficial to the arts and sciences than that of any of his predecessors' in the office of Prime Minister, 1828–30.[18]

Wellington was the villain of Wilkins's piece because he had failed to retrieve the Army Monument scheme, intended to immortalise the courage of the troops he had commanded. For himself, Wilkins complained, twelve months' work and 'upwards of five hundred pounds' in perfecting designs and producing a model were as nothing, but, far more reprehensible, 'the memory of Britannia's heroes' was merely 'perpetuated by the sod that covers them'.[19] More recently Wellington had, so Wilkins judged, manoeuvred him out of the commission for the Duke of York Monument. (He might have added that Wellington had also vigorously opposed the

University College Bill.) Wilkins then narrated the events as he saw them. Wellington had insisted that the monument to the Duke, who had died in the summer of 1827, be modelled upon the Roman Trajan Column, against the express wishes of the King who would have preferred a triumphal arch. Wilkins likened that column to a 'gigantic candlestick' in the *Letter*, and so had produced a version of his Dublin and Yarmouth Pillars, with a statue of the Duke at its pinnacle and a larger pedestal which was ornamented at each corner by symbolic figures seated above lists of British victories in the Napoleonic Wars (Pl. 90).[20] The pedestal would have served as the vestibule to an internal staircase, its interior articulated with statues in niches and lit by a clerestory (Pl. 91). The King, however, temporarily outflanked Wellington, and the competitors, drawn from the 'Attached Architects', the Academicians and Associates of the Academy, including Benjamin Wyatt, 'the Duke's architect' (he was altering Apsley House at the time), were invited to submit triumphal arch designs appropriate for an entrance to the Horse Guards Parade. Wilkins won that round on the recommendation of the King and the Committee of Taste with a design that has since disappeared, but which was briefly described in the *Gentleman's Magazine*, following its exhibition at the Academy in 1837, as a 'large arch between four columns, and an equestrian statue above, looking forward, accompanied by groups of trophies'.[21] The reviewer compared it with Nash's Marble Arch, which Wilkins would not have welcomed since, in the *Letter*, he had described that as 'a little piece of cabinet work'.[22] (In 1834 Wilkins was to form makeshift substitutes for the unexecuted Army and Navy Monuments by placing in the friezes of the east and west passage entrances of the National Gallery building reliefs of the battles of Trafalgar and Waterloo that Baily and Westmacott had originally executed for the Marble Arch.)[23] Yet, when all seemed set fair for Wilkins, Wellington engaged in a stubborn resistance, now with a monarch and not an emperor, and insisted that a column be erected. The competition lapsed until 1831 by which time George IV was dead. Wellington carried the day and Benjamin Wyatt captured the honours.

Thus Wilkins might be pardoned the volley of taunts fired against Wellington in this part of the *Letter*. He accused him of not being able to distinguish between the Athenian Parthenon and its pastiche at Edinburgh, the National Monument on Calton Hill, begun in 1822 but never completed – a barb also aimed at Cockerell who had received the commission through the good offices of Lord Aberdeen – and of taking no interest in sculpture beyond the manufacture of false limbs.[24] 'The only *columns* of which he knows anything', Wilkins punned, 'or that he contemplates with satisfaction are those which he could move to support the *capitals* of foreign potentates', while his correspondence with the architects competing for the Duke of York Monument 'was couched somewhat in the style of a man who may be supposed to have required from some half dozen of shoemakers, *Wellingtons*, on trial, and, having fitted himself to his satisfaction, desires them to send and take back their rejected samples'.[25]

Before he rashly charged and convicted that 'economist' and his like, Wilkins had commended the endeavours of the Society of Dilettanti to foster the arts, and especially architecture. The members had thrown their weight behind the creation of the Royal Academy and, in March 1774, had established two scholarships for students to work in Italy and Greece for three years, the first being awarded to Jefferys and Pars, and had also instituted the appointment of a painter and a sculptor to the society, beginning with Knapton and Adye.[26] As importantly, to Wilkins's mind, they had financed expeditions to Greece and Asia Minor and the publication of the findings. But their contribution to artistic education and cultural enlightenment would be limited in England without a policy of state patronage. Wilkins insisted that:

> The countenance of the government, and some assistance from the public purse, are essential to the due cultivation as well as to the proficiency of those who embrace the practice of the arts as a means of subsistence, if, through their agency, we hope to exult the national character...we may talk to all eternity of the elasticity of genius to spring up in spite of opposition or neglect.[27]

Governments should assign annually the 'trifling sum of six thousand pounds' for properly conducted competitions in each of the artistic disciplines and build a gallery for 'Native Art [foreshadowing one of the recommendations of the 1836 *Report* of the Select Committee on Arts and Manufactures]'. Such competitions would be preferable to the payment of subsidies to members of the Royal Academy, which could invite favouritism, and might help to redress the imbalance that existed, for example, between the prosperity of the portrait painter, Sir Thomas Lawrence, and the poverty of the History painter, William Hilton. He was impatient with the Directors of the British Institution (and thus with is president, Aberdeen) for having mounted in 1830 an exhibition of paintings by Lawrence, 'who in his life time enjoyed and abused' patronage 'to an extent beyond any one instance of previous occurence'.[28] The distribution of architectural commissions was equally irregular as exemplified by the 1818 Church Act and the National Monument débâcle. Taking issue with the Report of the 1828 Select Committee on Public Buildings, he thought that official competitions should be limited to experienced architects, not least because their chances of professional advancement had been diminished by the consolidation of the Board of Works with the Office of Woods and Forests; evidently he had forgotten his own dramatic entrance into the profession as an untried architect. More fundamental was the need for proper courses in architecture. 'On the subject of the study of architecture, which it is the main object of these pages to enforce and promote, much has yet to be performed, for hitherto the Academy has done little, and the government nothing.'[29] He wanted a separate school of architecture to be set up under the auspices of the Academy in part of St James's Palace, where students would be taught by full-time lecturers and the study of models and casts from celebrated buildings would be essential. Here Wilkins offered a response to widespread criticism summed up by a spokesman who, in an 1831 issue of *The Library of the Fine Arts*, had bewailed 'poor Architecture!... Why are its students deprived even of lectures? Why are there not rooms open for them to study the antique, and to draw from the most precious remains of antiquity?'[30]

Wilkins regarded education as the key to the reform and nurture of British culture. His views were progressive, and stimulated, as he acknowleged, by two contemporary books. The first was Charles Babbage's *On the Economy of Machines and Manufactures*, not actually published until 1832 though Wilkins surely read and discussed the manuscript with Babbage (1792–1871), who invented the adding machine and took over the Lucasian Chair in Mathematics at Cambridge University from Wilkins's brother-in-law, Robert Woodhouse. The second and more relevant book was James Millingen's *Some Remarks on the State of Learning and Fine Arts in Great Britain; on the deficiencies of public institutions, and the necessity of a better improvement of knowledge and taste* (1831). Millingen (1774–1845) was an antiquary celebrated for his work on Greek vase painting who, in the same year, published *Ancient Coins of Greek Cities and Kings from Various Collections principally in Great Britain.*

Millingen supplied Wilkins with the quotation from Necker which appeared on the frontispiece of the *Letter*, 'Learning and Science repay the State with usury the assistance which the State affords to those who profess and cultivate them (*Comptes Rendues* (1788), I, p. 157).' Millingen, too, contrasted the poverty of English patronage with that of the continental powers, stressing the gap between the professions made in the preface to the Report of the Elgin Marbles Select Committee and the actual situation pertaining in British art after 1816. He had also condemned English educational and cultural institutions. The old universities were, in his words, 'ill constructed or grown so corrupted, that they are far from presenting the advantages which might be expected from them', and none of 'our Societies can properly be called learned...except the Royal Academy, [these] are properly clubs'.[31] The organisation of the Royal Society was 'vicious', while of the Society of Antiquaries 'little can be said. It has slumbered for years and nothing but the voice of a total reform can rouse it from its lethargy.' Like Wilkins, he had praise only for the Society of Dilettanti:

> The active and enlightened zeal of various British artists and travellers, and, in particular, the mission of the Dilettanti Society, have affected of late an almost entire change in an important branch of the Fine Arts. The magnificent remains of Architecture existing in Greece and Asia Minor, have afforded models for imitation, on principles entirely new, as well as details of execution of a beauty and elegance previously unknown.[32]

But the influence of the Dilettanti was confounded by the ignorance of the 'pretenders to taste' who were appointed to the Boards of Trustees of institutions like the British Museum; from that group, which included Aberdeen, Millingen only excepted Richard Payne Knight, who had been of 'great service to the Museum' and who 'would have done more, if he had not been checked by ministerial influence' and the disinterest of the average Member of Parliament.[33] These were the men (chaired by Henry Bankes, 1757–1834) who had turned the Select Committee on the Elgin Marbles into 'an assembly of traders to settle a commercial concern, rather than...the Representatives of a great nation, to determine the remuneration due to an individual of high rank distinguished by his zeal and love for the Fine-Arts, and who had conferred a signal benefit on his country'.[34] They still wanted to tax imported works of art (a practice that Flaxman had managed to curtail to some extent in 1796 with the assistance of Long, who was Joint Paymaster-General), forgetting that the Hamilton Collection of Greek Vases, for one, had boosted English manufactures, notably the Wedgwood Pottery: 'In a fiscal point of view, there can be no doubt that the money expended for the purchase of the collection in question, has been repaid a hundredfold to the nation at large, and proportionally to the revenue.'[35] Wilkins added a further gloss to that theme by pointing out that public architectural commissions could help to reduce the high rate of unemployment in London, and he apostrophised Millingen's thesis when he wrote in the *Letter* that the 'cause, therefore, of the arts is the cause of the nation'.[36]

Both Millingen and Wilkins founded their arguments upon an ethical and social interpretation of the significance of the arts that recalled a passage from Prince Hoare's *Epochs*, in which he had written that the arts of design possess the 'power of imparting virtuous pleasure;...of giving splendour to a Nation;...of strengthening and diffusing moral and religious impressions;...of aiding and enhancing various manufactures'.[37] Millingen declared that the ' experience of all ages shews indeed, that the stability and happiness of a nation depend on the degree of religious and moral principle by which it is animated, and we have every reason to believe that many of the evils which afflict us at the present day, must be attributed to the neglect of this vital principle'.[38] He hoped that such ideals would inspire legislators to 'be solicitous of the national glory, and by a due encouragement of Learning and the Fine Arts...enable England to resume the exalted literary and scientific rank she once held'.[39]

Pursuing the same theme, Wilkins warned that the French Revolution had been caused less by the radical theories of the 'philosophes' than the 'ignorance and depravity of the noblesse and in the exemptions of the privileged classes from the onerous impositions which thus pressed with a double weight upon the lower orders'.[40] The political attitude implied in that sentence is more clearly articulated in a succeeding paragraph, ending, 'those who are closer observers of mankind, and reason upon the experience of past ages, see the expediency of more equally balancing the claims of the several orders of society, and endeavour to regulate their policy that intellect may constantly operate against the encroachments of rank and riches, and vice versa'.[41]

Wilkins, like Agar-Ellis and Beaumont, saw his scheme for the combined Gallery and Academy in that social context, and it is worthy of note that the last sentence quoted above actually anticipated a remark to the same effect made by the Tory leader, Peel, in the debate on the commission in the Commons in July 1832.[42] In the *Letter* Wilkins also tried to obviate a current myth that the general public were disinterested in the purchase of works of art, writing, ' It is true that there still exists a propensity to mutilate all works of art within the reach of a walking stick or of missiles; but this propensity to gratuitous mischief would only be overcome by a more familiar acquaintance with works of art, which will in time diffuse its beneficial effects over the minds of the community.'[43] Similar optimism was expressed in evidence presented to the Select Committee on Arts and Manufactures, to the calling of which both the *Letter* and Millingen's *Remarks* could have contributed, and before which Wilkins was summoned to explain the design of the Gallery. Indeed, Wilkins was voicing a belief in the beneficial influence of the arts that was to become virtually sacrosanct. T. Greenwood in *Museums and Art Galleries* (1888) averred that as 'reading increases and Museums and Art Galleries multiply, crime decreases, so that these ideal institutions of the future will play, as they do now, an important economical part in the nation's life'.[44]

Despite Wilkins's strictures upon Parliamentarians in the *Letter*, a majority endorsed the construction of the Gallery and Academy in 1832. They were prepared to increase the original grant of £35,000 by £15,000 so that the front and sides of the proposed building could be faced with Portland stone and accommodation for the Keeper of the Gallery be introduced. Early in 1833, therefore, the Grey administration felt able to allow two further improvements in consultation with Wilkins, the transference to the Gallery of the space reserved for the Public Records and the addition of a semi-circular single storey gallery at the centre of the north side for the Academy Life School. Another change involving extra expenditure was the projection of the entrances to the passages giving access through the building to the Barracks on the west and Castle Street on the east side, the provision of which had been written into the specification. Hoping to take advantage of the apparent flexibility of the Government, Wilkins proposed changes to his design up until its approval by William IV in September 1833, striving to give it more of the monumentality of University College and more of the magnificence of the British Museum, and, more distantly, of Klenze's Glyptothek and Pinakothek, Munich and of Schinkel's Altes Museum, Berlin.[45]

To this end Wilkins petitioned Grey to advance the façade line some sixty feet into the area of the present square so that the building would stand on the crest of rising ground, and at the same time to re-align it at ninety degrees to Smirke's College of Physicians. Both suggestions would have resulted in the obscuring of the view of the portico of St Martin-in-the-Fields from the west side of the square. Although Wilkins had some support in official circles, his proposals particularly outraged the Duke of Northumberland and his fellow members of the Church Council. In Shee's words, Wilkins brought on 'one of those violent fits of the picturesque' that periodically troubled the 'Metropolitan mind'.[46]

As disastrous for Wilkins was the fact that the Church Council and the public became aware of his proposals at the same time as an inaccurate and coarse version of his incompletely developed façade was printed without permission by the editor of the *Literary Gazette*, William Jerdan, on 23 February 1833. That was twenty days after Wilkins had most reluctantly shown a model of the projected building to a select group, including members of the press, at the Office of Woods and Forests, and seven days after the publication of the first of two letters he addressed to the editor of *The Athenaeum*; the second, shorter letter appeared on 2 March and included censure of Jerdan. Headed 'On the Change in the Line of Front of the Buildings for the National Gallery', the first was the more reckless because it spread antagonism and failed to achieve his aim; indeed, he was forced to retract the wings. Instead of concentrating upon the justifiable reasons for the alteration of the façade line, Wilkins lashed out at Gibbs, Vitruvius and, indirectly, at the rising generation of Synthetic Classicists. Equally foolhardy, he confused the issue by entering into an apology for his Greek Revival work and ideal, neither well represented in this design. Oppressed by the frustration of his genuine desire to make the best use of the site and lack of sympathy with his wish to improve the scheme, and depressed by rejection in two recent major competitions, those for the Duke of York Monument and the Cambridge University Library, he made the mistake of baring his wounded pride in public, as he grudgingly admitted in the second letter, 'as to the vanity I displayed in the letter I first addressed to you, I acknowledge myself to be guilty of the charge to any extent it may please anonymous writers to assume or assert'. He merely exacerbated the criticism and rendered the commission, in the words of W. H. Leeds, 'the object of more general, unqualified and invidious censure' than any of 'our lately erected buildings'.[47]

He began the first letter by pointing out that the chosen line would cram the east wing up to the parish workhouse and prevent the layout of the new square from being symmetrical. So far so good, but he then discounted the loss of the view of the portico of St Martin's, by boasting that the Gallery portico would be a finer example of the Classical style: 'I should have passed a great many years of useless study if I could not design something very superior to St. Martins Church.' Worse, he set himself up as the arbiter of Classical probity, taking Gibbs to task for not having fronted the whole church with the portico and pronouncing that every

> portico whether at the end or in the centre of a long range of buildings should be, or appear to be the ornamental termination of two flank walls...this is the stigma which attaches to the majority of our public edifices; it is a disregard of principle for which we are justly censured by our continental neighbours: our porticoes generally speaking, appear to be mere *appliqués* stuck against a range of wall, more or less extensive.

He offered St Pancras Church and his own University College as exemplars of true practice, conveniently forgetting that St Paul's, Nottingham or even Grange Park and, of course, the National Gallery, failed to match this standard. Here were grounds enough for two of his most vociferous critics, Gwilt and the 'Pseudo architect', Charles Purser, to have a field day.[48] And he supplied yet more when he claimed that study of the principles of composition, and the contemplation of the principal remains of architecture in Europe; comparing them with the productions of Italy, France and Germany [presumably seen on his tour of 1816] have qualified me to form a judgement upon the pretensions of all, and have forced me to the conviction that the comparative degree of superiority of one building over another depends mainly upon the observance of the principles of our great and inimitable masters, the Greeks.

Purser, reflecting the re-awakening of an appreciation for the Renaissance Classical tradition, exhibited by Cockerell in his winning design for the Cambridge University Library, asked 'But why should the merits of every building be judged merely by reference to Grecian examples?'.

Subjectivity also tainted his comments on Vitruvius to whom he attributed the faults he saw in Gibbs's portico. With the advantages of deeper study during the intervening years since the publication of *The Civil Architecture* and the 'valuable' edition of the Treatise published by J. G. Schneider (1750–1822), *M. Vitruvii Pollionis de Architectura libri decem* (Leipzig, 1807), Wilkins now regarded Vitruvius as 'a man of moderate qualifications, envious and jealous of his contemporaries, vain and a plagiarist'; ironically the last phrase was turned against Wilkins by his critics. But even Schneider, Wilkins continued, had not shown that Vitruvius had developed a system 'founded upon a Grecian basis, but made his own by variations which his vanity leads him to consider as improvements', as in the erroneous account of the rules for making the intervals between columns in the different types of portico. And so on to his climax that 'it would have been better for modern architecture that the work of Vitruvius had never reached us; the errors it has propagated are numerous, and so rooted, that it will require the greatest efforts to erradicate them'. Wilkins pledged himself to effect that purgation and allowed his readers to believe that the National Gallery emulated 'the pure basis of Grecian excellence', adding, 'I cannot sacrifice what I feel to be true, at the shrine of humility.' If only he had; at least more fully than the admission made in the second letter of some of the building's lesser deficiencies which, with good cause, he blamed upon the budget. As it transpired, the evident aesthetic weaknesses of the façade both in the designs and as executed – its meagre proportions, its disjointed massing, and its curious mixture of Greek, Roman and Palladian features with the suggestion of an almost Baroque movement towards the centre, increased by the recession of the wings – hastened the demise of the archaeological Greek Revival in the metropolis and ultimately in England. As he prophesied in the first letter, his attempts to introduce Greek purity would, 'in all probability, meet with but little suport in the present age', and he tagged on the forlorn hope that 'posterity will appreciate them'.

His chief mistake was to advance those polemical arguments while defending what he must have known to be a poor design. He had occupied safer ground when he had presented a similar thesis, saving the comments on Vitruvius, in the *Appeal to the Senate on the Subject of the Plans for the University Library* (Cambridge, 1831). For example, he regretted that 'In the generality of modern designs the portico is...something stuck on, either to form a center, or break the extent of a lengthened line' whereas, since it is 'the principal part on which we depend for the effect of a building, because the eye is directed immediately to the center, our study should be to render it as faultless as possible, and therefore as conformable, as circumstances will admit, with the best examples of antiquity'. He had in mind the portico of his design for the library, preserved in drawings and engravings at the c.u.l. (Pl. 92). The design merits study in the context of the National Gallery commission as proving that Wilkins was still capable of producing noble architecture if not confounded by unreasonable specifications.

The ten column Corinthian portico was derived from the Temple of Jupiter Olympius at Athens, but more accurately than at University College, being placed at ground level and occupying the height of the two storey building at the centre of the main façade. The portico was integrated by continuous mouldings, an attic that was only interrupted by the pediment and planned to mask the skylights of the library proper on the upper floor, and the repetition of the pyramidal composition of the openings on the flanking bays in the triple stepped doorcases behind the portico. It spanned that part of the old library which he retained (Pl. 93). The Reverend G. A. Peacock, F.R.S., previously lecturer in mathematics at Trinity College and a member of the First Syndicate appointed to superintend the competition for the library, and a propagandist for Cockerell, conceded that the 'portico in front of his [Wilkins's] buildings, with all its accompanying decorations, would be nearly unrivalled in this country for propriety and good taste. And the same character of appropriateness and simple elegance, presents itself on every one of the other fronts of his buildings.'[49] (That description precludes the association with the first competition of a wash perspective drawing at the C.U.L. which shows conically turreted belvederes, replete with sculpture, placed at the corners of the attic behind the main portico, and alterations to the side elevation, including the insertion of a pediment capping the four corner bays and the substitution of engaged columns for pilasters in the centre.[50] Almost certainly this is the revised elevation mentioned on page 20 of the *Appeal*. Though Wilkins expressed himself dissatisfied with the result, he may have entered it in the second competition of 1830, or the third in 1835, in an attempt to satisfy the preference of the Syndicate for more ornate designs.) The original design for the longer façade, to face King's Chapel, would have been equally imposing and refined. It harked back to Downing in the coupled antae, framing the slightly projected centre section, itself more reminiscent of Grange Park. The junction between the main portico and this side was nicely managed by two pilasters more widely separated than those at the other end of the elevation. The style was dignified, embodying the rational revivalism he advocated in the *Appeal*; architects ought to be directed by 'the spirit and genius which guided the great Architects of Antiquity'.

In the *Appeal* he also wrote more rationally than in *The Athenaeum* letters about the process of imitation and the quality of his own work.

> I will venture to assert that it [the style of his design for the library] is Grecian; although in the opinion of some it may be thought that style alone is entitled to the designation, wherein no other characters than those observed in ancient examples are introduced. The distinction between Greek and Roman Architecture does not consist in a difference of principles, but of proportions and details, and chiefly of the latter.

He admitted that the fenestration, including a quasi-Palladian opening in the court, and the attic in his design offended Classical practice but excused them on the grounds of necessity; he had read his Laugier (Pl. 94). The attic, too, added greater height without spoiling the proportions of the Greek columns. 'All modern Architecture must', he continued, 'therefore be regarded as the adaptation of the principal characteristics of Grecian or Roman edifices to the exigencies of modern life. We distinguish our buildings by either one or the other designation, according to the proportions and details we introduce, but we cannot call them pure examples of either style.'

The *Appeal* had been written to counter the partisan pamphlets of Peacock and the Reverend William Whewell (to be Master of Trinity from 1841 to 1866), who had campaigned respectively in support of Cockerell and of Rickman and Hutchinson, the winners of the first and second stages of the competition. Yet both had praise for Wilkins's design and it was one of the ironies of the competition that, had the judges abided by the instructions distributed to the competitors, he might have triumphed. Whewell hoped 'for the sake of fairness, that the plan of Mr. Wilkins would find, what it has many claims to, some intelligent and active advocates', and Peacock noted that Wilkins

> has followed very strictly the instructions of the Syndicate, and the arrangements of the interior of his building as well as its exterior, shew the hand of a great master of his art...His Library without much splendour or spaciousness, is full of accommodations; and though I might venture to point out many objections to the crowding together of his Museums and Lecture Rooms, I must consider them as originating in the precise instructions of the Syndicate.[51]

Those instructions had been agreed in July 1829 and sent to Burton, Cockerell, Rickman and Wilkins, who were asked to return designs by November.[52] The library was to be sufficiently high to accommodate galleries and 'to form a complete square' on the first floor above communicating Schools of Divinity, Law, Physic and Arts in that part of the building adjacent to King's Chapel. The Syndicate also required a Registry and Record Office at the east end of the Law School, well lit museums 'en suite' from the north west side for Geology, Mineralogy, Zoology and Botany, a workshop and two lecture theatres, respectively seating 400–500 and 250–300, situated on the north side and served by a model and apparatus room. The smaller theatre for the Plumian Professor of Astronomy should 'admit the *introduction* of the sun's light for two or three hours in the middle of the day'. These requirements stood, with certain changes including the stipulation that the designs be in the Greek style, for the second competition. This was forced by the outcry against Cockerell's wayward interpretation of the instructions, especially in his richer alternate design which the Syndicate wished to build.

As Peacock had to admit, Wilkins's compact plan cleverly fulfilled the original instructions, comprising a rectangle about a central court with a one storey three sided section. He was at his best in the octagonal vestibules linking the four parts of the library and masking pairs of circular stairs to the galleries. Wilkins published his *Letter to the Members of the Senate* in February and then his *Appeal* in March 1831 to claim common justice, writing in the latter that the particular indulgence granted to Cockerell by the Syndicate 'must very materially effect the confidence, which, in any future competition of a similar nature, would be reposed in their judgement'. He alluded to the greater cost of the rival designs and exposed two faults in Cockerell's ground-plan, one of measurement and the other of access to the work rooms, 'little omissions which only show that it may be necessary to look after an Architect'. The pamphleteers and Syndicate members had made the cardinal error of judging the designs 'NOT AS THEY NOW APPEAR, BUT FOR WHAT THEY MAY BE MADE'. The controversy and a lack of funds stalled progress towards the erection of the library until the winter of 1835 when the architects were invited to submit further designs; in 1834 each, excepting Cockerell, had accepted a payment of one hundred guineas. When the new plans were exhibited at the old library in April 1836 Romilly was unimpressed by Cockerell's winning design and unsympathetic towards Wilkins: 'Wilkins's is not exhibited because he had pettishly sd. he would send none, but afterwards changed his mind – his plan is worthless'.[53] Without conclusive evidence, it seems that Wilkins had re-entered his revised design, which despite the towers was in an outmoded style, specific in its classicism and precise in articulation, whereas Cockerell's elevations chart the change in taste, being eclectic and plastic.

Even three years earlier Wilkins's restrained style was losing favour and this partly explains the adverse reaction to his design for the National Gallery when it was published in February 1833. Nevertheless, the appearance of the pirated engraving of his model in the

Literary Gazette had some positive results for Wilkins. First of all the engraving greatly exaggerated the size of the arched openings then intended to front the passages, and of the lanterns above. This supplied useful, if unwelcome, ammunition for Wilkins in his successful effort to reduce the passages to footpaths and to redesign the entrances with square-headed openings. In the second place the engraving exaggerated the lowness of the façade which helped Wilkins, albeit to a small extent, to achieve an increase in its height. Indeed Colonel Sir Edward Cust (1794–1878), a vociferous Member of Parliament, distributed a print of the *Literary Gazette* engraving alongside a taller Neo-Renaissance scheme drawn for him by Charles Barry with the purpose of inducing the government to require of Wilkins another design for a loftier structure. On 25 April Wilkins wrote to Lord Duncannon, Commissioner of the Office of Woods and Forests, suggesting that the façade be raised by 5 feet, bringing it to the level of St Martin's and an adjacent house in Pall Mall East and masking the roof of the Barracks behind. He wrote again three days later arguing against an increase of more than 5 feet as it would interfere with the internal plan and diminish the illumination of the top-lit picture galleries. That was academic for, by then, he had agreed with the committee and the Government to restrict the increase to one foot as a means of effecting savings following the reception of the disquietingly high tenders. These finally determined that the wings should be retracted to reduce the quantity of building materials.

The lowest tender amounted to £76,867 as against Wilkins's revised estimate of £62,000. The sum shocked the Government, though it compared favourably with the £70,000 set aside for the construction of the north wing of the British Museum on which work had just begun. Fearing an outcry in Parliament, the Government virtually abandoned the scheme to build the Gallery and Academy, not least since Wilkins's explanation of the mounting costs was unconvincing and, on 12 August, Duncannon timidly proposed to the Commons that the National Collection be exhibited in Inigo Jones's Banqueting Hall. 'I should state how deeply I must be personally affected by such a decision', a distraught Wilkins wrote two days later, 'Your Lordship cannot be expected to be fully aware of this change of plans on my professional practice but I know it *must be* such as will leave me no option but that of retiring altogether from practice.'[54]

Ultimately, the Members of Parliament saved the commission and on 11 September Wilkins was ordered to proceed with the building. The favourable vote emboldened him to make at least one further attempt to improve the façade before September. Writing to Spring-Rice, the Chancellor of the Exchequer, on 24 August 1833, Wilkins sought his sanction not merely for the reduction of the passages to footpaths and the substitution of square-headed openings, but also for the omission of the flanking pairs of Corinthian columns salvaged from the Carlton House portico that he had been required to use, which would render the façade 'more in conformity with your notion of an unbroken line'.[55] Incidentally, Wilkins seems to have been prepared to adopt the Corinthian Order of Holland's Carlton House portico for the main portico of his building, since it was derived from the so-called 'Poikele Stoa' at Athens, published in the first volume of the *Antiquities of Athens* (1762). In a further letter dated 10 September, confirming that he would wait upon the King at three o'clock the next day at St James's, he wrote that he had canvassed the support of Lord Auckland.[56] The King agreed to the major changes but not to the exclusion of the columns (although it transpired that only the bases and capitals had escaped deterioration), nor to a minor revision to the rear elevation of the footpaths.

However, these may not have been the only improvements Wilkins tried to secure at the audience. The account printed in *The Athenaeum* on 14 September noted that 'Some alterations in the elevation' had been put to the King and referred to the examination of models. In addition to the models representing the building and its 'proportionate magnitudes' within the square, mentioned by Wilkins in his letter of 24 August to Spring-Rice, it is possible that he produced a model or a drawing of a more substantially revised structure similar to that exhibited at the Academy in 1835 on the same sheet as an elevation of the façade as built. Of this the critic of the *Gentleman's Magazine* wrote, 'It is shown as intended to be finished, compared with what Mr. Wilkins would have made it.'[57] The only clue he gave to the difference was a phrase about additional height which does not preclude the possibility that the sheet was copied by C. Aitchison, A.R.A. and exhibited at the Academy in 1891 (Pl. 95).[58] The upper elevation shows the buildings as executed, though the turrets at either side have openings without fretwork. The lower elevation, wrongly identified as Wilkins's original design in the inscription, has the revised articulation to the footpath entrances but is given greater monumentality by the projection of six column Corinthian porticoes topped by domes on either wing, resembling his original scheme for the side ranges of University College, London. The domes and sculpture would have augmented the grandeur and elevation of the façade, aspirations of Wilkins.

At the audience the King signed the floor plans Wilkins had drawn in May 1833, now preserved at the RA. (Pl. 96). Obviously maximum space at minimum cost had been the maxim forced upon him – the Working Drawing for the basement of the west wing actually includes accommodation, not executed, at the rear for soldiers from the Barracks (Pl. 97).[59] Only the Great Hall had the grand dimensions expected in a national building of such importance. Before alteration, initially by E. M. Barry in 1856, it spanned the whole space behind the portico as shown in the Working Drawings made in the spring of 1833 (Pls. 98 and 99). Still, at the lower level Wilkins crammed in two vestibules for the institutions, an office for the secretary of the Academy and a sculpture gallery, and above he raised the dome on a tall drum so as to insert a Drawing room for the students of the Academy, to the detriment of its external proportions. Subsequently the middle part of the Great Hall was handed over to the Gallery to provide hanging space for large paintings. The hall was also more ornamented than the unadorned interiors of the Gallery and Academy. Plain Neo-Renaissance doorways opened on to the staircases that led to the main, upper floors. At this level and in the centre stood eight columns and four pilasters of the Corinthian Order supporting a glazed lantern placed behind the dome, strengthened by cast iron plates and buttressed by cast iron beams to the side walls of the hall (Pl. 100). The beams also supported four large skylights, which, with the proto-Thrasyllan openings in the upper level of the rear wall, lit the vestibules (Pls. 101 and 102). The light from the former passed through pierced semi-circular coves.

Once beyond the Great Hall, the floor plans of each wing were virtually duplicated for economy. There were three large galleries, 50 by 35 feet, one 50 by 36 feet, two others 50 by 14 feet and a cabinet approximately 14 feet square, an arrangement partly determined by the toplighting and partly by Wilkins's wish to hang the paintings by School and size. The main difference occurred on the lower floor in the internal entrances from the passages, the disposition of the flanking interiors and their construction. On the Academy side, the west entrance was recessed behind two columns and led to the Hall of Casts, which had two thin piers along the centre line, while the east was a simple opening leading to separate doorways to the Council Room and library, which were divided by a wall with a communicating door in the middle. In the Gallery wing, the public had access by plain openings to the Halls of Casts of Antique Statues and Architectural Models, with piers forming central corridors. Incidentally, Wilkins struck another blow for his profession by assigning two rooms on the upper floor of the Academy, on either side of the staircase, to the display of architectural drawings and models.

Demolition of the Royal Mews began the day after the inspection of the plans by William IV. Almost immediately the excavations revealed 'the bed of an ancient rivulet, the stagnant weeds of which were ten feet deeper'.[60] So the foundations had to be dug deeper on the west side and extra concrete poured in, adding £912 to the costs, though Wilkins turned the problem to his advantage by introducing a basement underneath the Gallery wing. The work was carried on behind large hoardings and not dignified by a foundation laying ceremony, which led a contributor to the *Spectator* of 15 February 1834 to suggest that the Government wished to hide the 'Ministerial Folly' of building Wilkins's 'puny' and 'shapeless' architectural 'toadstool'. Over the ensuing year he was embroiled in wrangles with Cust over the installation of sculpture, so bothersome that he abandoned the idea after some statuary had been added on the side elevations and in the niches of the front. Thereafter the intended order of construction – the eastern wing, the centre, the western wing – caused him unwarranted difficulty. The National Collection was to have been placed temporarily in the Academy wing awaiting completion of the Gallery, but, despite the fact that in January 1834 Smirke had written to the Office of Woods and Forests expressing anxiety for the safety of the paintings, the Academicians forced their will upon the Government and took up their new quarters in September 1836, so that the collection was not installed in the Gallery until the spring of 1838.[61]

Meanwhile Wilkins was called before the Select Committee on Arts and Manufactures and questioned about the design of the Gallery on 1 and 8 July 1836.[62]. He had a good case to make about the toplighting in the galleries. The skylights, like the fire arches under the upper floor of the Gallery and other beams in the structure were made of cast iron (Pls. 103 and 104). 'In our galleries the skylights are immensely large and immensely heavy;...we have thirty-five feet long by twenty-six feet wide, there is ample light, there is abundance of light, it is so much more easy to modify the light than add to it, and I was determined that they should have enough.' The weight of the lanterns, however, restricted the dimensions of the galleries which consequently proved to be somewhat airless.

> Allow me to state [Wilkins told the Committee] all these walls are essential (pointing to plan) (Keeper's residence) ...These cross walls cannot be removed (Galleries) because all our skylights are constructed of cast iron, for the sake of durability, and they are so extremely heavy that we are obliged to make their span as short as possible, that restricts in a great measure the size of the Gallery.

In the choice of toplighting he doubtless followed the lead taken by Soane at Dulwich in 1812, and previously adopted by Turner for his private gallery. According to his son-in-law, the Reverend William Kingsley, Wilkins had consulted Turner: 'Old Turner told me that Wilkins made a wooden model for the rooms and the lighting of them & asked the opinion of most of the Royal Academy as to the fitness, and that he took all pains as to getting the rooms good for their purpose.'[63]

When asked if there was sufficient light in the front of the building Wilkins quite properly reminded his interrogators of the events of February 1833. 'Certainly and there would have been in the rear, only certain gentlemen amateurs chose to thrust us up into a corner where we could get no light.' There reason was on his side; not so in his defence of the small capacity of the Gallery. The problem loomed large at the Select Committee for there was concern that the available exhibition space would not allow for the future expansion of the National Collection. (Indeed, by April 1838 only 150 of the 160 paintings could be hung.) Wilkins started this part of his evidence on the wrong foot. Questioned whether he had followed the arrangement of any foreign gallery, he replied, 'O no;' because these were more calculated to show off the architecture of the rooms than to exhibit the greatest number of pictures in a given space...Now there is the Louvre, everybody talks in raptures of the magnificence and extent of the Louvre...They have altered the disposition of light since, but when I saw it there was only 1,770 feet of lineal measure, so that if you added to our gallery two rooms of fifty feet square you would have the same lineal extent as they originally had in the Louvre.

His bluster betrayed awareness of the practical and aesthetic superiority of the major continental galleries. Instead of quite fairly putting the blame on the Government's parsimony, he gave extravagant estimates of the capacity of his Gallery, and claimed that it would equal the best galleries in Europe for the exhibition of pictures. In his opinion it would be 'fifty years before you could occupy the whole' of the hanging space 'because I should hope that the Trustees of the National Gallery would never accept any picture but what is of the highest class'. And to a later question on the same theme he answered, 'There is ample space; there is not one of the three principal rooms that is not amply long to show any picture of any dimensions. In short, if you were to go to the end of these galleries to look at the "Lazarus" the distance would be too great, you would be obliged to approach it.'

He seems to have based his optimism on the hanging of two Schools in one gallery, an idea he proffered on 8 July, though earlier he had proposed that the trustees acquire the site to the west of the Gallery for an extension. One solution he totally rejected was the addition of another storey, not for structural reasons but because 'a gallery is perfectly useless unless is is lighted with a skylight; no pictures can be seen to advantage by any other light'. Later, in a letter to B. C. Stephenson, Commissioner of the Office of Woods and Forests, he offered another means of gaining space, which has become common practice, possibly inspired by the mounting of pictures on spur walls set at right angles to the windows in the Altes Museum:

The right hand division may be rendered capable of containing a numerous collection of Dutch and Flemish pictures, suspended on dwarf skreens extending from the central piers to the windows, in which situation they would receive a powerful & effective light; and although the Nation does not as yet possess any such collection, it is expedient that some provision should be made for such a purpose. The time will arrive when the highly finished productions of these Schools must have a place in a National Gallery, and it is desirable that they should be apart from the pictures of the Italian Masters.[64]

He was manifesting his appreciation of those Schools as well as prophesying the significant place these were to occupy in the National Gallery. There is also the possibility, considering the duplication of the first floor plans of the two institutions, that he foresaw the eventual occupation of the entire building by the collection, which happened in 1868 when the Academy moved into New Burlington House.

Yet the problem was undeniable, and at the Select Committee Wilkins was humiliated, if tactfully, first by the dealer, Solly, who stated that the Altes Museum could exhibit between 700 and 800 works, the Pinakothek, in Munich 1,600, and the Hermitage in St Petersburg between 4,000 and 5,000, and then by William Seguier, the first Keeper of the Gallery, who gave evidence in the presence of Wilkins. After expressing regret at the absence of a copying room in the Gallery, Seguier was asked a distinctly leading question: 'Then is this building (which ought to be on a great and comprehensive plan to be an eternal monument of the arts in this country) to be merely a gallery where pictures are to be placed without due distribution, and not a gallery worthy of this nation?' To which he replied, 'I should be afraid not; but Mr. Wilkins is better able to speak to that point than I am.'

It was left to the connoisseur, Samuel Woodburn, who also gave evidence in Wilkins's presence, to direct censure where it belonged.

I wish, equally with Mr. Wilkins, that the space had been five times as large, and then he could have made something which would have been more worthy of the country. I should say that owing to the public outcry, Mr. Wilkins has not made the best that could be made, but his being urged as he was by the public voice to curtail it, has been a misfortune.

Indeed, he thought that the plan of the Gallery was superior to its continental counterparts and said, 'I think, however, curtailed as Mr. Wilkins has been in the ground he could not have done better than he has done.'[65] At the session on 8 July Wilkins was also blamed for limiting the system of fireproofing to the Gallery, which, as the Surveyors of the Office of Woods and Forests were to concede in a report of 1837, was less complete than he had wanted.[66]

At the close of 1836 Wilkins made one final attempt to secure the commission to lay out Trafalgar Square so as to aggrandise the building. On 12 December he wrote to the Commissioner of the Office of Woods and Forests reviving the scheme he had presented in 1833 and illustrated in a site plan, dating from the early months of that year, since it shows the building after the insertion of the carriageways (Pl. 105).[67] The scheme comprised a semi-circular terrace, facing Whitehall, fronting a larger rectangular area with quadrants leading to a short flight of steps on the axis of the main portico; he also planned a pedestal, presumably for a monument, at the confluence of Whitehall, the Strand and Cockspur Street. As Wilkins explained, this layout would help to bind together the disparate façade lines of the various structures in the square (to which he wished to add a block between Duncannon Street and the Strand for the sake of symmetry) and to elevate his building without exaggerating the inclination of the ground or necessarily creating a space 'exposed to the Public or to Nuisances'. The whole might be enclosed apart from 'a circular sweep or road 16 feet in width, leading to a broad flight of steps in front of the Portico...as a drive and footway from the lower to the higher level' and was 'most essential to the general effect of the buildings'. He pleaded for 'common justice to the Architect, who relied for the effect of the whole upon a point so important & who had been so unjustly made the subject of attack and vituperation by those who have seen the building carried on in divisions & who have never considered the effect of the WHOLE design as originally intended'. Predictably it was ignored, on the grounds of economy and fear of public disorder, as in 1833. This was unjust to Wilkins since the square was soon to be laid out by Charles Barry in a comparable arrangement, and is still popular with demonstrators.

On 26 May 1837 Wilkins, exasperated by this latest spurning of his aspirations and debilitated physically and psychologically by the commission, wrote to Stephenson, 'I have determined therefore to make endeavour to divest myself of all further care and anxiety, and let things take their course without more interference or remonstrance.'[68]

So he kept his silence when the press reviled the Gallery at the time of its opening on 9 April 1838, two days after the young Queen Victoria had visited the newly hung collection. But the vitriol of his critics surely further weakened his failing health, and made impossible the award of an official honour by Melbourne's Whig administration. Even a more kindly notice printed in the *Civil Engineer and Architect's Journal* only praised the portico, 'a noble object...with an effect very different from that of any other piece of architecture of the kind in the metropolis'.[69] Yet the Academicians were delighted with their spacious domain. For all his fears that the National Gallery would encourage connoisseurship rather than the patronage of British artists, John Constable called it 'a very noble house'.[70] And G. D. Leslie, writing for those who were taught in the Academy, fondly remembered its 'lively and inspiriting' situation in the square and 'above all, the National Gallery with its priceless treasures, absolutely next door'.[71]

The building functioned as, even if it did not emulate the aesthetic distinction expected of, a temple of the arts. Certainly Wilkins deserves credit for risking his professional reputation to secure its completion under such miserable stipulations. For, in the absence of his practical initiative in 1832 and subsequent conformation to official dictate, the Government might well have converted an unsuitable building for the Gallery and/or the Academy. However cramped, he provided much improved quarters for both institutions behind a façade that remains, at least, memorable and that, with poetic justice, still commands Whitehall, from the denizens of which place issued most of its deficiencies. As James Fergusson, never a friend of revivalism, acknowledged in 1862:

> we know that Wilkins had talent enough to erect a creditable building if he had had fair play; but the public thought proper to impose conditions which rendered his doing so next to impossible. The sad result to the architect is well known; but on a fair review of the circumstances it does not appear that he was to blame for the painful result in Trafalgar Square.[72]

What would have consoled Wilkins even more was the comparison he drew with that other temple conceived to enshrine the 'great examples of art' for the edification of the British people and the inspiration of her artists: 'If the British Museum is not more successful than the National Gallery, it certainly is not so from the same causes. No architect had a fairer chance than Sir Robert Smirke had here.'

XIII
The ebb

Almost two years after the ancient Palace of Westminster had been ravaged by fire, the designs entered in the ensuing competition of 1835 for the new Houses of Parliament were exhibited in the Academy wing of the ill-fated temple of the arts.[1] Wilkins's Neo-Gothic scheme was not even chosen for inclusion among the five best submissions by the Parliamentary Commissioners, whose judgement cannot have been unaffected by the adverse publicity attending the National Gallery commission, as Wilkins suggested in the short pamphlet he published in 1836, *An Apology for the Designs of the Houses of Parliament.*

The chief interest of the *Apology* now is that it serves to confirm the attribution to Wilkins of three unsigned Neo-Gothic elevations preserved at the R.I.B.A. (perhaps those exhibited under the motto Phil-Archimedes in 1836), two of the river façade, one being a wash perspective, and a third of the front to Westminster Abbey (Pls. 106 and 107).[2] The stress he laid upon the Commissioners' injunction that they would judge the entries for the competition on the basis of the retention of 'those venerable and beautiful remains of antiquity, the cloisters and crypt of St. Stephen's Chapel' could explain the prominence given to the recessed chapel-like structure in the elevations, the style of which echoes the late-thirteenth-century articulation of the crypt that, together with Westminster Hall, had survived the fire. Yet, early in 1835 Wilkins had been one of those invited to survey the damage and 'at the head' of the group who considered that the crypt was beyond repair, as noted in the *Gentleman's Magazine*, the editor supporting the architects James Savage and L. N. Cottingham who took the opposite view.[3]

In the river elevation the chapel-like structure is made the focal point of a broad courtyard framed by two octagonal towers and linked by steps to the Thames. Perhaps Wilkins was alluding to that imaginative composition, wholly appropriate to a mercantile and naval power, when he criticised Charles Barry in the *Apology* for having ornamented the street more than the river façade in his competition design, reminding his readers that the re-alignment of the pulpitum of the Pnyx to face landwards had antedated the Athenians' loss of power. He also reproved Barry for having produced a monotonous Neo-Tudor design, suggesting that his own was more varied, as is the case with the R.I.B.A. elevations which have at least three distinct patterns of Neo-Gothic articulation. Conversely, the absence of towers in the elevations may be explained in two remarks, the first that 'the author' had not contemplated 'the absolute necessity...for the introduction of a tower to atone for the want of that which should have been reared above the meeting of the nave and transept of the Abbey', and the second that the taller tower in Barry's original winning design might invite comparison with Babel and was impractical as a place of storage for the Parliamentary Records, being difficult of access and requiring the formation of a special 'pidgeon company' or, more presciently, the installation of a 'patent railway'.

Positive substantiation for the attribution may also be discerned in the style and articulation of the three elevations. These comprise a series of separate symmetrical parts distinguished by different fenestration and ornament and more divided than integrated by the repeated turrets and pinnacles, much as in his work at Cambridge. The street elevation, especially, seems to bear the imprint of Wilkins's hand in the evident attempt to achieve regularity without monotony. Here again are the awkward breaks – or deliberate divisions of differing elements – of the hall and library ranges of King's College, most noticeable in the central, projected part of the street façade. That begins modestly at the New Palace Yard end with a symmetrical Neo-Tudor section reminiscent of the Trumpington Street façade of Corpus Christi College. Its eastern turret is echoed by one on the corner of the gabled block which might include an entrance lobby to Westminster Hall, judging by the position the hall appears to occupy in the wash elevation of the river front. The hall is apparently screened by the more ornate and spiky section which continues to what seems to be another recession in the façade line. Here a quadrant of Tudor elliptical arches abuts a gatehouse which forms the eastern end of another symmetrical Neo-Tudor section. This could have been intended as an entrance to the Commons, while the richer and turreted central gateway might be identified as the Peer's entrance to the Lords. Beyond the balancing gatehouse tower on the west end the composition peters out in a recessed two storey and arcaded segment. The street façade in particular exhibits the horizontality characteristic of Wilkins's work in this style. The turrets and pinnacles rise somewhat timorously above the almost continuous battlements rather than creating a graduated crescendo gathering to a climax in the new chapel or chamber.

That beauteous form magnifies his enduring inspiration, King's Chapel, though the tracery work of its broad windows is in the Geometrical style. The articulation of the façades that delineate the spacious open court before it on the river side closely resembles that of the halls of King's and Corpus Christi, clearly the source for the four projecting bays. The alternation of traceried windows and niches again recalls the designs for King's College, though on a more imposing scale. The linking and projection of windows on two storeys extend the configuration used at either end of the Trumpington Street front at Corpus Christi. The bastions below the terrace monumentalise those built at Dunmore and conceived for Tregothnan. New, for Wilkins, is the stronger massing and the two types of polygonal towers on the river side. If there is a precedent for the machicolation of those framing the court in the gatehouse of his Norfolk County Gaol, there is none in his earlier work for the steeply pitched roofs of the three other towers.

Accepting Wilkins to be the designer, he appears to have endowed his scheme with symbolical significance. A new, more splendid St Stephen's Chapel ascends phoenix-like above the three-storey ranges and four-storey turrets and towers as an emblem of historical continuity, for, from 1550, the old chapel had housed Parliament. It commands a conglomeration of differently styled blocks that evoke the piecemeal growth of the old Palace of Westminster. It also crowns the fine setting doubtless envisaged for the State Opening of Parliament. Surely the broad flight of steps from the Thames and the court were conceived as the scene of the landing of the Sovereign from the State Barge (which had been used to great effect at the opening of Waterloo Bridge, as recorded by Constable in a painting not exhibited until 1832 at the Royal Academy, no. 279). With more imagination than Barry, Wilkins would have exploited to the full both pageantry and the splendid riverside site. He would also have celebrated the history of British maritime endeavour and pointed up its contemporary consequence. And he sought to perpetuate other hallowed associations by retaining a clear sight of the roof and towers of Westminster Abbey in the views to be had from the opposite bank of the Thames.

However, when compared with Barry's design as executed, Wilkins's scheme lacks its panache, grandeur and cohesion. The illustrious nature of the commission and great compass of the site called for a more brilliant architectural display, foreign to Wilkins's measured style. But the design with which Barry won the competition was lugubrious and somewhat unbalanced due to its two unequal towers. The 'Classical' composition of the river façade, about which Pugin still complained after its erection, had been even more pronounced in Barry's competition design. And a large share of the aesthetic success of the new Parliament building belongs to the beauty of the detailing drawn by Pugin.

In the *Apology* Wilkins was quick to pounce on the shortcomings in Barry's submission and the criteria of judgement adopted by the Commissioners. He was indignant about the charge made by the editor of the *Atlas* that the notes, since lost, he had appended to his designs at the exhibition in the Academy wing decried 'the talents of my professional brethren... [while] extolling my own'. In the next sentence he challenged him 'to produce an instance wherein I have either published or spoken anything in disparagement of my contemporaries, unless I have been attacked without provocation'. So, to justify himself, he reminded his readers that in 1833 Cust had conspired with 'Mr. Barry to misrepresent my Design for the National Gallery, and to make it appear sixteen feet lower than it was at any time intended to be, and twenty one feet lower than it had been executed'. Moreover, he felt able to criticise the Commissioners because they had based their preference for Barry's scheme upon questionable grounds. For example, they claimed that Barry's Neo-Gothic design would prove to be more economical than any other when neither estimates nor detailed drawings had been required of the competitors.[4] Nor had they any technical expertise in acoustics, ventilation and heating. Doubtless founding his strictures on his practical experience in renovating the theatres of his circuit, Wilkins felt entitled to query the finality of their choice when, once again, they had publicly admitted their 'imperfect knowledge' of the 'theories of sound and artificial ventilation'. He punned that in Barry's Chamber each Member would need a hogshead to project his voice to the requisite 'Barry-tone pitch' and that the heating system would turn the 'whole floor [into] one great hypocaust' if possessing the advantage of reducing the length of speeches, the Members having to change leg constantly when speaking to a beat called by the Speaker. (The system might have proved effective, but the Commissioners later changed it at great expense.) He also found Barry's internal plan to be inconvenient, particularly in the elevation of the Parliamentary Library 50 feet above ground level and the relegation of the Records to the tower, both of which were altered subsequently. However, in the absence of Wilkins's floor plans there is no way of judging the comparative merits of his scheme.

Thus Wilkins had nothing but contempt for the failings of 'open competitions and amateur judges', which he may have thought to be the consequence of the recommendations of the Select Committee on Public Buildings of 1828. Most reprehensible, the competition had been rushed through, as the Commissioners conceded when they recorded that the architects 'had expressed their regret that they were prevented...from making such alterations as from time to time suggested themselves in the progress of work'. Though he does not appear to have been among those who petitioned Parliament to express their dissatisfaction with the competition, Wilkins summed up his exasperation in the last paragraph of the *Apology*, writing that, 'In every other profession, character and previous success leads to employment, but in architects the possession of such trifles has been found wholly unnecessary...hence we see that on the present occasion carpenters, bricklayers, house agents, artisans and *even* amateurs, submit their plans with the same confidence as the proved and experienced architects.'

He attributed the choice of Barry's design to Cust, a man who had persuaded the Government to dispense with the tradition of employing architects of attested competence because he supposed that they would perpetuate outdated 'taste and abilities'. In his own pamphlet on the Houses of Parliament competition Cust had argued for the adoption of the Gothic style and perhaps alluded to Wilkins when he accused the established architects of forcing John Bull to admire buildings inspired by 'undoubted Grecian authority'.[5] To Wilkins, the Colonel was one of a long line of unqualified amateurs who were engaged to judge architectural competitions and would be better advised to 'limit his opinions to field work and the important selection, not of plans and elevations, but of buttons and facings'. He had written of others in his *Letter to the Members of the Senate*:

> The relative merit of Designs after all can only be deter-
> mined by Professional judges. The Members of the Syndi-
> cates cannot be considered as critical arbitrators on the
> Designs of Architectural merit more than a company of
> artists, however accomplished, could be expected to decide
> between the classical attainments of Porson, Par and
> Burney. I could have wished that the Syndicate had called
> in the assistance of competent and indifferent Members of
> the Profession.

This was not sour grapes on his part. His antipathy for open competitions and amateur judges was shared by, among others, Sir John Soane and C. R. Cockerell. In an unpublished letter to James Spiller, concerning the employment of incompetent architects by the Church Commissioners, Sir John had written that proven members of the profession had to 'descend into the arena of Public competition in Design, not only with each other, but with all those who assume their profession' and bewailed the judging of competitions by 'those who are not qualified to determine their merits'.[6] Cockerell was more explicit in his evidence to the Select Committee on Arts and Manufactures in 1836. Only 'eminent' architects should participate in public competitions, the specifications of which should be drawn up and properly administered by qualified judges. The object must always be 'the competition of sound opinions'.[7] Despite the value of patronage in his own career, Wilkins, in the *Apology*, trusted that 'personal friendship or Party connections' would no longer determine the outcome of public competitions. The conduct of competitions continued to exercise the minds of English architects throughout the century, reports being prepared by the Institute of British Architects in 1839, and the Architectural Association in 1850. Little was resolved before Robert Kerr told a meeting of the R.I.B.A. in 1890 that competitions were 'radically unsound in principle and in practice most prejudicial to the profession of architects, both financially and morally'.[8]

The asperity of the *Apology* had another source. By 1835 Wilkins was a sick man suffering increasingly severe pain from gout and other complications attending a disease of the kidneys; it is worthy of remark that the publication of the pamphlets coincided with the deterioration of his health. His wife Alicia's account books for the period 1823 to 1827 refer to a number of sojourns in rented accommodation at Ealing, Hampstead and Hastings, and that for the months of March and April 1825 notes payments to a 'Monthly Nurse'. Writing to Shelford of Corpus Christi on 19 November 1828, Wilkins reported, 'I am confined to my bed by an attack of Gout brought on by the combinations of circumstances – One of my Servants was seized by the smallpox which threw the whole family into confusion and on the same day my sister arrived with her child and Nurse without any previous intimations.'[9]

Compounding the physical condition was the collapse of his theatrical business. At a shareholders' meeting held on 26 October 1840 Wilkins's eldest son, Henry, was to state that for some years past his father had borne a large personal deficit to sustain the circuit in the face of the 'wretched state of Theatrical Property throughout the whole Kingdom'. Owing to his 'high and honourable character' they had 'escaped the general ruin' and received dividends for the last ten years from 'the resources of an extensive and lucrative profession'.[10] This heavy loss had been sustained without complaint, but weighed heavily on his father's mind, 'overthrew a naturally strong constitution' and 'so aggravated the disease (not otherwise fatal) that it brought him to the grave, worn out by mental activities much more than by weight of years'.

The decline in returns during the mid twenties had been worsened by the debt of £4,000 incurred by the rebuilding of the Theatre Royal, Norwich, let alone the disadvantageous agreement with the Bury St Edmunds shareholders. By 1829 Wilkins had to stand a 35 per cent reduction in income from the Norwich Company. He described the bleak prospect in a letter dated 16 April 1830 to one of the shareholders of the Bury Theatre, Rupert Rashbrooke.[11] The chief causes were 'the increase of Sectarians, the change in the manners of English which renders them less desirous of dramatic entertainment, added to the gradually increasing distresses of the times and the increase of poor-rates and parochial assessments'. The Bury Theatre 'which used to contribute to the support of the other theatres which did not pay', but which were kept open 'at a loss, in order to give a respectable company constant employment, scarcely now pays its expenses, and the extent of the outlay in building scenery and repairs'. Therefore, he was 'most reluctantly compelled to lay the case before the Proprietors of the Theatre' hoping they would accept a reduction of interest on their shares, from 5 per cent to 3 per cent, an expedient that had received the unanimous support of the King's Lynn proprietors. He carried the same message to a meeting of the proprietors of the Theatre Royal, Norwich on 11 May 1830.[12] At 'the best of times' the theatre had 'occasioned a very considerable loss to the patentee' and had only been kept open by 'the profits arising from some of the Country Theatres'. He had been 'misled by the official statements of the Ministers as to the increasing prosperity of the Country and urged by the representations of some of the most respectable Inhabitants of Norwich that a new Theatre better adapted to the prevailing taste of the times and affording an elegant place of public amusement would be encouraged by the Norfolk public' and had spent nearly £5,000 on the property.

The decline in theatre attendance had been sufficiently disturbing to jolt the Government into calling a Select Committee on Dramatic Literature in 1832, at which Wilkins gave evidence as a leading proprietor. Besides being consulted on that problem, he was questioned on the methods of licensing, the quality of the provincial theatre, the standard of contemporary playwrights, the validity of their claim for the payment of royalties and the most suitable design for theatres. (His answer to the last has been quoted above in the introduction.) His theatres were licensed by the local magistrates, except at Norwich, which came under the Lord Chamberlain, and at Cambridge where none was required, though he hoped that the Vice-Chancellor of the University would grant one for performances during the vacations so that rowdies could be prosecuted. He claimed that the Norwich Theatre had the reputation of being a nursery for good performers, mentioning Mrs Siddons and a Mrs Sloman, who was then on tour in America; he did not take the opportunity to name any of the celebrated actors who had trodden its boards, such as

Irving, Kean and Macready, appearing mostly in productions of Shakespeare's plays, nor to mention that the wife of Berlioz had sung there in an opera in 1831.[13] Wilkins opposed any increase in the fees paid to playwrights by provincial theatre companies and saw no reason why it should improve the standard of writing. He spoke disparagingly about contemporary dramatists whom he lumped together as 'mere cookers-up of such drama'. The one modern play of which he approved was a piece entitled *The Hunchback* by Mr Knowles. Anxious to keep the provincial theatre running, but at the lowest cost, he had earlier prevailed on George Lamb to withdraw a Bill he was sponsoring in Parliament to force provincial managers to pay authors fees for the production of their works.[14] He believed that the public preferred 'melodramas and translations from the French and old plays modernised and adapted to our customs, and sometimes to particular performers'. Novelty was the best weapon with which to combat the fact that the British nation was not 'a play-going race generally'.

In answer to the main question, the reason for the decline in theatre-going, Wilkins repeated what he had told Rashbrooke, noting that sectarianism was most prevalent at Colchester and Norwich, and also remarked on the absence of royal patronage. This part of his evidence fills in the picture of his contracting finances. The income from the lessee to whom he rented his six theatres had dropped from £1,150 in 1825 to £800 in 1829 and was likely to be further reduced. To 'shut them up altogether' would be worse for there would be 'certain reserve rents' to pay.

Wilkins struggled on in this fashion during the closing years of his life, the circuit productions appealing alternately to the intellect and the senses of the dwindling audiences. The Norwich playbills for the previous decades betray a greater emphasis on the latter, although the company had acted *The Merchant of Venice* and *Richard III* within a fortnight of the opening of the theatre in 1826.[15] Throughout the Napoleonic wars the entertainment had been spiced with pieces of a military character to suit what he had described to Rashbrooke as '*the piping times of war*'. On 12 April 1804 *John Bull* and *The Poor Sailor* were staged, and the evening ended with the singing of 'God Save the King'. Two items presented on 1 May 1805 veered from the sublime to the ridiculous, a recitation, 'While the Dark Clouds of War', being followed by a musical farce called *The Deserter*. On 18 May the company performed *The English Fleet in 1742*, possibly based upon an incident in the War of Jenkins's Ear which had reopened hostilities with Spain and France. That was an excuse for an extravaganza of scenes which included a storm and shipwreck in Act I and, more surprisingly, in Act II 'The Equestrian Statue and Moresque Palace', concluded by one depicting the 'Infernal Regions'. Specially composed music was introduced into celebrated plays such as *Romeo and Juliet*; when Irving and Mrs O'Neil appeared in the tragedy on 9 September 1818 the whole company sang 'A solemn Dirge' in the fifth act. On 30 July 1818 *Bellamira or the Fall of Innis* was preceded by a 'Comic, Heroic, Operatic, Tragic Pantomime, Bruletta or Spectacular Extravaganza – Don Giovanni or a Spectre on Horseback'. If the titles were not sufficiently colourful, the 'cookers-up' of the playbills endeavoured to entice customers, for instance

> The Scenery (having most of it appeared before) has been (of course) received with unbounded applause, and will be repeated as often as authors can write pieces to introduce it. The Views are intended to represent several scenes in or near the City of Seville; with (by way of pictorial episodes) A view of Hyde Park Corner and Vauxhall Gardens. There will be exhibited a *New Moon*, which is expected to be *Full* about the time of *Half* price. The *Dresses* are as good as the Proprietor can possibly afford, and the *Properties* are of very *little use to any but* the owner.

Such diversions reached a fitting climax on 25 May 1820 during a benefit performance for Mr Thorne, the scene painter. After *Rosina* and *The Recruiting Sergeant* the audience was confronted by 'A Grand Scenic effect being a Correct representation of Madame Saqui on the Rope surrounded by Fire Works'. Before the concluding melodrama, *The Woodman's Hut*, with scenes 'of the River and Castle of the Baron Heinhausen, Interior of the Woodman's Cottage Exterior of ditto and the Burning Forest Bridge etc', Thorne sang the 'admired songs' of 'Molly Malone' and 'O Bring me Wine'. Yet these ploys failed and, sooner than abandon his responsibilities to the shareholders, actors and staff, Wilkins preferred to cushion the contraction of his theatre income by selling off paintings from his collection at Christie's, first on 22 May 1830 and then on 7 April 1838; there was a third sale after his death on 30 May 1840.[16]

The decline in his prosperity apparently accelerated from 1829 since the second sale included a Domenichino, 'Landscape with the Scripture story of Isaac and Abraham' (no. 22), acquired by Wilkins at the Christie sale held on 14 July 1828 (no. 100, from Litt); it was sold to the Marquis of Lansdowne for £204. 15s. Up to that time his style of life was relatively grand as can be pictured by taking random entries from Alicia's household account books, for instance, 7 May 1819 '130 to supper', 9 May '40 to supper' and 13 December 1820 'A Ball 90 to supper', all at his fashionable house in Weymouth Street. By the summer of 1838 the family was living permanently at Lensfield, though in part due to his ill health, where they entertained on a smaller scale. 'Dined with Wilkins', wrote Romilly, that gregarious Cambridge diarist. 'Indifferent ham doe venison that stunk...found the party very agreeable as I made the principal talk.'[17]

The first Christie's sale was described as 'Pictures of the Superior Class from the Cabinet of an Amateur', the second as 'A Catalogue of the Entire Collection of ITALIAN, French and Flemish Pictures of THE VERY FIRST CLASS of William Wilkins, Esq., R.A.' and the last as 'A FEW CAPITAL ITALIAN AND DUTCH PICTURES. The property of William Wilkins, Esq., R.A. etc.'. In the summer of 1837 he offered the remainder of his collection for sale to the trustees of the National Gallery. They examined the paintings but the secretary was instructed on 19 June to write that

> though they find them of considerable merit and impor-
> tance, yet having recently recommended to the Govrnt.
> the purchase of two Pictures at a large price, and the
> expenditure of a considerable sum for putting the National
> Collection into good order, regilding the Frames, etc,
> previously to their being brought before the public in the
> new Gallery, they feel at present reluctant to apply to the
> Government to sanction a further appeal to Parliament.[18]

On 3 March 1838 the trustees received another letter from Wilkins offering a selection of four pictures for £3,000 which again they declined to buy, and on 7 February 1842 George Wilkins received the same response with regard to an unspecified painting attributed to 'Parmegiano', possibly from Wilkins's estate.[19] Perhaps their decisions stemmed from knowledge of the results of the 1830 sale when, for example 'The Prodigal Son' (no. 14) ascribed to Rubens had failed to reach its reserve of £1,040. It was one of three paintings in his collection especially admired by no less an authority than Waagen, the others being 'St Peter and St John healing the impotent man' attributed to Nicolas Poussin and 'The Flight into Egypt' said to be by Titian.[20]

The opinion of the trustees was confirmed when, at the 1838 sale, the Poussin (no. 29), acquired from the Radstock Collection and published in Smith's *Catalogue Raisonée*, page 266, fetched only £219 paid by Johnson, the Rubens (no. 30) went for £246. 15s. to Farrar, while the Titian called 'The Holy Family' in the catalogue (no. 31) was passed at the sale but seemingly sold privately to the Earl of Upper Ossery since the painting, or another version, came up at the Christie's sale on 21 May 1842 (no. 101) and raised £451. 10s. John Pye had an enlightening note on this picture, later proved to be a copy, as were the Poussin and, almost certainly, the Rubens, in his book on the patronage of British art, *An Historical Sketch: comprising an account of the rise and progress of art and artists in London...* (1845). He offered the painting as an example of the defects of connoisseurship and misappropriation of funds better spent on the patronage of contemporary art, quoting from *The Athenaeum* for 28 May 1842:

> *A Repose in Egypt* by Titian. This picture belonged to the far-famed Orleans Collection, and was sold out of it for 250 guineas. Mr. Champernowne, swayed by the Orleans stamp, thought it a bargain for 2000 L., and we hope and believe that the late Mr. Wilkins (the architect) thought otherwise, as it was put up at 1600 L. A prudent public bid nothing then and not much now; – 430 gns rejected: it will probably, if put up again, come down still lower.

A puzzling factor emerges from a study of the auctioneers' copies of the catalogues. These suggest that Wilkins employed an agent or agents to buy back certain of his paintings. In 1830 an unidentified dealer paid £249 for a 'Ford' given to Berghem and Wouvermans (no. 5), £240 for 'The Retreat', said to be by Hackaert and A. Vandervelde (no. 9) and £175 for 'Italian Seaport', described as by Shellincks in the manner of Du Jardin (no. 6). These reappeared at the 1840 sale (nos. 82, 81 and 83) when the first two sold for £160. 13s. and £162. 15s., while the third was passed. Thus it would seem that at least £664 of the total of £2,908. 10s. made at the 1830 sale came from Wilkins's own dwindling resources. Perhaps he was to repeat the exercise in 1838 when the apparent earnings were £1,822. 17. 6d. A 'Deluge', claimed as the work of Perino del Vaga (no. 7), and a 'Diana and Actaeon' (no. 14), ascribed to Albano, seem to have been bought in at £5. 15s. and at £14. 3s. 6d., only to be passed in the 1840 sale (nos. 89 and 90). A 'St Catherine and St Theresa' (no. 24) and a 'St Ursula and St Carlo Borromeo' (no. 25), said to be by Domenichino, were sold to Johnson for £71. 8s. and £65 but came up again in 1840 (nos. 92 and 93) when they fetched £30. 19s. 6d. and £30. 9s.; a third painting attributed to Domenichino (no. 28) 'A grand Landscape from the Borghese gallery: some connoisseurs think it to be the production of A. Carracci' was bought by Peacock for £73. 10s. However, a 'Sleeping Nymphs, surprised by Bacchanals' (no. 19), given to Adrien Vanderwerff, bought for £22. 11s. 6d. by Collard was resold in 1840 (no. 91) for £28. 17s. 6d. The executors raised £706. 2s. 7d. at the last sale.

Still, these were not inconsiderable figures and Wilkins's connoisseurship compared reasonably well with that of his contemporaries. Four of the Flemish and Dutch paintings in the 1830 sale reached high figures: 'The Temptation of St Anthony' (no. 7), believed to be by Teniers, £315 to Bone; 'The Interior of a lofty Stable' by Wouvermans (no. 8), £313; 'Cattle driven out to Pasture' (no. 10) by Berghem, £750 to Foster; and 'A Stag Hunt' (no. 13) by Wouvermans, £525 to Peacock; this last had been acquired by Gavin Hamilton in Rome some sixty years before, possibly from the collection of Comtesse de Verrue, for the father of Henry Drummond of Grange Park, from whom Wilkins presumably had it. These prices show that the better pictures of his collection were from those Schools and he was regarded as something of an expert in this field. He was the chief witness at a case heard before the Court of King's Bench in 1831.[21] He appeared in support of Edward Gray of Harringay House, Hornsey, who sued a dealer named Nieuwenhays for misrepresentation. Wilkins was called to prove the authenticity of a Wouvermans which Nieuwenhays had persuaded Gray to exchange for a doubtful work which he claimed to be by the same artist. Apparently Wilkins had adjured Nieuwenhays not to perpetuate this deceit, pointing out that the genuine painting entitled 'Les Sables' was worth £600 while the other was a valueless fake. His judgement was entirely correct, since Gray's painting later entered the Wallace Collection as 'A Stream in Hilly Country' (no. 218), after having been returned to its rightful owner by the court. Another of Gray's pictures mentioned at the trial, Wouvermans' 'Stag Hunt', is now in the National Gallery (no. 975), for which Wilkins recommended, as has been noticed, the creation of a special collection of Dutch and Flemish paintings.

The sale catalogues provide some information on provenance and record the bulk of Wilkins's acquisitions, apart from the works retained by his family. These included a 'Holy Family' noted by Waagen as being by Annibale Carracci from the Radnor Collection, a version of Poussin's 'Phaeton begging the Chariot of Apollo' recorded by Professor A. Blunt, a 'Christ preaching from Lake Tiberius' by J. C. Eberlein, a number of pictures lent to the British Institution Old Master exhibitions and engravings by Dürer and Turner, one of Yarmouth Sands showing the Nelson Column, most of which were sold during the nineteenth century.[22]

The catalogues confirm that Wilkins was a collector rather than a patron, though *The Athenaeum* obituary stated that he was 'a great and ardent lover of the arts, which he encouraged to the extent of his means'. While clearly interested in contemporary art, being a member of the Academy Hanging Committee in 1828, of the council from 1835 and author of a resolution in 1837 'for introducing Sculpture into the exhibition', there is little evidence of his commissioning work from colleagues at the Academy besides the Chalon portrait and four others from his friend, Beechey.[23] The 1840 sale catalogue lists a 'Peasant Girl' (no. 100) by Henry Howard, which might have been bought directly from the artist. An undated letter written by Sir David Wilkie, owned by W. P. Wilkins, infers a close friendship but there is no record of purchase. Family tradition holds that Wilkins possessed a number of works by members of the Norwich School, including John Cotman, and he may have bought paintings from H. P. Briggs, whom he supported in the ballots for election to the Academy in 1828 and 1831. West's 'Banishment of Cleombrotus', given to the nation, was bought from W. Smith and not from the artist, though it is interesting to reflect that the subject of Leonidas's stoical government looks back to the period of Neo-Classicism associated with the 'impure' early Greek Revival. However, it is an example of the kind of History painting that Wilkins championed in the *Letter to Lord Goderich* and which he hoped to encourage by lending paintings from his collection to the British Institution exhibitions.

To those endeavours and his efforts to provide better accommodation and teaching facilities for the Royal Academy the obituarist might also have referred. Certainly Wilkins's views as to the best means of fostering art in England (greater state patronage aside) – reformed academic education and an increase in public collections – were echoed in the statements of most of the witnesses called before the Select Committee on Arts and Manufactures which sat between 1835 and 1836.[24] Although Wilkins was only asked to comment on the design of the National Gallery, his concern about the inadequacy of architectural training at the Academy was touched on by two witnesses, Howard and Donaldson, the latter then Honorary Secretary of the Institute of British Architects. Replying to one question, Donaldson unwittingly indicated how the antiquarian attitude tended to breed stylistic pluralism when he commended the use in art schools of a German pattern book, *Forbilder für Fabrikanten und Handwerker, herausgegeben von der König, technischen Deputation für Gewerbe* (Berlin, 1821), because it contained 'the choicest examples of ancient and modern art in their respective classes, not omitting even oriental and moresque. . . I have no doubt that if such a work were distributed over England, and easy reference could be had to the separate copies, the taste of our manufactures in regard to form would be materially improved.'

Learning by imitation from books and models seems to have been at the heart of Wilkins's plans for a revised architectural course at the Academy, outlined in the *Letter to Lord Goderich*. Naturally, his recommendations that the students should learn the principles of design from archaeological publications and from casts and models of celebrated buildings reflected his own dual career as well as current academic theory. If anything, he accorded a greater significance to this method than did most. 'Are you of opinion that the study of these originals would not be more useful to architects than drawings and casts?' he had been asked at the Select Committee on the Elgin Marbles, responding, 'I am not aware that any artist would obtain much more information than might be conveyed from drawings.' He even ventured to say that Elgin had not 'injured' the temples as 'schools' since he thought that 'drawings and models would convey all the information that these fragments will'. In 1832 he was able to effect part of his plan, as has been noted, by providing two rooms for displaying drawings and models on the upper floor of the Royal Academy. Five years later he presented the Academy with 'Some

Architectural Models' and advised that the Academicians 'procure others for the use of the Students'.[25]

The passages on architectural training in the *Letter* may well have been the initiation of a campaign to become the professor of architecture at the Royal Academy. That began in earnest with a letter to Sir John Soane, whose dilatory execution of the duties of the post in the 1820s provided Wilkins with his opportunity, there being no lectures between 1824 and 1830. Soane had the missive on 18 July 1836, which he marked as an 'Official letter'. Wilkins warned Soane of his 'intention at the General Meeting of the Royal Academicians tomorrow, to direct their attentions to the inadequacy of the present system, as far as related to Architecture, owing, as I conceive, to the supineness of those who ought to take the lead in all subjects relating to this branch of the Arts, in the body to which we both belong'. He had not raised the matter earlier 'from feelings of delicacy towards you and the situation you hold at the Academy'. He did not wish it to be thought that he harboured resentment against Soane for opposing his election to the Academy, but the institution was under fire from its critics and he thought 'the time has at length arrived when something *must be done* to put Architecture upon a different footing'.[26]

True to his word, the very next day Wilkins intervened at the General Assembly of the Academy to ask that the council consider two resolutions: that a professor who 'neglects for two successive years to deliver a course of lectures be compelled to resign' and that 'a Lecturer be appointed to give instruction in Perspective as before and possibly combine those duties with Architectural designing'.[27] He also asked two questions: 'whether the present state of the Arts be such as to warrant the abrogation of the Law which prohibits a Member of the Royal Academy from belonging to any other Society of Artists' and whether the law requiring their residence in England should be abolished. He withdrew these on 20 February 1837, following the death on 25 January of Soane, whose spectre, however, haunted Wilkins's election to the professorship on 30 March when four 'Noes' were registered against thirteen 'Ayes'.[28] Unfortunately Wilkins gave no lectures at the Academy before his death two years later, providing further ammunition for vociferous critics like the radical Member of Parliament, Joseph Hume.[29]

On the evidence of his earlier comments, the 'different footing'

Wilkins envisaged – apart from a regular course of lectures – would have been a higher standard of scholarship, more than likely centred on Greek and Gothic antiquities. Once more the loss of his personal papers precludes further comment on his plans, especially as to whether he would have introduced more extensive technical instruction than had Soane. Failing health robbed him of the chance to reform the Academy architectural course and the initiative passed from the Academy to the Institute of British Architects, founded in 1835 but in which Wilkins took little part though he attended the inaugural meeting, and later to Donaldson at University and Kerr at King's Colleges, London.

Some idea of the historical and aesthetic content of the lectures Wilkins would have given at the Academy may be gleaned from *Prolusiones Architectonicae or Essays on subjects connected with Roman and Greek architecture* published in June 1837. This was the opinion of the Royal Society obituarist who wrote that it had been 'designed, in some degree, as a substitute for those lectures, which, under other circumstances, he would have been called upon to deliver as Professor of Architecture, to the students of the Royal Academy'.

The publication of *Prolusiones* coincided with Wilkins's retirement from practice. B. C. Stephenson, in a letter dated 25 August 1837, welcomed the gift of the book, 'highly creditable of your Classical, and Professional acquirements', but regretted his retirement at a time when his 'Talents and Abilities are so necessary' for the support of the 'Profession'.[30] A reviewer, writing in the *Civil Engineer and Architect's Journal*, was even more appreciative of *Prolusiones*:

> as far as scholarship can be a qualification for the professorship we know of none in the profession who could have been opposed to him with equal pretensions. Even had he written nothing else, the present volume would fully make good his title to erudition, which, to say the truth, predominates in it to such a degree, that it will be quite a sealed book to many, and must content itself with 'audience fit, though few'.[31]

Prolusiones comprises six essays: 'The Erechtheum', 'The Iconography of the Erechtheum', 'On the Construction of the Erechtheum', 'The Athenian Inscription', 'On the Construction of the Roofs of Temples' (originally published in the *Unedited Antiquities of*

Attica), and 'The Temple at Jerusalem the Type of Grecian Architecture'. Thus it was a companion to his earlier publications. The first three essays were based upon parts of *Atheniensia*, the fourth upon the same work and the article in Walpole's *Memoirs* (an intermediate version had been read before the Royal Society of Literature by W. R. Hamilton on Wilkins's behalf and was summarised in the *Proceedings* of the Society, 1, 6 (1835), pp. 5–58), the fifth upon the *Unedited Antiquities* and *The Civil Architecture*, and the last upon *Magna Graecia*; some of the plates were again engraved by Lowry and Roffe, with others by F. Ollivier and three copied from Donaldson's *A Selection of the Most Approved Examples of Doorways from the Ancient Buildings in Greece and Italy* (1833).

In the first essay Wilkins partially revised his interpretation of the inscriptions on the Arch of Hadrian in a footnote on page 7. He admitted his failure to correct Chandler's translation, but persisted 'in the propriety of placing Hadrianopolis in that division of the ancient city, where the remains of many of the emperor's magnificent works are still to be seen'.[32] He was not in the mood to give ground and, in the same essay, disagreed with Leake on the number of entrances to the cella of the Parthenon, insisting that there was only one, although he acknowledged that the Colonel, who thought there were two, was a 'very learned writer on the topography of Athens'. In the fifth essay, which included a long section on the construction of the roof of the Parthenon, Wilkins took issue, in a footnote to page 96, with an unnamed author who had cited Leake, Cockerell and Kinnard in an attempt to prove that the temple had been hypaethral: 'With all my admiration for the talents and acquirements of these gentlemen, I must be permitted to remark that their conjoint opinion is not always infallible.' Elsewhere in the text he recalled that Cockerell had accepted the purport of his interpretation of the iconography of the pedimental sculpture of the Parthenon and that Leake had agreed that the small building near the Propylaea was a tomb and not, as later excavations proved it to be, the ruins of the Temple of Victory. To those references to Leake can be added another in a paper composed by Wilkins while 'looking over' the plates for the fourth volume of the new edition of the *Antiquities of Ionia*. Read before the Royal Society of Literature on 24 March 1836, again by Hamilton, and entitled 'The Lydo-Phrygian Inscription', it contained a revised reading of a four line memorial inscription found at 'Dongalu' and printed by Leake in his *Journal of a Tour in Asia Minor* (1824).[33] Before he corrected what he regarded as a number of inaccuracies in Leake's interpretation, Wilkins, perhaps sarcastically, described him as 'a giant in this way'. Certainly he confided a decidedly uncomplimentary opinion of Leake to Hudson Gurney in a letter dated 2 December 1834: 'The Colonel is celebrated not only for hypotheses, but for sacrificing everything to maintain them. I could prove to you in five seconds that one of his military suggestions as to the propylea of the Athenian Acropolis would be circuited by the merest tyro on military Architecture.'[34]

The contents of *Prolusiones* were not as retrospective or outdated as they might at first appear. The structure of the Parthenon and the iconography of the pedimental sculpture were still lively issues, not merely in England but also in Germany. Similarly, the Erechtheum and inscription had been the subject of more intensive study by English and German scholars, most notably H. W. Inwood, whose *The Erechtheion* was published in 1827, and K. O. Müller (1797–1840), author of *Minerva Poliadis Sacra et Aedes in Arce Athenarum* (Göttingen, 1820), to whom Wilkins referred in his last book. Another German authority mentioned in his text was August Boeckh (1785–1860), who had included a painstaking analysis of the Athenian Inscription in *Corpus Inscriptionum Graecorum* (Berlin, 1828). (Incidentally, Wilkins's son, William Bushby, noted in correspondence with his father that he had met another German archaeologist, Benjamin Schlick, 'a friend of yours', while visiting the excavations at Pompeii in February 1837 during his Grand Tour; when at Rome in January he had been to the Vatican Library to execute an unnamed task for his father.) Wilkins parted with Boeckh and Müller on the translation of the architectural terms in the inscription, but quoted the Latin preface to the *Corpus* in which he was lauded, and also recalled in *Prolusiones* that the late Reverend Peter Elmsley (1773–1825), a noted Oxford scholar of Classical texts and especially those of Euripides and Sophocles, had 'adopted some of my explanations in preference to his own preconceived notions'. Likewise the last essay on the relation between the Temple of Jerusalem and Greek architecture was by no means a dormant subject, *Essays on Chronology: being a vindication of the system of Sir Isaac Newton by a Member of the University* having been published anonymously at Cambridge in 1827.

Nevertheless, *Prolusiones* was a restatement of Wilkins's scholarship much as the re-exhibition of his designs for Downing and East India Colleges at the Academy in 1838 commemorated his youthful achievements. On those a reviewer commented acidly, 'They are very little to our taste, they betray too pedantic and frigid an affectation of that style carried *à la rigueur*, to show either much invention or happy conception in the application of it. There are a monotonousness and sameness of ideas in them that certainly do not evince an extraordinary stock of imagination.'[35]

While the drawings were on view Wilkins was mortally ill at Lensfield, but still active on the revision of the third part of the *Antiquities of Ionia* and also on behalf of Hudson Gurney. Gurney had asked Wilkins to superintend the redecoration of Keswick Hall in 1837, possibly to aid his friend financially. Over the ensuing two years Wilkins dictated a series of letters from his sick bed about the work and his physical and mental states.[36] The first that remains, dated 11 September 1837, is full of detailed and thoughtful advice on furnishings and decoration and ends hopefully, 'Although still confined to my bed I am already much better & advancing towards recovery. I should like before you finally decide on the paper to see the smaller drawing room as it has been fitted up.' Gurney also consulted Wilkins about the choice and placing of casts of celebrated Classical statues for the terrace, associated with a project for landscaping the grounds to be executed by W. S. Gilpin (1762–1843). Wilkins wrote from Lensfield on 15 February 1839 with something of his erstwhile wit:

> The Canephora for instance of the Townley Museum would make one excellent suggestion. The Basket on the head being hollow a large pot of the scarlet geranium might be inserted...The water bearer of the Elgin Collection of which a mould exists...would not be inappropriate...I think Mrs. Gurney would not approve of Canova's *Ballerina* although one should call them by the modest name of Graces and tripping Hebes.

Wilkins had already contacted C. H. Smith, the ornamental mason at University College, about the type, price and availability of casts. Smith replied on 5 February, sending drawings of six Classical figures between 5 and 8 feet high to be made either of 'Austin's Composition' or Portland stone. He had tracked down a cast of the Erechtheum Caryatid at Hamlet's Bazaar, which would be cheaper, though less durable, than a Coade stone copy of the Towneley Canephora. Wilkins communicated Smith's investigations to Gurney on 9 March, and recommended the purchase of casts of the

> Townley Cariatides. . . My *favourite lady* with the basket on her head would answer better than other for the niches, right & left, on the east front of the house, something rather higher should stand in the piers between the two little drawing room windows and I am well convinced that they will equally answer the purpose for the terrace where figures do not require that *indentation* of outline. It is only when they are placed far above the eye that it is required.

He sent another letter on 15 March, delighted to learn

> that Lord Aberdeen's authority for vases comes in aid of my recommendation of similar ornaments – I do not quite understand whether by the word *covers*, he means a temporary expedient against the alternation of wet and frost or whether said covers were part of the original design. Vases of this latter description were for the most part funereal, such would not be quite in character – There are some however which are not of a nature so *lugubrious* – Such for instance as No. 7. and No. 9 in room No. 2 in the Townley Gallery – These originally appear to have had covers, but I write to Austin for a sketch of these to send to Lord Aberdeen.

There followed more advice about the selection and disposition of statuary and the proposal that a few should be set between every two trees either side of the broad grass walk to 'make a mighty pretty walk for contemplation'. In the last paragraph he expressed embarrassment at accepting his friend's 'liberal offer' of a payment of £200, adding a postscript about the possible presence and use of artesian springs on the property.

Meticulous as ever, he did not spare his waning time in seeking to satisfy Gurney's wishes, which evidently gave him pleasure and a sense of purpose. In the last extant letter of their correspondence, written on 22 March, he was 'very much concerned to hear' that the wallpaper in the drawing-room was 'a failure – I know nothing more deceitful than to judge of the effect of a wall papered from a pattern'. Having proposed that the effect might be alleviated by the introduction of coloured blinds or carpets, and green instead of white muslin curtains, he owned himself to be 'very much obliged by what you have done in respect of Norwich Bank – I am still suffering very considerably – .' He made more suggestions about the installation of statuary and the discovery of artesian springs in a postscript, much of it, like the letter, underlined, denoting the anxiety of the sick.

Sandwiched between these practicalities are some distressing descriptions of his condition. On 15 February Wilkins excused himself from visiting Keswick because

> although the pain I suffer is considerably abated my excursions do not exceed the length of a few feet – The wound on the ankle is healing well though slowly, and it is really time, for it is as large as the palm of the hand (including the fingers) – I shall not think I am getting well until it reaches the italian admeasurement of the palmar piedi senza digiti.

And on 9 March he recounted the onset of what was indeed his final decline. He was experiencing long paroxysms of 'unabated pain' and failure of physical functions. His words are all the more poignant by virtue of his brave optimism, and faith in the rudimentary and ineffectual treatment administered. 'I eat a wing of a chicken with pudding and potatoes, and during the day two small tumblers of *English* Gin and water hot.' When he was 'labouring from an attack of something *very like* dropsy my body and limbs being very much swelled and my breathing difficult' he had taken daily an 'ounce of cream of Tartar in a tumbler of rice water for a fortnight, and from that period my body and limbs resumed their usual substance which they retained, until this long confinement' had emaciated his limbs. 'I have since done scarcely without my medicine whatever: and although I am obliged every night to take five and twenty drops of Laudanum to produce tranquility during the night, the usual effects of this costive narcotic are fully counteracted by eating dry toast with *honey*.' At the end he excused himself for having dictated the letter, quoting a tag from Cicero, '"Haec non scripsisse, ex *otie* abundantia sed amoris erga te" Cicero Ep.', and he struggled to write an apologetic sentence in his own hand. 'I am afraid you will think I have been very diffuse on a subject which seems personally to apply to myself but the improvement in my bodily health I cannot help attributing to the *regime* – the gout still hangs about me but the great pain I endured has considerably abated, but yet I *calculate six weeks confinement more.*' In fact he remained imprisoned in his bed for most of the next six months until his death on 31 August 1839. He never lacked courage and continued to entertain his friends to the end. Romilly recorded in his diary on 22 July 1839, 'To an Evening party at the Wilkins's played Whist – The concert ended in a dance . . . After 12 o'clock Mr. Wilkins's bedroom door (adjoining the drawing room) was opened and some supper was taken into him and he drank my health.'[37]

As an extraordinary coincidence, in the light of his respect for mathematical precision, he died at Lensfield on the same day and month of his birth sixty-one years earlier. Celebrated but disappointed, his undeniable tenacity and good humour had been sorely tried by public rejection and private suffering. Yet, like his dear Beechey, he died in the care of a loving family, still admired as a scholar and architect and, deservedly, the incumbent of the chief honorary position in his profession.

William Wilkins was buried under the sacrarium of the chapel of Corpus Christi College, in the heart of the learned grove that had quickened his intellect, and where, in the words of the obituarist of the *Gentleman's Magazine*, he had been 'left to exercise the full scope of his genius'.

ARCHITECTURAL DESIGNS AND DRAWINGS BY WILKINS

The location of drawings and associated documents is indicated in brackets at the end of each entry where known. The references to drawings exhibited at the R.A. are taken from A. Graves, *The Royal Academy of Arts. A Complete Dictionary of Contributors 1769–1904*, IV (1970 reprint); pp. 276–7.

1798?
Eleven measured drawings and sections of King's College Chapel, Cambridge, probably executed while his father completed minor repairs to the fabric, 1798–1802. Two were exhibited R.A. 1810 (nos. 826 and 840) and 1837 (nos. 1064 and 1079), each as 'King's College, Chapel, Cambridge', and the whole set S.A. 1813. (Phoenix Collection, Columbia University, New York)

Wash perspective drawing of Donington Park, Leicestershire, built to his father's design, 1790–1800, dedicated to Lady Charlotte Rawdon. (Sir John Summerson)

1799
'View of the Porta Honoris or entrance to Caius College', R.A. (no. 511). Lost.

'Design for improving the seat of a nobleman in Nottinghamshire', R.A. (no. 909). Possibly a design for Thoresby Park, Nottinghamshire, for the 1st Earl Manvers. Unexecuted and lost.

1805
Downing College, Cambridge. Wilkins submitted an unsolicited design in 1805, officially accepted in March 1806. Exhibited R.A. 1805 (no. 667) as 'Design for the new college proposed to be built at Cambridge' and (no.

673) 'Design for intended entrance proposed to be built at Cambridge', the last re-exhibited 1810 (no. 891) as 'Entrance to Downing College, Cambridge'. No. 667 might have been re-exhibited 1838 (no. 1069) as 'Downing College Cambridge'. Only the east and west ranges were built to Wilkins's designs, respectively 1807–13 and 1818–22. Contractors: S. Crowe, builder, J. De Carle, masonry, Coade Co. ornamental stonework. Enlarged to different designs from 1873. (D.C. and R.I.B.A.)

Osberton House, Nottinghamshire, for F. F. Foljambe, M.P., F.S.A. Wilkins added a Greek Doric portico to the entrance, altered the hall, redecorated the living-rooms and enlarged the offices. Altered on various occasions from 1847.

East India College, Hertfordshire; now Haileybury College. Wilkins prepared a design in November 1805 and prised the commission from Henry Holland in December. Exhibited R.A. 1805 (no. 934) as 'Design for East India College, Hertfordshire' and 1838 (no. 1077) as 'East India College, Haileybury'. Built 1806–9, but with the position of the side ranges reversed as requested by Wilkins in 1806. The entrance portico on the east side was redesigned by the Company Surveyor, S. P. Cockerell, who also persuaded the College Committee to enrich the decoration of the main rooms. Contractors: F. Stone and H. Wilkins. Enlarged from 1874. (I.O.L. and S.M.).

1806
Project for a theatre at Bentley Priory, near Stanmore, Middlesex, commissioned by Lord Aberdeen for the Marquess of Abercorn. Abandoned in 1810 by Abercorn in favour of one by Robert Smirke, according to Farington. Unexecuted and lost (B.M.)

Restoration Norwich Cathedral? Wilkins may have collaborated with his father on repairs to the interior and, given the quality of the detailing, to the exterior of St Ethelbert's Gate. (Diocesan Archive.)

1807
Nelson Pillar, Sackville Street, Dublin. Wilkins entered a Greek Doric columnar monument in the competition in December. Exhibited R.A. 1809 (no. 874) as 'Naval Column to the memory of Lord Nelson at Dublin'. Executed, under the superintendance of F. Johnston, with the exception of the substitution of a statue of Nelson for a Roman gallery atop the capital. Demolished 1966. (N.L.I.)

1808

Lower Assembly Rooms, Terrace Walk, Bath, Somerset. Wilkins added a Greek Doric portico on the main front and possibly the antis portico on one side, and refurbished the interior. Exhibited R.A. 1808 (no. 908) as 'New entrance to Lower Assembly Rooms, Bath' and 1809 (no. 764) as 'Entrance to Lower Assembly Rooms, Bath'; these tend to contradict Ison's date of 1806. Burned 1820, rebuilt 1823–5 by G. A. Underwood, incorporating Wilkins's porticoes, and demolished 1933.

Project for a villa, North Berwick, East Lothian, for Sir Hew Dalrymple Hamilton. Exhibited R.A. 1808 (nos. 911, 966 and 973) all as 'Villa at North Berwick for Sir H. D. Hamilton, Bt'. Unexecuted and lost.

1809

Grange Park (or The Grange), Hampshire, remodelling Samwell's house for Henry Drummond. Wilkins reordered the floor levels to match the scale of the Greek Doric columnar and antis porticoes he introduced, covering the façades with Roman cement and altering some internal apartments. Exhibited R.A. 1809 (nos. 752 and 773) as 'The Grange, Hampshire for H. Drummond Esq.' and 'The Grange, Hampshire', and 1820 (no. 917) as the latter. Crook and Redmill date the work from 1804 and Colvin from 1805, but Drummond had only just left Oxford and the handling of the transformation clearly post-dates Osberton. The later date is also supported by Drummond's marriage in 1808, a reference in the Aberdeen Correspondence and the year in which the designs were first exhibited. Enlarged Smirke and C. R. Cockerell and now in a ruinous condition. (B.M. and R.I.B.A.)

Argyll House, Argyll Street, London, alterations to the interior including the installation of a copy of the Parthenon Frieze in the salon. Demolished. (B.M.)

St Nicholas, Great Yarmouth, Norfolk? Wilkins may have assisted his father in the closing stages of the commission to replace the spire, since removed, and refurbish the interior. (Y.A.)

1810?

Pentillie Castle, Cornwall, addition of a new wing in the Gothic style for J. I. Coryton in collaboration with Wilkins senior. Dated c. 1811 by Colvin and after 1815 by Pevsner. Demolished 1962. (Pentillie)

1810

Theatre, Colchester, Essex, renovations to an existing structure. Demolished.

1811

Project for Theatre Royal, Drury Lane, London, in the Classical style. Commended by the judges of the competition, won by Benjamin Wyatt. Unexecuted and lost.

1811?

Lensfield, Lensfield Road, Cambridge, remodelling of an existing house for his family, including the addition of a Greek Doric antis portico, and therefore probably begun after his marriage in 1811. Dated c. 1815 by Colvin. Demolished 1955. (W.P.W.)

1814

Theatre, Newmarket Road, Cambridge. Wilkins probably assisted his father in the design. Remodelled.

Dalmeny House, West Lothian, new house for the 4th Earl of Rosebery. Wilkins submitted Greek and Tudor Gothic designs. Rosebery chose the latter, also in preference to a Gothic scheme by Jeffry Wyatt. Executed 1814–19 with two significant changes, the projection of the central tower on the southern façade rather than the turreted wings, and the addition of quarters for the Dowager Countess on the west side. Exhibited R.A. 1817 (no. 993) as 'Dalmeny, near Edinburgh, for the Earl of Rosebery'. Contractor: Coade Co. external ornamental stonework. (R.C.H.M.S.)

1815

Nelson Column, Great Yarmouth, Norfolk. The competition was advertised in January and awarded to Wilkins before his scheme was submitted to Trinity House in September. Before its completion in 1817 the design of the top section was altered from a Roman galley to a figure of Britannia standing on a globe and the dimensions of the Greek Doric column reduced. Exhibited R.A. 1821 (no. 959) as 'Nelson monument, Yarmouth'. Contractors: F. Braidwood, builder, Coade Co. statuary (Y.A.)

Tregothnan, Cornwall, remodelling and additions to the seventeenth-century house for the 4th Viscount Falmouth in the Tudor style. Wilkins took over the commission from Repton in 1815 and produced at least three schemes. The work was finished in 1818. Exhibited R.A. 1817 (no. 938) as 'Tregothnan, near Truro, for Lord Falmouth'. Enlarged 1842–6 by L. Vulliamy. (Tregothnan and Y.B.A.)

Project for the Wellington Testimonial, Dublin. Wilkins came third in the competition with a Neo-Greek design (N.L.I.)

Project for a new building to replace the Perse and Legge Building and structures at the south east corner, Gonville and Caius College, Cambridge, in the Tudor Gothic style. Unexecuted. (Gonville and Caius College)

Project for a Neo-Greek mausoleum or lodge in the Park at Stourhead, Wiltshire for Sir Richard Colt Hoare. Unexecuted but exhibited R.A. 1817 (no. 890) as 'Building for the Park of Sir R. C. Hoare, Bart'. (Stourhead and R.I.B.A.)

1816
Theatre, Great Yarmouth, Norfolk, reconstruction. Demolished. (N.N.R.O.)

Perse School, Cambridge, remodelling of three rooms to accommodate the Fitzwilliam Collection. Dismantled.

1817
Project for the Army Monument to be erected in Portland Place, London, drawn in collaboration with J. P. Gandy; shelved due to the economic recession. Wilkins and Gandy expressed their frustration with the Government by jointly exhibiting a model, R.A. 1826 (no. 1012) as 'Model of the tower of Waterloo, 280 feet high, as decided on by the Committee of Taste, to be erected pursuant to the unanimous Vote of the House of Commons, etc.' Gandy also showed a drawing of the Neo-Classical monument (no. 878) at that time. Unexecuted and lost.

Freemasons' Hall, York Street, Bath, Somerset. Notable for its fine Greek Ionic antis portico. Completed by the summer of 1818. A preliminary design might be that in the Avery Collection, Columbia University, New York, associated by Harris with Downing College. Afterwards Society of Friends' Meeting House.

Keswick Hall, Norfolk, remodelling and additions, having Neo-Greek and Renaissance features, for Hudson Gurney, including a bow-fronted block behind the old house containing a staircase tower. This work was finished by 1819. Contractors : S. Crowe, builder, Coade Co. ornamental stonework. In 1837 Wilkins advised Gurney on the redecoration of the interior and the installation of casts of Classical statuary on the terrace. Altered and enlarged 1951. (B.M. and N.N.R.O.)

Project for a church, Bothamsell, Nottinghamshire, for the 4th Duke of Newcastle. Exhibited R.A. 1817 (no. 878) as 'Bothamsell Church, Nottinghamshire'. Unexecuted and lost.

1818

King's Bridge, King's College, Cambridge (K.C.)

Theatre, Westgate Street, Bury St Edmunds, Suffolk. The plans in a Neo-Classical style placed before the Corporation in the winter of 1818 and built over the next year. Restored. (N.N.R.O. and Suffolk Record Office)

1819

Great St Mary's Church, Cambridge. Neo-Gothic alterations to the interior including addition of new gallery, west end. Largely removed 1863, excepting the gallery.

County Gaol, Bury St Edmunds, Suffolk, alterations in collaboration with the Governor, J. Orridge.

1820

Dunmore Park, Stirlingshire. New house for the 5th Earl of Dunmore. Built 1820–2 in the Tudor Gothic style with some minor changes from the original plans. Exhibited R.A. 1821 (no. 1005) as 'Dunmore Park, Stirlingshire, for the Earl of Dunmore'. Contractor: Coade Co. ornamental stonework. Demolished 1972. (R.C.H.M.S. and Y.B.A.)

New Norfolk Gaol and Shire House, Norwich, Norfolk. Wilkins submitted a scheme for constructing a prison and court house alongside the ancient Keep, the inspiration for the machicolation of the gatehouse, in 1820 following an open competition. His project was accepted, excepting the removal of the court to the foot of Castle Hill, and constructed 1822–4. Contractors: Fountain and Cattermoul, brickwork, Stannard, joinery, J. De Carle and Athow, masonry, T. J. Bramah, ironwork. Partly demolished, now Norwich Castle Museum; Shire House refaced in brick 1913. (N.N.R.O. and Castle Museum Norwich.)

Project for the Fitzwilliam Museum, Cambridge. Exhibited R.A. 1820 (no. 940) as 'Fitzwilliam Museum, etc. Cambridge'. Unexecuted and lost.

1821

St Paul's Church, George Street, Nottingham. The Neo-Greek design seems to have been made before August 1821. Exhibited R.A. 1821 (no. 991) as 'New church, Nottingham'. Consecrated in October 1822. Contractor: S. Crowe. Demolished 1926. (Ch.C.)

New Court, Trinity College, Cambridge. Wilkins was invited by the College Seniors to submit designs in May 1821. He supplied Greek and Gothic schemes, not executed. In 1823 the Seniors accepted a more substantial

Gothic design with a gatehouse to the Backs aligned to the Lime Avenue. Exhibited R.A. 1823 (no. 951) as 'Quadrangle, Trinity College, Cambridge' and 1827 (no. 1050) as 'King's Quadrangle of Trinity College, Cambridge' some eighteen months after its completion. Contractor: S. Crowe. (R.I.B.A. and T.C.)

1821

United University Club, corner Pall Mall East and Suffolk Street, London. Possibly designed with the aid of J. P. Gandy and notable for the use of casts from the Parthenon Frieze in the hall. Opened 13 February 1826. Attic storey added 1850–1. Demolished 1902.

New Quadrangle, Corpus Christi College, Cambridge. The college invited Wilkins to submit designs for a virtually complete new college at the 1822 Audit. Wilkins built a Neo-Gothic chapel, hall, library and accommodation for the fellows and undergraduates beside the Old Court, part of which he preserved, but demolished the Tudor chapel, gallery and lodge. Completed by 1827 Exhibited R.A. 1823 (no. 958) as 'Quadrangle, Corpus Christi College, Cambridge' and under the same title in 1824 (no. 855). Associated with the commission was an unexecuted project to reconstruct at least the façade of the adjacent church of St Botolph. Contractors: T. Phipps and G. Ward, builders, Bond, plumber. Chapel enlarged 1870 and attic storey added to the library and Trumpington Street block 1920. (C.C.C., R.I.B.A. and Y.B.A.)

Project for the University Observatory, Cambridge. Wilkins won second prize in the competition with a Greek Doric design. Unexecuted and lost.

Project for Bylaugh Hall, Bylaugh, Norfolk. Commissioned by Edward Lombe under the terms of the will of Sir John Lombe, Bt, the designs are in the English Renaissance style. Exhibited R.A. 1828 (no. 1003) as 'Mansion at Bylaugh, Norfolk, for Edward Lombe, Esq.'. Unexecuted (P.R.O.)

1823

Entrance screen and south range, King's College, Cambridge. Wilkins won the open competition organised by the Provost and Fellows in March 1823. Neo-Gothic design examined and approved by John Nash and Jeffry Wyatt in June, who instigated a change in the position of the library and a reduction in the decoration of the hall and screen. The plan to 'Gothicise' the Gibbs Building and link it to the new range was abandoned. The range comprised the Fellows' building, hall, Combination Room, library, Provost's

Lodge and offices. Exhibited R.A. 1824 (nos. 885 and 963) and 1825 (nos. 975 and 976) as 'New Building at King's College, Cambridge' and 'Gateway, etc. King's College, Cambridge' and 1827 (no. 972) as 'Quadrangle, King's College, Cambridge'. Completed 1828. Contractor: Stannard. Enlarged from 1873. (K.C., R.A. and Y.B.A.)

1824?

Project for Broomhall, Fife, for Lord Elgin. Unexecuted but possibly represented by a previously unattributed Neo-Greek design at the R.I.B.A., RAN.1/N/1.

1825

East India Company Military Seminary, Addiscombe, Surrey. Wilkins was engaged to build a dining-room, barracks and office blocks next to Vanburgh's house as part of his duties as Surveyor to the Company. Completed by 1827. Contractor: G. Harrison. Demolished 1861. (I.O.L.)

East India House, Leadenhall Street, London. Wilkins completed the alterations to the interior begun by S. P. Cockerell, re-laying the faulty foundations under the new Book Room added at the southeast corner, and constructed an accounting office on the third floor with water tanks and fire-fighting equipment on the roof. Completed by 1830 and demolished 1861 (I.O.L.)

Theatre Royal, Norwich. Wilkins proposed the reconstruction including a Greek Doric colonnade to the shareholders in April 1825 and the theatre re-opened in March 1826. Destroyed by fire in 1934. (N.N.R.O.)

Project for a new quadrangle, St John's College, Cambridge. Wilkins was awarded second prize in the competition. Unexecuted and lost.

1826

University College, Gower Street, London. Wilkins reluctantly agreed to enter the competition in the winter of 1825 which he won in April 1826 with his grandest Classical scheme. The college Governors could only afford to build a revised version of the central building with the Great Hall placed at the rear. Though J. P. Gandy did not collaborate on the design, he acted as unofficial assistant during its construction. Wilkins ceased working on the college in 1830. Exhibited R.A. 1827 (nos. 969 and 970) as 'University of London' and 1828 (no. 1016) as 'London University'. Contractors: H. Lee and Son, builder, C. H. Smith, ornamental masonry, T. J. Bramah and Rottam and Hallam, ironwork. Great Hall reconstructed following a fire as the library, 1848-9, and the wings added, to different designs, from 1869 (U.C.L. and W.P.W.)

St George's Hospital, Hyde Park Corner, London. Wilkins won the open competition in December 1826 with the simpler of two Neo-Greek schemes. He made four alterations to the original design, including the substitution on aesthetic grounds of Thrasyllan anta for Corinthian columns in the main portico. Exhibited R.A. 1828 (no. 1117) as 'St George's Hospital'. Contractors (three contracts): Martin, G. Harrison and Read, builders, T. J. Bramah, ironwork. Enlarged from 1859. (R.I.B.A. and St George's)

County Gaol, Huntingdon. The prison was built 1826–8 with James Gallier as Clerk of Works. Contractor: T. Phipps. (Huntingdon Record Office and Tulane University, New Orleans)

1827
Yorkshire Philosophical Society Museum, York. Early in 1827 Wilkins was invited to supply a sketch for the museum by the society's president. He provided a detailed design which was executed under the superintendence of R. H. Sharp and opened in 1830. Enlarged 1912. (York Museum.)

Restoration scheme for the Abbey church of St Mary, Sherborne, Dorset. Presented in the form of an illustrated report at the request of the Vestry. Unexecuted. (Dorset Record Office)

Project for Westminster Hospital, London. Wilkins unsuccessfully entered a Tudor Gothic design in the open competition. Exhibited R.A. 1837 (nos. 1014, 1016 and 1022) as 'Design for a Hospital'. Unexecuted and lost. (Westminster Hospital)

Project for Brooke Hall, Norfolk, for the Reverend J. Holmes. Wilkins sent a design to the 1827 R.A. Exhibition, which was not shown, almost certainly for the six bay two storey Neo-Classical addition executed in this period; the fenestration, pilasters and balustrade compare with the Keswick additions.

Before 1828
Kingweston, Somerset, addition of a Greek Doric antis portico to the side façade of the extant Georgian house for W. Dickinson.

1828
Project for Travellers' Club, Pall Mall, London. Unexecuted and lost. (Travellers' Club.)

Two projects for the Duke of York Monument, London. In the *Letter to Lord Viscount Goderich* Wilkins claimed that the competitors were first invited to enter columnar designs at the insistence of Wellington and then, upon the intervention of George IV, triumphal arch designs. Exhibited respectively R.A. (no. 984) as 'Design for Duke of York's Column', and 1837 (no. 1034) as 'Triumphal entrance to the Horse Guards, designed to commemorate the services of a deceased Field Marshal, and approved by His late Majesty George IV'. Upon the accession of William IV, Wellington, according to Wilkins, secured the commission for Benjamin Wyatt. Unexecuted, only the columnar design remains. (R.I.B.A.)

1829
Project for the University Library, Cambridge. Rejected in the competition of 1829 and that of 1830 when it was re-entered with the addition of turreted belvederes on the main façade; the latter was probably submitted in the final competition of 1835. Unexecuted. (C.U.L.)

1831
National Gallery and Royal Academy, Trafalgar Square, London. In 1831 the Trustees of the Gallery approved Wilkins's plan to convert the old Royal Mews to house both institutions. Immediately thereafter he was invited by the Government to submit a design for a new building in a limited competition. He was declared the winner in July 1832; plans approved by the King in September 1833 when construction began. Before and after that date Wilkins tussled with the authorities to alter the design and to incorporate it into a more regular layout of the square. East, Academy, wing and centre section finished by 1837 and the Gallery opened in 1838. Exhibited R.A. 1835 (no. 1031) as 'National Gallery and Royal Academy now in progress'. Contractors: S. Baker, builder, G. Harrison, brickwork, J. Mallcott, masonry, T. J. Bramah, ironwork. Enlarged and altered from 1856. (N.G., P.R.O. and R.A.)

1835
Project for the Houses of Parliament, London. Wilkins entered his designs in the open competition under the motto 'Pentalpha' in the Neo-Tudor style. Exhibited N.G. 1836. Unexecuted. (R.I.B.A.)

Project for the Fitzwilliam Museum, Cambridge. According to a document in the University Archive Wilkins entered a model, probably Neo-Classical in style, in the 1835 competition. Unexecuted and lost. (C.U.L.)

ADDENDUM

In 1977 the Y.B.A. acquired a series of designs, unsigned but attributed to Wilkins, from the collection of Mr John Harris. In the absence of reliable provenance or documentary evidence, B1977.14.1056–67 were tentatively identified by the Y.B.A. as designs for Cambridge colleges and B1977.14.1045–50 associated with two drawings having a comparable plan and articulation, inscribed 'Castle Fraser', also in the collection of the Y.B.A. (B1977.14.1053–4).

Three, B1977.14.1063 and 1066–7 are very probably by Wilkins as they correspond with a penultimate elevation for the side façade of the addition to Tregothnan in the bound volume of the house, the Trumpington Street façade of Corpus Christi College (inscribed 'William Wilkins M.A. Architect') and the south range of King's College. Three more appear to be by him. B1977.14.1064 is a wash elevation in the Tudor style for the façade of a house, judging by its scale and composition, which might be associated with the Tregothnan commission, though unrelated to any of the extant ground-plans. Comparable in articulation, and to some extent in composition, are B1977.14.1059–60, wash elevations for the façades of one or two country houses in the Tudor style.

To these might be added B1977.14.1065, a Neo-Tudor project for King's College, showing two three-storey blocks, one of twenty and the other of four bays, linked together with the chapel by one-storey battlemented walls pierced by pointed arches. While this design resembles his early collegiate Gothic style, it conflicts with a major feature of Wilkins's scheme for the college, namely the screen, and it is at least possible that it was drawn by one of the other architects who competed for the commission in 1823.

B1977.14.1045–50 are unlike Wilkins's designs in the mediaeval style and manner of rendering. For example, B1977.14.1045, an elevation for 'Castle Fraser' has weak perspective. B1977.14.1056, said to be a project for Downing College (in fact, it seems to represent a scheme for the enlargement of the Senate House, Cambridge) is uncharacteristic of Wilkins's work. B1977.14.1057, also described as a proposal for Downing College, cannot be related to any of Wilkins's known designs for it, and though the main structure is in the Greek style and capped by a dome similar to the one he built at University College, London, the composition, proportions and detailing suggest the work of an imitator, possibly even his son, William Bushby. B1977.14.1061 appears to be for a mansion in a Gothic style equally uncharacteristic of Wilkins. B1977.14.1058 and 1062, also in the Gothic style, appear to be designs for domestic structures but may not be by the same hand. The thin turrets of B1977.14.1058, the pinnacles and the central projected section with three slender pointed arches are reminiscent of the Neo-Gothic designs of Wilkins senior.

NOTES

Introduction

1 *Gentleman's Magazine*, CIX, 2 (1839), pp. 426–7, including quotations from *The Athenaeum*, 619 (1839), p. 685. Other laudatory obituaries appeared in *Art Union* (1839), p. 139, and *Civil Engineer and Architect's Journal*, II (1839), pp. 388–9. One fact omitted from the obituaries was his membership of the Architect's Club. J. M. Crook, 'The Pre-Victorian Architect: Professionalism and Patronage', *Architectural History*, XII (1969), n. 42.

Wilkins's will, signed 12 April 1832 (P.R.O., 1839 October, Item 663, Piece 1918) and witnessed by J. P. Deering (Gandy-Deering) and a Mary Borton, was proved on 17 October 1839; the trustees were his wife Alicia, brothers Henry and George, and his brother-in-law, J. C. Murphy of 'Castle Town'. Ireland. He bequeathed his 'real free-hold copyhold' to his brothers and Murphy, and to Alicia £500 for exigencies, her personal chattels, the residue of his Government Stocks after the deduction of funeral costs, and the rents from his remaining freeholds. The theatrical estates at Norwich, Colchester, Yarmouth, Cambridge and Bury St Edmunds were to be sold at the discretion of the trustees for his wife and children, with a portion reserved for his sisters.

2 In 1827 Wilkins submitted a design for Brooke Hall to the Academy Hanging Committee. The exhibition slip is owned by H. M. Colvin. This drawing may have been for the addition built on to the existing house in 1830, according to a reference in *Kelly's Directory* (1900). The style of the addition combines Neo-Greek and Neo-Renaissance features, respectively the pilasters framing the first floor and the nicely detailed architraves marking the floors, and the channelled rustication of the ground floor and fenestration and balustrading. However, N. Pevsner, *North-West and South Norfolk* (1962), p. 101, attributes it to B. Cozens-Hardy and dates it c. 1820.

In a letter to the Reverend Christopher Wordsworth sent in the spring of 1823, Hudson Gurney implied that Wilkins was going to alter a house in London for him (T.C., Records of New Court, Letter 34). Writing to T. Spring-Rice, 10 September 1833, Wilkins mentioned looking at the roof of his London house, perhaps with a view to alteration (N.G. Archive, Miscellaneous Letters).

3 In the possession of his descendants.

4 U.C.L., Records, Letter 219, undated.

5 S. D. Kitson, *The Life of J. S. Cotman* (1937), p. 305.

6 W.P.W.

7 *Abstracts of the Papers printed in the Philosophical Transactions of the Royal Society* (1837–43), pp. 176–7.

8 *Gentleman's Magazine*, CV, 2 (1835), pp. 181–2.

9 *Ibid.*, CIII, 1 (1833), p. 249.

10 *Civil Engineer and Architect's Journal*, I (1838), p. 248.

11 *Ibid.*, X (1847), p. 382.

12 J. Elmes, *Lectures* (2nd edn, 1823), pp. 77–8, though he praised Wilkins's scholarship, p. 193, and architecture, p. 401.

13 P. 55.

14 *R.I.B.A. Journal*, 3rd Series, XL (1932), p. 135.

15 T.C., Records of New Court, Letter 44, dated 8 May 1827.

16 W.P.W., dated 28 June 1833, referring to the alteration to part of the Broad Street Range, 1833–4. See N. Pevsner and J. Sherwood, *Oxfordshire* (1974), p. 137. However, the Exeter College register for 1833 has the following note: 'Mr. Wilkins of Cambridge...made some very questionable improvements but which were adopted on the authority of his name.'

17 The list compiled from Walkley, 'William Wilkins' (where it is suggested that Burton worked in his office), Colvin, *Biographical Dictionary*, and *Architectural Publications Society Dictionary of Architecture* (1848–92). Another pupil was John Bramah (I. McNeil, *Joseph Bramah* (1968), p. 186). Watkin, *Cockerell*, p. 200, adds Henry Case.

18 *History of the Modern Styles*, pp. 76 and 77; however, Fergusson went on to question whether 'he could be sincere in both, if he knew what architecture was', ignoring such factors as patron or site.

19 Select Committee on Dramatic Literature, *Reports from Committees*, VII (1832).

20 *Letter to the Members of the Senate of the University*, pp. 20–1.

21 Fergusson, *History of the Modern Styles*, p. 77. In a preceding sentence Fergusson wrote, 'in the portico in Gower Street he has certainly produced the most pleasing specimen of its class which has yet been attempted in this country. The stylobate is singularly beautiful and well proportioned: the Order itself is faultless, both in detail and as to the manner in which it stands; and the dome sits gracefully on the whole, and is itself as pleasing in outline and detail as any that ever was erected, in modern times at least.'

22 *Reports from Committees*, VII (1832).

23 From an unidentified newspaper in Wilkins's press cutting book, W.P.W.

24 Waagen, *Works of Art*, p. 261. Waagen wrote that Wilkins was 'a fine person' who was 'distinguished from most architects, by a solid, learned education'.

25 Aberdeen Correspondence, B.M., ADD. MS. 43229. CXCI. 177; see R. W. Liscombe, 'Aberdeen, Canova and the Pitt Monument, Cambridge', *Burlington Magazine*, CXIX (1977), pp. 700–5.

26 R. B. Beckett, *John Constable's Correspondence*, III 1965), p. 61, letter to C. R. Leslie dated 28 December 1831.

27 Knight in *An Analytical Inquiry* (1805) wrote on p. 235 that 'not one of these academies has yet produced an artist, whom public opinion has ranked among painters'. Thomas Hope replied to the Council of the Royal Academy on 15 July 1819 declining to lend one of his paintings to the School of Painting: 'No one can be more anxious than I am for the higher branches of the Art of Painting in this country, and I should think nothing more conducive to their advancement than the constant study of the living model – The celebrated old Masters arrived at the excellence they attained, not by copying their predecessors – for they had none worth copying – but by the unremitting study of Nature herself.' R.A., Minute Book, VI (1819), p. 83. In his lecture 'On the Present State of the Arts', revised 1824, Fuseli warned the students: 'But let none fondly believe that the importation of Greek and Italian works of art is an importation of Greek and Italian genius, taste, establishments and means of encouragement; without transplanting and disseminating these, the gorgeous accumulation of technic monuments is no more than a dead capital, and instead of a benefit, a check on living Art...' *Lectures* (1830), p. 133.

28 E. J. Willson and A. C. Pugin, *Specimens of Gothic Architecture* (1824), p. xx.

1 Beginnings

1 H. M. Colvin, 'Fifty New Churches', *Architectural Review*, CVII (1950), pp. 189–96.

2 R.C.H.M., *Cambridge*, pp. 369 and 375–6.

3 Coade Company Day Book, p. 251, 9 June 1819, P.R.O., CI11/106; the chimney caps cost £59. 10s. 10d. For all references to the Company see also Ruch, 'Regency Coade'.

4 Minute Books, Theatre Royal, Norwich, N.N.R.O. MS. 4697/2. 10F. The records of the theatre show that a member of the Wilkins family had been a proprietor as early as 1768; one of the later proprietors was Bartlett Gurney.

5 D. Stroud, *Humphry Repton* (1962), pp. 39 and 126.

6 *Ibid.*, respectively pp. 50, 66–7, 79, 49, 68, 66 and 39. See also Colvin, *Biographical Dictionary*, for a list of the works of Wilkins senior.

7 The design for Locko Park is preserved in the Manuscripts Department of the University of Nottingham Library, where there is also a letter written by Wilkins senior to the 3rd Duke of Portland, Pw. F. 9470.

8 Quoted Stroud, *Humphry Repton*, p. 67.

9 Quoted J. C. Loudon, *The Landscape Gardening and Landscape Architecture of the Late Humphry Repton* (1840), pp. 57–8.

10 H. Repton, *Observations on...Landscape Gardening* (1803), p. 174; for Donington, J. Brushe, 'Wilkins Senior's Original Designs for Donington Park as Proposed by Repton', *Burlington Magazine*, cxxi, 1979, pp. 113–14, though he understates the differences between the Gothic Revival domestic styles of Wilkins father and son.

11 B.M., ADD. MS. 18. 37917.F244, 7 May 1794. The B.M. has another letter written by Wilkins to Windham dated 23 May 1796 (ADD. MS. 18. 37908.F237), containing a testimonial for one Hardingham who had deserted from the Surrey Militia but who had supported Windham in the recent General Election, and Windham's election address. D.C. Library has a bound volume recording an investigation conducted into the legality of Windham's election in that year.

12 S. R. Pierce, *Norwich Cathedral at the End of the 18th Century with Descriptive Notes by William Wilkins* (1965), introduction.

13 Noted, with an account of the study Wilkins and Repton later made of the cathedral, by Pierce, *Norwich Cathedral*.

14 Willis and Clark, *Architectural History*, I, pp. 531–2.

15 R. Fitch, *Views of the Gates of Norwich* (1861), pp. xxxii–xxxiii and xxxiv.

16 N. Pevsner, *North-East Norfolk and Norwich* (1973), p. 232.

17 'An Act for Repairing the Parish Church of *Great Yarmouth* in the County of *Norfolk*, and Rebuilding of the Tower Thereof' (1806). The Act enabled the trustees to levy duty on the coal, culm and cinders landed at Yarmouth to finance the repair work. Various records associated with the commission are at the Y.A. The top of the old spire was dismantled by Messrs J. Catlove and Company and rebuilt by Messrs Norton Simpson with a timber frame covered with sheets of an alloy of copper and tin, costing £2,595. Brief descriptions of the renovations appear in J. P. Neale and J. Le Keux, *Views of the most Interesting Collegiate and Parochial Churches in Great Britain* (1824), with illustrations, and Preston, *Yarmouth*, p. 39. Neither book mentions the re-roofing of the church to which Wilkins referred in a letter dated 13 November 1809 addressed to the Town Clerk, John Watson (Y.A.).

18 P. 226.

19 N.N.R.O., Gurney Papers, RQG. 363.

20 Quoted Crook, *The Greek Revival*, p. 137.

21 Phoenix Collection, Avery Library, Columbia University, P727.3/w65. 1–11; these are listed in Harris, *Catalogue of British Drawings*, p. 276.

22 S.A., Minute Book. XXVIII, p. 225, Thursday 4 December 1800; the Vice-President, Alexander Aubert, was in the chair and Charles Towneley and Samuel Lysons were present; the testimonial had been lodged on 3 July 1800 (p. 166).

23 The Varsity antiquaries are discussed by Watkin, *Thomas Hope*, and Crook, *The Greek Revival*.

24 Another example is the earlier traveller in Greece, James Dallaway, who, in 1801, wrote *Observations on English Architecture*, covering both Classical and mediaeval styles and attributing the source of the Gothic to France; for this book see N. Pevsner, *Some Architectural Writers of the Nineteenth Century* (Oxford, 1972), p. 18.

25 The other contributors included C. R. Cockerell, J. N. Fazakerley, Edward Hawkins, Dr Philip Hunt, Henry Raikes and the military topographers, Captain Light and Lieutenant Colonel Squire.

26 *Greek Marbles Brought from the Shores of the Euxine, Archipelago and Mediterranean and Deposited in the Vestibule of the Public Library of the University of Cambridge* (Cambridge, 1809); in a footnote to p. iii he noted that William's eldest sister had 'completed a drawing upon a very large scale which is suspended in the University Library'. For the caryatid, L. Budde and R. Nicholls, *A Catalogue of the Greek and Roman Sculpture in the Fitzwilliam Museum Cambridge* (Cambridge, 1964), pp. 46–9.

27 For Whittington, Pevsner, *Architectural Writers*, pp. 18–19; see also pp. 16–22 for a review of contemporary writings on the origins of Gothic architecture, and G. Germann, *The Gothic Revival in Europe and Britain: Sources, Influences and Ideas* (1972).
   The Aberdeen Correspondence in the B.M. includes verses addressed by him 'To the Revd. Mr. Whittington on his Grace after Meals' (ADD. MS. 43347.CCCIX).

28 S.A., Minute Book, XXVIII, pp. 415–21, 30 April 1801, when he was first admitted a Fellow; it was published in *Archaeologia*, XXIV (1801), pp. 105–12. The secretary was the Reverend James Brand (1744–1806).

29 P. 162, in which he claimed that Moorish and Gothic architecture were corruptions of the Classical.

30 B.M., ADD. MS. 43229.CXCI.31.

31 B.M., ADD. MS. 43229.CXCI.62, dated St Johns College, 28 April 1805.

32 B.M., ADD. MS. 43229.CXCI.81.

33 B.M., ADD. MS. 43229.CXCI.180. written from Ditton.

34 B.M., ADD. MS. 43229.CXCI.272, dated Betchworth [?], 2 December. In an earlier passage Raikes wrote, 'His family who have been most sensible throughout to your recollections of him, were gratified by your wish to evince it so strongly in preparing his Architectural work for publication...'
   A draft for the preface and for the contents remain in the Aberdeen Correspondence at the B.M., respectively ADD. MS. 43229.CXCI.370 and 368.

35 B.M., ADD. MS. 43229.CXCI.318, dated Betchworth, 22 August.

II Antiquaries abroad

1 B.M., ADD. MS. 43229.CXCI.35, dated Ryde, 22 October.

2 The University Grace Book for 1801 records that only one Bachelorship was awarded.

3 The four remaining letters Wilkins wrote in Latin to the Vice-Chancellor are preserved in the C.U.L., Oo.96.16.
   The author is greatly indebted to Mr B. Caven, M.A., of Birkbeck College, University of London, for the translation of the letters which appear in the text.

4 The information on H.M.S. *Malta* is taken from the Log Books preserved at the P.R.O.

5 E. Croft-Murray, *Decorative Painting in England*, II (1970), p. 159. Murray states that Aglio met Wilkins in Rome in 1801, travelled with him to Greece, returning to Rome in 1802, and going to Cambridge in December 1803 only to leave for London after six months following a quarrel with Wilkins. For Aglio's career, U. Thieme and F. Becker, *Allgemeines Lexicon der Bilden Künstler* (Berlin, 1967).

6 Three gouaches by Aglio, W.P.W.: the Bay of Naples, signed 'A. Aglio Feci 180[2]'; the interior of a cave near Syracuse, inscribed 'Veduta interna d'una delle Satonne a Siracuse ad uso communementa dei fabricatori di Corde ed'attiva gente di similforte – depinta e diqe. da Agostino Aglio Pitte', and a river scene signed 'A Aglio feci' and inscribed verso, 'Veduta della Corrente ossa [?] Camate [?] dessng e dep. da Agostin Aglio Pitt'. A line drawing of a distant view of ruins in this collection may also be by Aglio.

7 Quoted A. J. Bolton, *The Portrait of Sir John Soane* (1927), p. 135.

8 *Ibid.*, p. 247, with references to the books by Antonini and Pigonati. For Mylne's projected work and preceding publications on Paestum see Wiebenson, *Greek Revival Architecture*, p. 35, n. 73, and p. 124, and pp. 44–5.

9 *The Topography of Athens* (1821), p. cxiv.

10 B.M., ADD. MS. 43229.CXCI. 97.

11 B.M., ADD. MS. 43229.CXCI.99, dated Thebeston Hall, 27 October. John Hayter (1756–1818) graduated from King's College, Cambridge and was sent to Naples by the Prince of Wales to decipher the Papyri.

12 B.M., ADD. MS. 43229.CXCI.109, written from Thebeston Hall.

13 B.M., ADD. MS. 43229.CXCI.10; Pitt replied from Downing Street on 27 October 1805 that theatricals could not harm Aberdeen's 'character for the attention to real business'. The play was Sheridan's *The Rivals*. Aberdeen's theatrical exploits are recounted by Sir Arthur Gordon, *The Earl of Aberdeen* (1893), p. 14.

14 B.M., ADD. MS. 43229.CXCI.129.

15 B.M. Typescript, p. 4647.

16 B.M., ADD. MS. 43229.CXCI.228.

17 For the Stanmore circle see Gordon, *Earl of Aberdeen*, p. 13.

18 The identity of Findlay remains a mystery unclarified by Gordon, *Earl of Aberdeen*, pp. 9–10; Venn, *Alumni Cantabrigienses* states that Whittington accompanied Aberdeen through France and Italy.

19 Departure date noted B.M., ADD. MS. 43336.CCXCVIII, p. 4, the second

volume of the diary Aberdeen kept in France and Italy. The letter from Pitt is dated Park Place, 20 December 1801 (ADD. MS. 43229.CXCI.5); in it Pitt gave Aberdeen permission to visit Napoleon if he so desired.

20 B.M., ADD. MS. 43335.CCXCVII, the first volume of the diary kept in France and Italy.

21 B.M., ADD. MS. 43335.CCXCVII, p. 26 v.

22 B.M., ADD. MS. 43335.CCXCVII, pp. 24 v-25.

23 B.M., Department of Greek and Roman Antiquities, ABE 65, II, p. 66.

24 B.M., ADD. MS. 43335.CCXCVII, p. 38 v.

25 B.M., ADD. MS. 43335.CCXCVII, pp. 39 v-40.

26 B.M., ADD. MS. 43336.CCXCVIII, pp. 27-9.

27 B.M., ADD. MS. 43336.CCXCVIII, pp. 42-3.

28 According to Gordon, *Earl of Aberdeen*, p. 10, he met the Countess of Albany at Florence and conversed on Italian literature with her lover, the poet, Alfieri, though this is not recorded in the diaries.

29 B.M., Department of Greek and Roman Antiquities, ABE 65, I, respectively pp. 36, 83 and 121.

30 B.M., Department of Greek and Roman Antiquities (no. 1600), purchased by the museum at the sale held at Argyll House, London, in 1862; see A. H. Smith, *Catalogue of Sculpture in the Department of Greek and Roman Antiquities*, III (1904), pp. 39-40, said to be similar to the statue executed by Praxiteles. Other marbles Aberdeen had collected in Greece were presented to the museum by his son in May and June 1861 (Minutes of the Standing Committee and General Meeting, pp. 2260, 9973 and 9982).

31 B.M., Department of Greek and Roman Antiquities, ABE 65, I, p. 39 v.

32 For the Greek Committee, C. M. Woodhouse, *The Philhellenes* (1969) and W. St Clair, *That Greece might Still be Free* (1972), p. 58, where it is recorded that Aberdeen contributed with Lansdowne and Elgin to the ad hoc committee formed by Lemprière, though he declined to join the 1823 London Greek Committee.

The report of the Turkish atrocity is B.M., Department of Greek and Roman Antiquities, ABE 65, I, pp. 137-8.

33 *Ibid.*, p. 50.

34 *Ibid.*, respectively pp. 69, 105 and 113.

35 R.A., LAW/1/95, addressed from Whitehall. The references to Troy are *ibid.*, pp. 75 and 143 v; under the second heading Aberdeen wrote, 'It is my object to insist strongly upon the length of time between The War and Homer. I indeed think it great.'

36 See J. V. Luce, *Homer and the Heroic Age* (1975), especially pp. 125-6, and J. M. Cook, *The Troad: An Archaeological and Topographical Study* (Oxford, 1973), pp. 28-29 for Aberdeen.

37 B.M., Department of Greek and Roman Antiquities, ABE 65, I, pp. 73-5.

38 *Ibid.*, p. 132.

39 B.M., ADD. MS. 43229.CXCI.240. Published E. D. Clarke, *Greek Marbles* (1809), pp. 67-9 and xxvii.

40 B.M., Department of Greek and Roman Antiquities, ABE 65, II, p. 7, 26 September 1803, where he refused to buy a small gold coin for 500 piastres; a rough plan of the temple appears on p. 7 v.

41 *Ibid.*, pp. 22–5, inscribed ground-plan on p. 43 v.

42 *Ibid.*, p. 32. R. Walpole (ed.), *Memoirs relating to European and Asiatic Turkey* (1817), 'Remarks on Two Sculptural Marbles brought from Amyclae', pp. 446–51, written as a letter to Walpole dated Argyll House, 26 May 1817, and R. Walpole (ed.), *Travels in Various Countries* (1820), 'Letter from the Earl of Aberdeen to the Editor, relating to some Statements made by M. R. Rochette, ... on the Authenticity of the Inscriptions of Fourmont', pp. 489–503, dated Argyll House, September 1819.
    The reference in the Aberdeen Correspondence is B.M., ADD. MS. 43230.CXCII.332, dated 1819.

43 B.M., ADD. MS. 43229.CXCI.360, from First Lieutenant C. A. Lennock.

44 'The Topography of Troy', *Edinburgh Review*, VI, 12 (1805), pp. 257–83. There is a draft in the Aberdeen Correspondence (ADD. MS. 43344.CCCVI).

45 B.M., ADD. MS. 43229.CXCI.72, dated only Friday. Earlier in an undated letter (no. 44), Drummond had written to Aberdeen hoping that he had finished the Review. Writing from Twickenham on 13 August 1805, Drummond told Aberdeen, 'I have received a letter from Knight [see note 46] in which he attacks our *critique* on Gell.' In a subsequent undated letter (no. 79), he wrote, 'I dined yesterday at Holland House, and heard the *Edinr. Review* discussed. I saw that they thought *highly* of our performance but said it was too severe. I did not drop a hint. I wish you would undertake Clarke [a reference to Clarke's comments on Troy in *Travels in Various Countries*, II (1810)].'

46 B.M., ADD. MS. 43229.CXCI.75. On 18 July 1805 Knight wrote to Aberdeen from Downton (no. 87): 'As for poor Gell he is certainly not capable of contending either with you or Drummond either as a Scholar or as a Writer. But I have obtained some useful Information from his Drawings; and think sometimes you treat him rather horribly, particularly as to the *long Grass* on the tumulus of Hector.'

47 'The Topography of Troy', p. 261 n.

48 *Ibid.*, p. 279.

49 *Ibid.*, p. 268.

50 *Ibid.*, p. 282.

51 *Ibid.*, p. 283.

52 B.M., ADD. MS. 43229.CXCI.46 and 71; in the second Whittington began 'I have not gone through you yet in the *Edinburgh Review* but it looks well.'

53 B.M., ADD. MS. 43229.CXCI.177 and 178.

54 S.D., Minute Book, III. Wilkins was proposed for membership on 5 March 1809 and almost immediately elected to the Committee of Publications, which then included Lord Aberdeen.

55 B.M., ADD. MS. 43230.CXCII.8.

56 B.M., ADD. MS. 43229.CXCI.116, headed Cambridge.

III Temples of learning

1 For the commission, Willis and Clark, *Architectural History*, II, pp. 753–69, and for annotated illustrations of Wilkins's designs, Watkin, *Triumph of the Classical*, nos. 13–18.

2 The case for Hope is made by Walkley, 'A James Wyatt Design', with illustrations of the designs by Wilkins and Wyatt, and Watkin, *Thomas Hope*, pp. 62–3 and 68–9; see also A. Dale, *James Wyatt* (1936), pp. 87ff.

3 D.C., Minute Book, Report of the Referees, 26 March 1806.

4 D. Stroud, *Henry Holland. His Life and Architecture* (1966), p. 142, and pl. 128 for Hertford Castle which Holland enlarged in 1805.

5 The specification is given in the Minutes and Reports of the College Committee (I.O.L., J/2/1, p. 31). For a review of the commission based on the records at the I.O.L., Crook, 'Haileybury'.

6 Minutes and Reports of the College Committee, 12 December 1805 (I.O.L., J/2/1, pp. 67–8).

7 Little, 'Cambridge and the Campus'.

8 The alteration was proposed in a letter dated Hertford, 6 April 1806, recorded in the Committee of College References (I.O.L., J/1/22, p. 406). Wilkins wrote, 'Having been for the last week resident upon the spot, I find that the plan may be considerably improved by changing the East for the West side, *mutatis mutandis*; the approach will, in this case, face the road,...and the other offices be thrown into the background and perfectly concealed from the view.' S.M., Drawer LXXIII, Set 2.

9 Committee of Colleges References (I.O.L., J/1/23, pp. 409–10). Cockerell persuaded the Committee to add 'a portico of the Ionic order with stone Entablature and other decoration' to the entrance at a cost of £956. 4s. 8d., and to embellish the ceilings of the chapel and library at a cost of £344. These are illustrated, with other views of the college, in eight water-colours at the I.O.L., Western Drawings, 541/1–8, dated c. 1855 by M. Archer, *British Drawings in the India Office Library* I (1969), p. 85.

10 Minutes and Reports of the College Committee, 3 March 1809, I.O.L., J/2/1, p. 325.

11 Repton's scheme was finally adopted by the Court of Directors on 6 April 1809 (Proceedings, I.O.L., J/3/1) after nearly two years of discussion. The total cost was £4,237. 18s. 9d.

12 The final account dated 15 March 1814 and signed by T. W. Rundall is set out on pp. 469–70 of the Committee of College References (I.O.L., J/1/29). In a footnote Rundall stated that the original contract had been for £50,855 but noted that £3,351. 10s. 1d. of additional expenses had been sanctioned in 1807 and another £1,311. 13s. 5d. in 1809, while Wilkins had been paid £600 for his Working Drawings.

The sources for Addiscombe and the East India House, apart from the Court Books, 1825–30 (I.O.L., B/178–82), are Vibart, *Addiscombe*, Leeds,

Public Buildings of London, p. 82 and Foster, *East India House*, p. 145. There are photographs of Addiscombe and plans of East India House at the I.O.L., respectively Misc. Series H/763 and Maps A1x7.

13 Report of the Committee of Buying and Warehouses read 8 June 1825 (Court Book, I.O.L., B/178, p. 136); for Cockerell, Watkin, *Cockerell*, p. 250.

14 P.R.O., Works 17/10/1, Wilkins to Alexander Mylne, Weymouth Street 19 January 1833: 'I have said Wednesday instead of Tuesday the latter being my day at the India House.'

15 The details of Alicia's background are obscure. Those given were kindly supplied by W. P. Wilkins, who owns her account books for the 1820s, which record the Colonel's visits.

16 D.C., Minute Book, 24 January 1818.

17 P.R.O., CI11/106, Order and Memorandum Book, 1 July 1819, Letter Book, 17 June 1820 and Day Book, 25 July 1820; the cost was £402.

18 R.C.H.M., *Cambridge*, p. 374.

19 Avery Collection, Columbia University, IB/15; see Harris, *Catalogue of British Drawings*, p. 276.

20 Crook, *The Greek Revival*, pp. 130-1. However, Downing established a pattern for classically styled educational institutions beginning with J. Sanders's Sandhurst, 1807, and including Mill Hill, Hackney and Highbury Colleges.

IV 'The true proportions of that noble architecture'

1 *Reports of the Yorkshire Philosophical Society* (1827), p. 33.

2 Farington Diary, B.M. Typescript, p. 4453, Friday, 8 September 1809: 'at the Royal Society Club yesterday...Cavendish...Wilkins...Simmonds and Cockerell all criticising and objecting one way or another to the design of Covent Garden Theatre viz. the *Front*.' For Soane's attack and a review of the design, Crook, *The Greek Revival*, pp. 117-19.

3 Pls. 60-1; Donington, pls. 31-5.

4 R. Southey, *The Life of Nelson* (1929), p. 267.

5 'Nelson's Pillar. A Description of the Pillar with a List of Subscribers. Published by order of the Committee' (1811, reprinted 1846). For the commission, Henchy, 'Nelson's Pillar' and 'Francis Johnston'; his doubts on Wilkins's authorship are disproved by the pamphlet.

6 Pevsner lists some of the preceding columns in his entry on the Yarmouth Column, *North-East Norfolk and Norwich*, p. 154.

7 'Nelson's Pillar...Published by order of the Committee'.

8 W. Ison, *Georgian Buildings of Bath*, pp. 45 and 49.

9 R.C.H.M., *Cambridge*, p. 373.

10 Britton, *Bath and Bristol*, p. 52, and N. Pevsner, *South and West Somerset* (1958), p. 215.

11 P. 152.

12 Crook, 'Grange Park' (and for the original house, E. Mercer in *The Country Seat*, ed. H. M. Colvin and J. Harris (1970), pp. 48–54), and Redmill, 'The Grange'.

13 N. Pevsner and D. Lloyd, *Hampshire* (1967), p. 47.

14 Gallier, *Autobiography*, pp. 12, 15 and 16.

15 R.I.B.A., E4/10(1–2).

16 Watkin, *Cockerell*, pp. 71 and 69.

17 *Repository of Art*, 3rd Series, IV (1825), p. 250.

18 Fergusson, *History of the Modern Styles*, pp. 83–4.

19 P. 184, quoting J. Stuart and N. Revett's description, *Antiquities of Athens*, III (1794), ed. W. Revely, chapter 1.

20 The designs were kindly made available by the present Earl of Rosebery and are now preserved at the R.C.H.M.S. There are also elevations in the Neo-Greek style by Burnes the Younger and, closer in composition to those of Wilkins though dating from 1805, by William Atkinson.

21 R.I.B.A., E4/13. The Stourhead Archive has a letter of payment to Wilkins for the design (T(ST)383. 4). See Woodbridge, *Landscape and Antiquity*, p. 133.

22 R.I.B.A., RAN.1/N/1.

23 Watkin, *Cockerell*, p. 170; see also Crook, 'Broomhall, Fife'.

v The Civil Architecture of Vitruvius

1 *Quarterly Review*, XXI (1819), pp. 25–40; the reviewer praised the book and largely concurred with the criticisms of Vitruvius as an historian of Greek architecture. 'Shanaghan' also complimented it in the *Gentleman's Magazine*, I (1819), p. 507. *The Civil Architecture* was listed as one of the 'Authorities' consulted in J. Britton, *A Dictionary of Architecture and Archaeology of the Middle Ages* (1838).

The critique in the *Quarterly Review* emphasises a problematical feature of the publication of the book, for the volume is described as 'part II'. This is unresolved by the references in the Longman Archive now preserved at Reading University Library. These record that the book was commissioned 27 June 1808 (Commission Ledger, CI, fo. 321), that 'part I' was published 9 June 1813 (Divide Ledger, DI, fo. 237), and that 'part II' was entered at Stationer's Hall 10 September 1817. However, the title-pages of copies thus far discovered are dated 1812 and the dedication 31 December 1812. Since the title given in the list of recent publications in the *Edinburgh Review*, XXI (1813), is a shortened form of that in the *Quarterly Review*, and since the Divide Ledger also has entries dated 14 January 1818, referring to the engraving of plates by Lowry, costing £600, of which Wilkins paid £200, it may be that part II denotes the inclusion of illustrations.

Wilkins subsequently contemplated republishing the translation, possibly with revised notes, as indicated by the announcement in the *Architectural*

Magazine, I (1834), p. 372, that he was preparing an edition of two of the 'principal' books of the Treatise.

2 *Inquiry into the Principles of Beauty in Grecian Architecture* (1822), p. 36.

3 B.M., ADD. MS. 43230.CXCII, respectively nos. 13, dated 30 Bedford Place, 23 August 1809; 15, dated London, 25 August 1809; 31, dated London, 10 October 1809; 38, undated, and the draft no. 33.

4 F. Granger, *Vitruvius on Architecture* (1931), p. 170; and Wilkins, *The Civil Architecture*, pp. 9–10. The translation was praised by Edward Hawkins in his essay on the topography of Athens (in Walpole, *Memoirs*, p. 489), and the whole footnote quoted by W. Kinnard in the second volume of his new edition of the *Antiquities of Athens* (1825), p. 30, n. b.

5 W. Newton, *The Architecture of M. Vitruvius Pollio*, I (1771), p. 49. Newton, apart from editing Stuart's papers for the second volume of the *Antiquities of Athens* (1787), wrote *Commentaires sur Vitruve*... (1780).

6 James Stuart, *Antiquities of Athens*, I (1762), chapter 5, and II (1787), chapter 1. The latter opinion was reiterated in chapter 2 of the third volume (1794), edited by W. Reveley.

7 The manuscript copies at the British Museum are Arundel 122.xv (acquired 1831); Cotton Cleoparra DI.x–xI, and Harleianus 2508.xv, 2760.xIV–xV, 2767.IX–x, 3859.xI–xII and 4870.xv (each acquired in 1753). For the manuscripts see C. H. Krinsky, 'Seventy-eight Vitruvius Manuscripts', *Journal of the Warburg and Courtauld Institutes*, xxx (1967), pp. 49–52.

8 *The Architecture of M. Vitruvius Pollio*, preface, p. v.

9 The review, from an unidentified journal in Wilkins's press cutting book (W.P.W.), appears to have been of L. Marini's, *Discorso...del methodo di descrivare la voluta Ionica vitruviani*... (Rome, 1821), which criticised *The Civil Architecture*.

10 *The Civil Architecture*, pp. 21–2, n. 2.

11 The history of these and later studies is recounted by W. H. Goodyear, *Greek Refinements, Studies in Temperamental Architecture* (New Haven, 1912). For Cockerell's investigation of entasis, Watkin, *Cockerell*, p. 17, acknowledged by Aberdeen in the *Inquiry*, p. 157. T. Jenkins briefly examined the use of entasis in *Antiquities of Athens*, IV (1830), and quoted Wilkins's explanation on p. 5, n.c.

12 Penrose, *An Investigation of the Principles of Athenian Architecture* (1851, reprinted 1888), p. 23. On p. 77 Penrose complimented Wilkins on his translation of the problematical passage on the temple of Jupiter Olympius.

J. Gwilt, *The Architecture of Marius Vitruvius Pollio in Ten Books* (1826). Wilkins was a subscriber. Gwilt preferred Newton's translation, only referring to that by Wilkins on p. xxix.

13 Penrose, *Investigation*, p. 22, n. 2.

14 *Ibid.*, p. 23, n. 1.

15 *Ibid.*, pp. 37 and 38.

16 In the fourth volume (1830), T. L. Donaldson praised Wilkins's commentary on Vitruvius's description of the Classical theatre, p. 43, n. b.

17 The Aberdeen Correspondence at the B.M. includes a letter with a rough plan for the ground floor of Argyll House dated 4 June 1808 and signed Ignatius Bonomi (ADD. MS. 43229.CXCI.314). Argyll House is fully documented with illustrations in *The Survey of London*, XXXI, *St James Westminster, Pt II* (1963), pp. 295–7, and XXXII, pls. 132 and 133.

18 For these commissions and a review of the influence of the Marbles, Liscombe, 'The Commencement of Real Art'.

19 B.M., ADD. MS. 43230.CXCII.147, dated Stonebrook Cottage, 28 September.

20 W.P.W. The reference may be to Knight's *Carmina Homerica* (1808 and 1820).

21 B.M., ADD. MS. 43229.CXCI.228, dated Malta, April 1807.

22 B.M., Department of Greek and Roman Antiquities, ABE 65, II, pp. 67–78.

23 The volume inscribed 'Miscellaneous Notices Tending to Illustrate Grecian Subjects; Ancient and Modern', B.M., Department of Greek and Roman Antiquities, ABE 65a, especially pp. 17–25. There are a series of writings on numismatics: B.M., ADD. MS. 43229.CXCI; 43345.CCCVII; and 43346.CCCXIII. The article is Walpole, *Memoirs*, pp. 425–45.

24 The purchase seems to stem from correspondence between Knight and Aberdeen dating back to the summer of 1805 (B.M., ADD. MS. 43229.CXCI). During this period Aberdeen gave Knight two bronzes from Paramythia. A. Michaelis, *Ancient Marbles in Great Britain* (Cambridge, 1882), p. 118; for Knight's collection, pp. 119–22.

25 B.M., ADD. MS. 43229.CXCI.201, addressed from Portland Place. There remain four earlier letters written in 1807, Nos. 191, 193, 195 and 199.

26 B.M., ADD. MS. 43229.CXCI.207, dated Soho Square, Saturday.

27 B.M., ADD. MS. 43230.CXCII.74, Knight to Aberdeen, dated 12 October [1810].

28 Price wrote to Aberdeen from Foxley on 27 February 1813 (ADD. MS. 43228.CXC.12): 'I shall be most happy to go a picture hunting with you...' Aberdeen's loans to the British Institution are recorded in the Exhibition Catalogues, 1815, 1816, 1828, 1830, 1832 and 1836.

29 B.M., ADD. MS. 43229.CXCI.87, addressed from Downton.

30 *The Civil Architecture*, Introduction, p. lxxvi.

31 *Inquiry*, p. 73 and *The Civil Architecture*, Introduction, p. xli.

32 B.M., ADD. MS. 43230.CXCII.58.

33 *The Civil Architecture*, Introduction, p. xxii.

34 *Ibid.*, p. xiii.

35 B.M., ADD. MS. 43230.CXCII.74; for the argument between Knight and Price, N. Pevsner, 'Richard Payne Knight', *Art Bulletin*, XXXI (1949), pp. 293–320, and W. Hipple, *The Beautiful, the Sublime and the Picturesque in Eighteenth Century British Aesthetic Theory* (Carbondale, Ill., 1957).

For Aberdeen's correspondence with Price, B.M., ADD. MS. 43228.CXC; the earliest letter is dated 22 May 1810. References to the Introduction occur

in nos. 22. 27, 30, 32, 44, 47, 51, 53 and 61 in which Aberdeen replied to
Price's criticisms, dated Priory, 23 September 1816, beginning, 'As I have
no particular wish to bear such a close resemblance to the sturdy hero of
Homer as may be discovered in our friend Knight...I shall not scruple to
confess that I have been a good deal shaken in my opinions by much that
you have said.' However, Aberdeen did not alter his argument for the
Inquiry.

36 Aberdeen's synthesis of current ideas on aesthetic response was probably
   influenced by two short quotations from Stervent and Hume, written into
   his Commonplace Book, B.M., ADD. MS. 43342.CCCIV, respectively pp. 33
   and 42. This contains notes for the Introduction, including a draft for the
   beginning, p. 33.

   For further discussion of these theories, *The Civil Architecture*, Introduction, pp. iii–xv, and *Inquiry*, pp. 5–48.

37 *The Civil Architecture*, Introduction, p. xvii.

38 *Ibid.*, p. xix. This surmise has received support in general terms by J.
   Boardman, 'Chian and Early Ionic Architecture', *Antiquaries Journal*,
   XXXIX (1959), esp. pp. 212–18.

39 *The Civil Architecture*, Introduction, p. xx.

40 *Ibid.*, p. xx and pp. xxxv–xxxvii.

41 *Ibid.*, p. lii.

42 *Ibid.*, p. lv–lxiii.

43 *Ibid.*, pp. lxvii and lxviii.

44 *Ibid.*, p. lxxvi.

45 *Inquiry*, p. 214.

46 *Ibid.*, p. 215.

47 *Ibid.*, p. 216.

48 *Ibid.*, p. 216; R. P. Knight, *Analytical Inquiry* (1805), pp. 177 and 178. See
   also J. Gwilt, *An Examination of the Elements of Beauty in Grecian Architecture*
   (1825), and *Elements of Architectural Criticism* (1837), including this sentence,
   p. 23: 'The truth is that the arrangements which Greek architecture
   require, in order to produce effect, are unsuitable to modern habits.'
   Aberdeen's ideas were reiterated by J. Pennethorne, *The Geometry and Optics
   of Ancient Architecture* (1878), p. 83.

49 *The Civil Architecture*, Introduction, p. xv.

50 A. Hirt, *Die Baukunst nach den Grundsätzen der Alten* (Berlin, 1809).

51 *The Civil Architecture*, Introduction, p. xvi, referring to B. Galiani,
   L'Architettura di M. Vitruvio Pollione (Rome, 1758 and 1790).

52 *Inquiry*, p. 52.

53 U.C.L., Records, Document 1167, pt 10.

54 In a second letter, 2 March 1833, Wilkins wrote, 'Far from propagating
   the errors of Vitruvius, the aim of my translation is to separate them from
   such parts of his system as are in conformity with Grecian principles.'

55 *Inquiry*, p. 216.

56 The Testimonial read: 'William Wilkins Esq R.A. F.S.A. of Weymouth
   Street a Gentleman well versed in various branches of Science. Author of

"The Antiquities of Magna Graecia" "The Civil Architecture of Vitruvius" and other works being desirous of becoming a Fellow of the Royal Society, we whose names are underwritten here do, from our personal knowledge recommend him as highly deserving of that honour and likely to become an useful and valuable member', signed by J. A. Paris, D. Gilbert, J. Gage, T. J. Pettigrew, J. Ealey, T. Amyot, C. Konig, H. Ellis, C. Wilkins, G. Peacock, T. Phillipps, C. F. Barnwell and E. Hawkins.

57 B.M., ADD. MS. 43230.CXCII.66.
58 Lawrence Correspondence, R.A., LAW/1/228.
59 B.M., ADD. MS. 43230.CXCII.88. For the election and Aberdeen's presidency, J. Evans, *A History of the Society of Antiquaries* (1956), pp. 225–51.
60 Lawrence Correspondence, R.A., LAW/1/286, addressed from Mirables.
61 B.M., ADD. MS. 43230.CXCII.112.
62 S.A., Minute Book, XXXIV, p. 274, 25 November 1819; Aberdeen, in the chair, gave Knight 'full power and authority...in my absence to supply my place of President', to counter criticism of his lack of attendance. Evans, *Society of Antiquaries*, p. 241, n. 1.
63 S.D., Minute Book, IV. Apart from serving as the society's editor, Wilkins belonged to committees on the restoration and engraving of the Reynolds Group Portraits and finances, 1818, 1819, 1829 and 1830. In 1835 he was made auditor of the Antiquaries with William Ottley, Bishop of Chichester, and Lord Prudhoe (*Gentleman's Magazine*, CV, 1 (1835), p. 420).

VI The Gothic mode

1 Figures taken from N.N.R.O., Minute Books, Theatre Royal Norwich, MS. 4697/2.10F and Wilkins's evidence to the Select Committee on Dramatic Literature, 1832, Q.3805. The Norwich Local History Library has indistinct illustrations of the Colchester and Ipswich theatres; those at Yarmouth and King's Lynn are illustrated in Preston, *Yarmouth*, and T. Burley, *Playhouses and Players of East Anglia* (Norwich, 1928).
2 H. G. Wayment, *The Windows of King's College Chapel Cambridge* (1972), pp. 118b–119a.
3 Christie's Sale Catalogue, Saturday 7 April 1838 (no. 4); possibly bought by Wilkins at Hermon's Sale Room, 8 June 1814 (no. 74) for £10 (A. Graves, *Art Sales* (1921)).
4 B.M., Typescript, p. 5722.
5 Stroud, *Humphry Repton*, p. 72; at a later date Repton talked of being 'engaged in the greater works of Pentillie and Tregothnan'. For Pentillie, W. P. Wilkins, 'Pentillie', and N. Pevsner, *Cornwall* (1970), p. 137.
6 S.A., Minute Book, XXXIII, p. 256, 25 February 1813; vote of thanks, p. 257.
7 Macaulay, *The Gothic Revival*, pp. 318–19, pl. 176.
8 *Ibid.*, p. 320; for William Burn, pp. 321–37, and for others, pp. 216–18.

9 Cockerells' criticisms are quoted fully in Watkin, *Cockerell*, pp. 82–3 and pl. 11.

10 Letter Book, p. 344, 7 July 1818; Notes and Memorandum Book, p. 11a, 28 October 1815, the original order with additions on pp. 12a, 13, 20 and 20a, and Day Book, pp. 207–8, August 1818 with complete account amounting to £3,822. 5s. 4d. P.R.O., CI11/106.

11 Day Book, p. 333, 2 March 1821. P.R.O., CI11/106.

12 Fergusson, *History of the Modern Styles*, p. 84.

13 Press cutting book. W.P.W.; see also *Survey of London*, XXXIV, *St Anne, Soho* (1970), pp. 20ff.

14 Hussey, 'Tregothnan' and *English Country Houses*. He attributes the drawings to Wyatville and dates them c. 1816, i.e., after Wilkins had been commissioned by Falmouth; their composition and style seem closer to that of the Reptons or Robert Lugar.

15 Macaulay, *The Gothic Revival*, pp. 320–1, pls. 177 and 178 (wrongly attributed to Burn in the captions), from the bound volume of designs for Dunmore, R.C.H.M.S., STD/86/1 (1–7). A perspective wash drawing of the main and entrance fronts conforming exactly with these and probably that exhibited R.A. 1820 is now at the Y.B.A., hitherto confused with Dalmeny (Harris, *Catalogue of British Drawings*, p. 278, B1975.2.637). Dunmore is reviewed in R.C.H.M.S., *Inventory of Stirling* (1963), p. 341.

VII Dilettanti

1 'Report of the Committee of the Society of Dilettanti appointed by the Society to superintend the expedition lately sent by them to Greece and Ionia', 1814, p. 15.

2 *The Antiquities of Ionia*, V (1915), ed. R. P. Pullan, introduction, p. 3; the introduction contains a full account of the expedition and the compilation of the books published on its findings, and also the extracts from Wilkins's correspondence with members of the society quoted in this chapter.

3 See G. Martin, 'The Birth of the British Institution', *Country Life*, CLI (1972), p. 186–8. Prince Hoare was censured by the Academicians for having praised the Institution in *Academic Annals* (1809), pp. 56–8 (R.A., Council Minute Book, IV, p. 96).

4 R.A., Council Minute Book, V, p. 299; compare Lord Darnley, who lent Titian's 'Venus and Adonis'; 'I am indeed persuaded that nothing will tend more effectually to form and improve the Taste or more usefully to direct the hand of the young English Artist than a careful study of the peculiar excellencies of the great Italian Masters.'

5 R.A., Council Minute Book, IV, p. 104, receipt of Will 15 March 1809; opened 13 May 1824, VII, pp. 4–5; but on 26 June, p. 7, a letter was read from T. A. Knight stating that Payne Knight had remade it in 1814 in favour of the B.M.

6 The improvements date from 1802 and continued into the early 1820s,

listed Council Minute Books, III–V, and briefly mentioned by Whitley, *Art, 1800–1820*, pp. 111, 212, 253–4 and 262. Flaxman expressed the opinion of most Academicians in the revised version of his introductory lecture on sculpture: the Prince Regent's 'munificent gift of the extensive and valuable collection of casts from the most sublime works of Greek sculpture' would be essential to the 'diffusion of knowledge and taste [and] the elevation of national character in noble and useful arts'. *Lectures* (1838), p. 20.

On 18 July 1831 Wilkins, seconded by Reinagle, moved in the General Assembly (IV, p. 127) that the collection of architectural casts purchased from the Lawrence executors be presented to the B.M. and be conveniently arranged 'for the study of Artists and the improvement of the public Taste'.

7 J. Barry, *A Letter to the Dilettanti Society* (1797), p. 6.
8 Artists elected to the societies are listed in Evans, *Society of Antiquaries*, and L. H. Cust, *A History of the Society of Dilettanti*, ed. S. Colvin (1914).
9 S. C. Hutchison, *The History of the Royal Academy* (1968).
10 This paragraph condenses Liscombe, 'The Commencement of Real Art'.
11 B.M., Letter Books, Fellows, XXV, 10 August 1843, retrospective account of Aberdeen's aid; Tatham, XXI, 12 and 13 August 1842.
12 W. Gell, *The Itinerary of Greece* (1827), p. 46.
13 Colvin, *Biographical Dictionary*.
14 Reconstructed on the Athenian Agora (J. Travlos, *A Pictorial Dictionary of Ancient Athens* (New York, 1971), pp. 104 and 199, fig. 150).
15 S.D., Minute Book, IV.
16 Wilkins, *Atheniensia*, p. vi.
17 *Ibid.*, p. vii.
18 *Ibid.*, pp. vii–viii.
19 'The Pediment Sculptures of the Parthenon', pt VI of C. R. Cockerell, *A Description of the Collection of Ancient Marbles in the British Museum* (1830).
20 Walpole, *Memoirs*, pp. 580–603, entitled 'Remarks on the Architectural Inscription brought from Athens, and Now Preserved in the British Museum'; Hawkins's essay was entitled 'On the Topography of Athens', pp. 475–516.

The 'Athenian Inscription' and Wilkins's contribution to its translation, and to the study of the Erechtheum, are examined in *The Erechtheum*, ed. J. M. Paton (Cambridge, Mass., 1927), pp. 93, 182, 301, 543, 545, 552, 554, 596, 597, 600 and 620 where his description of the temple is said to be 'intelligent and, on the whole, accurate', but his translation to be 'vitiated by his misunderstanding of the architectural terms.'

21 Wilkins, *Atheniensia*, p. 15.
22 *Ibid.*, pp. 28–30.
23 *Ibid.*, p. 9–10.
24 In the *Inquiry*, p. 56, Aberdeen wrote that numerous prototypes for Greek architecture existed in 'nature, or among accidental combinations of natural objects'.
25 Pennethorne, *Geometry and Optics*, p. 112.

26 Wilkins, *Atheniensia*, p. 37.

27 *The Antiquities of Athens*, Bohn Library (3rd edn, 1849), p. 43.

28 *Ibid*., pp. 56 and 65; further complimentary references, pp. 60, 63, 68, 70, 74, 76, 79, 81 and 103.

29 Wilkins, *Atheniensia*, pp. 48–9.

30 *Ibid*., p. 49.

31 Bolton, *Sir John Soane*, p. 276.

32 In Walpole, *Travels*, pp. 409–19. Wilkins acknowledged the aid of Clarke on pp. 148–9 of *Atheniensia* and described him as the 'learned' professor of mineralogy.

33 Wilkins, *Atheniensia*, p. 101, argument pp. 97–109.

34 *Ibid*., p. 86.

35 The biography of Hittorf in *Allgemeines Deutsche Biographie*, XII (Leipzig, 1880), p. 505, states: 'Later he translated…William Wilkins's *Unedited Antiquities of Attica*. He used the book in many ways and defined it through notes and drawings.'

36 Gell, *Pompeiana* (1817), p. 160, n. 1; compare *Antiquities of Athens* (3rd edn, 1849), p. 12: 'but that Ictinus and Callimachus, to say nothing of Phidias and Praxiteles, practised these atrocities, while Pericles approved and patronised, can only be believed – quia impossible est'.

    The Standing Committee of the B.M. trustees ordered a scientific investigation for traces of colour on the marbles in the collection by two chemists, two sculptors and two painters at the instigation of W. R. Hamilton on 12 November 1836 (Minutes, XV, pp. 4380–2).

37 Walpole, *Travels*, p. 410.

38 B. Schweitzer, 'Pheidias der Parthenonmeister', *Jahrbuch der Kunsthistorischen Instituts, Berlin*, LIII (1938), pp. 1–89, and B. Ashmole, *The Classical Ideal in Greek Sculpture* (1964).

39 Wilkins, *Atheniensia*, pp. 121–2.

40 B.M. Typescript, p. 6895.

41 St Clair, *Lord Elgin*.

42 *Atheniensia*, p. 144.

43 'On the Sculptures of the Parthenon', p. 418.

44 S.D., Minute Book, IV; Elgin was rejected in April and May 1817.

45 *Atheniensia*, pp. 119–20; Wilkins referred to the 'learned and accomplished author of a recent essay on ancient sculpture, whose taste and judgement upon such subjects is undisputed'.

46 B.M., ADD. MS. 43229.CXCI.237, postmarked July.

47 B.M., ADD. MS. 43229.CXCI.260, addressed from Petersham.

48 B.M., ADD. MS. 43229.CXCI.312, addressed from Soho Square.

49 B.M., ADD. MS. 43230.CXCII.108, dated 14 May, in which Knight confided there was 'no society or conversation for which I more willingly exchange them than your own'; no. 117, dated 13 June, Soho Square and no. 147, dated 28 September, Stonebrook Cottage.

50 B.M., ADD. MS. 43230.CXCII.310, addressed from Soho Square. In his evidence, Aberdeen equated the friezes aesthetically but found the

Parthenon of greater historical value. Knight in *Explanation of part of the evidence of...Knight concerning the Elgin Marbles* (1816) called the Phigaleian frieze 'unquestionably inferior to the best specimens from Athens'.

VIII National monuments and private commissions

1 Treasury Records, P.R.O., T1.1526.4583; formally joined 6 April.
2 B.M. Typescript, p. 7174.
3 B.M. Typescript, p. 7162, Friday 23 May 1817.
4 Beckett, *Constable's Correspondence*, p. 61, letter undated but c. 10 January 1832.
5 *Gentleman's Magazine*, LXXXVII, 1 (1817), p. 624, stating that construction of the monuments would relieve the high rate of unemployment.
6 R. W. Liscombe, 'Economy, Character and Durability: Specimen Designs for the Church Commissioners, 1818', *Architectural History*, XIII (1970), pp. 54–5, fig. 27.
7 *Gentleman's Magazine*, LXXXVII, 1 (1817), p. 624; see also J. M. Crook, 'The Career of Sir Robert Smirke, R.A.', D.PHIL. Thesis (Oxford, 1961).
8 B.M. Typescript, p. 7171, Friday 6 June 1817.
9 Number of entries given in a letter written by A. Robertson to Constable after the publication of Wilkins's *Letter to Lord Goderich* (*John Constable: Further Documents and Correspondence*, ed. I. Fleming-Williams (1975), pt II, 'Correspondence', pp. 281–2. Robertson claimed that Wilkins and Gandy were favoured by the committee, sending their tower design late, which then became the preferred type of monument, but the Government had proposed an 'Ornamental tower' (R.A. Council Minute Book, V, p. 281). Robertson named James Wyatt as a competitor. Nash and J. B. Papworth also entered designs (J. Summerson, *John Nash, Architect to George IV* (1935), app. 1 and pp. 268–9 and W. Papworth, *John B. Papworth* (1879), p. 39).
0 Brief accounts of the competition appear in Papworth, *John B. Papworth*, and Crook, 'Sir Robert Smirke', pp. 8off. In the *Letter to Lord Goderich*, p. 73, Wilkins quoted the Speaker's Address following that vote: 'To consecrate the trophies and perpetuate the fame of our brave countrymen who fell in that unrivalled victory...we have declared it to be our ardent desire...to erect in the metropolis of the empire such a lofty and durable monument of their military renown and our national gratitude as may command the veneration of our latest posterity.'
1 Printed by Hoare in the *Inquiry into the requisite Cultivation and present State of the Art of Design in England* (1806), and in his own *Lectures on Painting* (1809).
2 J. Sandby, *The Royal Academy and its Members* (1862), I, p. 280.
3 Crook, 'Sir Robert Smirke', p. 81.
4 Preston also described the column as 'an emulating object to British seamen, who are daily passing and repassing the Roads within its view' (p. 167).

15 H. Mallalieu, *The Norwich School. Crome, Cotman and their followers* (1974), p. 79.

16 Preston, *Yarmouth*, p. 188, and, renovations, Minute Book, Theatre Royal Norwich, N.N.R.O., MS. 4697/2.10F.

17 Southey, *Life of Nelson*, p. 214.

18 Pamphlet distributed by the Committee preserved at Y.A. with other documents (Tc. 32.F).

19 For example, Walkley, 'William Wilkins', and Crook, 'Haileybury'.

20 R. Gunnis, *Dictionary of British Sculptors 1660–1851* (1951), p. 93.

21 P.R.O., CI11/106, Notes and Memorandum Book, pp. 39–40, and Day Book, pp. 198, 210, 247, 254 and 264, 27 June 1818 to 30 September 1819. The final account amounted to £950. 13s. 0d., sundry expenses £412. 8s. 6d.

22 Kitson, *J. S. Cotman*, fig. 30. W.P.W. has an engraving said to be by Cotman showing the column as built.

23 Preston, *Yarmouth*, p. 168. The address noted in a press cutting (Y.A.).

24 Crook, *The Greek Revival*, p. 133; for the hall, Ison, *Georgian Buildings of Bath*, pp. 45 and 83–4, pl. 37a.

25 Pevsner, *North-West and South Norfolk*, p. 217.

26 Liscombe, 'Bylaugh Hall, Norfolk'.

27 D. Linstrum, *Sir Jeffry Wyatville* (1972), pp. 53–67. For the Renaissance Revival in country house design, M. Girouard, *The Victorian Country House* (Oxford, 1972).

28 N.N.R.O., Gurney Papers, RQG.363. The estimate comprised: £6,453. 9s. 6d., foundations and structure, £200 white brick facing to three fronts of old house, £50 bells, £100 adding seven feet to the dining-room and bedroom above, £68 estimate, £1,030 builder's profit, £390 architect's commission and £30 for Wilkins's travelling expenses. In August 1818 Wilkins ordered two shields of arms for the house from the Coade Company (Notes and Memorandum Book, p. 26, P.R.O., CI11/106).

29 Correspondence concerning the theatre 1818–46 preserved at the Bury St Edmunds and West Suffolk Record Office, Acc. 421/1–88, used Rosenfeld, 'William Wilkins'. See also S. Tidworth, *Theatres. An Illustrated History* (1973), p. 140, illus. 123, and for the restoration *National Trust Newsletter*, XXI (1974), pp. 22–3.

IX Alma Mater

1 Willis and Clark, *Architectural History*, I, p. 189, and Venn, *Gonville and Caius*, II, p. 137. Three drawings, almost certainly by Wilkins, preserved at the college.

2 Willis and Clark, *Architectural History*, p. 198.

3 Willis and Clark, *Architectural History*, I. p. 573. The King's Congregation Book records that the bridge, like the later extensions, was financed by the

sale of trees from their estates. For Cockerell's opinion, Watkin, *Cockerell*,
p. 69.
4 Verse, Walkley, 'William Wilkins'; reports, *Cambridge Chronicle*, 11
February and 10 October 1814, R.C.H.M., *Cambridge*. pp. 369b–370a.
5 In September 1819 Wilkins ordered a 'Cast of Gothic'. Notes and
Memorandum Book, p. 54, Coade Company, P.R.O.: and Day Book, p.
264, 29 September 1819, noting despatch of plaster model of Gothic
mouldings to Mr William Browne at Cambridge, costing £3. 9s. 0d. For
Bernasconi, Macaulay, *The Gothic Revival*, pp. 196, 198 and 300, and the
commission, R.C.H.M.. *Cambridge*, p. 279a.
6 T.C., Records of New Court, Letter 14a. The Seniors were also greatly
disturbed by the immorality of the undergraduates. For the commission,
Willis and Clark, *Architectural History*, II, pp. 651–9.
7 Willis and Clark, *Architectural History*, III, pp. 192–5.
8 *Ibid.*, II, pp. 277–8.
9 *Ibid.*, I, p. 303; for the commission pp. 302–4.
10 *Ibid.*, I, pp. 564–5.
11 'Exhibition of Designs for Completing King's College Cambridge,
submitted to the Provost and Fellows', S.M. Library 55.2.
12 Wilkins was consulted by the Commissioners of the Woods and Forests
after Nash had accused Burton, and the sculptor, Bubb, of departing from
the contract (Sanders, *Regent's Park*, p. 124).
13 T.C., Records of New Court, Gurney, Letter 34. The others were also
favourable.
14 C.C.C., Records of New Court, dated 5 February 1828; the inscription is
now on the library staircase.
15 Oswald, 'Corpus Christi', and Willis and Clark, *Architectural History*, I,
p. 302.
16 Apart from the elevation for this front at the R.I.B.A., E6/11, there is
another signed version, Y.B.A., B1977.14.1066.
17 Watkin, *Cockerell*, p. 83.
18 Report, preserved at King's; Willis and Clark, *Architectural History*, I,
p. 64, appear to have confused Wyatt's Christian name with the surname of
another architect.
   N. Pevsner, *Cambridgeshire* (1970), p. 96; with reviews of Wilkins's other
work at Cambridge.
19 W. P. Hunt, 'A plan for King's Parade, Cambridge', *Country Life*, CVII
(1950), pp. 1798–1800, illus. 4, design exhibited at the R.A. 1797 (1150).
20 T.C., Records of New Court, Letter 39, dated 12 May 1821. Watkin,
Triumph of the Classical, illustrates one of the Classical designs, no. 19.
21 T.C., Records of New Court; another letter, 290, from a Mr Judgson to
the bursar implies that the Seniors chose the Gothic style as more
compatible with the Avenue trees.
22 T.C., Records of New Court.
23 R.I.B.A., E4/11.
24 Trevelyan, *Trinity College*, p. 92.

25 Willis and Clark, *Architectural History*, I, pp. 348–9.
26 Y.B.A. has a design for the south range, B1977.14.1067.
27 Classical designs were submitted by Barry, Burton, Donaldson, Forbes, Goldicutt, Goodwin, Jenkins, Meade, M'Intosh, Poynter, Wallace and Wolfe; some illustrated ('King's College, Cambridge in the Making').
28 Wilkins does not appear to have made a drawing for such a cloister.
29 Minute Book, Theatre Royal Norwich, N.N.R.O., MS 4697/2.10F.
30 C.U.L., 6245.I.146.
31 B. Harcourt, *The Theatre Royal Norwich* (Norwich, 1903), p. 5.
32 The letters in the press-cutting book are signed 'A Member of the Senate', which Wilkins was even after resigning his fellowship in 1811. Both are full of privy information about the commissions for Trinity, Corpus Christi and King's Colleges and University College, London. As conclusive are first, the comment regarding the proposed museum that hypaethral temples 'were of so rare occurrence, that Vitruvius is obliged to resort to Athens to prove that such buildings were sometimes erected', adding that the passage in the manuscripts was corrupt, and second, the statement that the plan to rebuild the façade of St Botolph, for which he had made a design, 'might be accomplished without any great expense and certainly without any inconvenience or loss of character'.
33 Willis and Clark, *Architectural History*, III, pp. 198–205.
34 J. P. T. Bury, ed., *Romilly's Cambridge Diary 1832–1842* (Cambridge, 1967), p. 74, 13 April 1835.
35 N.N.R.O.. Gurney Papers., RQG.363, dated Dalmeny Park, 12 July 1817.

x Institutional Architecture

1 T.C., Records of New Court, Letter 44.
2 N. Pevsner, *Nottinghamshire* (1951), p. 40.
3 R.I.B.A., E6/11, inscribed, 'Elevation of Corpus Christi College Cambridge with St. Botolph redesigned'.
4 Ch.C., Records, File 18074, pt. 1.
5 *Gentleman's Magazine*, XCVII, 1 (1827), p. 9.
6 Ch.C., Records, File 18074, pt 1.
7 *Gentleman's Magazine*, XCVII, 1 (1827), p. 9.
8 *Ibid.*, XCVII, 2 (1827), p. 10.
9 Liscombe, 'Economy, Character and Durability'.
10 M. H. Port, *Six Hundred Churches* (1961).
11 Pp. 48–9.
12 Britton and Pugin, *Public Buildings of London*, p. 131; for the commission pp. 130–4.
13 *Respository of Arts*, X (1827), p. 306. Cockerell disliked its design (Watkin, *Cockerell*, p. 69).
14 *Architecture in Britain 1530–1830* (1970), p. 501.

15 *Survey of London*, XXIX, *St James, Westminster Pt I* (1960), p. 399.

16 B.M., ADD. MS. 43230, CXCII. 332, undated; 335, dated 1 November 1819; and 339, dated 16 November 1819, Stonebrook Cottage.

17 H. Rosenau, *Social Purpose in Architecture* (1970), pp. 52–76; also N. Pevsner, *A History of Building Types* (Princeton, 1976), pp. 159–68.

18 Orridge, *The Gaol at Bury St Edmunds*, p. viii. The Bury Gaol was brought into the discussions of Wilkins's scheme on 18 April 1826 (Proceedings of the Committee for Improving the Castle Hill and the Courts of Justice, Quarter Sessions Order Book, N.N.R.O., C.S4/4).

19 P. 20. For Soane's Neo-Gothic Gaol and an illustration, D. Stroud, *The Architecture of Sir John Soane* (1961), p. 34, pl. 46.

20 Wilkins defeated the painter, Allan, by fourteen to seven votes. R.A., General Assembly Minute Book, III, p. 392; and IV, p. 1 for his election as Academician. He attended his first General Assembly on 6 November 1826.

21 S.M., Soane Correspondence; Soane noted on it: 'An impudent letter from William Wilkins. No answer returned.' Cup. 1, Div. 2.

22 S.M., Soane Correspondence, dated 21 February. On the letter Soane wrote: 'Another impudent letter from William Wilkins. No answer returned.' Cup. 1, Div. 2.

23 Quarter Sessions Order Book, N.N.R.O., C.S4/4.

24 *Ibid.*. The figure comprises: £35,543 Shire House and gaol; £3,006. 15s. 11d. exterior granite wall; £1,720. 5s. 5d. restoration of the Keep; £2,033. 12s. 2d. mill; £2,768. 13s. 11d. alterations and additions to Shire House and gaol, £699. 15s. extra foundations; £150. 9s. 8d. sundry repairs to castle; £2,949 fees for Wilkins and the clerk of works – totalling some £2,000 more than the estimate. Additional expenses not in the original contract: £392. 162. od. stone paving to yards; £510. 18s. 6d. additional drainage; £596. 17s. 5d. earth removal and levelling; £147. 13s. 11d. erection of wall behind Shire House; £110. 3s. 4d. lobby for prisoners in Shire House; £1,059. 13s. 10. palisades around Shire House; £87 arch to strengthen part of castle wall; £142. 10s. od. expenses incurred by death of clerk of works; £910. 11s. od. furnishing courts and £433. 11s. 2d. Act of Parliament and advertisements for plans and contracts.

25 The water colour perspective is reproduced in Harris, *Catalogue of British Drawings*, pl. 68. For the gaol, Hatfield, *The County of Huntingdon*, in which Wilkins is misnamed Thomas Wilkins and the cost given as £14,000 instead of £11,440. Hatfield also confused some of Wilkins's work with those additions executed by a local architect, Thomas Smith, in 1850.

26 Rosenau, *Social Purpose in Architecture*, and F. N. L. Poynter, *The Evolution of the Hospital in Britain* (1964), pp. 210ff., and for the subject generally, J. D. Thompson and G. Goldin, *The Hospital: A Social and Architectural History* (New Haven, 1975), and Pevsner, *History of Building Types*, pp. 159–68.

27 *Morning Herald*, June 1828.

28 J. L. Davies, *Westminster Hospital* (1952).

29 St George's Hospital, London, Minute Books, and Liscombe, 'St George's Fate'.

30 Anecdote kindly supplied by Dr Humble, Honorary Historian to Westminster Hospital.
31 *Gentleman's Magazine*, cvii, 2 (1837), p. 174.
32 Blomfield, *St George's Hospital*, pp. 40–1.
33 R.I.B.A., E4/9(8). E4/9(7 and 9–13) are Working Drawings for the hospital as built.
34 R.I.B.A., E4/9(1–6). The elevations are not attributed to Wilkins in M. Binney, 'Future of St. George's Hospital', *Country Life*, CLX (1976), pp. 1354–6.
35 St George's Hospital, Minute Books, 28 September 1831.
36 Quoted in description of the hospital by Leeds, *Public Buildings of London*, pp. 41–7.
37 The foundation of the college is recounted by Bellot, *University College London*. For Bentham, J. Bowring, *The Works of Jeremy Bentham* (1838–43); the University College Archive has writings by Bentham on the college and education.
38 D. J. Watkin, 'Charles Kelsall: the quintessence of Neo-Classicism', *Architectural Review*, CXL (1966), pp. 109–12.
39 For Brougham's activities, C. W. New, *The Life of Henry Brougham to 1830* (Oxford, 1961), expecially chapters 19 and 20.
40 Britton and Pugin, *Public Buildings of London*, introduction, p. xxvii. W.P.W. elevation exhibited 'Age of Neo-Classicism', London, 1972, cat. no. 1387.
41 Leeds, *Public Buildings of London*, p. 86; for preceding comments on the design, pp. 78–88. Hosking also declared, 'The portico of the London University is of almost unequalled magnificence and beauty', while Wightwick averred, 'Here Athens is nobly accredited; Rome accredited; and England honoured.'
42 The other members of the first council listed in University College *Calendar* (1969), apart from those given in the text, included Sir Alexander Baring, George Birkbeck, Sir James Mackintosh (Professor of Law, East India College, Haileybury, 1818–24), James Mills (a Director of the East India Company) and Benjamin Shaw, M.P.
43 For Cockerell's scheme, Watkin, *Cockerell*, pp. 153–4, pl. 41.
44 Wilkins sent a copy to Horner, U.C.L., Records, Letter 219, adding that the 'subject should be constantly pursued to the eye of the public or interest in this establishment may decline'.
45 *Survey of London*, XXI, *St Pancras Pt III* (1949), pp. 87–8.
46 U.C.L., Records, Document 1167, pt. 10; this reference includes the extant reports from Atkinson, dated 18 March 1826, Gandy, dated 17 March, and Wyatville (with Lewis Wyatt) dated 20 April.
47 U.C.L., Records, Letter 1, dated Lensfield, 1 November 1825.
48 U.C.L., Records, Document 1167, pt 15.
49 U.C.L., Records, Document 1167, pt 9.
50 U.C.L., Records, Council Minute Book, app. 3, p. 13, read at Ninth Session, 29 April 1826.
51 U.C.L., Records, Document 1167, pt 13.

52 U.C.L., Records, Council Minute Book, app. 3, p. 13.

53 Leeds *Public Buildings of London*, opp. p. 77, and more recently, *R.I.B.A. Journal*, 3rd ser. XL (1933), p. 151, and Summerson, *Architecture in Britain*, pl. 410.

54 U.C.L., Records, unnumbered letter written from Weymouth Street. Among other corroborative documents are the Building Committee report, 25 November 1826: 'Mr. Gandy (who attended upon them in consequence of the illness of Mr. Wilkins)'; Council Minute Book, app. 14; and Letter 210, Wilkins to Brougham, 7 November 1827: 'I think if you will look to the wording of the Resolution you will find Mr. Wilkins. Mr. Deering (who by the bye has nothing whatsoever to do with the Commission) and Messrs Lee and Sons are informed that they are to receive his (Mr. Horner's) *instructions*. Now Messrs Lee and Sons, the Clerk of Works and all minor superintendents ought to receive *instructions* only from me.' The only reference to Gandy having contributed to the design appears in a note in an unpaginated bound specification, c. 1830, 'Room 76 . . . Mr. Deering's plan for the w.c.'

55 U.C.L., Records, Council Minute Book, p. 29.

56 U.C.L., Records, Document 34240, written from Ketterbrook.

57 U.C.L., Records, Document 34245.

58 The thirty-seven Working Drawings remaining at U.C.L. are signed by James Walter, Clerk of Works, Horner, the Warden and Henry Lee junior, but undated, though having the Great Hall behind the main block as ordered at the 46th session of the council on 16 May 1827.

59 U.C.L., Records, Letter 1118, written from Weymouth Street.

60 U.C.L., Records, Letter 1127. R. D. Owen in *Hints on Public Architecture* (New York and London, 1849), p. 43, noted that a flue had to be inserted for the chemical laboratory, spoiling the contiguous staircase, and that Sir Charles Bell, professor of anatomy, had the seating in the anatomical theatre altered from the semi-circular to the circular form.

61 U.C.L., Records, unnumbered letter, written from Weymouth Street.

62 U.C.L., Records, Building Committee Book, 2 June 1829, in a letter from Wilkins.

XI Preservation

1 E. W. Harcourt, ed., *The Harcourt Papers*, XIII (1904), pp. 180–1.

2 C. B. Knight, *This is York* (York, 1954), p. 124. For a fuller history, Wilmot, 'Yorkshire Philosophical Society Museum'.

3 Y.P.S., Minutes of the Council; on 2 November 1829 they agreed to pay Sharp £4 for his survey.

4 Harcourt, *Harcourt Papers*, pp. 182–3.

5 *Ibid.*, pp. 183–4.

6 Y.P.S., *Reports*, 1827, p. 32.

7 *Ibid.*, p. 31.

8 *Ibid.*, p. 33.

9 An engraving of Sharp's elevation appears in the end papers of the *Reports*, 1823–6.

10 *Y.P.S., Reports*, 1827, p. 33.

11 *Yorkshire Gazette*, 27 October 1827.

12 N.N.R.O., Quarter Sessions Order Book, C.S4/4. The report, dated 19 October 1826, and Wilkins's letter were discussed at the Easter Sessions, 25 April 1827.

13 B.M., Minutes of the Standing Committee of Trustees, XIV, p. 3897. The *Essay* was dated 8 November 1834.

14 N.N.R.O., Gurney Papers, RQG.363.

15 *Report on the State of Repair of Sherborne Church by William Wilkins Esq. M.A. R.A.* (1828), addressed from 36 Weymouth Street. The choice of Wilkins from a list of other architects recorded Vestry Minutes, Dorset Record Office.

16 Vestry Minutes, Dorset Record Office.

17 For a modern study, J. Newman and N. Pevsner, *Dorset* (1972), pp. 368–77; the church was restored in the 1850s by R. C. Carpenter and W. Slater.

18 Regarding the use of iron Wilkins wrote, pp. 15–16:

Some observations have been made, and some stress laid upon the report drawn up by Sir Christopher Wren, on the subject of Salisbury Cathedral [1668]... According, however, to my understanding of the passage, he decidedly condemns the use of iron as 'against the rules of good architecture', not only because it is corruptible by rust, but because it is fallacious, having unequal veins in the same metal, some pieces in the same bar being three times stronger than others, and yet all sound to appearance.

It is singular enough, that Sir Christopher Wren, who condemns the use of Iron as applied to prevent the spread of the Tower of Salisbury, where the spire sits upon it, has adopted it in St. Paul's for a similar purpose, around the Attic order from which the dome springs!! The two cases of Salisbury and Sherborne are totally dissimilar; and no argument deduced from the employment of iron in the former is applicable to the latter, where the iron work is calculated to hold the ceiling *suspended*, and not to prevent the spread of the Tower itself.

19 One example, surely studied by Wilkins, was the thirteenth-century detached bell-tower at West Walton, Norfolk.

20 For the issue of restoration, Pevsner, *Architectural Writers*, pp. 168–82. In *Contrasts*, A. W. N. Pugin wrote, 'If casts of all the effigies of royal and ecclesiastical persons, remaining in the cathedral and other churches, were carefully taken, coloured fac-simile from the originals and arranged in chronological order, what a splendid historical and national series they would form.' (2nd edn, 1841), p. 16n.

XII A temple of the arts

1 The best review of the events surrounding the commission is Martin, 'Founding of the National Gallery'; for Wilkins's design, Martin, 'Wilkins and the National Gallery' and Crook and Port, 'The King's Works, pp. 461-70, including a summary of expenditure; the total cost, not accounting for the fireproofing of the Gallery, was £81,793. In The Greek Revival, p. 101, Crook argues that Wilkins's design for the Gallery and comments on the layout of the square were influenced by the Picturesque.

2 D. Farr, William Etty (1958), p. 84, from a review in Frazer's Magazine, June 1838; Samuel Woodburn, however, told the Select Committee on Arts and Manufactures in 1836 that the Gallery would keep people from the gin shops.

3 N.G., Board of Trustees' Minutes, I, pp. 22-3, when Aberdeen, Goderich, Farnborough, Dover and Peel were present; they further resolved, 'That Mr. Wilkins's plan be submitted to the First Lord of the Treasury, and that Lord Goderich, Lord Farnborough and Lord Dover be empowered on the part of the Trustees to communicate with him on the subject.'

4 Wilkins, Letter to Lord Viscount Goderich, p. 66; signed copy presented to R.A. Library.

5 Ibid., p. 42.

6 R.A., General Assembly Minute Book, III, p. 439, 18 July 1825; the other members were Chantrey, Flaxman, Hilton, Phillips and Turner, their report read on 15 March 1826 (IV). On 20 June 1832 another committee, consisting of Shee, Howard, Chantrey, Mulready, Phillips, Smirke, Turner, Westmacott, Wilkie and Wyatville, was appointed by the General Assembly 'to confer with Mr. Wilkins as to the appropriation of the space which appears to be allotted to them by the Government for the purposes of the Royal Academy' (IV). Two weeks earlier the council sent an Address to the King: 'Highly honourable and beneficial as a National Gallery must be to the interests of Taste, it cannot, we conceive, be reasonably consider'd of more importance in a great state than an establishment like the Royal Academy for the immediate cultivation of its native Art – nor do we apprehend that any well-understood principle of economy can be advanced in opposition to the object which we thus presume to advocate – since the Fine Arts are amongst the first utilities as well as the brightest ornaments of Society; and there is no branch of science, no department of mechanical productions which is not benefitted through their agency to an extent that repays tenfold the expense necessary to provide for their due cultivation' (Council Minute Book, VII, pp. 506-7; this volume contains correspondence between Shee and Grey and Spring-Rice concerning the Academy's tenure of their quarters in the new building, pp. 96-102, dated May 1834).

7 B.M., Minutes of the Standing Committee of the Trustees, X, p. 3005,

10 February 1827, and N.G. Archive, Miscellaneous Letters, H. Ellis of the
B.M. to the N.G. Keeper, W. Seguier, dated 12 February 1827. The
painting is now in Tate Gallery, no. 121.

8 *Reports from Committees*, IX, 1836.

9 Nash's design, Summerson, *John Nash*, p. 70 and app. I, and Cockerell's,
Watkin, *Cockerell*, pp. xii, 106, 232, 246 and 252. N.G. Archive has a plan
submitted by Sidney Smirke in 1830 'for converting the building called the
King's Mews, at Charing Cross, into a Gallery for the permanent reception
of the National Collection of Pictures'. The Minutes of the Board Meeting
of the Trustees include a resolution sent to the Surveyor-General of
Works, J. Stewart, on 15 December 1830, stating their preference for the
construction of a brick building 'adjoining St. James's Palace, and on the
space left vacant by the fire which destroyed part of that edifice some
years ago – provided that the suggestion should meet with His Majesty's
Approbation' (I, p. 17).

10 *Hansard*, 3rd Series, IV (1831), p. 991.

11 Whitley, *Art, 1821–1837*, p. 268.

12 Barry, *Letter to the Dilettanti Society*, p. 25.

13 *Ibid.*, p. 5.

14 Pp. 183–4.

15 *An Account of the British Institution* (1805), p. 24.

16 *Ibid.*, (2nd edn, 1805), p. x.

17 *Letter to Lord Viscount Goderich*, p. 22.

18 *Ibid.*, p. 53.

19 *Ibid.*, pp. 75 and 80.

20 *Ibid.*, p. 64; two of Wilkins's designs, an elevation and a section, are at the
R.I.B.A., E6/10(1–2). The R.I.B.A. has recently acquired a wash drawing
identified as for the monument and attributed to Wilkins, E4/118, but
which does not correspond with the description of his designs in the *Letter*.

21 *Gentleman's Magazine*, CVII, 2 (1837), p. 174.

22 P. 78. The Arch was 'copied from that of the Tuileries, itself a copy in
miniature of the Arch of Constantine' and a 'petty bauble'.

23 For this episode, Martin, 'Wilkins and the National Gallery', pp. 325–6.

24 *Letter to Lord Viscount Goderich*, p. 53; for the Edinburgh Monument,
Watkin, *Cockerell*, pp. 151–3.

25 *Letter to Lord Viscount Goderich*, p. 63.

26 *Ibid.*, p. 34.

27 *Ibid.*, p. 40; proposals pp. 70–2. See also Shee in *Letter to the President and
Directors of the British Institution, Containing the Outlines of a Plan for the
National Encouragement of Historical Painting in the United Kingdom* (1809), and
B. R. Haydon in memorials to the Government after 1823, Q. Bell, *The
Schools of Design* (1963).

28 *Letter to Lord Viscount Goderich*, p. 56. 'The British Institution by this act
have in some degree neutralized the great benefits they had hitherto
conferred on the arts.'

29 *Ibid.*, pp. 46–7; in 1810 James Elmes had attempted to found a Royal
Academy of Architecture (Crook, 'Pre-Victorian Architect', n. 45).

30 Crook, 'Pre-Victorian Architect', p. 61; the lack of lectures was also castigated in the Report, Select Committee on Arts and Manufactures, 1836.

31 J. Millingen, *Some Remarks on the State of Learning and Fine Arts in Great Britain*...(1831), p. 8. In the *Letter* Wilkins quoted an anonymous scholar who had described Germany as a 'hot bed of Greek', noting that many Classical texts used in England came from Germany (p. 52).

32 Millingen, *Some Remarks*, p. 51.

33 *Ibid.*, p. 24.

34 *Ibid.*, p. 41.

35 *Ibid.*, p. 30.

36 *Letter to Lord Viscount Goderich*, p. 72.

37 P. 351.

38 Millingen, *Some Remarks*, p. 82.

39 *Ibid.*, pp. 81–2.

40 *Letter to Lord Viscount Goderich*, p. 15.

41 *Ibid.*, p. 16.

42 Peel declared, 'The erection of the edifice would not only contribute to the cultivation of the arts, but also to the cementing of the bonds of union between the richer and poorer orders of the state.' Quoted Martin, 'Founding of the National Gallery', VII, p. 113; in VIII Martin reviews the attitudes of Beaumont, Dover and Farnborough.

43 Pp. 44–5.

44 Greenwood quoted Ruskin's quip that the Gallery was an 'European Jest'. *The Times*, 20 April 1832, carried a letter signed 'Technes' hoping that the Government would not save 'some pounds, shillings and pence, at the costly price of national taste and civilization'.

45 For these and earlier museums, Pevsner, *History of Building Types*, pp. 111–38.

46 M. A. Shee, *The Life of Sir Martin Arthur Shee*, II (1860), p. 11.

47 Leeds, *Public Buildings of London*, p. 56. In his second letter to the editor of *The Athenaeum* (almost the only journal to give him qualified support, publishing an engraving of the façade on 31 May 1834, p. 409 with description p. 408), Wilkins referred to 'poisonous' articles in the *Albion* and *Globe*, and attacked Jerdan for having published an inaccurate print of his design without permission. Critical reports appeared in, among other journals, the *New Anti-Jacobin Magazine* (April 1833), *Gentleman's Magazine*, CV, I (1835), pp. 181–2, *Penny Magazine* (13 November 1836), pp. 466–9 and *Architectural Magazine*, IV (January and February 1837), pp. 19–28 and 57–63. However, Wilkins received some praise in 'A Letter from an Obstinate Observer', published *Lo Studio* (May–November 1833), p. 237, including 'in the management of which job, the architect has been made to feel the weight of impotent conclusions and impertinent economy'.

48 J. Gwilt, *Observations on the Communication of Mr. Wilkins To The Athenaeum* (1833) and C. Purser, *The Prospects of the Nation in regard to its National Gallery* (1833); Wilkins's description of Purser occurs in a letter to Spring-Rice dated 24 August 1832, N.G. Archive. The Gallery was also

criticised by A. W. Hakewill, *An Apology for the Architectural Monstrosities of London* (1835). By comparison J. Weale, in *Quarterly Papers on Architecture*, II (1844), p. 11, thought the Gallery portico exposed the incorrect intercolumniation of St Martin's.

49 *Observations on the Plan for the New Library by a Member of the First Syndicate* (1831); the first of three pamphlets by Peacock.

50 C.U.L., Map Room, MS., Plans X. 2; reproduced Watkin, *Triumph of the Classical*, no. 30, pl. 19.

51 *Remarks on the Replies to the Observations on the Plans for the New Library* (1831).

52 For the competition, Willis and Clark, *Architectural History*, III, pp. 97–128, and Watkin, *Cockerell*, pp. 183–96.

53 14 April 1836, Bury, *Romilly's Cambridge Diary*, pp. 100–1; entry for 11 May states that Wilkins's design received no votes (p. 101).

54 P.R.O., Works 17/10/1, dated 14 August 1833.

55 N.G. Archive, Miscellaneous Letters; Martin, 'Wilkins and the National Gallery', limits the change to the alteration of the entrances of the passages.

56 N.G. Archive, Miscellaneous Letters.

57 *Gentleman's Magazine*, CV, 2, 1835, p. 181.

58 R.I.B.A., W13/11.

59 P.R.O., Works 33/929, signed and dated (last digit missing) and inscribed, 'National Gallery No. 25 Basement floor of the west wing'; Wilkins wrote in his second letter to the editor of *The Athenaeum*, 'The building will be infested with soldiers, and cooped in by Barracks.'

The extant Working Drawings are P.R.O., Works 33/909–65, the earliest date, 1832, is on 33/953, 'No. 57 Details of the Cast-iron Girders'.

60 Whitley, *Art, 1821–1837*, p. 267.

61 N.G. Archive, Miscellaneous Letters, dated 7 January 1834, forwarded to the Trustees.

The council of the Academy asked Wilkins to prepare the Exhibition Room in the new building on 2 August 1836 (Minute Book, VIII, p. 223). On the same day Wilkins seconded Phillip's motion that the Address requesting the removal of the Academy to the new building be laid before the General Assembly, passed 29 August (Minute Book, IV). On 3 September the council discussed the arrangements for the removal of the library, casts and paintings, and on 5 November the installation of gas lighting with Wilkins (handed over to Cockerell on 19 January 1837) (Minute Book, VIII, pp. 234–6, 244 and 272–3). In the spring of 1837 Wilkins and the council made various alterations to the interior, including on 6 March (VIII, pp. 290–1), closing the communication between the Great Hall and the Academy.

62 *Reports from Committees*, XI (1836).

63 W.P.W., Kingsley to Wilkins's grandson, dated The Rectory, South Kilvington, Thirsk, 21 October 1898.

64 P.R.O., Works 17/10/1, dated 5 August 1837. For Schinkel's ideas on the exhibition of pictures see Pevsner, *History of Building Types*, pp. 128ff.

65 Compare also Waagen, *Works of Art*, p. 261, who criticised the cramped
dimensions of the Gallery and the insufficient elevation of its façade, but
praised the toplighting (though he preferred high side lighting as most
akin to that in the artist's studio) and continued, 'The main object,
therefore, of the edifice, to see the masterpieces of the National
Gallery to advantage, will, at all events be obtained, if they are judiciously
arranged...'

66 Report, N.G. Archive.

67 P.R.O., Works 17/10/1, pt 256. Wilkins estimated the cost at between
£5,000 and £6,000. The first ground-plan is Works 33/908; a similar plan
is signed and dated 1837, Works 33/966. For the layout of the square, R.
Mace. *Trafalgar Square Emblem of Empire* (1976).

68 W.P.W.

69 *Civil Engineer and Architect's Journal*, I (1838), p. 10. On p. 248 'J.H.',
writing on recent metropolitan architecture, complimented the internal
arrangements of the Gallery and blamed the Government for most of the
aesthetic faults of the building.

70 17 February 1837, Beckett, *Constable's Correspondence*, V (1967), p. 37. In
1837 Constable sent Wilkins a case of wine; for Wilkins's reply,
Fleming-Williams, *John Constable*, pp. 318–19, and p. 322 for Shee's
recommendation that Wilkins be appointed a vice-president of the Artists'
General Benevolent Institution, chaired by Turner.

71 G. D. Leslie, *The Inner Life of the Royal Academy* (1914), p. 44.

72 *History of the Modern Styles*, p. 78, condensing remarks in his *Observations on
the British Museum, National Gallery and National Record Office* (1849),
especially pp. 48–50.

XIII The ebb

1 P.R.O., Works 17/10/1, Wilkins informed the Commissioners of the Office
of Woods and Forests on 25 April 1836 that the principal floor of the
Academy would be ready 'after the end of the present exhibition'. For the
competition, Crook and Port, *The King's Works*, pp. 573–88, and Port, *The
Houses of Parliament*, pl. 25, illustrating the R.I.B.A. line elevation of the
river front (see note 2 below) attributed to Wilkins.

  Q. Hughes, *Seaport* (1964), p. 95, lists Wilkins as a competitor for the St
George's Hall, Liverpool, commission, 1836, though it is more likely that the
design was entered by his son, Henry.

2 R.I.B.A., OS1/12A(3, 4 and 5).

  The *Apology* was examined in the *Quarterly Review*, LVIII (1837), pp.
61–82, esp. p. 79, with Cust's *Letter* (see note 5 below), Hakewill's *An
Apology* and Purser's *Prospects*; the reviewer commended the simplicity and
majesty of Neo-Greek architecture, 'the Athenian style is, indeed, the *source
and fountain* of good architecture', but discounted most of Wilkins's
criticisms of Barry's design.

3 *Gentleman's Magazine*, cv, 2 (1835), pp. 257–61.

4 'Report of the Commissioners Appointed to Consider the Plans for Building the Houses of Parliament', *Reports from Committees*, xxxvi (1836), pp. 487–90.

5 E. Cust, *A letter to the Rt. Hon. Sir Robert Peel, On the expedience of a better system of control over buildings erected at the public expense and on the subject of rebuilding the Houses of Parliament* (1835).

6 S.M., Soane Correspondence, Cup. II, Div. 11, Letter IV, p. 25.

7 *Reports from Committees*, IX (1836).

8 *Building News* (13 February 1890), pp. 186–7.

9 C.C.C., Records of New Court.

10 Minute Book, Theatre Royal, Norwich, N.N.R.O.. MS. 4697/2.1OF. The Theatre Royal, Norwich, failed under the Wilkins family management in 1852 (*The Oxford Companion to the Theatre* (Oxford, 1967), p. 689).

11 Rosenfeld, 'William Wilkins', p. 22.

12 Minute Book, Theatre Royal, Norwich, N.N.R.O.. MS. 4697/2.1OF.

13 Theatre Royal Playbills, N.N.R.O., Box 1OF. p. The appearances of Kean and Macready are taken from Harcourt, *Theatre Royal Norwich* and W. Toynbee, *The Diaries of Macready* (1912).

14 Rosenfeld, 'William Wilkins' p. 23; Wilkins's evidence *Reports from Committees*, VII (1832).

15 Theatre Royal Playbills, N.N.R.O., Box 1OF. 9. Illustrating popular taste, the York Theatre advertised a 'GRAND MOVING PANORAMA executed upon 20,000 square feet of Canvas...in 14 extensive different Views, Comprising the latest struggles and Victories of the GREEKS at sea and upon land against the TURKS...views of the cities of *Athens* etc...Portrait of Lord Byron' (*Yorkshire Gazette*, 28 July 1817).

16 In the following list of paintings from the collection of Wilkins sold at Christie's the information on provenance printed in the catalogues appears in brackets, and those marked with an asterisk were said to have been exhibited at the British Institution, though not necessarily by Wilkins. 1830

    1. Van Dalen and Teniers. The Peristyle of a Mansion. (Panné)

    2. J. B. Weenix. The Prodigal Son. (Orleans collection)

    3. G. Dow. A Girl at a Window with a Brass Milk-can.

    4. Netscher. Hagar.* (Orleans collection)

    5. Berghem and Wouvermans. The Ford.*

    6. Schellincks, in the manner of Du Jardin. An Italian Seaport.*

    7. Teniers. The Temptation of St Anthony.*

    8. Wouvermans. The Interior of a Lofty Stable.* (Prince Reebempere, Mad. Hogguer, and Le Rouge)

    9. Hackaert and A. Vandervelde. The Retreat.*

    10. Berghem. Cattle Driven out to Pasture.* (M. di Beltrano)

    11. Rubens. Descent from the Cross.

    12. Gherardo delle Notte. Repas des Courtissanes. (Palazzo Pitti)

    13. Wouvermans. A Stag Hunt. (Comtesse de Verrue, A Drummond)

14. Rubens. The Prodigal Son.* (M. Pieters, M. Stiers d'Aertselaer)

1838

1a. A highly finished sketch of 'Raffaelle's' Murder of the Innocents; said to be for the engraving by Marc Antonio.

1. Francesco Francia. Adoration of the Saviour.

2. Luca Cambiaso. Martyrdom of St Stephen.

3. Cornelius Van Harlaem. The Marriage of Thetis and Peleus.

4. Parmegiano. Holy Family.

5. Domenico Feti. The Deaths of Hero and Leander. (Archduke Leopold)

6. Rubens. Descent from the Cross.

7. Pierino Del Vaga. The Deluge.

8. Pietro Da Cortona. A Reposo.

8[a] Spanish School, repainted Sir Joshua Reynolds. The Garden of Love.*

9. Giulio Romano. The Battle of Constantine and Maxentius, cartoon.

10. C. Maratti. The Holy Family.

11. Garofalo. The Holy Family with St Mark. (Gray)

12. School of Raffaelle. The Baptism of St John. (Sir Gregory Page Turner)

13. Bronzino. Noli me Tangere.

14. Albano. Diana and Actaeon.

15. Schedone. Adoration of the Shepherds. (Grand Ducal collection at Parma, Elwin)

16. Andrea del Sarto. St Sebastian. (Sir Henry Englefield)

17. Elzeimer. A Landscape.

18. Steenwyck. Interior of a Church.

19. Adrien Vanderwerff. Sleeping Nymphs, Surprised by Bacchanals.

20. Correggio. La Madonna Della Scudella, cartoon.

21. Agostino Carracci. Martyrdom of St Justine.

22. Domenichino. Landscape, with Isaac and Abraham. (Orleans Collection)

23. Raffaelle. The Judgement of Paris.

24. Domenichino. St Catherine and St Theresa.

25. Domenichino. St Ursula and Cardinal Borromeo. (Altieri Collection, Davenport)

26. P. Veronese. The Temptation of St Barbara.

27. Gaspar Poussin. The Campagna Di Roma. (Gray)

28. Domenichino. A Grand Landscape. (Borghese Gallery)

29. N. Poussin. St Peter and St John Healing the Impotent Man. (Lord Radstock)

30. Rubens. The Prodigal Son. (M. Pieters, M. Stiers d'Aertselaer)

31. Titian. The Holy Family. (Orleans Collection)

1840

81. Hackaert and Van De Velde. The Retreat.

82. Berghem and Wouvermans. The Ford.

83. Schellincks. An Italian Seaport.

84. G. Romano. The Transfiguration; a beautiful small copy from Raffaelle.

85. Correggio. The Holy Family.

86. Van Dyck. The Descent from the Cross.

87. Oizonti. A Classical Landscape.

88. Raffaelle School. Diana and Actaeon.

89. P. Del Vaga. The Deluge.

90. Albano. Diana and Actaeon.

91. Van Der Werff. Sleeping Nymphs.

92. Domenichino. St Catherine and St Theresa. (Altieri Collection, Davenport)

93. Domenichino. St Ursula and St Carlo Boromeo [sic]. (Altieri Collection, Davenport)

94. Raffaelle. The Nativity.

95. Towne. A Landscape.

96. Guido. The Virgin and Child with St John.

97. Correggio. The Nativity. (From the French Chapel at Rome)

98. Ruysch. A Vase of Flowers.

99. Van Dyck. A Gentleman in a Crimson Dress.

100. Howard. A Peasant Girl.

101. Titian. Portrait of a Gentleman in a Black Dress.

102. Domenichino. The Virgin and Child.

103. Leonardo Da Vinci. The Virgin and Child, with the columbine. (Royal Gallery at Madrid)

17 4 January 1838, Bury, *Romilly's Cambridge Diary*, p. 137.

18 N.G., Minutes, I, p. 105, Aberdeen present. The paintings to which the secretary referred are: 'The Two Trinities', by Murillo (no. 13) and 'The Brazen Serpent', by Rubens (no. 59), respectively N. Maclaren, *The Spanish School*, ed. A. Braham (1970), pp. 61–3 and G. Martin, *The Flemish School* (1970), pp. 133–7.

19 N.G., Minutes, I, p. 120. Aberdeen present, and p. 185, 7 February 1842.

20 Waagen, *Works of Art*, p. 264, noting that the Rubens had been brought to England in 1823. He also praised Wilkins's A. Carracci, 'Holy Family and Landscape' (not in the sale catalogues), and G. Poussin, 'View of Tivoli' (no. 27 in the 1838 sale) exhibited at the British Institution, 1831, no. 134. The Rubens had been exhibited at the Institution in 1829, no. 53, together with Teniers, 'Temptation of St. Anthony'. no. 22 (1830 sale, no. 7), Wouvermans, 'Interior of a Stable', no. 26 (1830 sale no. 8), Berghem, 'Cattle and Figures', no. 27, Moucheron and A. Van Der Velde, 'Landscape with Cattle', no. 76, Moucheron and A. Van Der Velde, 'Seaport', no. 152, and Netscher, 'Abraham and Rebecca', no. 183. The Titian, 'Flight into Egypt', was probably exhibited in 1831, no. 5, as 'Holy Family'; that year Wilkins also lent Domenichino (as Tibaldi), 'St Catherine and St Theresa', no. 25 and 'Cardinal Borromeo and St Ursula', no. 31 (1838 sale nos. 24 and 25), Schedoni, 'Nativity', no. 127 (1838 sale no. 15) and Domenichino, 'Meleager and Atalanta', no. 168

(1838 sale no. 28?). In 1832 Wilkins lent Bronzino, 'Christ in the Garden', no. 18 (1838 sale no. 13), Teniers, 'Virgin and Child with St John', no. 94, and Schalken, 'Bacchanalians by Torchlight', no. 159.

For paintings ascribed to Poussin and Titian, A. Blunt, *The Paintings of Nicolas Poussin. A Critical Catalogue* (1966), p. 58, no. 84, and H. E. Wethey, *The Paintings of Titian. The Religious Paintings* (1969), p. 94, no. 43, and Graves, *Art Sales*.

21 Whitley, *Art, 1821–1837*, p. 238. For Nieuwenhays, D. Robertson, *Sir Charles Eastlake and the Victorian Art World* (Princeton, N.J., 1978), pp. 86–7.
22 Blunt, *Paintings of Nicolas Poussin*, p. 123, no. 172. See note 20 above for the pictures Wilkins lent to the British Institution but which are not listed in the sale catalogues.
23 W. Roberts, *Sir William Beechey R.A.* (1907), pp. 241 and 257.
24 *Reports from Committees*, v (1835) and ix (1836); for the committee and issues preceding its formation, Bell, *Schools of Design*.
25 R.A., Council Minute Book, viii, 2 November 1837. On 16 November Cockerell seconded by Smirke proposed the purchase of 'Architectural casts', p. 370, and on 5 December Cockerell purchased a cast of a capital from the Pantheon in Rome for the Academy, p. 381.
26 s.m., Soane Correspondence, Cup. 1, Div. 2.
27 R.A., General Assembly Minute Book, iv, p. 233.
28 R.A., General Assembly Minute Book, iv, p. 251; Wilkins was the only candidate.
29 R.A., Council Minute Book, viii, p. 329, 22 June 1837, letter from Hume requesting that entrance to the Annual Exhibition be free on one or more days. His campaign against the Academy which, in the House of Commons, he called 'the *meanest* and most *stingy* of all institutions', provoked Shee into writing *A Letter to Joseph Hume Esq. M.P. in reply to his aspersions on the character and proceedings of the Royal Academy* (1838); the frontispiece is inscribed with a quotation from the Count Stroganoff, President of the Imperial Academy at St Petersburg: 'Délivre nous grand Dieu! de ces amateurs sans amour, de ces connoisseurs sans connaissance.'
30 w.p.w., who also possesses a letter from Rogers, dated Bowood, 20 October 1837, thanking Wilkins for the 'very beautiful volume' and for arousing his interest in 'the most interesting city in the world – a city which, alas, I shall never, I fear, see but in my dreams'. He hoped Wilkins's health would improve following a 'change of air and leisure of mind'.
31 *Civil Engineer and Architect's Journal*, 1 (1838), p. 34; however, the reviewer dismissed his theory about the relationship between ancient Greek temples and the Temple of Solomon, noting that Wilkins had overlooked the reference to a tall tower over the entrance of the latter in the second Book of Chronicles. It was reviewed uncritically in *Architectural Magazine*, v (1838), pp. 42–4. Penrose, *Principles of Athenian Architecture*, includes two complimentary references to *Prolusiones*, p. 46, n. 3, tiling of Greek temples, and p. 71, n. 1, translation of Athenian Inscription.
32 *Prolusiones Architectonicae*, p. 7. In this section Wilkins stated that Hadrian

had not completed the building of the Temple of Jupiter Olympius, though he had added statuary.

33 *Transactions of the Royal Society of Literature*, III (1839), pp. 155–60; Leake, *Journal*, p. 21. The copy of *Prolusiones* in the Victoria and Albert Museum Library contains an off-print of the paper with a note in Wilkins's hand including the following: 'The MS of this was sent to Hamilton to correct before presenting it to the Society. To my great dismay I found it presented just as I sent it although I had pointed out two very doubtful parts [neither specified]...Originally the Inscription was – I presume in four lines following each other.'

34 N.N.R.O., Gurney Papers, RQG.363.

35 *Civil Engineer and Architect's Journal*, I (1838), p. 24.

36 This and following letters, N.N.R.O., Gurney Papers, RQG. 363.

37 Bury, *Romilly's Cambridge Diary*, p. 175. On Wednesday 4 September 1839 Romilly lamented, 'Find that poor Mr. Wilkins was dead' (p. 176).

SELECT BIBLIOGRAPHY

PLACE OF PUBLICATION IS LONDON
UNLESS OTHERWISE STATED

WRITINGS BY WILKINS

1801. 'Some Account of the Prior's Chapel at Ely', *Archaeologia*, XIV, pp. 105–12.

1807. *The Antiquities of Magna Graecia.* Printed at the Cambridge University Press, published Longman, Hurst, Orme and Rees and dedicated to the Rt Hon. Francis Rawdon Hastings, [2nd] Earl of Moira. Fol.

1809. 'Observations on the Porta Honoris of Caius College, Cambridge', *Vetusta Monumenta*, IV, pls. 21, 22 and 23.

1813 and 1817 (title-page 1812). *The Civil Architecture of Vitruvius: Comprising those Books of the Author which relate to the Public and Private Edifices of the Ancients,* prefaced by an Introduction, written anonymously by Lord Aberdeen, entitled 'An Historical View of the Rise and Progress of Architecture amongst the Greeks'. Published Longman, Hurst, Rees, Orme and Brown and dedicated to George [Gordon, 4th] Earl of Aberdeen, K.T., F.R.S., F.S.A. Fol. and 4to.

1816. *Atheniensia, or Remarks on the Topography and Buildings in Athens.* Published John Murray and dedicated to Henry Pelham, [4th] Duke of Newcastle, K.G. 8vo.

1817. 'Remarks on the Architectural Inscription Brought from Athens, and Now Preserved in the British Museum', in *Memoirs relating to European and Asiatic Turkey*, edited by the Reverend Robert Walpole, pp. 580–603.

1820. 'On the Sculptures of the Parthenon', in *Travels in Various Countries*, edited by the Reverend Robert Walpole, pp. 409–19.

1828. *Report on the State of Repair of Sherborne Church.* Printed by Harker and Penny, Sherborne.

1831. *Letter to the Members of the Senate of the University*, dated 9 February and published J. Smith, Cambridge.

– *An Appeal to the Senate on the Subject of the Plans for the University Library*, dated 15 April and published J. Smith, Cambridge.

1832. *A Letter to Lord Viscount Goderich on the Patronage of the Arts by the English Government*, dated 20 November 1831 and printed by G. Whittingham (reprinted *Library of the Fine Arts* (1832)).

1836. *An Apology for the Designs of the Houses of Parliament marked Phil-Archimedes now exhibiting at the National Gallery, Trafalgar Square, with a defence of the Report of the Commissioners appointed by His Majesty to examine and report upon the plans which might be offered by the competitors for re-building the Houses of Parliament.* Printed W. Clowes (reprinted 1837).

1837. *Prolusiones Architectonicae or Essays on Subjects connected with Grecian and Roman Architecture.* Published by John Weale and dedicated to the Rt Hon. Charles [Grey, 2nd] Earl Grey. 4to.

1839. 'The Lydo-Phrygian Inscription', *Transactions of the Royal Society of Literature of the United Kingdom*, III (1839), pp. 155–60.

Published letters and evidence to Select Committees

1816. Evidence to the Select Committee on the Elgin Marbles, *Reports from Committees*, III, pp. 91–5.

1817. 'Topography of Athens', *Literary Gazette*, I (1817), ii, pp. 213–14 and 331–2, reprinted *Gentleman's Magazine*, LXXXVII, 2 (1817), pp. 401–3.

1826. 'Architectural improvements in Cambridge', signed 'A Member of the Senate', addressed to the editor of the *Cambridge Chronicle*, 3 and 10 November.

1828. Letter on the Bull Inn, King's Lane, Cambridge, addressed to the editor of the *Cambridge Chronicle*, 21 March.

1832. Evidence to the Select Committee on Dramatic Literature, *Reports from Committees*, VII, pp. 209–14.

1833. 'On the Change in the Line of Front of the Buildings for the National Gallery', addressed to the editor of *The Athenaeum*, 277, 16 February, pp. 104–6.

– 'The National Gallery', addressed to the editor of *The Athenaeum*, 279, 2 March (letter dated 26 February), pp. 135–6.

1836. Evidence to the Select Committee on Arts and Manufactures, *Reports from Committees*, IX, pp. 280–4 (and 284–99).

WRITINGS ON WILKINS

Arts Council of Great Britain, Exhibition Catalogue, *The Age of Neo-Classicism* (1972), pp. 649–51.
Beresford-Pite, A. 'The Work of William Wilkins, R.A.', *R.I.B.A. Journal*, 3rd ser., XL (1932), pp. 121–33, with discussion pp. 133–6.
Bellot, H. H. *University College London 1828–1928* (1929).
Blomfield, J. *St. George's Hospital 1733–1933* (1933).
Blyth, G. K. *The Norwich Guide* (Norwich, 1843).
Britton, J. *Bath and Bristol* (1829).
Britton, J. and Brayley, E. W. *Cornwall Illustrated* (1831).
Britton, J. and Pugin, A. C. *The Public Buildings of London*, II (1828).
Burley, T. *Playhouses and Players of East Anglia* (1928).

Colvin, H. M. *A Biographical Dictionary of British Architects 1660–1840* (2nd edn, 1978), pp. 893–6.

Crook, J. M. 'Haileybury and the Greek Revival: the Architecture of William Wilkins', *Haileyburian and I.S.C. Chronicle* (Hoddesdon, 1964).

– 'Grange Park Transformed', *The Country Seat*, ed. H. M. Colvin and J. Harris (1970), pp. 220–8.

– 'Broomhall, Fife', *Country Life*, CXLVII (1970), pp. 242–6.

– *The Greek Revival. Neo-Classical Attitudes in British Architecture 1760–1870* (1972).

Crook, J. M. and Port, M. H. *A History of the King's Works 1782–1851*, VI (1973).

Dictionary of National Biography, XXI (1917), pp. 267–9.

Eastlake, C. *A History of the Gothic Revival*, ed. J. M. Crook (Leicester, 1970).

Fergusson, J. *The History of the Modern Styles of Architecture*, ed. R. Kerr, II (3rd edn, 1891).

Foster, Sir W. *The East India House* (1924).

Gallier, J. *The Autobiography of James Gallier* (Paris, 1864).

Harris, J. *A Catalogue of British Drawings for Architecture, Decoration and Landscape Gardening 1550–1900 in American Collections* (New Jersey, 1971).

Hatfield, J. *History, Gazetteer and Directory of the County of Huntingdon* (Huntingdon, 1854).

Henchy, P. 'Nelson's Pillar', *Dublin Historical Record* (Dublin, 1949), pp. 53–63.

– 'Francis Johnston, Architect', *Dublin Historical Record* (Dublin, 1950), pp. 1–16.

Hussey, C. 'Tregothnan, Cornwall I & II', *Country Life*, CXXI (1956), pp. 1051–4 and 1112–15.

– *English Country Houses. Late Georgian 1800–1840* (1958), pp. 140–50.

Ison, W. *The Georgian Buildings of Bath from 1700 to 1800* (1948).

'King's College, Cambridge in the making', *Architect and Building News*, CXXXIV (1933), pp. 340–5.

Leeds, W. H. *The Public Buildings of London*, supplement (1838).

Liscombe, R. W. 'William Wilkins', *Atti del Convegno internazionale promosso dal Comité International d'Histoire de l'Art, 1971 Neoclassicismo* (Genoa, 1973), pp. 58–63.

– 'St George's Fate', *Architectural Review*, CLIV (1973), pp. 401–2.

– 'Designs by William Wilkins for Bylaugh Hall, Norfolk', *Burlington Magazine*, CXVI (1974), pp. 396–8.

– 'The Commencement of Real Art', *Apollo*, CIII (1976), pp. 34–9.

– '"That Noble Architecture", The Work of William Wilkins', *Country Life*, CLXIII (1978), pp. 540–4.

– 'Alma Mater. The Architecture of William Wilkins at Cambridge', *Architectural Review*, CLXIV (1978), pp. 42–6.

Little, B. 'Cambridge and the Campus', *Virginia Magazine of History and Biography*, LXXIV (1971), pp. 190–201.

Lysons, D. and S. *Magna Britannia*, III (1814).

Macaulay, J. *The Gothic Revival 1745–1845* (1975).

Martin, G. 'Wilkins and the National Gallery', *Burlington Magazine*, CXIII (1971), pp. 318–29.
– 'The Founding of the National Gallery London I-VIII', *Connoisseur*, 186 and 187 (1974), esp. pp. 124–38, 200–7, 272–9 and 48–53.
Neale, J. P. *Views of the Seats of Noblemen and Gentlemen*, 1st ser., I (1818), II (1819) and 2nd ser., III (1826).
Orridge, J. *Description of the Gaol at Bury St Edmunds* (Bury, 1819).
Oswald, C. 'Corpus Christi, Cambridge, II', *Country Life*, LXX (1931), pp. 420–6.
Port, M. H. *The Houses of Parliament* (New Haven, 1976).
Preston, J. *Picture of Yarmouth* (Yarmouth, 1819).
Prosser, G. F. *Select Illustrations of Hampshire* (1833).
Redgrave, S. *A Dictionary of Artists of the English School* (1878).
Redmill, J. 'The Grange, Hampshire II', *Country Life*, CLVII (1975), pp. 1242–5.
Rosenfeld, S. 'William Wilkins and the Bury St Edmunds Theatre', *Theatre Notebook*, XIII (1958), pp. 20–5.
Royal Commission on the Ancient and Historical Monuments of England. *An Inventory of the Historical Monuments in the City of Cambridge*, II (1959).
– *An Inventory of the Historical Monuments in the City of York*, IV (1975).
Ruch, J. E. 'Regency Coade', *Architectural History*, XI (1968), pp. 34–56.
Sanders, A. *Regent's Park* (Newton Abbot, 1969).
St Clair, W. *Lord Elgin and the Marbles* (Oxford, 1967).
Stacy, J. *A Topographical and Historical Account of...Norwich* (Norwich, 1819).
Summerson, Sir J. *Architecture in Britain 1530–1830*, 5th edn (1970).
– *Georgian London*, 2nd edn (1962).
Survey of London, XXI (1949), XXIX (1960), XXXI and XXXII (1963) and XXXIV (1970).
Trevelyan, G. M. *Trinity College. An Historical Sketch* (Cambridge, 1946).
'University College, London', *Country Life*, LXI (1927), pp. 973–7.
Venn, J. A., ed. *The Annals of Gonville and Caius College* (Cambridge, 1904).
– *Alumni Cantabrigienses, Part II* (Cambridge, 1940), VI, p. 471.
Vibart, H. M. *Addiscombe, its Heroes and Men of Note* (1894).
Waagen, G. F. *Works of Art and Artists in England*, I (1838).
Walkley, G. 'A Recently found James Wyatt Design', *R.I.B.A. Journal*, 3rd ser., XLV (1938), pp. 970–4.
– 'Designs for Downing College', *R.I.B.A. Journal*, 3rd ser., XLV (1938), p. 1014.
– 'William Wilkins Architect. 1839–1939', *Country Life*, LXXXV (1939), p. 689.
– 'William Wilkins', R.I.B.A. Silver Medal Prize Essay (1947).
Watkin, D. J. *Thomas Hope 1769–1821 and the Neo-Classical Idea* (1968).
– *The Life and Work of C. R. Cockerell, R.A.* (1974).
– *The Triumph of the Classical. Cambridge Architecture 1804–1834* (Cambridge, 1977).
Wearing, S. J. *Georgian Norwich and its Buildings* (Norwich, 1926).
Whitley, W. T. *Art in England, 1800–1820* (Cambridge, 1928).
– *Art in England, 1821–1837* (Cambridge, 1930).
Wiebenson, D. *Sources of Greek Revival Architecture* (1969).

Wilkins, W. P. 'Pentillie Castle', *Architectural Review*, 143 (1968), pp. 469–71.

Willis, R. and Clark, J. W. *An Architectural History of the University of Cambridge*, I–IV (Cambridge, 1886).

Wilmot, G. F. 'The Yorkshire Philosophical Society Museum', *Museums Journal*, 53 (1953), pp. 143–6.

Woodbridge, K. *Landscape and Antiquity* (Oxford, 1970).

THE PLATES

1. King's College screen, Cambridge. 1823–8.

2. National Gallery, London. 1833–8.

3. University College, London. Main façade. 1826–30.

4. A. E. Chalon. William Wilkins and his family. c. 1824.

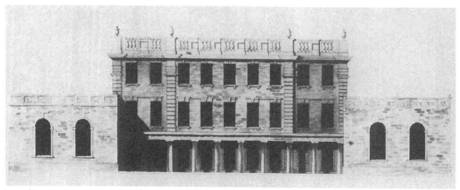

5. William Wilkins senior. Design for alterations to Locko Park, Nottinghamshire.
c. 1803.

6. Wash perspective of Donington Park, Leicestershire. 1790–1800. Dedicated to Lady Charlotte Rawdon. c. 1798.

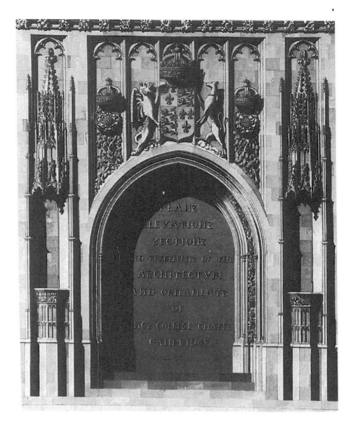

7. Frontispiece, drawings of King's College Chapel,
Cambridge. c. 1798.

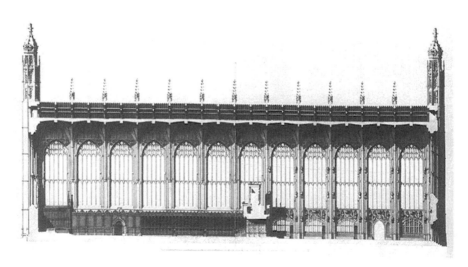

8. East–west section, King's College Chapel. c. 1798.

9. A. Aglio. A scene near Syracuse. c. 1802. Gouache.

10. Design for the south front, Downing College, Cambridge. 1805.

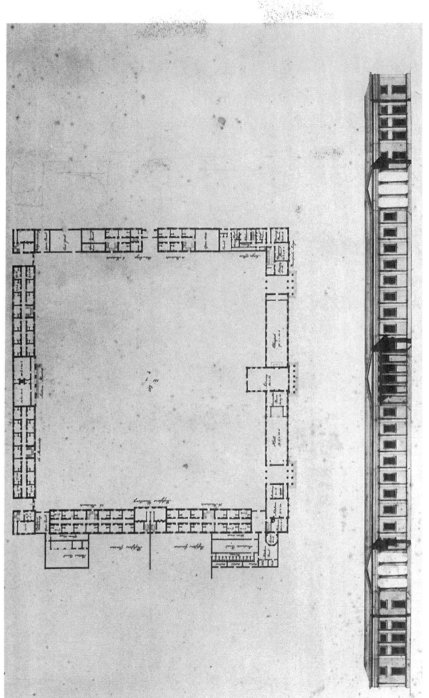

11. East India College, Haileybury, Hertfordshire. South front and revised ground-plan. 1806.

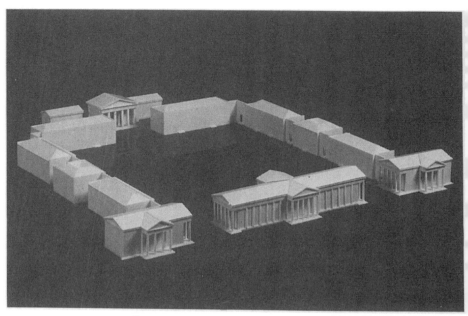

12. Proposed layout for Downing College. 1805.

13. East India College. South side of the quadrangle.

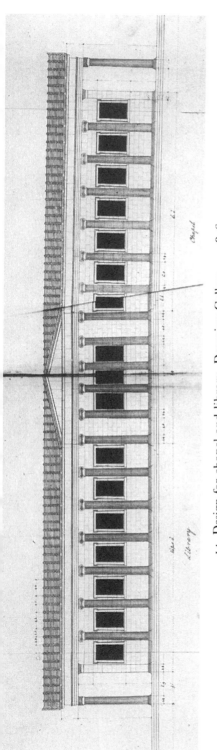

14. Design for chapel and library, Downing College. c. 1806.

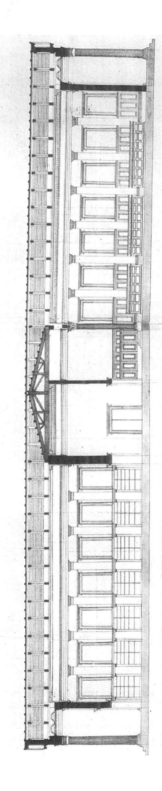

15. Section of chapel and library, Downing College. c. 1806.

16. Downing College. Hall. 1818–20.

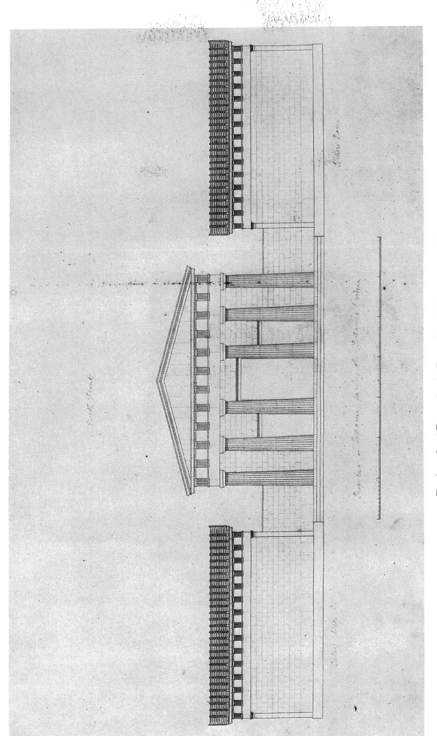

17. Design for 'Propylea', Downing College. c. 1806.

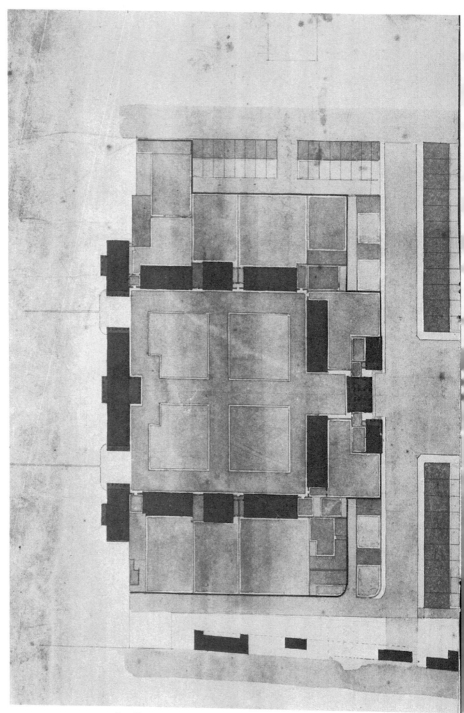

18. 'Ground Plan of Downing and Streets', 1817.

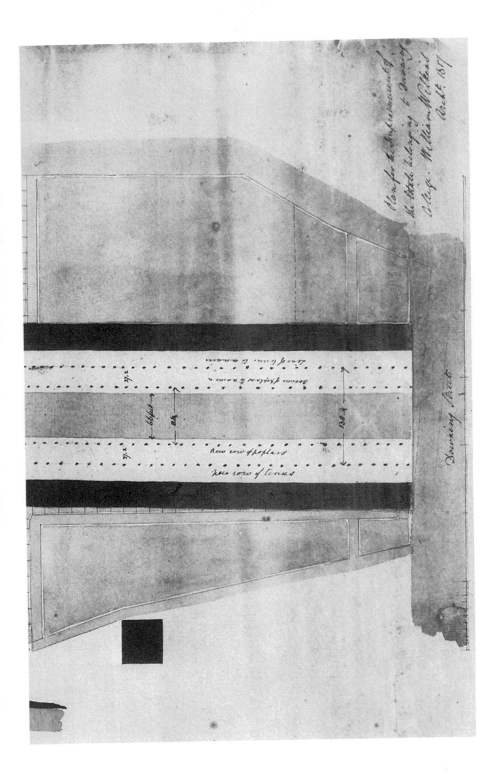

Plan for the improvement of
the streets belonging to Providence
College. William McKail
Oct. 1st 1817

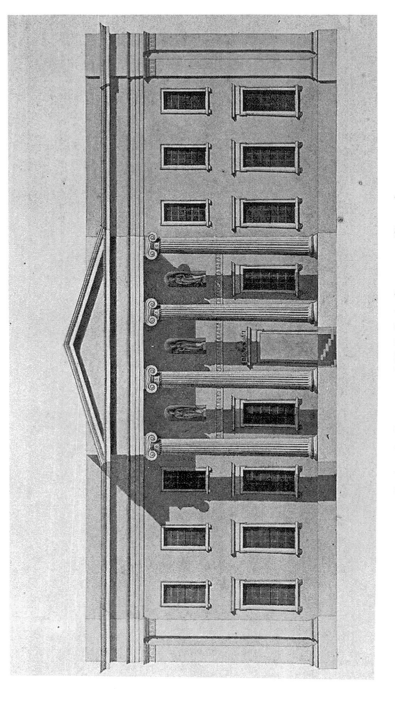

19. Design for Freemasons' Hall, Bath, Somerset. (?) c. 1817.

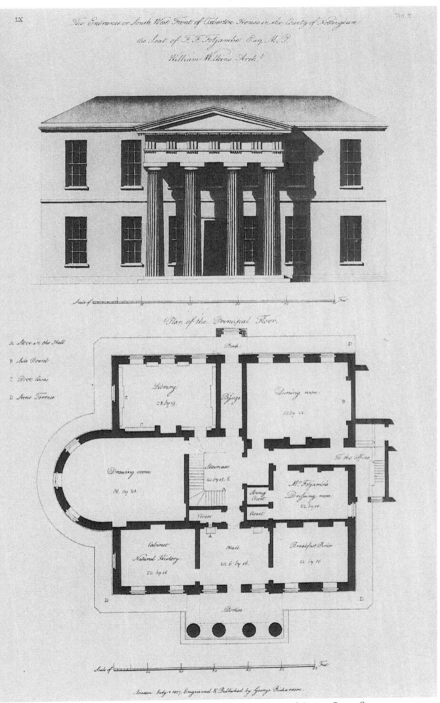

20. Osberton House, Nottinghamshire. 1805–6.

21. Competition design for Nelson Pillar, Dublin. 1807.

22. Lower Assembly Rooms, Bath. 1808–9.

23. Lensfield, Cambridge. Portico. c. 1812.

24. Kingweston, Somerset. Portico. Before 1828.

25. Design for east front, Grange Park, Hampshire. c. 1809.

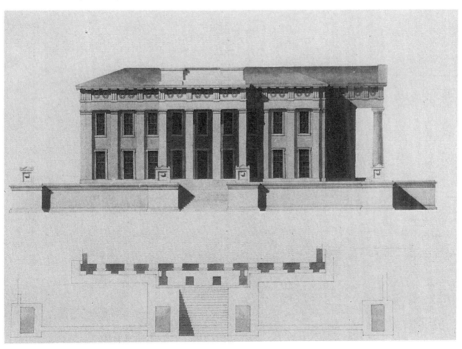

26. Design for south front, Grange Park. c. 1809.

27. Grange Park. Entrance. c. 1809–10.

28. Design for Dalmeny House, West Lothian. c. 1814.

29. Design for Dalmeny House. c. 1814.

30. Design for a building in the Park, Stourhead, Wiltshire. 1815.

31. Design for Broomhall, Fife. (?) c. 1822.

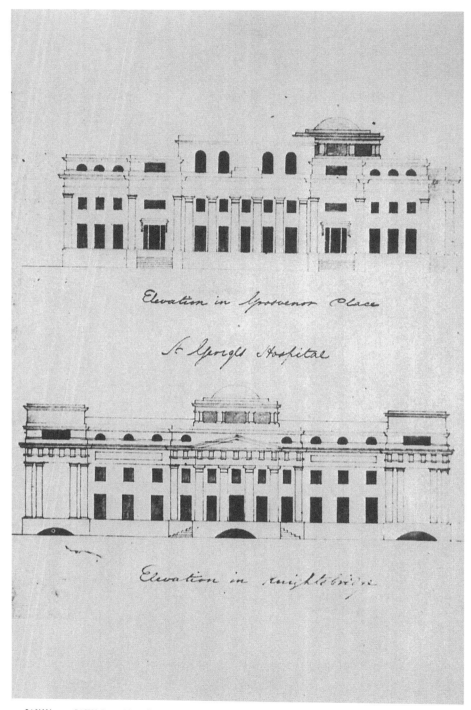

Elevation in Grosvenor Place

St Georges Hospital

Elevation in Knightsbridge

32. William Wilkins (?). Designs for Grosvenor Place and Knightsbridge façades, St George's Hospital, London. 1826.

33. Wilkins senior and junior. Pentillie Castle, Cornwall. South wing addition before demolition. c. 1810–11.

34. East Barsham Manor, Norfolk. Built by Sir Henry Fermor. c. 1520–30.

35. Dalmeny House. 1814–18.

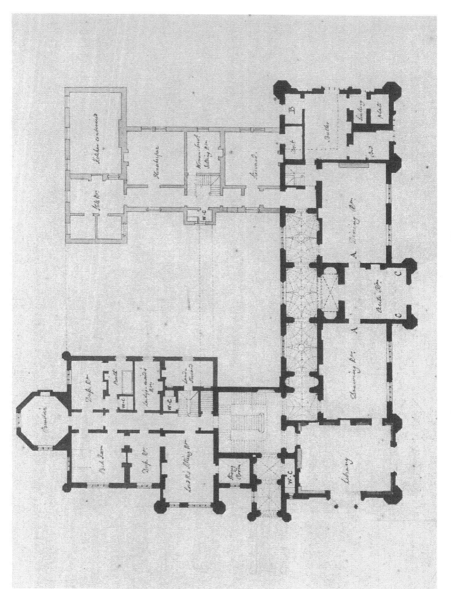

36. Ground floor plan for Dalmeny House. 1814.

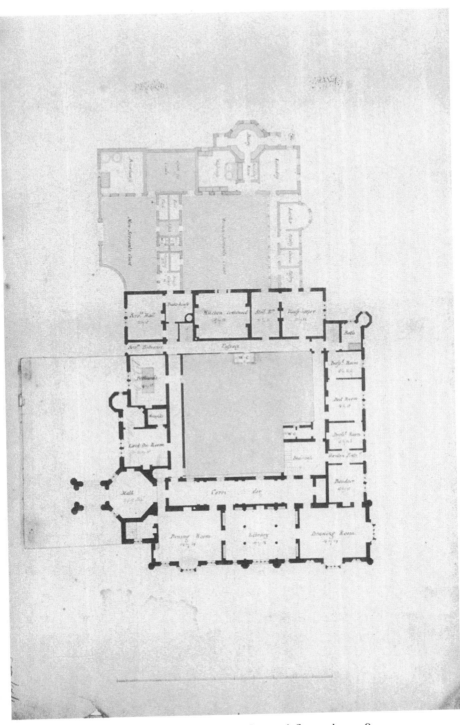

37. Dunmore Park, Stirlingshire. Ground floor plan. 1820.

38. G. Repton, wash drawing of Tregothnan, Cornwall, and proposed alteration.
c. 1810.

39. Design for entrance front, Tregothnan. 1815.

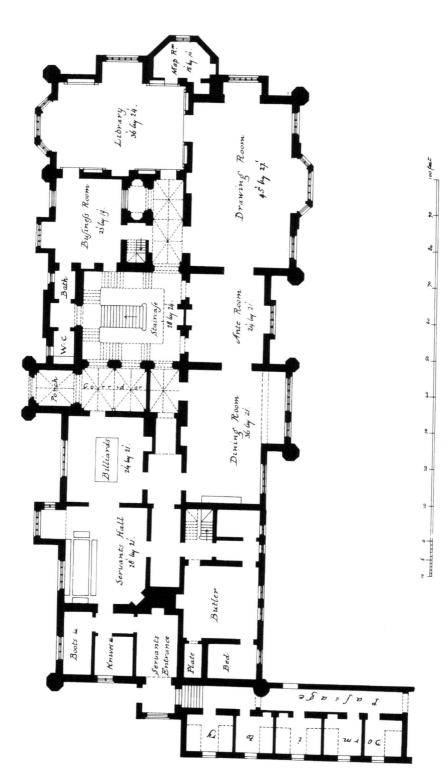

Map Rm. 15 by 10.

Library 36 by 24.

Business Room 23 by 19

Bath

W.C.

Porch

Corridor

Staircase 28 by 24.

Drawing Room 45 by 27.

Ante Room 24 by 21.

Dining Room 36 by 21.

Billiards 24 by 21.

Servants Hall 28 by 21.

Books &c

Knives &c

Servants Entrance

Butler

Plate

Bed

Passage

Dorm

40. Ground floor plan for Tregothnan. 1815.

41. Design for garden and side façades, Tregothnan. 1815.

42. Tregothnan. Entrance front. 1815–17, with additions by L. Vulliamy, 1842–6.

43. Dunmore Park, Stirlingshire. 1820–2.

44. Dunmore Park, Wash elevation as executed. 1820.

45. Nelson Column, Great Yarmouth, Norfolk, 1815–17.

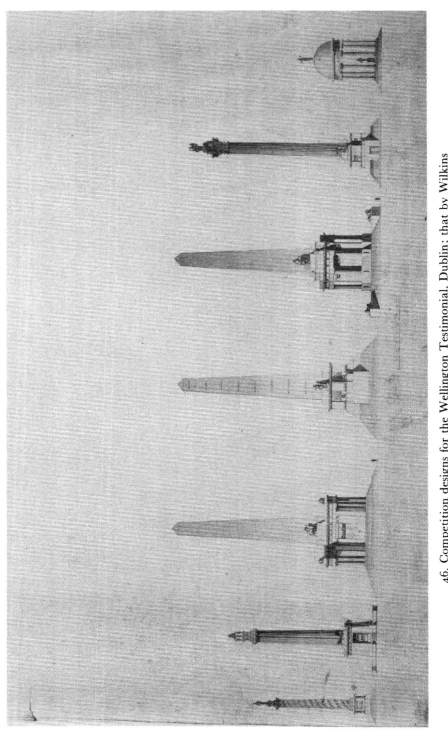

46. Competition designs for the Wellington Testimonial, Dublin; that by Wilkins second from left. 1815.

47. Freemasons' Hall (later Friends' Meeting House), Bath. 1817.

48. Keswick Hall, Norfolk. Wash elevation as executed. 1817–18.

49. Design for Bylaugh Hall, Norfolk. 1822.

50. Alternate design for Bylaugh Hall. 1822.

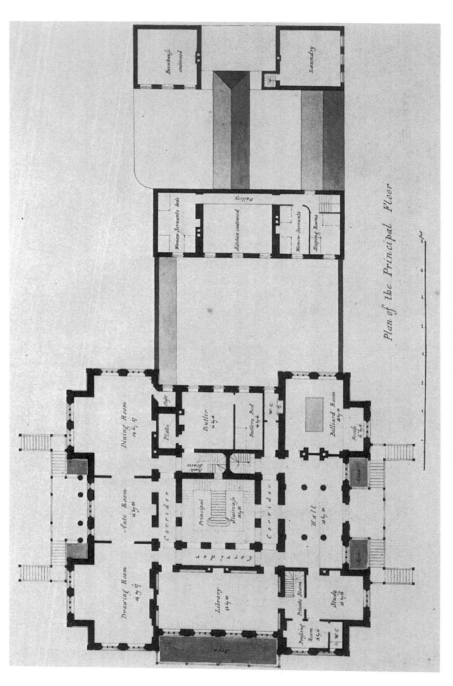

Plan of the Principal Floor

51. Principal floor plan for Bylaugh Hall. 1822.

52. Theatre Royal, Bury St Edmunds, Suffolk. 1818–20.

53. Theatre Royal, Bury St Edmunds. Auditorium. 1818–20.

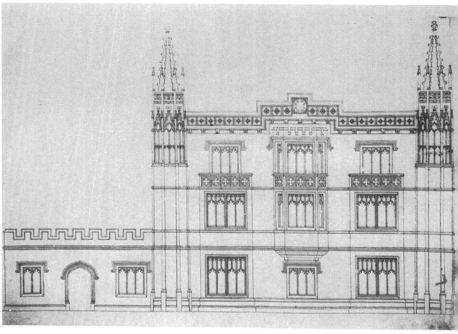

54. Design for a new building, Gonville and Caius College, Cambridge, attributed to Wilkins. c. 1815.

55. King's College Bridge, Cambridge. 1818.

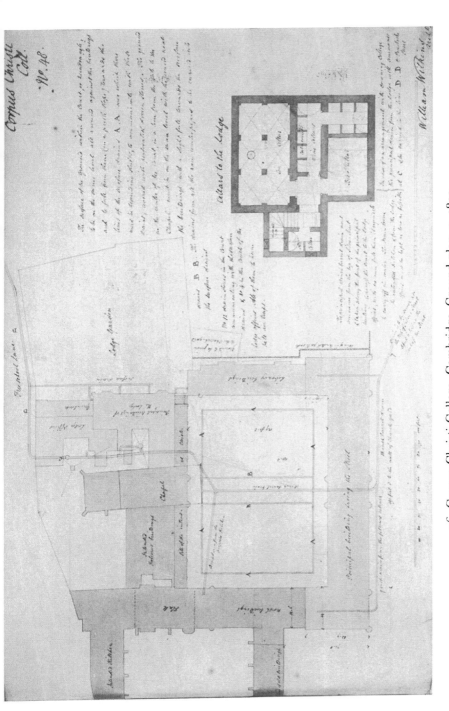

56. Corpus Christi College, Cambridge. Ground-plan. c. 1823.

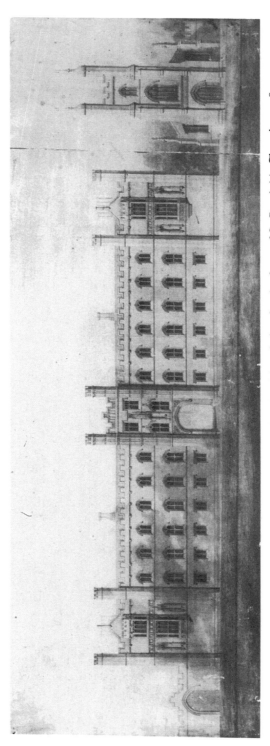

57. Corpus Christi College. Trumpington Street façade with a design for the front of St Botolph's Church. c. 1823.

58. Corpus Christi College. Chapel. 1822–7.

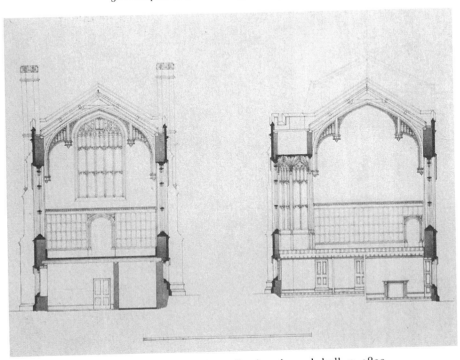

59. Corpus Christi College. Section through hall. c. 1823.

60. King's College, Cambridge. Hall range. 1823–8.

61. Corpus Christi College. Library interior. 1822–7.

62. King's College. Hall interior. 1823–8.

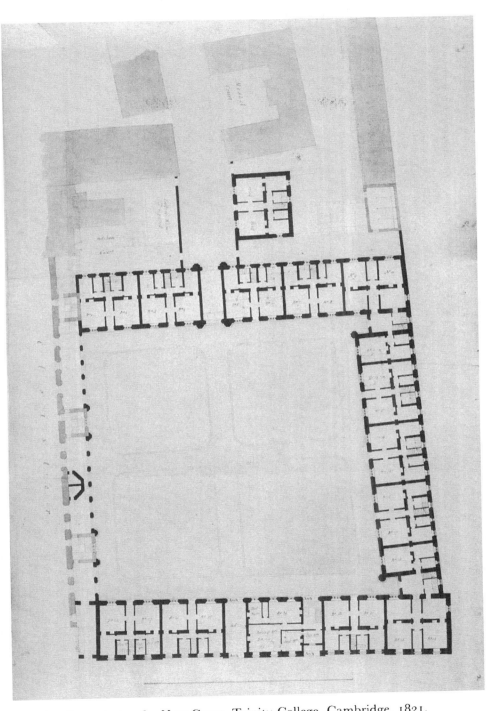

63. Ground-plan for New Court, Trinity College, Cambridge. 1821.

64. Design for Backs façade of New Court, showing Wren's Library,
Trinity College. 1821.

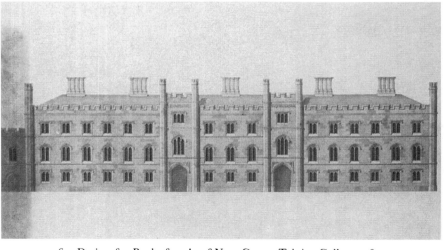

65. Design for Backs façade of New Court, Trinity College. 1821.

66. Trinity College. Wash elevation of Backs façade. c. 1823.

67. Trinity College. New Court. 1823–5.

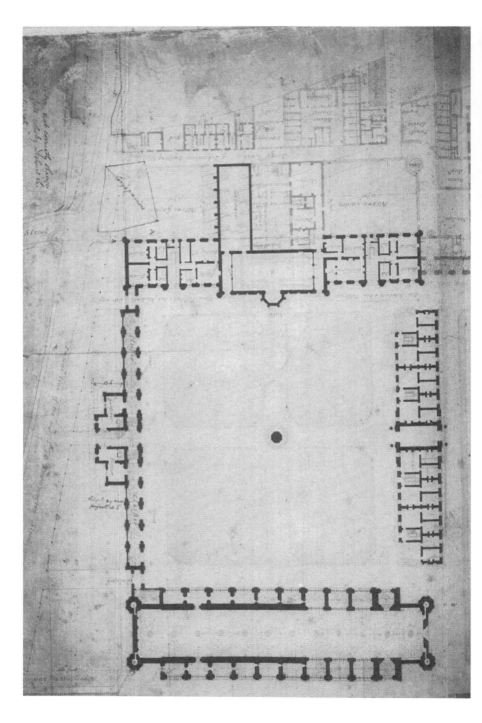

68. First ground-plan for additions to King's College. Signed and dated 1831.

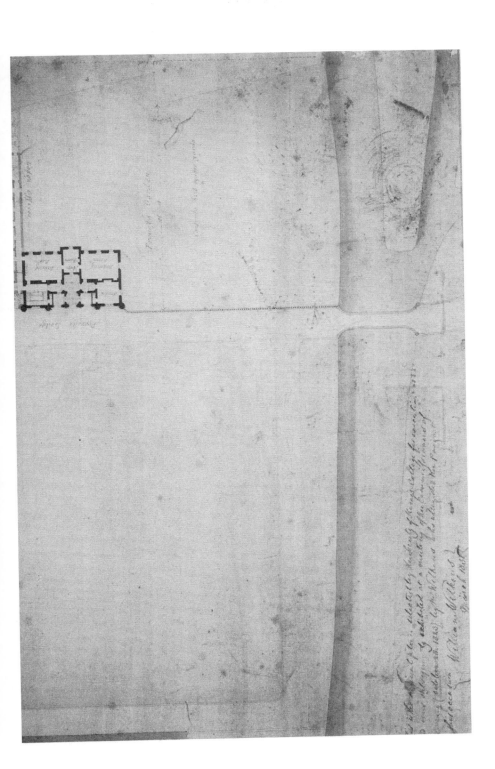

69. First design for additions to King's College. c. 1823.

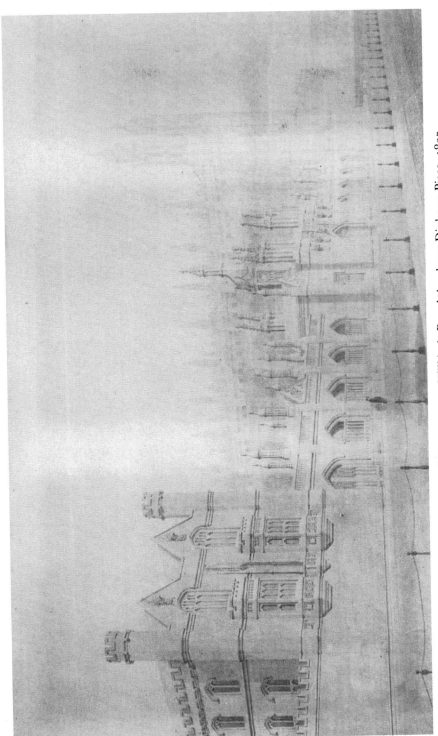

70. First design for King's College screen; Wilkins's Royal Academy Diploma Piece, 1827.

71. King's College. Library and Provost's Lodge. 1823–8.

72. Theatre Royal, Norwich, Norfolk. 1820–1. Photograph 1926.

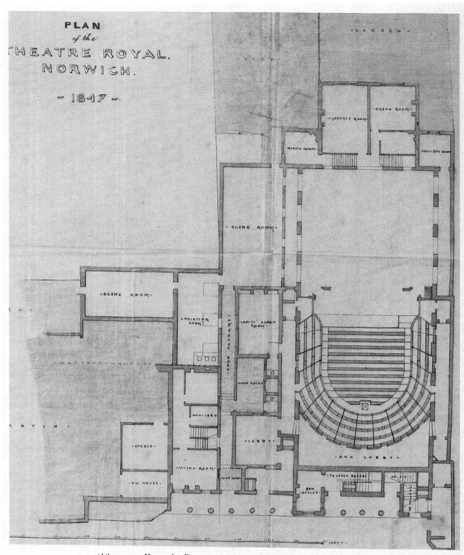

73. Theatre Royal. Ground-plan. Drawn by R. Kitton. 1847.

74. St Paul's Church, Nottingham, 1821–2. Photograph c. 1926.

75. St Paul's Church. Nave looking to entrance. 1821–2. Photograph c. 1926.

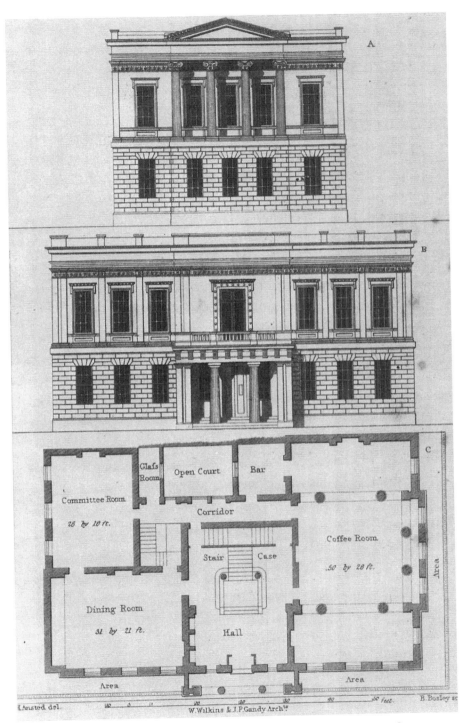

Labels within the plan:

A

B

C

Glass Room

Open Court

Bar

Committee Room

26 by 10 ft.

Corridor

Stair   Case

Coffee Room

50 by 28 ft.

Area

Dining Room

31 by 21 ft.

Hall

Area

Area

L.Ansted del.   W.Wilkins & J.P.Gandy Arch.ᵗˢ   B.Bosley sc

76. United University Club, London. Façades and ground-plan. 1822–3.

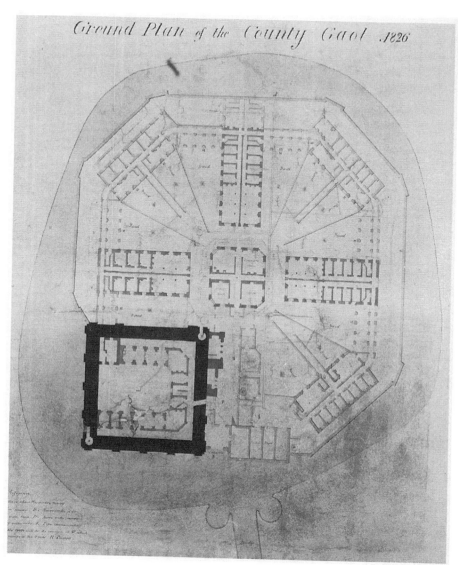

77. Norfolk County Gaol, Norwich. Ground-plan.

78. Norfolk County Gaol, showing the Gatehouse and Keep. 1822–6.

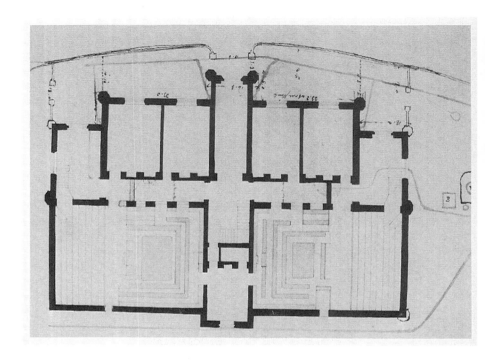

79. Shire Hall, Norwich. Ground-plan of courts. 1822–6.

80. Huntingdon County Gaol, Huntingdon, Huntingdonshire. 1826–8.

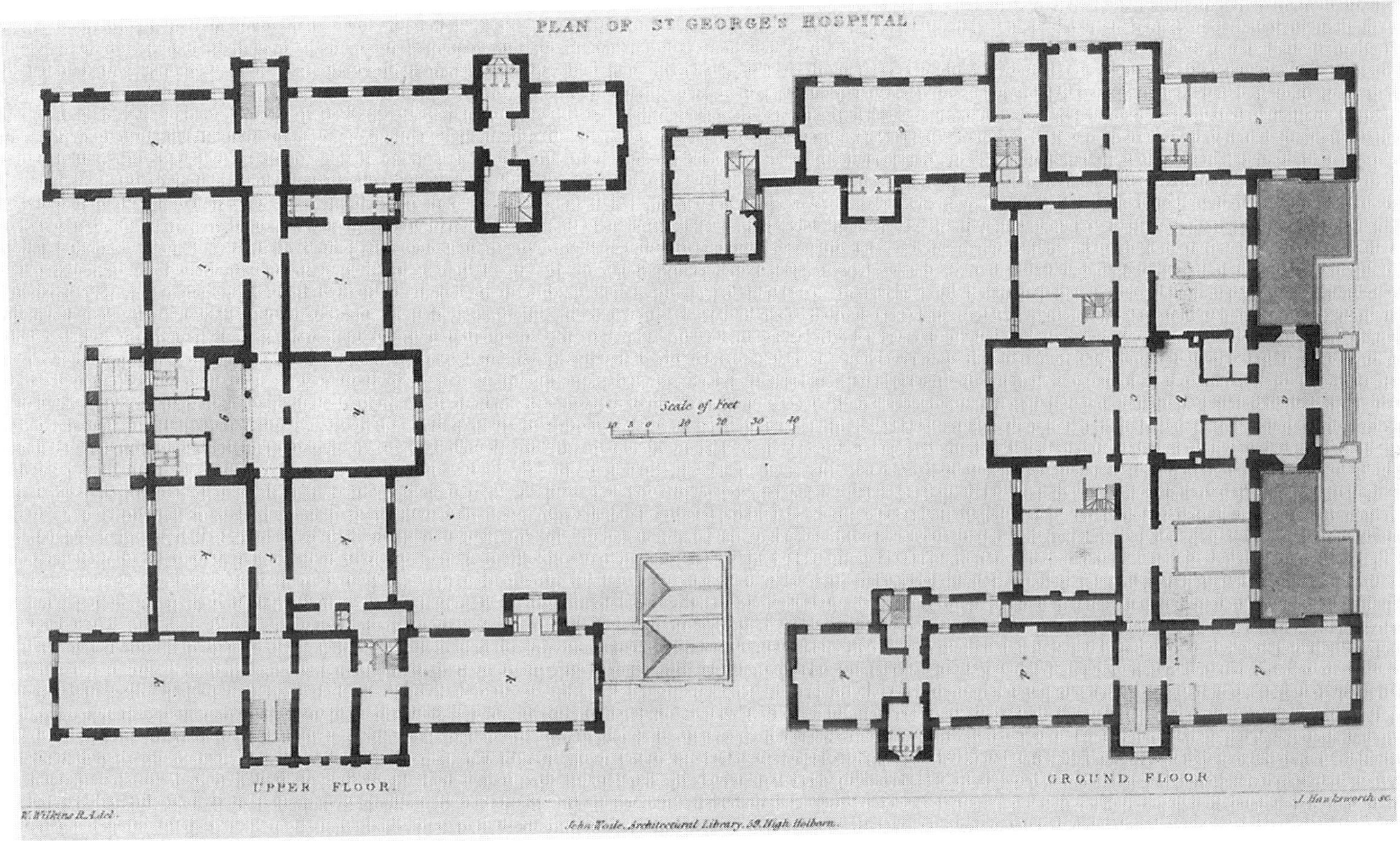

PLAN OF ST GEORGE'S HOSPITAL

a

b

c

e

d

d

d

GROUND FLOOR.

i

i

i

i

i

i

h

f

g

f

k

k

k

k

k

UPPER FLOOR.

Scale of Feet

81. St George's Hospital, London. Floor plans. 1826-8.

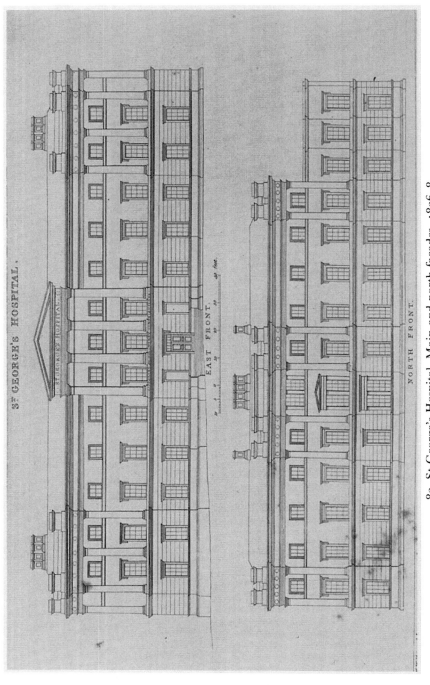

ST GEORGE'S HOSPITAL.

ST GEORGE'S HOSPITAL.

EAST FRONT.

NORTH FRONT.

82. St George's Hospital. Main and north façades. 1826–8.

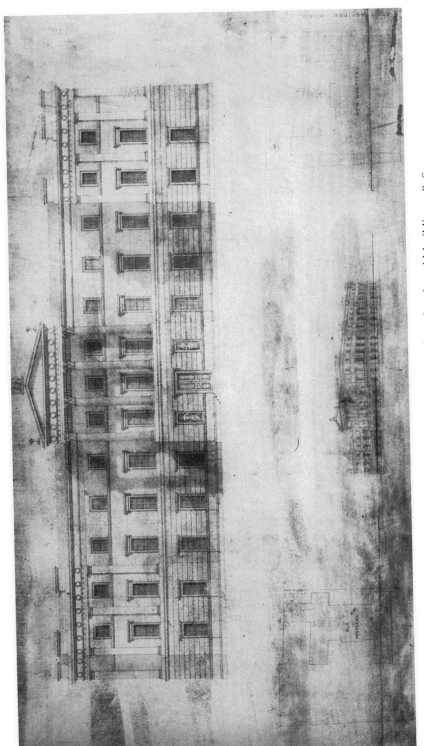

83. St George's Hospital. Design and site plan, showing old building. 1826.

84. Design for University College, London. 1826.

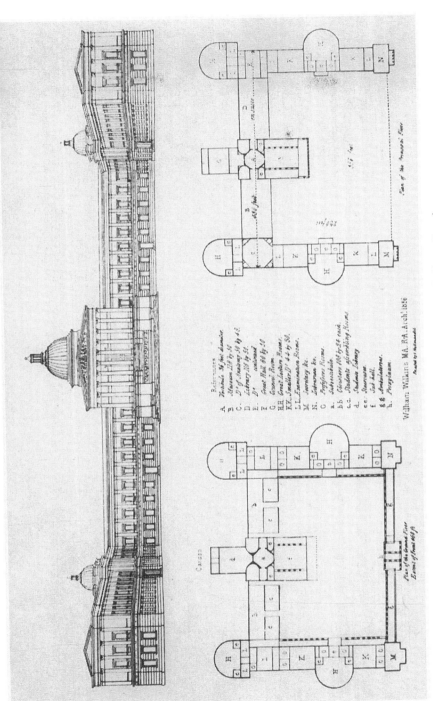

85. Design and floor plans for University College, London.

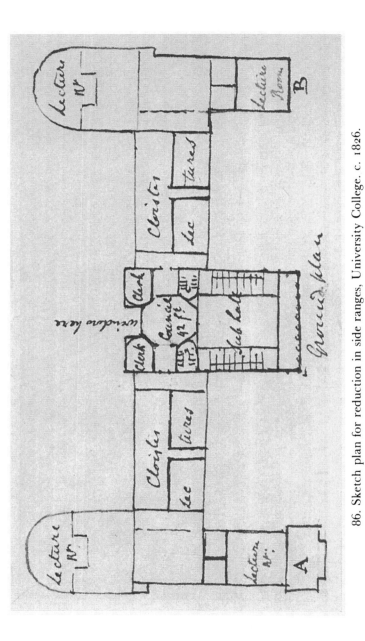

86. Sketch plan for reduction in side ranges, University College. c. 1826.

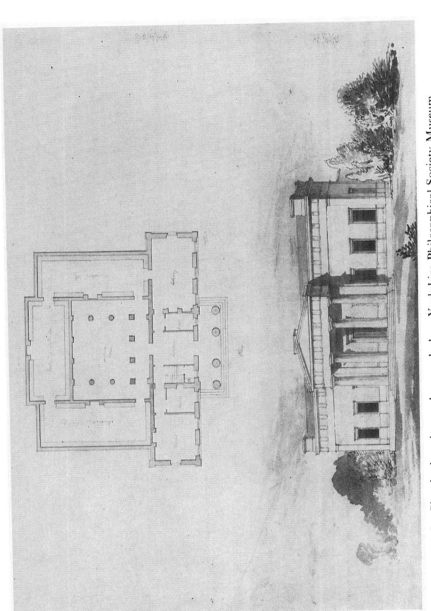

87. Sketch elevation and ground-plan, Yorkshire Philosophical Society Museum (now York Museum) York. c. 1827.

88. Yorkshire Philosophical Society Museum. 1827–8.

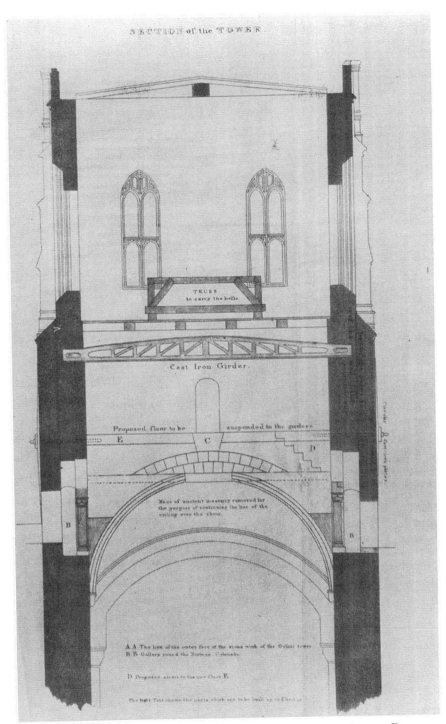

89. Section of the crossing tower, St Mary's Abbey, Sherborne, Dorset showing projected renovations.

90. Design for Duke of York Monument, London. c. 1828

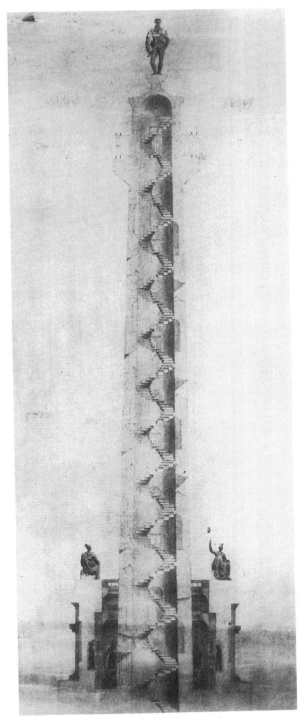

91. Section of projected Duke of York Monument. c 1828.

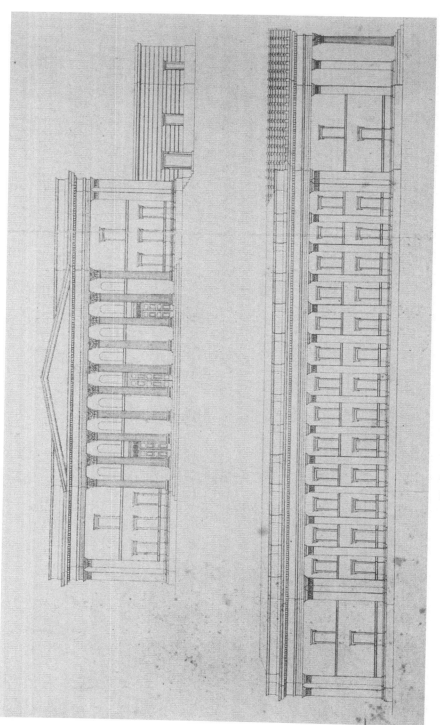

92. Design for University Library, Cambridge. 1829.

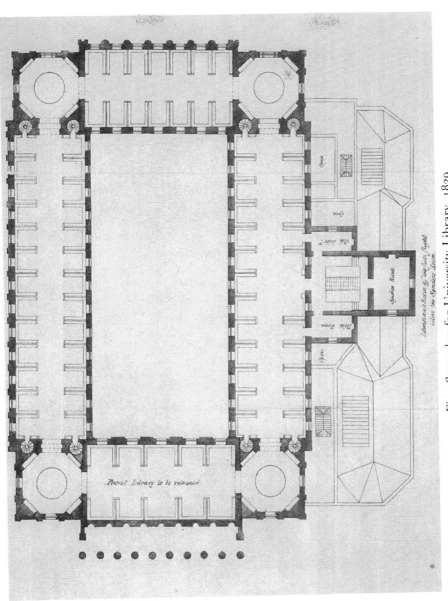

93. First floor plan for University Library. 1829.

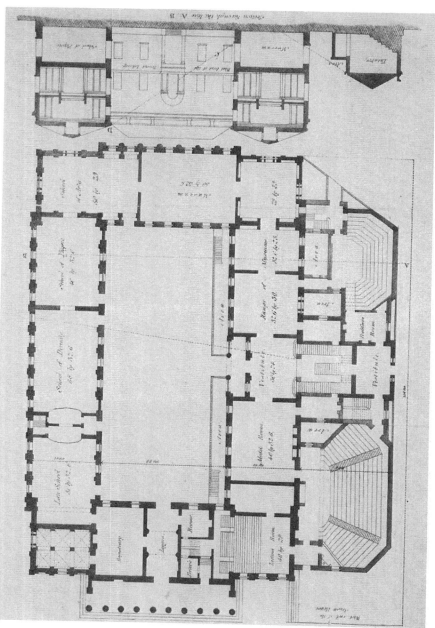

94. Ground floor plan for University Library. 1829.

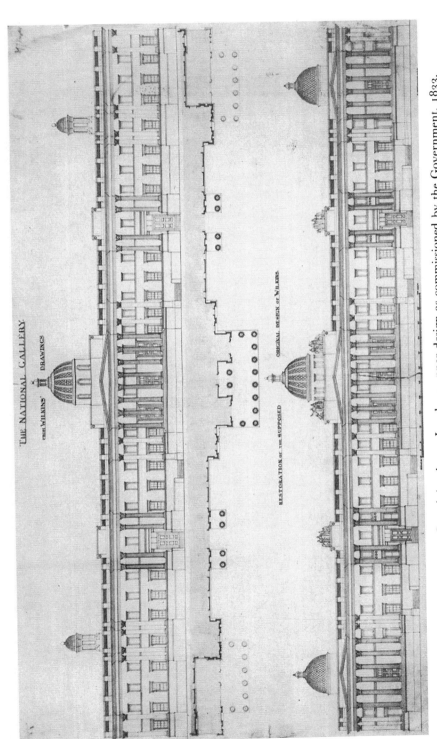

95. National Gallery and Royal Academy, London; upper design as commissioned by the Government, 1833, and lower design proposed improvement (?).

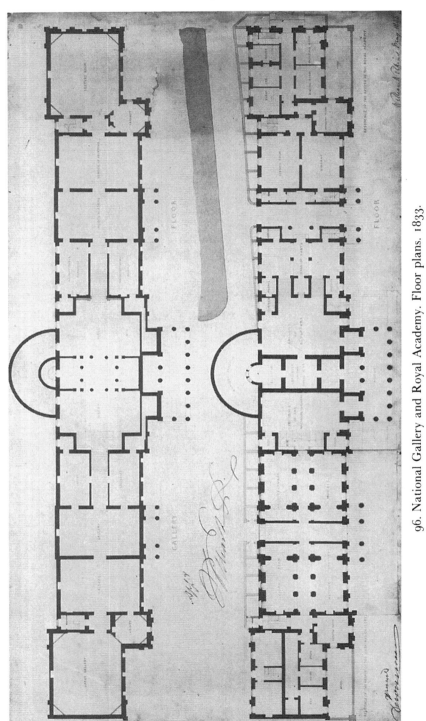

96. National Gallery and Royal Academy. Floor plans. 1833.

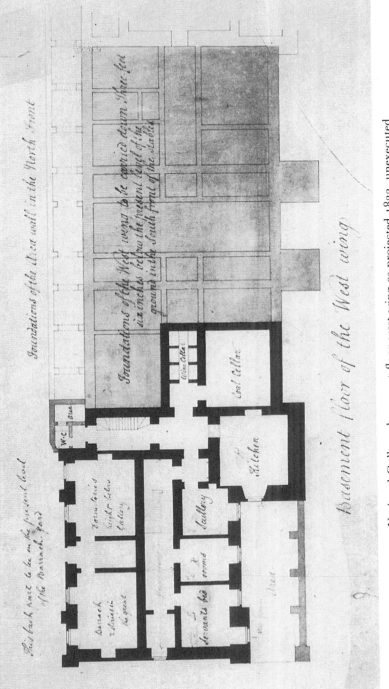

Foundations of the Area wall in the North Front

This back wall to be in the finished level of the Barrack yard

Foundations of the West wing to be carried down three feet six inches below the present level of the ground in the South front of the Stables

W.C

Area

Coal Cellar

Kitchen

Wine Cellar

Scullery

Servants' Hall

Store

Barrack & Chelsea Pensioners

Yeomen Guard light robes rooms

97. National Gallery, basement floor west wing as projected 1833, unexecuted.

basement floor of the West wing

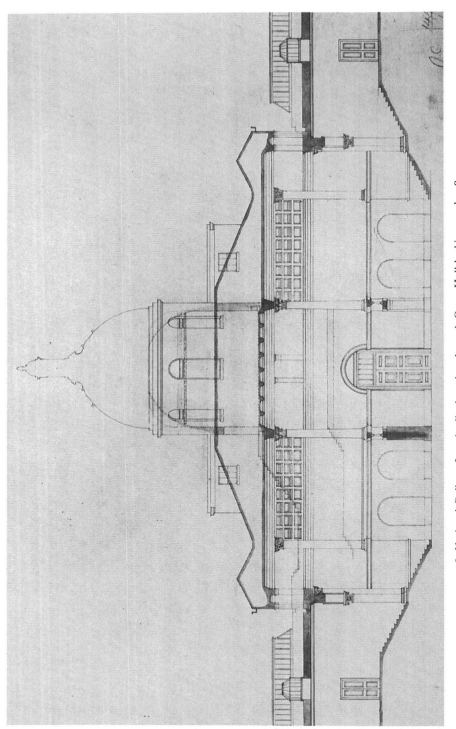

98. National Gallery. Longitudinal section through Great Hall looking south. 1833.

National Gallery &c
No 10

Transverse Section taken through the Portico and Vestibule

99. National Gallery. Transverse section through Great Hall and portico. 1833.

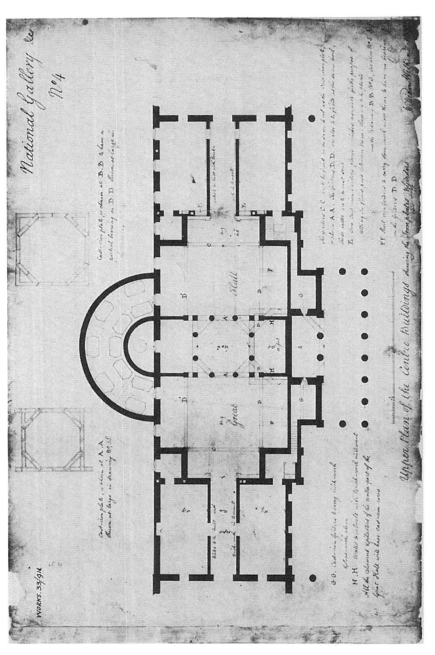

100. National Gallery. Upper plan central section, showing cast ironwork. 1833.

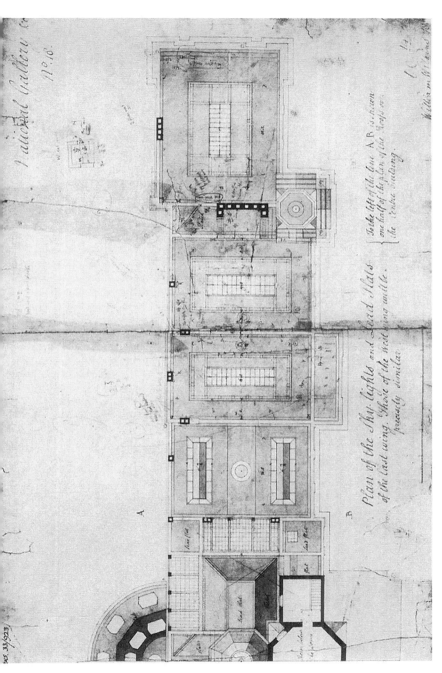

101. National Gallery. Plan of skylights, east wing. 1833.

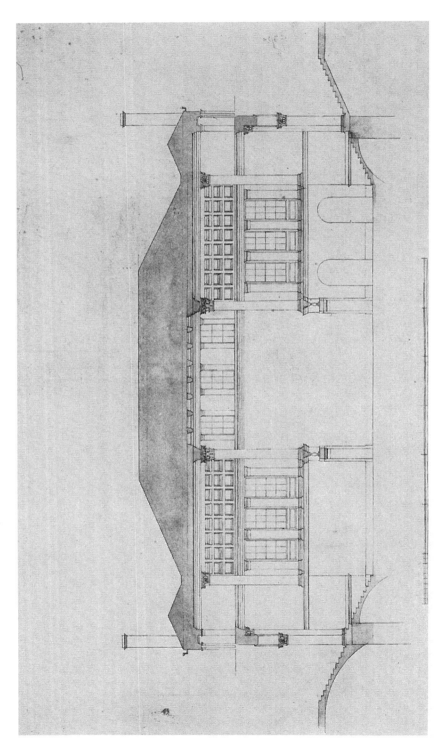

102. National Gallery. Longitudinal section through Great Hall, looking north. 1833.

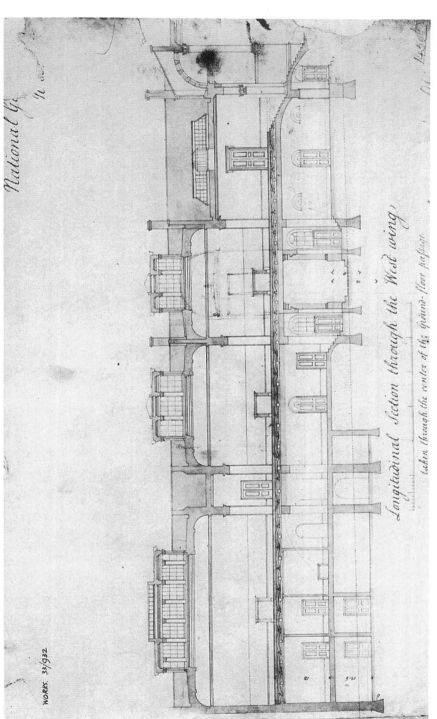

National Ga...

Longitudinal Section through the West wing

taken through the centre of the ground-floor passage

103. National Gallery. Longitudinal section through west wing. 1833.

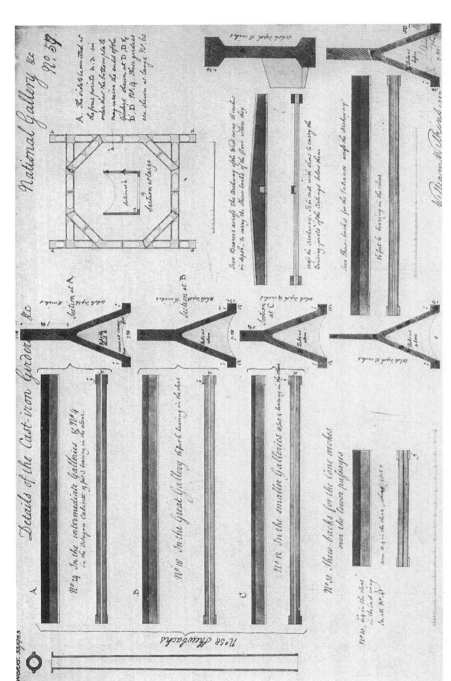

104. National Gallery. Details of cast ironwork. 1832.

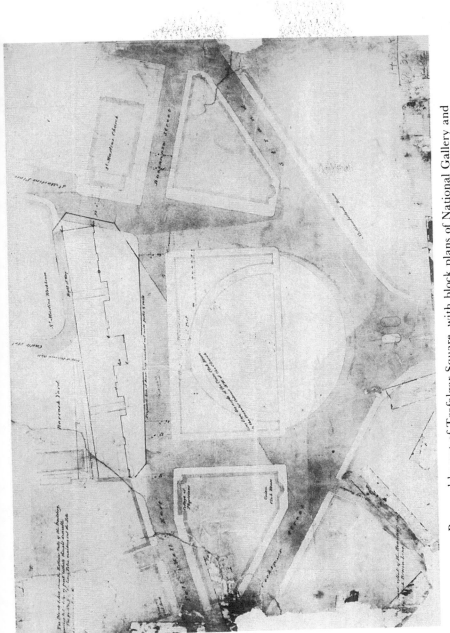

105. Proposed layout of Trafalgar Square, with block plans of National Gallery and Royal Academy as conceived January 1833.

106. Design for Houses of Parliament, London. River façade. 1835.

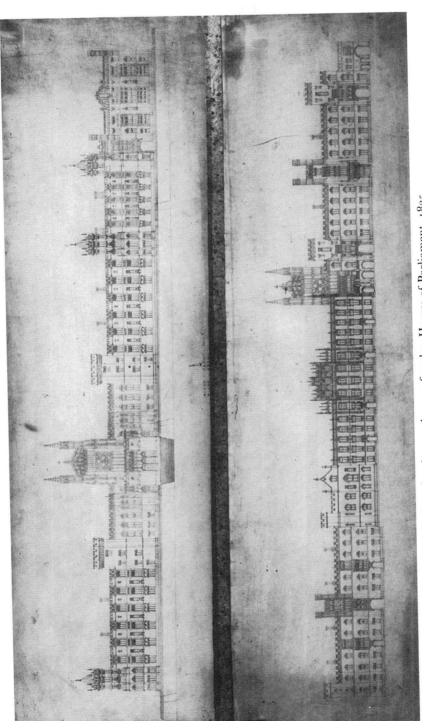

107. Designs for river and street façades, Houses of Parliament. 1835.

SELECT INDEX

Printed in Great Britain
by Amazon